SCIENCE AND THOUGHT
IN THE
FIFTEENTH CENTURY

12–18 + 32
37 50
70
118 142
144 150
168 182–188
235 240–241
247 182
255
258

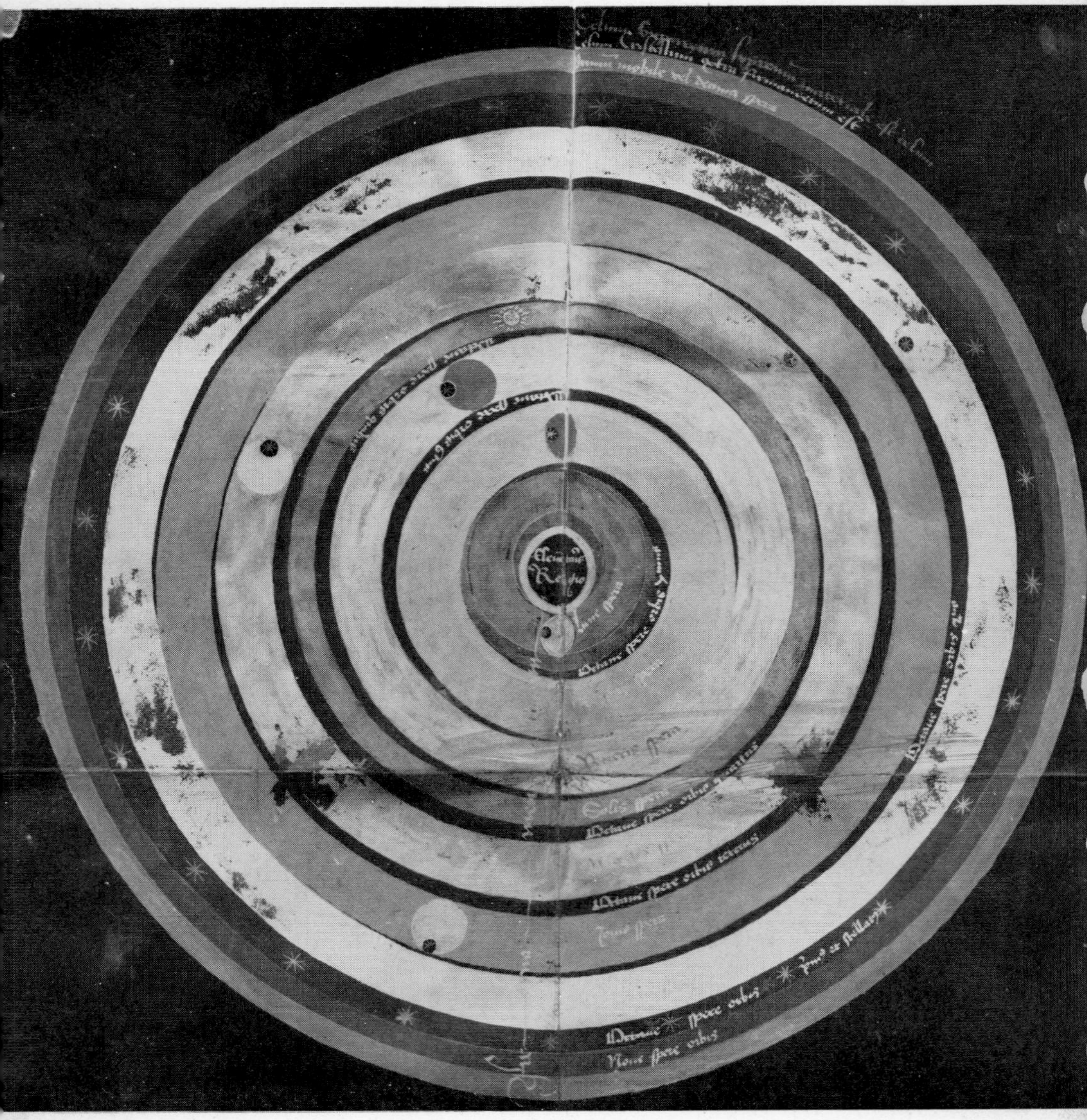

PLATE I

JOHN TOLHOPF'S SCHEME OF THE MOVEMENTS OF THE HEAVENS

Vatican Latin MS 3103, fols. 20–21

(About three-fourths diameter)

SCIENCE AND THOUGHT
IN THE
FIFTEENTH CENTURY

Studies in the History of Medicine and Surgery
Natural and Mathematical Science
Philosophy and Politics

BY
LYNN THORNDIKE

New York
COLUMBIA UNIVERSITY PRESS
1929

Printed from type. Published May, 1929

PRINTED IN THE UNITED STATES OF AMERICA
BY THE PLIMPTON PRESS, NORWOOD, MASS.

TO MY COLLEAGUES
IN THE DEPARTMENT OF HISTORY
OF COLUMBIA UNIVERSITY

THE WILLIAM A. DUNNING FUND

In the publication of this book the author has received assistance from the fund for the encouragement of historical studies bequeathed to Columbia University by Professor William A. Dunning.

PREFACE

This volume consists chiefly of special studies in the science and thought of the fifteenth century, based in large measure upon manuscript and unpublished materials. Of these last, some further idea will be given by reproducing their tables of contents or certain illustrative passages from their texts. It is hardly possible as yet to draw a general picture of fifteenth-century thought and science, although one might think so from the sweeping generalizations which have long been bandied about with reference to the decline of scholasticism, the so-called Italian Renaissance, and the pre-Reformation period. One result of the special studies that follow should be to suggest that such generalizations have been to a considerable extent unwarranted. Resting primarily upon the humanistic bias which has prevailed ever since the fifteenth century — and which has, rather oddly, infected even modern men of science who have no taste for the classics with its distaste for things medieval — these generalizations must give way as soon as the period is scrutinized from the neutral ground of the history of science and in relation to the medieval centuries immediately antecedent. But in order to develop such neglected aspects, detailed investigation is required.

The first chapter is, however, more general in character, introducing the reader to the scientific and other thought of the fifteenth century by some consideration of the fourteenth as well, and aiming to give him some notion of what has been done and what remains to be done in the way of historical investigation thereof. Then follow the more specialized studies — arranged in a combined topical and chronological order — concerning medicine and law; surgery and medicine; astronomy and mathematics; speculative, moral, natural, and political philosophy.

The majority of these chapters are a revision, or enlargement and development, of articles which have appeared in learned periodicals — *The Romanic Review*, *Isis*, *Medical Life*, *Annals of Medical History*, *American Mathematical Monthly*, and *Political Science Quarterly* — whose editors have courteously assented to their utilization here in book form. But several of the chapters and the two long appendices from Niccolò da Foligno are now published for the first time. The others have been corrected by a reëxamination of the manuscripts on which they were based, or have been altered as a consequence of finding more manuscripts of the works in question and other additional materials. My best thanks are due to the European libraries — the Biblioteca Apostolica Vaticana, Biblioteca Nazionale di San Marco in Venezia, British Museum (Department of Manuscripts), National-Bibliothek of Vienna, R. Biblioteca Medicea Laurenziana of Florence, and Bibliothèque Sainte-Geneviève, Paris — which have enabled and permitted me thus to publish some of their treasures and to reproduce certain pages from the manuscripts in the plates which illustrate this volume.

The phrase "Fifteenth Century" is introduced into the title of this volume mainly as a matter of rough convenience. One or two of the works which we shall discuss were written in the closing years of the fourteenth; one or two others came after 1500. And sometimes, for purposes of comparison or to trace influences and continuities, we turn back to the thirteenth, or forward to the sixteenth, seventeenth, and even eighteenth centuries. But everything will be seen to have its connection with fifteenth-century thought and science, and most of our discussion will lie well within the strict chronological limits of that hundred years.

In the publication of this volume I have received financial assistance from the William A. Dunning Fund, which that genial scholar and beloved teacher left at the disposal of the Department of which he was for so many years a leading member, for the encouragement and support of historical research.

I knew him somewhat as a student, better as a fellow member of the American Historical Association, and it is no small satisfaction to have a work of mine the first to appear in connection with the William A. Dunning Fund. I would also gratefully acknowledge assistance received from two other sources. The purchase of rotographs of manuscripts utilized in this volume has been made under a grant from the Special Research Fund of Columbia University. In the last stages of revising proofs the research assistance made possible by a recent subvention from the Council on Research in the Humanities has proved very helpful.

In preparing this volume, or the articles which preceded it, for publication I have sought and received help on various points from my colleagues or other scholars, some of whose names will be found mentioned in the footnotes. Dr. George Sarton has very obligingly lent me certain recent European publications and allowed me to make use of his notes on the fourteenth and fifteenth centuries, which will soon appear as a part of the second volume of his *Introduction to the History of Science*. In correcting the proofs I have been aided by Professor Austin P. Evans, Dr. Richard McKeon, Miss Pearl Kibre, and Professor Dino Bigongiari. The last named in especial, by his mastery of the Latin language and literature, his broad familiarity with medieval learning, and his knowledge of Italian custom and speech of the period herein treated, has rendered invaluable assistance in correcting a number of my readings of the manuscripts.

CONTENTS

APPENDICES

INDICES

PLATES

Il viendra un tems pour l'histoire comme pour la connoissance de la nature, où la lumiere succédant tout à fait aux ténebres tous ces morceaux épars prendront d'eux-mêmes leur place et s'ajusteront au système géneral de la verité. — P. Liron, *Singularités historiques et littéraires*, I (1738), Preface, p. xii.

CHAPTER I

INTRODUCTION: THE STUDY OF WESTERN SCIENCE OF THE FOURTEENTH AND FIFTEENTH CENTURIES[1]

Generally speaking, the amount of extant and available historical material and records increases during the fourteenth and fifteenth centuries. Notarial papers become abundant; account books, public and private, begin to multiply; the records of towns and gilds and universities grow fuller; what had been customary is now set down in writing. This does not necessarily imply that these centuries accomplished more that deserved recording than the twelfth and thirteenth, or that they produced more in literature, learning, art, and institutions. If anything, the contrary seems to have been the case. But, coming after that more creative epoch, they either consumed and obliterated many of its memorials and substituted their own counterparts thereof, or for the first time reduced its achievements to written form. Writing material in the form of paper, as against parchment, had become more abundant. The invention of printing with moveable types not only increased the number of books and probably testifies to an increasing demand, but, by throwing manuscripts into disuse, perhaps contributed to the preservation and survival of those already in existence. The growing distaste for things medieval, and aversion from the immediate past, which accompanied the humanistic movement and so-called Italian Renaissance and "birth of modern times," likewise tended to bury many of the old records beneath the sand of salutary neglect until they should be excavated by recent historical research.

When interest in the medieval period began to revive, it at first concerned itself more with the early middle ages — the

[1] Recast and enlarged from *Medical Life*, Vol. XXXII, 1925, pp. 117–27.

decline and fall of Rome, the early church, the work of the monks — or with medieval civilization at its height than with its closing centuries. Bibliographers, historians of literature, and editors of texts commonly started their enterprises at the very beginning of the middle ages and have either ceased from their labors without reaching the fourteenth and fifteenth centuries or are still slowly making their way down the ages in that general direction. Thus Migne's *Patrologia Latina* extends only to the time of Innocent III; Manitius's history of the Latin literature of the middle ages has yet hardly reached the twelfth century; and the great *Histoire littéraire de la France*, so valuable a guide for the thirteenth and earlier centuries, is foundering about in the first years of the fourteenth century, to which it has devoted volume after volume without perceptible chronological progress — a sign of that greater amount of material available to which we have already alluded. The older histories of scholasticism, such as those of Prantl and Hauréau, chose to stigmatize the scholasticism of the fourteenth century as decadent and to halt there a story which they might well have prolonged for several centuries. Even Karl Werner's *Die Scholastik des späteren Mittelalters*, published in four volumes between 1881 and 1887, retained something of this attitude.

Indeed, the feeling that medieval civilization in general began to decline in the fourteenth century and the practice by some of terminating their treatment of the middle ages as a period with the date 1328 or 1300 or 1270 or even 1250, tended to discourage study of the fourteenth and fifteenth centuries by medievalists, especially since so much was found to study in the twelfth and thirteenth centuries. Therefore the two later centuries were left, for the most part, at the mercy of those seeking forerunners and background for the Reformation and to those devoted to the misleading conception of an Italian Renaissance. Now, writers on the so-called Renaissance have recently been described even by one in sympathy with them as "notoriously unscientific," and Burckhardt, the author of a work on the Renaissance commonly regarded as standard, frankly admitted his total ignorance of the scientific writings of the period. More catholic was the plan and outlook of Tiraboschi in the eighteenth century, who devoted chapters of his history of Italian literature to Latin works on law and medicine, mathematics and astronomy, in the fourteenth and fifteenth centuries — chapters which are still, for the want of a better, a valuable guide to one beginning to investigate the thought and science of those times.

General histories of science, and even the histories of particular scientific fields,[2] have usually been so meager and unsatisfactory in their discussion of medieval thought and science — although they give more space to the closing medieval centuries than to any others — that the whole subject has seemed to require rehabilitation. It is therefore not surprising that Professor Haskins confined his *Studies in the History of Medieval Science* to the twelfth century and the early thirteenth, while my *History of Magic and Experimental Science* ends at 1327. Duhem's *Système du monde*, or history of cosmological doctrines from Plato to Copernicus, leads us a certain way into the fourteenth and fifteenth centuries, but the author's death prevented his reaching his intended goal.[3] Special investigations and the publication of texts have also devoted more attention to the twelfth and thirteenth than to the fourteenth and fifteenth centuries, as can be seen by an examination of the past monographs in such series as the

[2] Some, of course, are better than others. Cantor's history of mathematics is useful for the fourteenth and fifteenth centuries, yet he has almost nothing concerning such a personage as Richard Suiseth, whom both Scaliger and Cardan, in the sixteenth century, ranked among the world's greatest wits (Moritz Cantor, *Vorlesungen über Geschichte der Mathematik*, 1880–92). Our period is treated in the second volume, which has not been revised since this first edition, although a so-called "second edition" of it appeared in 1913. For the medicine of the period, Neuburger's *Geschichte der Medizin* is also useful, but always within limits, and in Playfair's English translation it has unfortunately been shorn of much of its scholarly apparatus and detail.

[3] There are, however, other volumes of his work in manuscript which have not yet been printed. Equally valuable are his three volumes of studies on Leonardo da Vinci.

Abhandlungen zur Geschichte der mathematischen Wissenschaften or *Beiträge zur Geschichte der Philosophie des Mittelalters*. Since I first made this statement, however, there have appeared the first volumes of a new series, E. Droz's *Documents scientifiques du XVe siècle*.

The mass of material available for historical investigation in general of the fourteenth and fifteenth centuries has been receiving attention in researches such as those into the archives of the Avignon popes, the representative assemblies or Estates of various parts of Europe, the development of the gilds during that time, the libraries of the later middle ages, or the statutes and other documents bearing upon the history of the universities. Moreover, the thought of the period is being increasingly investigated from other than the humanistic standpoint. Gerhard Ritter's *Studien zur Spätscholastik* appeared in two volumes in 1921–22, and the latest edition of De Wulf's history of scholastic philosophy provides at least a summary account of scholastic thinkers through to 1500.[4] And instead of one or two outstanding individuals, such as Roger Bacon in the thirteenth, or Nicholas of Cusa and Leonardo da Vinci in the fifteenth century, receiving a notice disproportionate to their importance, the tendency is growing to study the science of the time impartially as a whole.

In the field of the history of medicine and surgery Karl Sudhoff and those who have worked under his inspiration have made many successful raids into the medical literature, pictorial material, instruments and other remains of the fourteenth and fifteenth as of other centuries. An imposing list of their contributions in this regard will be found in the volume published under the editorship of Charles Singer and Henry Sigerist to celebrate Sudhoff's seventieth birthday. In the same volume is an essay by Paul Diepgen on "The Significance of the Middle Ages for the Progress in Medicine,"[5] which should be read by anyone retaining the old-fashioned

[4] See Vol. II of the English translation, 1926.
[5] *Essays on the History of Medicine*, Zurich, 1924, pp. 99–120.

derogatory notions concerning medieval medicine and surgery. Summing up the recent researches of various investigators, he shows the practice of systematic dissection of the human body in the fourteenth century for purposes of instruction; the advance made in measures against infection as the source of disease, so that far more diseases were recognized as contagious than in antiquity, while leprosy largely disappeared in the fourteenth and fifteenth centuries; the use of mercury salve against syphilis long before the close of the fifteenth century, when it used to be thought that that disease first appeared in Europe (its American origin is still maintained by Barduzzi and others); the invention in southern France in the fourteenth century of the dental instrument of extraction known as the pelican; the employment of inhaled narcotics or *Spongia somnifera*;[6] the fact that medieval surgery did not slavishly follow tradition but went its own way; the development of hospitals; the progress in legal regulation of the medical profession; and the inclusion in university instruction of seminar exercises, clinics, and bedside instruction. The work of Henry of Mondeville, written between 1306 and 1320, but first edited by Pagel at Berlin in 1890–91, and translated into French by Nicaise in 1893, reveals him as a pioneer in antiseptic surgery. It was unfortunate that Guy de Chauliac, later in the century, followed Lanfranc and William of Saliceto in abandoning the pusless treatment of wounds which Hugh of Lucca, Theodoric, and Henry of Mondeville had developed.[7] I might further add some points brought out by the late Mr. Wylie: that most medieval towns of that time maintained municipal physicians; that in a hospital like the Hôtel-Dieu in Paris the patients were frequently washed, and the bed

[6] But see the subsequent articles of Marguerite G. Baur, "Recherches sur l'histoire de l'anesthésie avant 1846," *Janus*, Vol. XXXI, 1927, pp. 24–39, 63–90, 124–37, 170–82, 213–25, 264–70. She found that the medieval soporific sponges would not put even a guinea pig to sleep.

[7] See Walter von Brunn, "Die Stellung des Guy de Chauliac in der Chirurgie des Mittelalters," *Archiv f. Gesch. d. Medizin*, July, 1921, pp. 65–106. But see "Pus" in my Index for later cases of pusless treatment.

linen was changed every week or even every day, "while the extraordinarily large number of brooms used up is another indication of the thoroughness bestowed on the housework." At Troyes, iron stoves were wheeled up to the bedsides in winter to keep the patients warm.[8]

French as well as German scholars have made incursions into the medical history of the fourteenth and fifteenth centuries. Ernest Wickersheimer has contributed a number of papers and has edited various minor medical texts. Nicaise in 1890 edited Guy de Chauliac's great work of 1363 on surgery. Pansier since the opening of the present century published studies on the faculty of Montpellier, the physicians of the popes at Avignon, and the Jewish physicians at Avignon, and printed for the first time such works on the sense of sight as that written in 1308 by Arnald of Villanova or that written in 1346 by John of Casso. In Belgium a portion of the work of John of Ypres, known as the father of Flemish surgery, who died in or after 1329, was published as long ago as 1854, while in Switzerland, Meyer-Ahrens, *Die Aerzte und die Medizin der Schweiz im Mittelalter*, which dealt chiefly with the fifteenth century, was published in 1862. In English we have such publications as Henslow's *Medical Works of the Fourteenth Century*, 1899; Cholmeley's *John of Gaddesden and the Rosa Medicinae*, 1912; D'Arcy Power's edition of John Arderne, and Brennan's recent translation, *Guy de Chauliac on Wounds and Fractures*. In Italy among significant studies were Ferrari's *A Chair of Medicine in the Fifteenth Century*, which Sir Clifford Allbutt has summarized in English in one of the supplementary historical essays at the close of his *Greek Medicine in Rome*, 1921; Segarizzi's brochure on Michael Savonarola, noted physician and uncle of the yet more famous reformer; that of Simonini on Maino de Maineri; and such regional descriptive and biographical works as those of Chiapelli and Viviani on the physicians and surgeons of Pistoia and Arezzo respectively.

[8] J. H. Wylie, *The Reign of Henry the Fifth*, Vol. I (1413–15), Cambridge University Press, 1914.

In the field of mathematics and related subjects, there may be mentioned the article of Gloria in the *Atti* of the Venetian Institute on the two marvelous mechanical clocks invented by James and John de Dondis, or that of Favaro on Prosdocimo de' Beldomandi in Boncompagni's *Bullettino*, or his paper on another fifteenth-century Italian mathematician, Leonardo Mainardi of Cremona, in the *Bibliotheca mathematica*. The French mathematician, Jean de Meurs, has been treated of by Hirschfeld, Nagl, and Karpinski. In Germany Maximilian Curtze (1837–1903) edited a number of mathematical works from the closing medieval centuries. R. T. Gunther's *Early Science in Oxford* treats of such topics as the Merton school of astronomy in the fourteenth century. The importance of Richard of Wallingford, who died in 1336, in the history of trigonometry has been demonstrated by J. D. Bond in several issues of *Isis*.

Since we have just mentioned several periodicals which are devoted in whole or part to the history of science, we should not fail to state that there are others where articles may occasionally be found upon the late medieval period, such as the Dutch *Janus*, the German *Archiv für Geschichte der Medizin* and *Mitteilungen zur Geschichte der Medizin und der Naturwissenschaften*,[9] the Italian *Archivio di storia della scienza* (now *Archeion*) and *Rivista di storia delle scienze mediche e naturali*, and the French *Bulletin de la Société française d'histoire de la médecine*.

The source material for the study of science in the fourteenth and fifteenth centuries is found preëminently, of course, in the scientific writings of those times. Of these, relatively few have been printed or are accessible, and it would be an excellent idea for learned societies and councils or foundations for the stimulation and support of research to publish some

[9] *Jenaer medizin-historische Beiträge* ceased to be published after 1920, and the *Archiv für die Geschichte der Naturwissenschaften und Technik* after 1922. The latter was revived in July, 1927 as the *Archiv für Geschichte der Mathematik, der Naturwissenschaften und der Technik*.

of these late medieval science texts. We have too long been dependent for our knowledge of the middle ages upon collections made in the theological or ecclesiastical interest, like Migne's *Patrologia* or the *Acta Sanctorum*, or from the standpoint of the national state or language, like the *Monumenta Germaniae historica* and *Histoire littéraire de la France*. A *corpus* of scientific writings is a pressing desideratum. Two other kinds of records may be noted. The lives of men of science in the fourteenth and fifteenth centuries will be found set forth by such contemporary — or nearly so — biographers as Filippo Villani, Bartolomeo Fazio, Michael Savonarola, Vespasiano da Bisticci, and Trithemius, although their notices are usually all too brief and often are difficult to control. The universities were then as now the home and source of most scientific activity; they increased greatly in number in the fourteenth and fifteenth centuries, and their records and statutes tend to grow more voluminous as time goes on. Unfortunately, like the minutes of faculty meetings today, these records are apt to be concerned mainly with matters not closely related to scientific content, such as organization. However, they are occasionally helpful. Such documents, together with any private papers bearing upon the university personnel, are being increasingly published. The annual salary lists for university faculties and the records of those presenting or examining candidates for degrees give us a host of names of teachers of natural philosophy, mathematics, astronomy, medicine, and surgery, or a number of definite dates in the career of any given individual.[10] For instance, through Gloria's researches into the monuments of the university of Padua we know by name some 2200 men who were professors, doctors, licentiates, or scholars there between 1222 and 1405, and the vast majority of them in the fourteenth century. From 1318 to 1405 in

[10] Two notable publications of this type are: Umberto Dallari, *I rotuli dei lettori legisti e artisti dello Studio bolognese dal 1384 al 1799*, 4 vols., 1888–1924; and Rodolfo Maiocchi, *Codice diplomatico dell' Università di Pavia*, 1905–1915, 2 vols., covering the years 1361–1450. Both works have full indices of names.

medicine, surgery, and astrology alone we know at this single university of 78 professors, 125 persons who received the doctorate, 22 licentiates, and 120 scholars.[11] Of recent years several works have dealt with the faculties of medicine of individual universities during the closing middle ages.[12]

I shall now venture to throw out some feelers as to further investigation of this field and even hazard some conjectures as to the general character of the science of the period. First may be raised the question, are we to treat this period only as the vestibule to the theories or discoveries of Copernicus, Harvey, and Newton, and measure every astronomer then by the standard of the heliocentric hypothesis, every medical man by his approach to the discovery of the circulation of the blood, and apply the scale of the Newtonian formula to every physicist of the fourteenth and fifteenth century? Or shall we, instead of condemning most of their industry as misplaced, try to see what *they* were working for and towards, and trace their own progress according to their own lights? I have, of course, just put two extreme points of view; perhaps the best method will be found to lie somewhere between them. But if some of our own scientific tenets come in their turn to be abandoned, we shall be found to have doubly erred in our presentation of medieval error, and our account will have no value for future students. Historically, therefore, the safer method would seem to be simply to reproduce the medieval view.

The old slurs and disparaging generalizations at the expense of the middle ages are now repeated only by mechanical

[11] Andrea Gloria, *Monumenti della Università di Padova (1222–1318)*, 1884, in *Memorie del Reale Istituto Veneto di Scienze, Lettere ed Arti*, Vol. XXII; *Monumenti della Università di Padova (1318–1405)*, 1888, in *Studi editi dalla Università di Padova*, Vols. I–II. For the years 1406–50 has appeared *Acta graduum academicorum Gymnasii Patavini*, ed. C. Zonta et Ioh. Brotto, 1922.

[12] Ernest Wickersheimer, *Commentaires de la faculté de médecine de l'Université de Paris (1395–1516)*, 1915, xciii + 561 pp.; Eberhard Stübler, *Geschichte der medizinischen Fakultät der Universität Heidelberg, 1386–1925*, Heidelberg, 1926 (pp. 1–73 cover from 1386 to 1558); J. Barbot, *Les chroniques de la faculté de médecine de Toulouse du XIIIe au XXe siècle*, 1905, 2 vols.

creatures of habit, by those who stopped thinking and reading twenty or thirty years ago, and who refuse to give up any catchword or prejudice that was instilled into their minds in childhood. Candid inquirers are becoming increasingly convinced that the true Renaissance occurred around the twelfth rather than the fifteenth century,[13] that medieval Latin and scholasticism possessed great merits, that Gothic painting has been neglected just as Gothic architecture and sculpture once were, that democracy and popular education declined rather than advanced in early modern times, that organized charity and care for public health received much attention in medieval towns, whose unsanitary streets seem largely a figment of the modern imagination.[14] Every intelligent person should, if necessary, revise his former estimate of the middle age and think of it, at its height and best, especially in the life of the towns, as having much closer and more vital connections with our present civilization and way of looking at things than used to be held.[15]

Another problem is, whether there was not a falling off in civilization in general and in scientific productiveness in particular after the remarkable activity of the twelfth and thirteenth centuries — in short, whether instead of a renaissance something of a backsliding did not set in with Petrarch. Conceited as he was in many ways, he hardly thought of his own time as a renaissance. On the other hand, his frequently expressed pessimism as to his *own* time has been misinterpreted and distorted into a condemnation of the medieval period in general. It was not the thirteenth century, or even the early years of the fourteenth century in which his boyhood and student days were spent, that he condemned. On them

[13] See C. H. Haskins, *The Renaissance of the Twelfth Century*, 1927.

[14] See my article on "Medieval Sanitation, Public Baths, and Street Cleaning," in *Speculum* for April, Vol. III, pp. 192–203, 1928. Part of the material used will be found in the following chapter.

[15] See the revised edition of my *History of Medieval Europe*, 1928, especially Chapters 17 to 22; or my *Short History of Civilization*, Book VI, "Revival of Civilization in the West."

he looked back as glorious halcyon days. Then the university towns of Montpellier and Bologna were thronged with students, rich with merchandise, full of merrymaking, tranquillity, order, and freedom. Then there was no need to close the town gates after dark or to keep the walls in repair. He used to wander alone at night securely on the mountains near Avignon which now are invested with wolves and robbers. When he first visited ruined Rome, there were still some sparks in its ashes; now all is cold and extinct. All the towns of Northern Italy and Tuscany are changed for the worse, and even Venice, though still prosperous compared to others, is less prosperous than it used to be. The younger generation, which has grown up among these ills, is so used to them that it is incredulous when you tell it that times once were much better; but Petrarch is certain that piety, truth, faith, and peace have disappeared before impiety, falsehood, perfidy, war, and discord.

What were the causes contributing to this change? Were they the Hundred Years War, the ravages of the mercenaries, the sinister development of absolutism in the despotisms of the Italian cities, and the unscrupulous aggrandizement of the French monarchy? Petrarch notes that Montpellier's ruin began when it passed from the hands of the kings of Aragon and Majorca into those of the kings of France. Academic freedom began to disappear in the fourteenth century when, as Sir Clifford Allbutt has noted, the *ius ubique docendi* yielded to dependence on charter from pope, king, or bishop, royal interference increased, and universities became national instead of international. With the first years of that century, too, appeared a race of royal jackals, writers like Pierre Dubois, Jean de Jandun, and Marsiglio of Padua, who were ready to sell their services to a Philip the Fair or a Louis of Bavaria, and to doctor their thought accordingly.

What was the effect on science, thought, and intellectual productivity of the destructive Black Death of 1348, which has been so often estimated to have reduced the population from one-third to one-half, and of its repeated subsequent outbreaks? That it was a stimulus to medical literature Sudhoff, Mrs. Singer, Klebs,[16] and others have shown, and it was perhaps equally so to astrological writers. But did it result in something of a break in the continuity of civilization, in something of a decline in medieval culture, which will help to explain the notion, largely chimerical, of an Italian Renaissance after it, and the more certain fact of a growing distaste for medieval customs, institutions, and modes of thought? Was the human mind seriously affected by the repeated ravages of the plague? To what extent did schools and popular education decline? May we ascribe the inferior handwriting in manuscripts of the fourteenth and fifteenth centuries, as compared to those of the twelfth and thirteenth, to this cause, and also the inferior Latin style of many of the later schoolmen? Did the intellectual class suffer both in quantity and quality? How many can be shown to have died from the plague? How many are known to have lived through it? Is it true, as seems to have been the case, that there were more noted scientific writers and more important books in the half century preceding than in that following the fatal year of 1348? How seriously were the universities affected by the plague?[17]

Then there is the problem of the relation of humanism to science in the fourteenth and fifteenth centuries. Did humanism retard science or divert attention from it? Certainly it did very little to further the growth of natural or mathematical science, and the scientific knowledge of the average humanist seldom rose above the level of the second-rate bestiaries and lapidaries of the preceding period, whose marvels and moraliz-

[16] Dorothea Waley Singer, "Some Plague Tractates (Fourteenth and Fifteenth Centuries)," *Proceedings of the Royal Society of Medicine*, Vol. IX, 1916, Section of the History of Medicine, pp. 159–212. A. C. Klebs and E. Droz, *Remedies against the Plague*, 1925; A. C. Klebs and K. Sudhoff, *Die ersten gedruckten Pest-schriften*, 1926; and, above all, Sudhoff's series of nineteen articles on "Pestschriften aus den ersten 150 Jahren nach der Epidemie des 'schwarzen Todes,' 1348," running in the *Archiv für Geschichte der Medizin* from Vol. IV, 1910, to Vol. XVII, 1925.

[17] For a more detailed investigation of these questions than has hitherto been attempted, see the forthcoming Columbia dissertation of Anna Campbell, *The Effect of the Black Death upon Men of Learning*.

ings he repeated unquestioningly. This, however, is practically equivalent to saying that humanism and science were separate developments which had little effect upon each other. Humanism would hardly check science so much as it checked scholasticism, and it really seems to have checked scholasticism but very slightly. The humanists themselves continued to indulge in debates and disputations, only they argued whether Hannibal or Scipio was the greater man, instead of whether universals were real. The Hellenists were for the most part still devoted to Aristotle. In short, scholasticism continued almost unabated until Descartes or later, and the making of many commentaries on the *Sentences* of Peter Lombard and the *Metaphysics* of Aristotle was still going on merrily in the eighteenth century. Was not humanism in part an easier way for princes and their sons who found the existing university requirements too harsh, and for those in general who preferred to write poems, letters, and orations, instead of following intricate arguments and arranging their own thought in a systematic, orderly manner? To escape this stern necessity, the humanists glorified what had been a grammar-school subject, Latin, into the sum and substance of culture, and it has remained for us today to make things still easier for ambitious youth by dropping that same grammar-school subject from the curriculum as too difficult. Indeed, leisure and cultured ease were the ideal of many humanists, as against either great literary productivity or sustained reasoning.

Whether it was due to humanism or not, Duhem was impressed in the course of his investigation by a decline of astronomy in Italy of the fourteenth and fifteenth centuries. In western Europe generally, the natural encyclopedias of the thirteenth century seem not to have been improved upon during the two following centuries, and little evidence has yet been brought to light of further advance in zoology, botany, and mineralogy. In these fields, such thirteenth-century writers as Albertus Magnus and even Bartholomew of England continued to be cited as authorities in the sixteenth century.

The *Lumen animae* or *Liber moralitatum rerum naturalium* [18] has usually been printed and referred to under the name of Matthias Farinator, who, however, on his own statement in the preface, appears to have been simply its fifteenth-century editor. In a Strasburg manuscript a work of that title at least is ascribed to Johannes Modernior, whose name, suggesting that he was a very up-to-date citizen, might incline one to place him late, but the manuscript is of the thirteenth and fourteenth centuries.[19] In another manuscript, of the monastery of Saints Ulrich and Afra at Augsburg, the author gives his name as Berengarius (of Londora), a Dominican who was archbishop of Compostela from 1317 to 1325.[20] I have also seen the work ascribed to Hermann von Gottschalk, a canon of Vorau in the pontificate of John XXII (1316–34), but I do not know upon what authority. The work cites few, if any, authors later than the thirteenth century and might have been written then so far as its contents are concerned. In fact, since it appears to have been dedicated to John XXII and its author says he has worked on it for twenty-nine years, it was presumably begun in the thirteenth century.

In a general way it resembles the *Septiformis de moralitatibus rerum nature*,[21] which was apparently addressed by an

[18] The edition of 1477 was very kindly sent to New York for my use by the library of Princeton University.

[19] Strasburg 86 (Latin 83), 13th–14th centuries, fols. 49–86, Johannis Modernioris Lumen animae.

[20] R. Cruel, *Geschichte der deutschen Predigt im Mittelalter*, 1879, p. 460, citing Braun, *De codd. S. Ulrici*, etc., V. 112, quotes the following Latin passage, not found in the printed text, from the MS: "Tandem ego frater Berengarius, quondam magister ordinis fratrum Predicatorum, nunc autem quamvis indignus Compostellis Archiepiscopus, hunc sic fundatus librum edidi ad utilitatem mei ordinis et ad edificationem hominibus universis."

[21] L. Delisle discussed the work in the first part of his long article, "Traités divers sur les propriétés des choses," *Histoire littéraire de la France*, Vol. XXX, 1888, pp. 334–53. He corrected the false or dubious assumptions of Narducci, "Intorno ad una Enciclopedia finora sconosciuta di Egidio Colonna, romano, ed al plagio fattone dall' inglese, Bartolomeo Glanville," *Atti della R. Accad. dei Lincei*, January 18, 1885. Besides the Munich MS in which I have examined the work (CLM 8809, A. D. 1426, fols. 2r–236r), and which Delisle used in penning his notice, there is the MS used by Narducci (Q. 5. 26 of the Angelica Library, Rome). Both Narducci and Delisle failed to note a third

anonymous author [22] between 1281 and 1291 to Benedict Cajetan, the future Boniface VIII,[23] the *Summa de exemplis ac similitudinibus rerum* of John of San Gimignano,[24] who wrote about 1350, and the *Reductorium, repertorium, et dictionarium morale utriusque Testamenti* [25] of Petrus Berchorius, or Pierre Bersuire, a Benedictine of Poitou, who died in 1362. These works continued the biblical, moralizing, and marvelizing strain which had often characterized works written by the medieval clergy, and added little to the scientific information contained in the *De proprietatibus rerum*, composed by Bartholomew of England in the first half of the thirteenth century.

In the vernacular the *Dittamondo* of Fazio degli Uberti,[26] who died in 1367, was an attempt, somewhat like the *Acerba* of Cecco d'Ascoli half a century earlier, to describe the world of nature in imitation of Dante's depiction of the other world, but marked no advance upon the thirteenth-century treatise of Ristoro d'Arezzo, *La composizione del mondo*.[27]

The *De mundi fabrica* or *Fons memorabilium mundi* of Dominicus Bandinus (*c.* 1335–1418) of Arezzo, a work written

---

(Antoniana XVIII, 388, 14th century, 232 fols., at Padua), which is hardly favorable to their contention that the work was written between 1281 and 1291. Another MS is Oxford, New College 157, 14th century, 156 fols.

22 But according to Antonio Maria Iosa, *I codici manoscritti della biblioteca Antoniana di Padova*, Padua, 1886, p. 231, the copy of it in MS XVIII, 388 of that library ascribes the work to Thomas Vallensis, who was a Domincan of the first half of the fourteenth century, according to the *Apparatus Sacri* of Possevino (1553–1611). This Paduan copy is of the fourteenth century, and has the same Incipit and Explicit as the other two MSS.

23 Presumably it was this dedication to Cardinal Cajetan which led Angiolgabriello da Santa Maria, in his *Biblioteca e storia di quei scrittori cosi della città coma del territorio di Vicenza*, 1772–82, 6 vols., to list the *Septiformis* among the works of Gaietanus de Thienis (1387–1465)!

24 Printed at Venice, 1499, Joa. et Greg. de Gregoriis. Cruel, *op. cit.*, p. 460, says that some make Helvicus Teutonicus the author, rather than John of San Gimignano.

25 It appeared in many editions: for example, Strasburg, 1474; Deventer and Cologne, 1477; Nürnberg, Koburger, 1489: Paris, 1521–22; Venice, 1575. It continued to be printed in the seventeenth century, in 1609, 1620, and even as late as 1692, Cologne — the edition which I have used.

26 First edition at Vicenza, 1474.

27 Edited by Enrico Narducci, Rome, 1859; Milan, 1864.

about 1400, appears to have made little impression. It seems not to have been printed, and to be found in manuscript form rarely and in scattered portions.[28] In a letter of 1462 it was described as a compilation useful chiefly to those who had few other books of reference.[29]

George Valla of Piacenza wrote a voluminous résumé of all the arts and sciences in forty-nine books, which, after his death, was published by his son in 1501 in two folio volumes.[30] The work was of no especial merit unless as an industrious but uninspired compilation. On most topics it is not as full as the thirteenth-century encyclopedia of Vincent of Beauvais. Its chief novel feature was the inclusion of more excerpts from ancient Greek writers, but this gain was nullified by the omission of most medieval authorities. Brief compendiums of natural science or of the works of Aristotle were produced by the reformer, Savonarola,[31] by Theophilus Cremonensis de Ferrariis,[32] by Nicolaus de Orbellis,[33] by Johannes Peyligk,[34] and by Hermolaus Barbarus.[35]

[28] Such as, at Venice, S. Marco, XIV, 47 (Valentinelli), paper, A.D. 1429, *Liber de herbis, leguminibus, et oleribus et de virtutibus herbarum;* and S. Michael de Muriano, 22, 15th century, "De populis, de aedificiis, de provinciis, de civitatibus, de insulis" (quarta pars immensi operis *Fons memorabilium universi*). The following items, ascribed to "Dominicus de Aretio" in a Vatican MS, are probably extracts from the work of Bandinus: Vatic. lat. 3121, fol. 1, de celo signis et imaginibus celestibus, opening, 'Iuvat me diu versatum . . ."; fol. 23, de stellis errantibus, opening, "Quoniam celos . . ." Bandinus went to see Petrarch about the book in 1374, lost his manuscript for some years after 1381, and completed the work later. See Mehus' account of Bandinus in his long *Praefatio* to the 1759 edition of the Latin letters of Ambrogio Traversari, pp. cxxix–cxxxviii.

[29] Ugo Viviani, *Medici, fisici e cerusici della provincia Aretina*, 1923, pp. 47–49.

[30] *Georgii Vallae Placentini De expetendis et fugiendis rebus opus in libros xlix tributum*, Venice, Aldine, 1501.

[31] Frater Hieronymus Savonarola de Ferraria ordinis praedicatorum, *Compendium totius philosophiae tam naturalis quam moralis*, Venet., apud Iuntas, 1542.

[32] *Propositiones ex omnibus Aristotelis libris*, Venetiis, Joh. et Greg. Gregoriis, 1493.

[33] N. de Orbellis, *Cursus librorum philosophie naturalis secundum viam doctoris subtilis Scoti*, 1494, 1503, etc.

[34] *Philosophiae naturalis compendium*, 1499.

[35] *Compendium scientiae naturalis ex Aristotele*, Paris, Jean Roigny, 1547.

Commentaries upon the *Physics* and the psychological treatises of Aristotle seem to have continued to pour forth, but these were the more theoretical of the Aristotelian treatises, although it may be that a diligent search would reveal some precious kernels of scientific development concealed within the intricate and voluminous folds of the scholastic argumentation of these commentaries. Duhem has shown that out of the scholastic discussion of and commentaries upon Aristotle at the University of Paris in the first half of the fourteenth century, which used to be stigmatized as a period of sterile verbosity, were engendered new hypotheses and theories marking the birth of modern dynamics. Occam attacked the Aristotelian physics; Buridan and Albert of Saxony (bishop of Halberstadt from 1366 to 1390) [36] developed a clear and complete theory of impetus. Buridan furthermore held that the same mechanics apply to celestial as to sublunar bodies and, in describing the quantity of first matter, used almost the same terms as Sir Isaac Newton did concerning mass. Albert of Saxony suggested that the fall of a heavy body is a motion uniformly accelerated. Like his predecessor, Franciscus de Mayronis, and his contemporary, Nicolas Oresme, he suggested that it might be better to regard the eighth sphere of the fixed stars as immobile and the earth as in motion.[37] This suggestion would seem superior to that for which Nicholas of Cusa, in the next century, has been given so much credit, namely, that the eighth sphere revolved twice about its poles while the earth revolved once.

The impression should not prevail, therefore, that the period was mainly one of decline or setback or standstill. Just as many gilds and representative bodies did not come into existence until the fourteenth and fifteenth centuries, just as many towns reached the height of their development not in the thirteenth but in the fifteenth century, so we have, at least

[36] Georg Heidingsfelder, *Albert von Sachsen, sein Lebensgang und sein Kommentar zur Nikomachischen Ethik des Aristoteles*, 1921, in Baeumker's *Beiträge*, Vol. XXII.

[37] Pierre Duhem, *Études sur Léonard de Vinci, ceux qu'il a lus et ceux qui l'ont lu*, Paris, Vol. III, 1913, pp. vii–xi, 29–43, 263, etc.

in certain regions and subjects, further intellectual activity and advance. In legal thought and writing the Bartolists with their innovations replaced the earlier Glossators. In theology we find a controversy raging between the "moderns" — or perhaps I should say, modernists — as the followers of the fourteenth-century writers, such as John Buridan and Marsilius d'Inghen, were called, and the "ancients," an epithet now applied to thirteenth-century writers such as Alexander of Hales, Albertus Magnus, Aquinas, Egidius Romanus, and Bonaventura. In medicine the works of Marsilius de Sancta Sophia Junior, who died about 1411, and of Jacopo da Forlì, who died in 1414, by the time of Michael Savonarola, about thirty years later, "occupy all the schools of our time." Or already in fourteenth-century France we find Nicolas Oresme suggesting the use of coördinates and apparently the first to employ fractional exponents. He also is important for his works on the depreciation of coinage and his several criticisms of astrologers and magic. Much attention was given throughout our period to the matter of calendar reform: John of Meurs and others urged it in 1337; Pope Clement VI considered it in 1345; it was again urged by Cardinal Pierre d'Ailly at the beginning of the fifteenth century, Regiomontanus was summoned to Rome concerning it in 1474–75, and Paul of Middelburg addressed Innocent VIII (1484–1492) on the theme. Another frequent scientific occupation was the compilation of astronomical tables.

The work of translation from the Arabic had largely ceased, and Arabic science was on the decline, now that Persia and Mesopotamia had been desolated by the Mongol hordes. But translation from the Greek, which had gone on indeed all through the middle ages, increased in the fourteenth and fifteenth centuries, although this increase was manifest in the realm of pure literature rather than of science. However, Nicholas of Reggio translated additional works of Galen from Greek into Latin for King Robert of Naples, and such an important work as the *Geography* of Ptolemy was translated into Latin for the first time by Jacobus Angelus for Pope Alexander V in 1409. But medieval geographical knowledge had hitherto been steadily growing without its assistance. Indeed, the translation had the bad effect that, as the age of the discoveries began to open, too much confidence was placed by cartographers and others in the mistaken theories of Ptolemy, to the neglect of the medieval geographical knowledge and maps which constitute the true background and basis of the evolution of modern geographical science.

The inventiveness of the middle ages continued to manifest itself in the fourteenth and fifteenth centuries, and seems to offer a promising, though difficult, field for further investigation. Printing is about the only invention of the period that has thus far been adequately studied. We have both practical inventions and the development of scientific instruments. The invention of the mariner's compass in the twelfth century was followed about 1300 by that of the rudder, and by changes in the build of shipping and in masts, spars, and rigging in the fourteenth and fifteenth centuries. Similarly the invention of gunpowder in the thirteenth century was followed in the fourteenth and fifteenth centuries by further developments in fortifications and armor and by the invention of artillery and firearms. The fourteenth century also saw the introduction of the blast furnace and progress in ironworking. Indeed, by 1300 almost all the coal fields of England were being worked, and her iron and textile industries were already in existence; but she did not yet have an empire to which to sell.

The mechanical clock of the early fourteenth century was in a way the parent of all subsequent machinery, and not a few of the inventors of the time of the industrial revolution in the eighteenth century resorted to clock-makers in order to perfect their ideas and made them practicable. Our division of the hour into minutes and seconds was not known to Bartholomew of England in the first half of the thirteenth century, but was employed as customary by John of Meurs and Firminus of Bellavalle in 1345. Various astronomers made marvelous instruments representing the movements of the celestial bodies and in the fifteenth century Giovanni Bianchini devised an instrument for measuring the distance and height of inaccessible bodies. In 1342 Peter of Alexandria had translated into Latin for Pope Clement VI, under the title "The Instrument That Reveals Secrets," a passage from Levi ben Gerson dealing with Jacob's staff, an instrument to determine the altitude of the stars, which was subsequently employed by the Portuguese mariners.

Only thirty years ago the following statement was made, not by some crude American unacquainted with the more recent findings of European scholarship, but by the Gallic author of a history of French literature in the sixteenth century: "The world has been discovered for only a trifle over three hundred years. The time has not been more than that during which men have known that the world is round, that it is small and the sky infinite. This [discovery] has changed all ideas." [38] This utterance represents one of the worst slanders current against the fair name of the middle ages, when every astronomical textbook or lecturer taught that the earth was a sphere, and this was well known to any educated layman such as Dante. The southern hemisphere and likewise the western hemisphere were unknown, but progress was being made in geographical science and discovery.[39] The thirteenth century had opened up the entire Far East to European ambassadors and travelers such as William of Rubruk and Marco Polo. "The thirteenth century knew China better than we

[38] E. Faguet, *Seizième siècle*, 1898, pp. vi–vii: "Le monde a été découvert il y a un peu plus de trois cent ans. Il n'y a pas plus de temps que les hommes savent que la terre est ronde, qu'elle est petite et que le ciel est infini. Cela a changé toutes les idées." Of course, if such an author were discussing Sir Isaac Newton, he would think nothing of veering completely about and representing the middle ages as having regarded the heavens as eternal and incorruptible and far removed from the inferior creation of earth, whereas Newton showed the heavenly bodies to be subject to the same mechanical laws as terrestrial matter.

[39] On the whole subject consult C. Raymond Beazley, *Dawn of Modern Geography*, 3 vols., 1897–1906.

knew it in the middle of the nineteenth century." Jordan the Catalan, writing about 1324, gave the best account of India by any medieval Christian writer. Caravans crossed the Sahara to the interior of Africa, and Genoese vessels made an attempt to circumnavigate that continent. In 1316 Dominican missionaries went far up the Nile, and William Adam began a cruise of twenty months duration in the Indian Ocean. Architects from Granada constructed a royal palace on the Niger.[40]

Indeed, sufficient records remain to reveal the middle of the fourteenth century to us as an age of globe-trotters and world-wide adventurers. Francesch des Valers, who in 1342 commanded two vessels sent to the Canaries, about twelve years later took the eastward route to Tartary. Forty years thereafter the memory of his mission was still green, for the King of Aragon called in a survivor of the party to tell him the story of his travels in the Far East. Or, if we turn from Christian Spain to the westernmost Moslem world, we have the case of Ibn Batuta of Morocco, whose account of his travels was rediscovered in the modern French occupation of Algeria. He visited not merely Asia Minor and Russia, but India, the Maldives, and China, spending much time *en route*. On his return, he crossed the Sahara to the Sudan on a mission for the Sultan of Fez in 1352. While on his way, far south of the Atlas Mountains, he met a man whom he had seen in China.

Such intercourse with the distant parts of Asia and Africa fell off after the middle of the fourteenth century, perhaps as a result of the loss of life and disorganization of society in the Black Death, but its traces remain in the Italian and Catalan *portolani* which revolutionized, or rather, created the science of cartography from about 1300 on.[41] They also show us that westward Atlantic exploration had begun and that such groups of islands as the Canaries and even the Azores were known and

[40] Charles de la Roncière, *La découverte de l'Afrique au moyen âge*, 1925, 2 vols.

[41] E. L. Stevenson, *Portolan Charts, Their Origin and Characteristics*, 1911.

charted. But it appears that the Portuguese had to rediscover the Madeiras and Azores in the first half of the fifteenth century, perhaps because of a confusion following the Black Death such as we have suggested. In 1455 Cadamosto ascended the Senegal and Gambia rivers, and the next year he discovered the Cape Verde Islands. Fra Mauro's world map of 1457–59, made for King Alfonso V of Portugal, showed a surprising knowledge of Abyssinia and the Galla countries lying south of it.[42] In 1472–73 the Portuguese crossed the equator.

The occult sciences lost nothing of their hold upon the human mind during the fourteenth and fifteenth centuries, and continued to be inextricably combined with the natural and mathematical science of the time. Nicholas Oresme and Henry of Hesse, in the fourteenth, and Pico della Mirandola, in the fifteenth century, might criticize astrology, but almost every astronomer of the time wrote or lectured on astrology, and many of them made particular predictions. The literature of alchemy becomes increasingly abundant, and works now appeared under the great names of the thirteenth century — Aquinas, Albertus Magnus, Raymond Lull, and so on. One wonders if there is any relation between the enigmatical alchemistic treatises and the prevalence of mysticism during this period.

But I would close this chapter rather with an instance of practical surgical skill of the fifteenth century. We have heard a good deal lately of the wonderful plastic surgery performed during the recent war, as if it were an entirely modern development. But hear the following passage from Bartolommeo Fazio's *De viris illustribus*, written in 1456:[43]

I have thought peculiarly worthy of being remembered and included in this number the Brancas, father and son, remarkable

[42] E. Heawood, *A History of Geographical Discovery in the Seventeenth and Eighteenth Centuries*, 1912, p. 144.

[43] I use the eighteenth-century edition with introduction by Laurentius Mehus, where the passage concerning the Brancas is found at pp. 38–39 of the text of Facius.

Sicilian surgeons, of whom Branca the father was the inventor of an admirable and almost incredible process. For he thought out a way to reform and complete dissected and mutilated noses, and accomplished all this with wonderful art. Moreover, Antony, his son, added not a little to the beautiful invention of his father. For he devised a process by which mutilated lips and ears, as well as noses, could be repaired. And while the father had cut skin to piece out the nose from the face of the mutilated person, he took it from the arm, so that no facial deformity resulted therefrom. And he inserted the remains of the mutilated nose, and bound them up so tightly that the mutilated person could not even move his head. After fifteen or sometimes twenty days, he would little by little cut open the bit of flesh which adhered to the nose and reform it into nostrils with such skill that the eye could scarcely detect where it had been joined on, and all facial deformity was completely removed. He healed many wounds which it seemed that no resource of medical art could heal.

However, according to a note by Tiraboschi, this facial reconstruction did not immediately die out with Brancas, father and son, but continued to be characteristic of surgery through the sixteenth century.

CHAPTER II

MEDICINE VERSUS LAW AT FLORENCE[1]

In the manuscript collections of the Laurentian Library at Florence are preserved several codices of the fifteenth century containing discussions of the relative importance of law and medicine. Some of the treatises on this theme appear to have never been printed, and on the whole perhaps hardly deserve to be printed at this late date. Taken together, however, the works on this theme, which was discussed by such well-known men of the time as Coluccio Salutati and Poggio Bracciolini, merit some attention and are of some interest in the history of law and of medicine, of thought and its expression, and in consideration of the period of declining scholasticism and of the so-called Italian Renaissance or Quattrocento.

Of the treatises to be here considered, the oldest and longest was composed on the verge of the fifteenth century in 1399 by Coluccio Salutati, the celebrated Florentine secretary and humanist, and bears the title, *Tractatus de nobilitate legum et medicinae* (On the Nobility of Law and Medicine). There are two well-written manuscript copies of it in the Laurentian Library, namely, Strozzi 95 and Laurent. Plut. 78, cod. 11.[2]

[1] Revised and enlarged from the *Romanic Review*, Vol. XVII, No. 1, January–March, 1926, pp. 8–31.

[2] Strozzianae 95, 15th century, nitide exaratus, 62 fols. Incipit cap. 1, Quid sit nobilitas, "Scio quam arduum quamque grave sit Doctor egregie frater charissime. . . ."

"Explicit feliciter tractatus de nobilitate legum et medicine editus per Colucium Pyeri Salutatum ad magistrum Bernardum phisicum de Florentia qui perfectus fuit anno Domini MCCCLXXXXVIIII indictione septima IIII Idus Augusti."

Laurent. Plut. 78, cod. 11, early 15th century, has the same Explicit. It is beautifully written and illuminated upon membrane. At fol. 1r occurs the rubric, "Colucii pyeri Salutati de nobilitate legum et medicine ad Bernardum physicum de Florentia tractatus incipit et primo proemium." Both in this rubric and the Explicit, the word "Florentia" appears to have been half erased.

In both Strozzi 96, 15th century, nitidissimus, 38 fols., and Laurent. Plut. 78,

The work was printed for the first and only time at Venice in 1542,[3] but this edition seems to be rare; the British Museum, for example, has no copy of it.[4] I have examined this printed edition at Florence and noted only slight variations between it and the manuscripts.

The second in order of time and much the shortest of our treatises, entitled *Disputatio an medicina sit legibus politicis preferenda vel econtra* (A Disputation whether Medicine is to be Preferred to Laws Politic or Contrariwise), is, in part at least, by John Baldus, physician and citizen of Florence, whose medical work, *De temporibus partus*, addressed, as it happens, to the noble doctor of laws, Alexander Salvi Philippi, likewise a citizen of Florence, precedes it in Gaddi reliq. 74, where our treatise occupies fols. 102–105v (old numbering, fols. 97r–101v). At the close it is stated that it was copied in 1488 from a text written in 1415.[5] I shall usually refer to it as the treatise of 1415. The *De temporibus partus* occurs with other treatises by the same author in another manu-

---

cod. 12, is another work by Salutati on the theme that physicians should study eloquence, "Coluccii Salutati tractatus quod medici eloquentiae studeant."

There is some indication that the Strozzi MS of the *De nobilitate legum et medicine* is a copy made from the Laurentian MS. Thus at the bottom of fol. 45v the Strozzi MS inserts two lines which are found in their proper place in the Laurentian MS.

[3] "Tractatus insignis et elegans Colutii Pieri Salutati de nobilitate legum et medicinae in quo terminatur illa quaestio versatilis in studiis utrum dignior sit scientia legalis vel medicinalis. Venetiis. In aedibus Ioanni Baptistae Pederzani, MDXXXXII."

The treatise of Salutati is preceded by a letter to its editor urging him to publish it: "Hieronymus Gradonius iurecons. clarissimo oratori et iureconsulto Hieronymo Giganti Forosemproniensi S. P. D."

Then follows: "Colutii Pieri Salutati Tractatus de nobilitate legum et medicinae ad Bernardum medicum de Florentia per Hieronymum Gigantem Iureconsultum Forosemproniensem Nunc primum in lucem edictum."

[4] There is, however, a copy of this edition in the Surgeon General's Library at Washington, D. C.

[5] Gaddi reliq. 74, chart., double-columned page, fol. 105v, col. 2: "Ex exemplari corrupto scripto in anno 1415, 23 aprilis fuit hec extracta in anno 1488 die 28 aprilis." The preceding *De temporibus partus*, at fols. 97r–101v, is dated at the close "15 kal. maii 1488," indicating that it was copied on April 17. The juxtaposition of the two methods of dating in the same MS is interesting.

script of the Laurentian library,[6] in which he designates himself as John Baldus de Tambenis of Faenza, a citizen of Florence.

The leading treatise in this other manuscript is a discussion, in three sections, whether the science of the Gentiles, that is to say, profane learning, is contrary to the Catholic faith.[7] Baldus maintains that science is not contrary to the Faith, against Rainaldus dominus Masii de Albicis of Florence, whose arguments against science occupy the first section.[8] The second section [9] consists chiefly of the establishing by Baldus of ten main conclusions with various subordinate "reasons" and corrollaries. In the third section he demolishes one by one the twenty arguments of his adversary. The work is dedicated to Malatesta de' Malatesti, ruler of Pesaro from 1373 to 1429, and in closing the dedicatory epistle John Baldus speaks of his lectures at the Universities of Bologna and Florence. He epigrammatically describes his intellectual life as consisting in harassing his equals, teaching his scholars, and asking questions of those who know more than he does. What he knows, he teaches, and what he has seen or doubted concerning, he tries to pry into. He praises frequent disputations as training the intellect just as physical exercise strengthens the body. Medicine is his main interest, but he sometimes enters the fields of other sciences as in the present work. Even in it, however, he treats more fully of medicine than of any other

[6] Laurent. Plut. 19, cod. 30, 15th century, membr., 45 fols. and not 44 as stated by Bandini. The *De temporibus partus* occurs at fols. 38r–44r (not 37–43, as given by Bandini) with the rubric, "Tractatus de temporibus partus ad nobilem legum doctorem dominum Alexandrum salvi phylipi utilem florintinum civem per Magistrum Iohannem baldum physicum civem florintinum."

[7] *Ibid.*, fols. 1r–30v (and not 29v, as in Bandini). The rubric reads: "Incipit tractatus quo concluditur nullam gentilium scientiam chatolice [*sic*] fidei christiane esse contrariam, ymo quamlibet talem ad ipsius veritatem cognoscendam parare viam, ad Magnificum dominum malatestam de malatestis de pesaurio editus cum obedientia per Magistrum Iohannem baldum de tambenis de faventia civem florintinum." Bandini gives the Incipit and Desinit for each part, but his pagination should be advanced one in each case.

[8] *Ibid.*, fols. 2r–6v.

[9] *Ibid.*, fols. 6v–19r.

science [10] and discusses again the question of the relative superiority of medicine and law.

Of the remaining three treatises in this manuscript, two are addressed to or concern members of the Medici family. One of these deals with the choice of a physician and is addressed by John Baldus to Cosimo as a youth;[11] the other is a moral discussion of anger.[12] The third treatise seems to be an attempt to console a noble count on the death of his son by resort to a sophistical form, it being argued, first, that it is not possible for a man to have had a son; second, that if he can have one, he cannot lose him; third, that if he can lose him, he should not grieve at his death.[13] The person who is being argued with keeps repeating the same refrain in each of the three sections, namely, "Filium habui," "Filium a[d]misi," and "Filii mei morte doleo," like the similar interlocutor in Petrarch's *De remediis utriusque fortunae.*

It will be seen that these other treatises substantiate rather than conflict with 1415 as the date of composition of John Baldus's discussion of the relative importance of law and medicine. From such *rotuli* of the University of Bologna as are extant we learn that Master John Baldus of Faenza taught there from 1385 to 1389. During the first two years he taught natural philosophy; during the last two he taught logic in addition, receiving a humble stipend of twenty-five pounds Bolognese for his lectures in natural philosophy, and fifty

[10] Laurent. Plut. 19, cod. 30, fols. 5r, 15v–16r, 26v–28r.

[11] *Ibid.*, fols. 44r–45r (not 43–44 as in Bandini): "De electione medici ad nobilem florintinum [*sic*] iuvenem cosmum Iohannis bitii de medicis per Magistrum Iohannem [bal]dum physicum civem florintinum."

[12] *Ibid.*, fols. 30v–31v: "Extirpatio ire a nobili iuvene florentino Nicola domini verii de medicis utiliter quesita per Iohannem baldum physicum de tambenis civem florentium [?] desideranda veritate edita vigore illius cuius lumine lumen videmus." Alternate sentences or paragraphs begin with the phrases, "Irasci licet" and "Non licet irasci."

[13] *Ibid.*, fols. 32r–37v: "Incipit tractatus quo ratione concluditur non esse possibile hominem filium habuisse, et si potest haberi quod non possit amicti, et si possit amicti quod non sit illius morte dolere, ad nobilem comitem Antonium de monte Garnneli [Carmeli?] editus per Magistrum Iohannem baldum de faventia civem florintinum."

pounds for the instruction in logic.[14] Since the dedicatory epistle to Malatesta de' Malatesti represents his teaching at Bologna as a thing of the past, before he came to Florence, and since he would naturally teach such subjects as natural philosophy and logic for the salaries indicated when a young man and not yet far advanced in medicine, these dates, too, agree well with 1415 for the writing of our treatise.

A third Florentine, if I may so term him, to discuss the case of medicine versus law was John of Arezzo [15] who addressed Lorenzo de' Medici on this subject while he was still young and soon after the death of his father, Piero de' Medici. John of Arezzo's work on the heart, dedicated to the aforesaid Piero, occurs in another Laurentian manuscript (Plut. 73, cod. 29, 15th century, membr., 68 fols., *De procuratione cordis*) and will be discussed in a later chapter.[16] The treatise at present under consideration, entitled *De medicina et legum prestantia* (Of the Superiority of Medicine and Law), is contained in a very neatly and even elegantly written and beautifully illuminated manuscript, Laurent. Plut. 77, cod. 22, of 45 brief leaves.[17] Like many of the Laurentian manuscripts, it has chains attached to it.

Our theme was also utilized by the noted humanist, Poggio Bracciolini, in one of the three brief dialogues which constitute

[14] U. Dallari, *I rotuli dei lettori legisti e artisti dello studio Bolognese dal 1384 al 1799*, 4 vols., 1888–1924, Vol. I, p. 7; Vol. IV, pp. 11, 12, 14.

[15] On John's identity see Ugo Viviani, *Medici, fisici e cerusici della Provincia Aretina dal V al XVII secolo*, 1923, pp. 79–82, where he is identified with a Giovanni Lippi. Ambrogio Traversari refers in a letter to a bookseller of the same name, "Hodie mecum diutius fuit Johannes Aretinus librarius multaque invicem contulimus": Martène et Durand, *Veterum scriptorum . . . collectio*, 1724, Vol. III, p. 536.

[16] See chapter 5, "Some Minor Medical Works of the Florentine Renaissance."

[17] Rubric at the top of fol. 1r: "IOHANNIS ARRETINI PHISICI DE MEDICINE ET LEGUM PRESTANTIA AD CLARISSIMUM IUVENEM LAURENTIUM MEDICEM."

Incipit, "Cum animum antea aplicuerim ad te conscribere, Laurenti adolescens spectatissime. . . ." The second day's dialogue, "De legum ac medicine scientia que prestantior sit?" begins only at fol. 28r. Most of the leaves of this MS are unnumbered. Mehus, 1759, p. 58, described the MS briefly and noted some of its mentions of Niccolò Niccoli.

his *Historia Tripartita*, written in 1450, and printed in the 1513 edition of his works.[18] It has already been discussed by Walser in his recent work on Poggio and briefly contrasted with Salutati's treatment of the same theme.[19] But Walser did not know of our other two treatises. It will therefore be advisable for us to refer occasionally to Poggio's dialogue for purposes of comparison with our other treatises. Chronologically it precedes the treatise of John of Arezzo, who was perhaps influenced by Poggio's previous treatment. Poggio's probable debt to other previous literature has already been discussed by Walser.

Yet a striking circumstance about these three treatises — or four, if we include Poggio's — all composed in the same city [20] within a space of about seventy years and found — except Poggio's — in the same library, is that the later writers take no notice of their predecessors, although they employ very similar, not to say identical, arguments. Perhaps the relative merits of legal and medical studies and professions were a favorite theme of scholastic disputation then. Walser implies that this was the case, but he does not name any specific instance of a scholastic discussion of this theme before Salutati. And while he asserts that "the old useless controversy between the doctors and jurists" finds in Poggio's dialogue "realistic, Machiavellian treatment instead of "rhetorizing prize-fighting" anent soul and body, subject and accident, and the like,[21] Salutati's treatise is really the only example he offers of such scholastic debate.

[18] *Historia tripartita*, or *Disceptationes convivales tres*, *Opera*, 1513, fols. 13–24. Poggio also wrote orations in praise of the laws and of medicine. There is a manuscript containing them at the Vatican: Latin MS 3923, fol. 9–, Oratio in laudem legum, "Si quis ea esset facultas . . ."; fol. 19–, Oratio in laudem medicinae, "Vellem . . ."

[19] E. Walser, *Poggius Florentinus: Leben und Werke*, 1914, pp. 248–58. Voigt, *Wiederbelebung des classischen Alterthums*, 3d edition, 1893, Vol. II, p. 480, also refers to Salutati's treatise but had evidently not seen it and misinterprets its attitude. Alfred von Martin makes use of Salutati's treatise in his *Mittelalterliche Welt- und Lebensanschauung im Spiegel der Schriften Coluccio Salutatis*, 1913, and *Coluccio Salutati und das humanistische Lebensideal*, 1916, but does not mention our other two treatises.

[20] With the possible exception of Poggio's. The scene is laid at his villa in Terranuova in 1449. He had hitherto been papal secretary at Rome, but on April 27, 1450, became chancellor of Florence.

[21] Walser, 1914, p. 258.

But Salutati himself at the beginning of his treatise states that it was an ancient and much debated controversy,[22] and in Appendix 1 at the close of this volume I shall note some further instances of it, which are mainly of the fifteenth century, however. But it is noteworthy that in a work written especially for Lorenzo the Magnificent, who is commonly represented as one of the most intellectual patrons of the Renaissance and who at least had access to the library started by Cosimo de' Medici, John of Arezzo should put the discussion of the relative merits of law and medicine into the mouths of such celebrated men of the Quattrocento as Carlo Marsupi, or Marsuppini, of Arezzo, poet laureate, Niccolò Niccoli of Florence,[23] and Leonardo Aretino,[24] but say nothing of Coluccio Salutati, John Baldus, and Poggio, who had all three previously written on his very theme. Indeed, Carlo Marsuppini had already appeared in Poggio's dialogue as one of the interlocutors, although Poggio referred to him as state chancellor of Florence rather than as poet laureate, and although the chief disputants were the jurist Benedetto Accolti against the physician Niccolò da Foligno,[25] whereas in John of Arezzo's dialogue Carlo presents the arguments for the law.

[22] "Scio quam arduum quamque grave sit, doctor egregie fraterque karissime, controversiam antiquam ingentem et quam crediderim ventilatam a multis, a te vero nuper determinatam . . ."

[23] Giuseppe Zippel, *Nicolò Niccoli*, 1890, pp. 61–62, anent the mention of the library of a Giovanni Aretino in a letter by Pier Candido Decembrio to Nicolò about 1412, asks, "E questi l'autore del dialogo *de legum et medicinae praestantia*, oppure quel Giovanni Aretino libraio, di cui parla il Traversari in una sua lettera? (Cfr. Martène et Durand, III, 536)". This seems to indicate that he was aware of the existence of our treatise but neither knew the date of its composition (1469 or later) nor the fact that Niccolò Niccoli figures in it.

[24] "Carolus arretinus laureatus poeta et Nicolaus nicolus florentinus litterarum amantissimus ad Leonardum arretinum istoricum et philosophum doctissimum veniunt: sed a Nicolao primo sermo oritur." This rubric follows the close of the preface to Lorenzo de' Medici at fol. 4v. Then with a finely illuminated capital *S* and a first line in small capitals the text proper begins, "Sepenumero confabulari soleo, Leonarde vir excellens, cum hoc Carlo, ornatissimo viro . . ." Previously in the preface (at fol. 4r-v) John said, "Introduxi autem meos [?] consocios loquentes ac disceptantes Carolum arretinum et Nicolaum nicolum florentinum ut assolebant et Leonardum arretinum respondentem."

[25] Poggio, *Opera*, 1513, fol. 14r: "ac Nycholaus Fulginus [*sic*] insignis philo-

One wonders if both John of Arezzo and Lorenzo de' Medici were ignorant of the very existence of these previous works.[26] While it would be going too far to suggest that John was inclined to trade upon Lorenzo's ignorance, we obtain a slight hint that he regarded Lorenzo as less of an intellectual, or at least as less of a bookworm, than his father Piero, from a comparison of the prefaces and texts of the two works which he addressed to them. In that addressed to the father, John states that Piero has always cultivated the mind, and that even in his boyhood days "dogs or hawks or horses, in which many of less sound judgment delight, were not agreeable to your free and elevated spirit." [27] In the preface to the son, on the other hand, while he professes the conviction that gifts of the spirit (*munera ingenio elaborata*) will be more grateful to Lorenzo [28] "than horses or dogs or hawks," he adds, "although you have an abundance of these and they agree well enough with your time of life." [29] This repeated reference to animals

sophia atque arte medicus." He has been usually identified with the Niccolò da Foligno who addressed to Lorenzo de' Medici a quite scholastic work upon the Platonic conception of ideas and its relation to the philosophy of Aristotle of which we treat in Chapter 10.

[26] One might infer that Salutati's discussion was well known in Lorenzo's time from the statement in Fabroni, *Hist. Acad. Pisanae*, Vol. I, 1791, p. 294, that Bernard Tornius (1452–97), who taught medicine at Pisa and of whom we treat in our fifth chapter, wrote a confutation of it. But Fabroni was mistaken. Tiraquellus (1480–1558), *Tract. de nobilitate*, cap. 31, no. 360, whom he cites, says nothing of the sort and does not mention Bernard Tornius. What Tiraquellus says is that Salutati wrote a confutation of the disputation on the subject by Bernard, a physician of Florence, which, as we have seen, is stated by Salutati himself in the treatise in question.

[27] Laurent. Plut. 73, cod. 29, 15th century, fol. 1: "Nam optime novi etiam in tua pueritia canes aut aucipitres vel equos quibus plerique iuditio minus integri summopere delectantur tuo libero ac elevato animo non convenire."

[28] Anent Lorenzo's relation to medicine may be cited two monographs on his friend and physician, Pierleone of Spoleto: L. Guerra Coppioli, "Maestro Pierleone da Spoleto, medico e filosofo," in *Bollettino della R. Deputazione di Storia Patria per l'Umbria*, 1915; *Il Bagno a Morba nel Volterrano e M. Pierleone da Spoleto medico di Lorenzo il Magnifico*, Siena, 1915.

[29] Laurent. Plut. 77, cod. 22, 15th century, fol. 3v: "Intellexi enim munera ingenio elaborata tibi grata magis esse quam equos vel canes aut accipitres [corrected from "ancipitres"] quamvis eorum apud te copia sit et tue etati satis conveniant. . . ." Angelo Fabroni, *Laurentii Medicis Magnifici vita*, Pisa, 1784, Vol. I, pp. 5–6, speaks of Lorenzo's youthful zest for horses and knightly

employed in the chase is, it may be incidentally remarked, a good illustration of the paucity of ideas of the average humanist [30] as well as of John's poor memory or carelessness or lack of tact, as the case may be. Moreover, while John wrote for Piero a serious work on the heart, its diseases and their cure, and poisons, he represents his treatise to Lorenzo as a facetious trifle, "being convinced that it is not unseemly sometimes to mingle stories and light reading with the worthy and authoritative works which you possess in abundance." [31] At first sight it may not seem that a discussion of the relative merits of law

---

sports: "nam vel a pueritia equorum studiosissimus et equitandi peritissimus fuit . . . Edidit et spectacula splendidissima . . . Conveniebant autem ad ea ex universa fere Italia strenui et nobiles adolescentes, quibuscum ita certavit in illis equestribus hastatorum ludis, ut non semel victor discesserit."

[30] The same expression is also found earlier in Poggio, who said that to sustain the virtue of one's ancestors only by a great number of dogs, hawks, and horses was to seek nobility among the beasts.

[31] *Ibid.* "Mihi tamen ipsi suasus etiam fabulas vel res leves cum dignis et autenticis libris quibus plurimum abundas interdum consotiari non indecens esse."

In a later passage John treats the question, Is the legal or medical profession more agreeable in actual practice? in a spirit of somewhat unbecoming levity, or rather of levity which he appears to have thought becoming to the youthful years of Lorenzo de' Medici and to the general reading public of his day. When Carlo argued that medical practice was very unpleasant, since doctors have to visit the poor and the slums, and bring home vermin, or inspect foul substances such as *stercus et urina*, while the lawyer sits comfortably at home and his clients come to consult him, Niccolò replied that doctors also had opportunities to visit fine houses and courts, to receive big fees as well as vermin, and to hold the wrists or touch the breasts of soft, pretty girls, while lawyers are also likely to have to visit low dives or to hold offices which are far from profitable.

Fols. 38v–39r: "Sunt etiam puellarum ac iuvencularum interdum amene indoles molles quod manuum ac brachiorum pulsus et tenere mamille dulcia fercula atque tibiarum et pectinis suaves aspectus que pro illis satagere valde videntur. Legiste autem si non domos aut vicos queritent petunt tamen vilia et sordida officia que ipsi birrarias vocant ut ibi magna cum calamitate ac incommoditate agrestem ducant vitam. Nec solum pulicibus ac cimicibus pleni domum suam repetunt sed sepe animantibus aliis magis domesticis nisi dixerint filomenarum domesticarum cantus suavis atque rugitus continui ipsos plurimum delectare que non vestes aut libros solum verum interdum aures sibi corrodere invente sunt. Sed si hec omnia insontes aut sospites pretereant, non tamen arbitratum officii quem sindacatum [or *sindocatum*] vocant effugere possunt ut interdum nonnulli ad plus valde reddendum damnati moliantur quam fuerint unde domum suam leviores multo repetunt quam inde abierint et mundiores ac nitidiores pecuniis quam barberiorum bacile pulveribus."

and medicine can be appropriately termed a facetious trifle, but part of the time John of Arezzo treats the subject in a somewhat light vein, and indulges in slightly risqué anecdotes. There is something of this same tendency in Poggio, who shows the influence of the tales, *fabliaux*, or *novelle* of vernacular literature in his *Historia tripartita*, Walser thinks, as well as in his *Facetiae*. It goes back even to Salutati, in whose treatise we can match Poggio's funny story concerning Angelus, bishop of Arezzo, who refused to take medicine, with an anecdote over a page in length telling how Andreas de Luco got the laugh on the doctors of Florence.[32] In both cases the patient surreptitiously deposited in the vessel under the bed the medicines which had been prescribed for him and afterwards, when he had recovered and the doctors began to plume themselves upon their successful treatment of his case, showed them what had become of their drugs.[33]

Such resemblances between our treatises suggest a comparison of their character and form. That of Salutati is in the nature of a reply to a work by master Bernard, a physician of Florence, who had urged the superiority of medicine, whereas Salutati defends against him the preëminence of the law. The work of this Bernard seems not to have been preserved, at least not in the Laurentian Library. But we get some notion of his argument from Salutati's reply to it. Bernard's work was, according to Salutati, a very copious one, so that it would require a large volume to answer all its arguments *seriatim*.[34] We are not moved to lament Salutati's failure to do this as much as we might, for as it is, his own treatise is very long drawn out, repetitious, and confused in arrangement, although superficially it has the appearance of being systematically ordered. It is divided into thirty-nine chapters, each with its heading, usually in the form of a distinct topic or thesis. But across this arrangement runs another of numbered conclusions, which

[32] In the nineteenth chapter of Salutati's treatise.

[33] This story is repeated in Theodor Zwinger's *Theatrum vitae humanae*, edited by his son, Jacob Zwinger, Basel, 1604, p. 1248. Zwinger's work is a vast compilation and encyclopedia in twenty-nine parts.

[34] Cap. 20.

occur in the course of the text singly or in groups. Thus his 19th to 23rd conclusions will be found in Chapter 12, while Chapter 17 consists simply of conclusions 27 to 42 inclusive, and is indeed entitled "Sixteen conclusions which are reached concerning the topic of certitude." With Chapter 20, Salutati turns to Bernard's arguments, and, having by Chapter 36 demolished them to his heart's content, relents sufficiently to give medicine what he considers its due mead of praise in his closing chapters. But in the text of his earlier chapters he anticipates many of his later conclusions and chapter headings, and he employs over and over again the same arguments to reach what are supposed to be different successive conclusions. Sometimes even the chapter headings are repetitious. Thus both Chapter 6 and Chapter 16 deal with the relative certainty of law and medicine. On the whole, the form of Salutati's treatise is that of scholastic argumentation and disputation,[35] although it is far from being an example of scholastic presentation at its best, and occasionally displays an oratorical tendency which we might regard as a step towards humanism, were it not equally likely to be simply a continuation of medieval rhetoric. I cannot agree with Walser that, aside from its scholastic arguing, which is tiresome to the modern reader, it provides enjoyable and charming reading.[36]

Our second treatise too may be regarded as distinctly

[35] Indeed, he is represented as regretting the neglect of disputation by the younger generation in a treatise written two years after his own by Leonardo Bruni or Aretino — *Libellus de disputationum exercitationisque studiorum usu*, 1401. Bruni's treatise, in the form of a dialogue between himself and two other pupils of Salutati and their master, is of further interest to us because not only is its form similar to those of Poggio and John of Arezzo, but two of its interlocutors, namely, Niccolò Niccoli and Leonardo himself, reappear in John of Arezzo's work. But whereas John's work has never been printed, there have been no less than three modern editions of Leonardo's *Libellus*, which is also briefly described by Philippe Monnier, *Le Quattrocento*, 8th ed., 1924, Vol. I, pp. 106–08.

[36] Walser, 1914, p. 253: "Das Werk Coluccios, trotz Gegenstand und Gründen die uns heute müssig erscheinen, bildet eine erfreuliche und liebenswürdige Lektüre. Eine behaglich erzählte Anekdote, die massvolle Disputation, die das Gute des Gegners ohne Weiteres in reichsten Masse anerkennt, der versöhnliche Ton, die bescheidene Versicherung, sich gerne eines Besseren belehren zu lassen: alles stimmt zu der edlen feinen Gestalt Salutatis."

scholastic in form and arrangement, albeit with exceptional consideration for the convenience and time of the reader. On a double-columned page, one column is devoted to the cause of law, the other to that of medicine, the various paragraphs or arguments being placed opposite one another so that contrasting paragraphs commonly begin on the same line across the page, and if one paragraph is longer than its fellow, a space is left blank in the other column to cover this. After six pages of this parallel discourse, the seventh page begins with a rubric which may be translated thus: "To settle this litigation Reason admonishes me, John Baldus, physician, to offer the following remarks." [37] He continues, however, to hold an even balance between the rival subjects, which, he says, may be compared with respect to either their origins, their relations, or their ends.[38] If you look at the question from the standpoint of God's relation to man,[39] medicine is superior. But if from the standpoint of man's relation to God,[40] then civil justice is to be preferred to medicine. If you have regard to the *finis quo*, that is, knowledge or science, medicine again leads. But if you regard the *finis gratia cuius*, which is God, law takes precedence. The conclusion of the whole matter, therefore, is that either subject and profession is superior to the other in certain respects and that their practitioners should live upon good terms and in honor prefer one another.[41] In his discussion of the compatibility of science and the Catholic faith he is less impartial, stating that medicine is known to be superior to law in honor by two irrefragable lines of reasoning.[42]

Both Poggio and John of Arezzo, by giving their works the

[37] Gaddi reliq. 74, fol. 105r: "Ad huius litigii pacem me Johannem baldum physicum hec dicenda dicturum Iubendo ratio monet."

[38] "Aut comparatur ratione principii aut ratione ordinis aut ratione finis."

[39] "Si ratione ordinis dei in hominem tunc sic."

[40] "Si ratione ordinis hominis in deum tunc sic."

[41] Fol. 105v, col. 2: "Quia variis respectibus una alteri prevalet est quod ipsarum artifices se in caritate diligant et individualibus considerationibus alter alterum in honore preponat."

[42] Laurent. Plut. 19, cod. 30, fol. 26v: "et duplici infrangibili ratione scitur ipsum in honoribus legistis anteponi."

form of informal and conversational dialogues between men of note, evade any charge of discursiveness or lack of logical arrangement that might otherwise be laid at their doors, and, unlike John of Baldus, both tip the scales in favor of medicine. In Poggio's dialogue the representative of medicine, Niccolò da Foligno, is allowed more space than the jurist, Benedetto Accolti, who is also put somewhat on the defensive. In John of Arezzo's dialogue Niccolò Niccoli pleads the cause of medicine aggressively; Carlo more mildly, not to say apologetically, presents the arguments in favor of the law, while Leonardo adds the weight of his judgment to the side of medicine. It should be said that the discussion as to the respective merits of law and medicine is really only half of the short work by John of Arezzo, representing the second day of discussion between Carlo Marsuppini, Niccolò Niccoli, and Leonardo Aretino. The first day had been devoted to indignant discussion of the high popular reputation which ignoramuses and quacks enjoyed as physicians, particularly in the Florence of that time, and the neglect by the crowd of truly learned and wise medical men. Here again John of Arezzo might seem to be following a lead given by Poggio, in whose *Historia tripartita* the merits of law and medicine is the second of three questions which his guests debate after breakfast. Poggio himself, however, participates in his dialogues, which are laid in the present; John of Arezzo puts his in the past and has only the three interlocutors.

John of Arezzo further resembles Poggio in manifesting more effort to make his work agreeable and even popular reading than did the authors of the other two treatises. He says on this score in the last sentence of his preface: "If, indeed, I have treated the matter with some slight or humble elegance, I have thought that this was to be done the more readily in order that the common herd and old wives may the more easily discern their errors." [43] In fact, I should say that John has

[43] Laurent. Plut. 77, cod. 22, fol. 4v: "Si vero rem modica aut humili quadam elegantia agitaverim, id libentius faciundum duxi ut vulgares et muliercule suos facilius intueantur errores."

carried this popularizing tendency farther than Poggio, and that his work makes more agreeable reading, the listing of arguments in Poggio's treatise being too condensed and bare. Despite this popularizing tendency and the informal three-cornered dialogue form, a scholastic flavor occasionally appears in John's work, as when Leonardo, summing up an argument, says, "But if we wish an invincible demonstration of this matter by dialectic," and then proceeds to syllogize. Nor should the employment of the dialogue form by Poggio and John of Arezzo be over-emphasized as a sign of Quattrocento change from the middle ages under the influence of Cicero and Plato; for an occasional shaft of sly satire directed against his own age by John of Arezzo reminds one of the spirit of Adelard of Bath's dialogue between uncle and nephew on Natural Questions in the twelfth century.[44] As a matter of fact the dialogue form was employed frequently during the middle ages from the time of Boethius on. John, however, introduces a number of humanistic phrases and classical catchwords such as calling a university a "ginnasium."

From Salutati's reply to the physician Bernard, it is evident that they differed not only as to law and medicine, but concerning the nature and purpose of science in general. On the one hand, Salutati complains that Bernard is so devoted to study and intellectual pursuits that he regards all other human activities as of no account,[45] whereas Salutati denies that speculation is the ultimate end of man.[46] On the other hand, he refuses to accept Bernard's view that science deals with particulars,[47] and asserts that all science, properly conceived, is concerned with incorruptible and eternal matters.[48] He keeps throwing up against medicine its empirical and experimental character, and the fact, as he supposes, that it originated in connection with magic and the empirical use of remedies cen-

[44] As it happens, Adelard's work is the first treatise in the manuscript in which one of the treatises that we are considering — that of 1415 — is the last.

[45] Cap. 1. [46] Cap. 22. [47] Cap. 16. [48] Cap. 6.

turies before Hippocrates developed its logical side.[49] The law was handed down direct from God amid thunders at Sinai and on various other occasions.[50] The law, as Cicero saith, is supreme reason implanted in nature.[51] The law has never departed from reason.[52] The medical art, on the other hand, is always changing and being improved; old traditions are abandoned daily.[53] And it not only got its start from magical incantations and experiments, but keeps growing not merely by the use of man's noble reason, "but by magic inventions of remedies and daily experiments" [54] (or "experiences," if one insists on reserving the word "experiments" exclusively for such precise and delicate operations as are carried on in modern laboratories). Salutati therefore questions whether medicine is a science at all and not rather one of the mechanical arts.[55] On the other hand, he says that Bernard is wrong in denying that the law is a science, "since it proceeds by definitions and divisions, and since it has its universals which cannot be otherwise." [56]

From which discussion emerges not only some confirmation of the close historical connection between magic and experimental science, but also the revelation that Coluccio Salutati, commonly represented as one of the founders of Italian humanism and Renaissance, held fast to the *a priori* and theoretical conception of science which used to be charged up solely to the account of medieval scholasticism, rejected the modern ideal

[49] Caps. 4, 11, etc. Similarly, in a sketch of the antiquity of medicine which John Jacob Bartholoti of Parma delivered at the University of Ferrara in 1498 at the beginning of his course of extraordinary lectures on the Canon of Avicenna and which he dedicated to Niccolò Maria d'Este, bishop of Adria (1487–1507), the first headings in the text, as given in Vatican Latin MS 5376, are: fol. 2r, "Medicina ex divinatione et vaticiniis"; fol. 2v, "Medicina ex cognitione herbarum simpliciumque medicaminum"; fol. 3r, "Medicina experimento habita"; fol. 3v, "Medicina a casu, Medicina ex insomniis"; fol. 4v, "De medicina ex magia"; fol. 5r, "Medicina ex astrologia et immaginibus."

[50] Cap. 9. [51] Cap. 3. [52] Cap. 11. [53] Cap. 10.

[54] Cap. 11: ". . . sed remediorum magicis inventionibus quotidianisque experimentis processisse."

[55] Cap. 4. The treatise of 1415 also questions whether medicine is a science.

[56] Cap. 35: ". . . cum diffiniendo dividendoque procedant [leges] et cum habeant universalia sua que non possint aliter se habere."

of experimental science which had already been taking form in the middle ages, and apparently had little faith in human progress and the evolution of thought. Little did he realize that those Aristotelian genera and species, which he regarded as incorruptible and eternal matters with which science might properly concern itself, would one day, as a result of that experimental study of particulars which he decried, be shown to be very far from being incorruptible and eternal. Bernard, also, would seem to have been too given to the theoretical side of medicine, if Salutati was justified in saying, "since the whole basis of your arguments rests upon the dignity of [medicine as a] speculation and the prerogative of certainty," [57] and in charging that Bernard wished to separate medicine from all practice.[58] If so, the art was already superior to its advocate in this respect, as we shall presently hear Salutati unwittingly admit.

Poggio rose to no such height as a discussion of the nature and purpose of science in his dialogue, although he briefly asserted that medicine is a part of natural philosophy and based upon unchanging nature, has reason as its leader, and is universal and invariable. And that, on the contrary, lawyers really have nothing to do with law of divine or natural origin, but deal with the historic Roman law, "made by human judgment," changing with place and time, and full of doubtful points. That the law requires no subtle investigation or theory, but merely "memory of things written down and inextricable reading of commentaries."[59] And that it is useful only in the same way as cooking, weaving, carpentry, and other mechanical arts are useful.

John of Arezzo turned the dictum that "science is not concerned with particulars" [60] against the law, declaring that laws

[57] Cap. 5: ". . . cum omne tuarum rationum fundamentum stet in speculationis dignitate et certitudinis prerogativa."

[58] Cap. 36.

[59] Poggio, *Opera*, 1513, fol. 17r: ". . . sed scriptarum rerum memoria et inextricabilis commentariorum lectio."

[60] "Scientia est vix de particularibus."

are partial and individual rules pertaining to temporal goods. On the other hand, in the first book of John of Arezzo's dialogue Leonardo Aretino protested that Carlo Marsuppini was confusing empiricism and experimental method when he called experiences or experiments the apparent cures worked by quack surgeons among the populace. "You call that experience, Carlo, which is directly opposed to experience. For experience is some particular knowledge, gleaned from many single instances, which, to attain truth, lays down seven conditions for itself." These are no doubt the seven requirements of medical experimentation which John of St. Amand collected from the works of Galen in the thirteenth century, and to which other medieval medical writers refer. Leonardo continues, "If you search for these in your empirics, you will rarely or never find them. Wherefore you are speaking not of true, but false experiments. For effects which sometimes take place without reason are no doubt due to chance or accident. But chance is opposed to true experience. One or two swallows, as you well know, do not make a spring, and so neither do one or two experiences make a doctor." [61]

John of Arezzo would also separate medicine from that connection with magic with which Salutati twitted it. According to John, it is only the populace who regard enchanters as great medical men because they pour forth an abundance of words. Basterius, who used to make saddles for donkeys, won

[61] Laurent. Plut. 77, cod. 22, fols. 16v–17r: "Tu id experientia [*sic*] vocas, carole, quod prorsus experientie adversatur. Nam est experientia particularis quedam notitia e plurimis singularibus collecta que ut veritatem claudat septem sibi prepostulat conditiones quas si in tuis queras emperiis per raro vel numquam invenies. Quocirca he quas narras non vere sed false sunt emperie. Effectus enim qui interdum sine ratione contingunt forte non dubium vel casu prodeunt. Sors autem vere experientie adversatur. Nec una ut bene nosti vel due irundines ver faciunt, sic etiam nec una vel due experientie medicum."

In our English version of the proverb quoted, we of course often say "summer" instead of "spring." For use of the same proverb by another Florentine writer of the late fifteenth century, see the account of John Nesius in our eleventh chapter. Another common proverb found in John of Arezzo's first book is that about closing the barn door after the horse has been stolen: "Ut vilicus post perditos boves stabulum claudit."

all his great popular medical reputation in Florence by means of a single incantation that he learned from a hermit who brought his ass to him to have its saddle repaired.[62] Pelacanus, another popular impostor, pretended to invoke demons to bring him an image or form of the patient, which he would then eviscerate by the light of consecrated candles, and carefully examine the state of the internal organs in order to be able to prescribe intelligently for the patient.[63] He furthermore insisted on knowing the patient's name and his mother's name. He did not care for the father's name, saying that the name of the true father was uncertain anyway. John of Arezzo grants, however, that the profundity of medicine makes fraud the more possible, and he seems to admit that even the wise man may sometimes be misled by secret books said to have been found in the ark of the covenant or the tomb of Apollo, or left in the mountains of Nurcia by the Sibyl.[64] Thus the science of the fifteenth century still knew the same secret books of magic which had been current in the thirteenth century. On this matter of quacks Poggio was chiefly concerned to maintain that ignorant empirics and impostors were quite as common in legal as in medical practice, and were even given the LL. D. degree. In an invective against the doctors of laws Niccolò da Foligno charges them with ignorance of their art, inability to speak decent Latin, villainy and malpractice.[65]

Returning to the subject of medical quacks, a word of qualification must be uttered concerning Bistichius or Bisticius, mention of whom had started John of Arezzo's whole discussion of the matter. He was spoken of as "a silversmith of Florence and man ignorant of letters" who "suddenly became the leading physician of the whole city."[66] But from other sources we obtain a more favorable estimate of Bistichius. Mehus, in the preface

[62] Laurent. Plut. 77, cod. 22, fols. 21v–22r.

[63] *Ibid.*, fol. 22v.

[64] *Ibid.*, fol. 12v.

[65] Poggio, *Opera*, 1513, fols. 18r–19v.

[66] Laurent. Plut. 77, cod. 22, fol. 5r: "Bisticius quidam florentinus faber argentarius atque homo litterarum ignarus repente summus in tota urbe evasit medicus."

to his life of Traversari,[67] mentions the donation by him at his death in 1478 of codices to the library of the monastery of San Marco. In the notes made in these codices recording the gift, his full name is given as Magister Laurentius Magistri Iacobi Philippi de Bisticcio, and he is further described as "a famous professor of physic." [68] Moreover, in a Venetian manuscript of the sixteenth century,[69] containing alchemical and medical treatises, a Bartholomaeus Marcellus *abia cirra*, who furtively copied works of the noted alchemist, John of Rupecissa, in the space of eight days in 1462 "from Bistichius's corroded and smoke-stained codices," praises the latter highly. He states that, following the teaching of a certain Raymond — perhaps the pseudo-Lull — Bistichius, "since he was a goldsmith (rather than silversmith, as above stated) and experienced in sublimations, . . . became a marvelous doctor, beyond the other most learned physicians of this age, so that he seemed no Empiric but the supreme monarch of medicine, and was so courted by all the nobles, lords, and princes of Italy, as if he had been the oracle of Apollo and with immense gain for himself, that there seemed to be in him the soul and reason of most holy Hippocrates of yore." [70]

[67] Laurentius Mehus, *Vita Ambrosii Traversari*, Florence, 1759, Praefatio, p. lxvii.

[68] " . . . praeclarus artis physicae professor." Mehus repeats this flattering designation in his text, though he also quotes John of Arezzo's slur on Bisticius.

[69] S. Marco Latin MS, VI, 282 (Valentinelli, XIV, 39). It contains John of Rupecissa's *De philosophiae famulatu* and *De consideratione quintae essentiae*, and Raimundus *De arte practica medicinalium*.

[70] The Latin, as given by Valentinelli, *Bibl. MS. ad S. Marci Venet.*, 1868–74, Vol. V, p. 111, runs: "Raimundi doctissimi et sanctissimi divinum de philosophiae famulatu opus explicit, quo duce Bistichius florentinus cum esset aurifex et sublimationes experiretur, quas opus hoc copiosissime docet, mirabilis supra ceteros huius aetatis physicos doctissimos medicus evasit, ut non empericus videretur, sed summus physicorum monarcha adeoque a nobilibus omnibus et Italiae dominis et principibus, tanquam Apollonis oraculum, suo cum lucro maximo observaretur, ut in eo vetustissimi ac sanctissimi Hippocratis anima ac ratio esse videretur." Later occurs another passage of about the same tenor, of which also Valentinelli reproduces the Latin. But, according to Valentinelli, neither of these remarks made by Bartholomaeus Marcellus in 1462 was included in the printed edition.

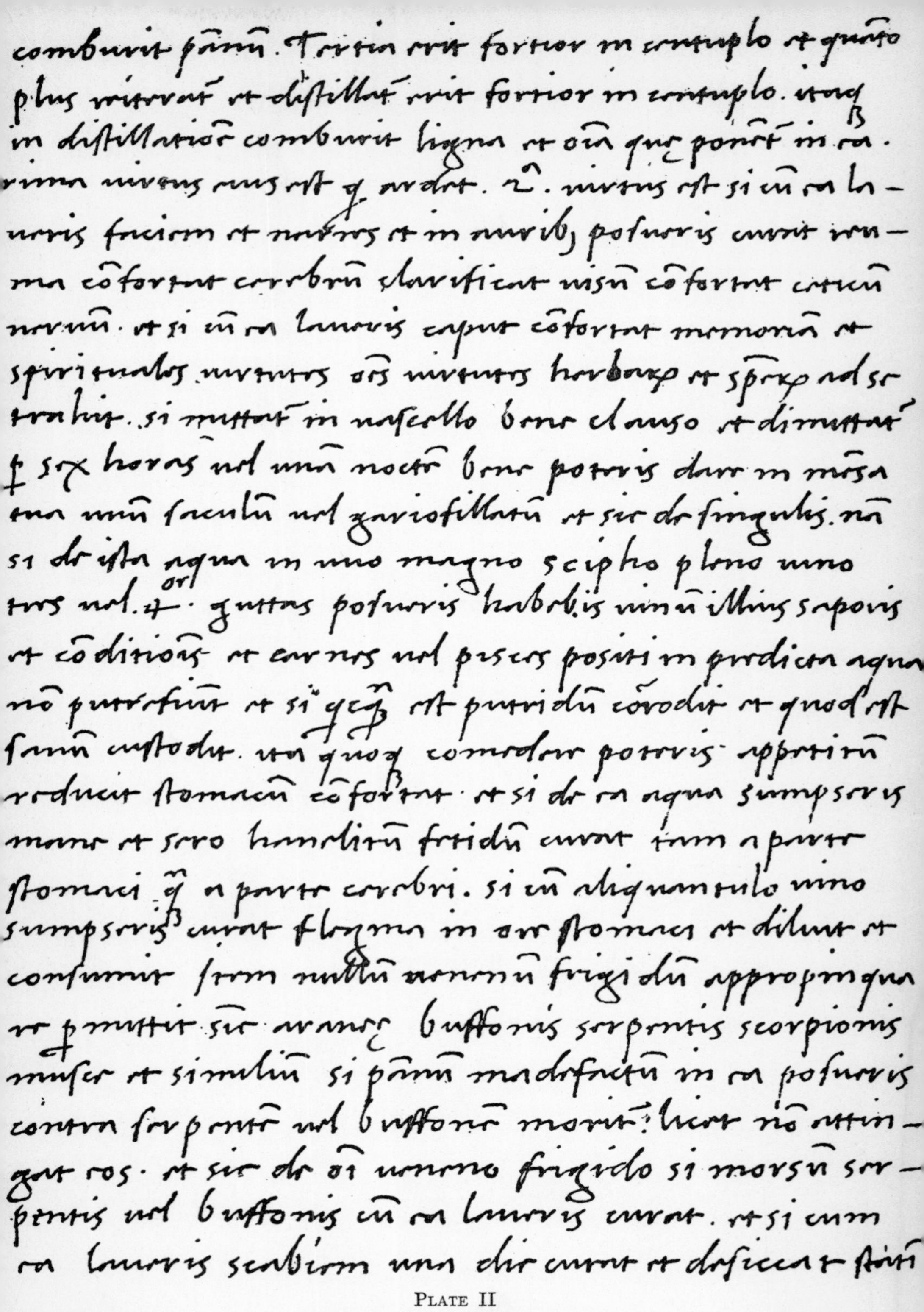
comburit pannum. Tertia erit fortior in centuplo et quanto
plus reiteratur et distillatur erit fortior in centuplo. itaque
in distillatione comburit ligna et omnia que ponit in ca-
rinna virtus eius est quod ardet. 2a. virtus est si cum ea laueris faciem et ueneos et in auribus posueris curat ven-
ma cōfortat cerebrum clarificat visum cōfortat certum
neruum. et si cum ea laueris caput cōfortat memoriam et
spirituales virtutes oēs virtutes herbarum et specierum ad se
trahit. si mittatur in vasello bene clauso et dimittatur
per sex horas vel unam noctem bene poteris dare in mensa
tua vinum saculum vel gariofillatum et sic de singulis. nam
si de ista aqua in uno magno sciphe pleno vino
tres vel .4or. guttas posueris habebis vinum illius saporis
et cōditionis et carnes vel pisces positi in predicta aqua
nō putrefiunt et si quod est putridum cōrodit et quod est
sanum custodit. ita quoque comedere poteris appetitum
reducit stomacum cōfortat. et si de ea aqua sumpseris
mane et sero tanc calidum frigidum curat tam a parte
stomaci quam a parte cerebri. si cum aliquantulo vino
sumpseris curat flegma in ore stomaci et diluit et
consumit sicut nullum venenum frigidum appropinqua-
re permittit sicut aranee buffonis serpentis scorpionis
muscae et similium si pannum madefactum in ea posueris
contra serpentem vel buffonem moritur licet nō attin-
gat eos. et sic de oī veneno frigido si morsum serpentis vel buffonis cum ea laueris curat. et si cum
ea laueris scabiem una die curat et desiccat statim

PLATE II

MEDICAL RECIPES OF BISTICHIUS

S. Marco MS L.VI. 282, fol. 78v.

Moreover, Bistichius not merely copied alchemistical treatises of earlier authors: the same manuscript contains various medical recipes which he wrote with his own hand, and of which the first is against quartan and tertian fever.[71] He was thus at least able to write Latin, however "ignorant of letters" he may have been according to the standards of classical and medical education upheld by the humanists participating in John of Arezzo's dialogue. And he would seem to have been a sort of forerunner of Paracelsus in his close association of chemistry, especially that of metals, with medicines. His recipes, however, are sufficiently superstitious, including the use of the ashes of a burnt live hare for the stone, the prescription of ground glass or burnt human excrement for clouded eyes of beasts, the recital of Paternosters and Ave Marias and the name of Christ in the plucking of medicinal herbs, the writing of other pious phrases on three leaves of salvia which the patient is to eat on an empty stomach, one on each of three days, and similar insistence upon number, position, and ceremonial procedure. Of one "Marvelous Water" for the eyes Bisticius says, "And believe me that a certain man who had been blind for ten years by using this water for forty days recovered his sight.[72] The recipes of Bisticius were in part, at least, derived from other authors. He cites John of Toledo and Ugo or Hugh the Cardinal; the book of the latter on the virtues of waters;

[71] S. Marco Latin MS VI, 282 (Valentinelli, XIV, 39), fols. 77–82, opening "Prima medicina per me Bistichium expertissima est contra quartanam et tertianam."

[72] In Appendix 2 at the close of this volume, I give the Latin text and an English translation of a few specimens of Bisticius's recipes. While we are on the theme of Florentine physicians of the fifteenth century, it may be noted that Mario Battistini has resuscitated the names of several fourteenth-century practitioners from the archives. See his "Note d'archivio," in *Archivio di storia della scienza*, Vol. II, 1921, pp. 211–14, where he treats of "Andrea di Bartolo, un medico del carceri," of Maestro Gregorio da Pisa and Maestro Beltramo da Cortona, both oculists at Florence, of the condemnation and pardon of Maestro Stefano degl' Impiastri in 1341, and of Maestro Cristofano dei Brandaglini at the close of the century. Attention may also be called to the recent book of R. Ciasca, *L'arte dei medici e speziali nella storia e nel commercio Fiorentino dal secolo XII al XV*, 1927, a work of over 800 pages, coming down to 1435.

Peter, brother of the abbot of Sancta Justina of Padua; and Joannes de Sancta Brizida.[73]

Underlying much of the discussion of our treatises are two premises concerning which the advocates of the law and of medicine cannot agree, namely, to what extent the law or laws may be identified with moral philosophy and politics, and how far medicine may be identified with natural science. The advocates of medicine are inclined to restrict the scope of the law to the defense of private property and the punishment of evildoers. Salutati protests that Bernard should not deny that politics and law are the same.[74] Salutati would have it that law embraces all parts of moral philosophy, and things divine as well as human,[75] that it is not merely punitive and coercive, that it distinguishes between the just and the unjust, and that it follows nature.[76] But if it did merely punish the wicked, even so it would do something that medicine does not accomplish.[77] His opponent, Bernard, he says, admitted that medicine had nothing to do with morals.[78] On the other hand, Salutati will not admit that medicine is a sister or even a branch of physical science.[79] As against this, John of Arezzo insists that law is only a small part of moral philosophy. Into this dispute Poggio hardly enters, simply affirming that medicine, as a part of natural philosophy, is superior to law, as a part of moral philosophy.[80]

But this introduces another fundamental question — whether moral or natural philosophy is the loftier. This is disputed in the treatise of 1415, while John of Arezzo makes Leonardo Aretino say that medicine alone is worthier than moral philos-

[73] S. Marco Latin MS VI, 282, fols. 79r, 79v, 80v.

[74] Salutati, cap. 20.

[75] *Ibid.*, cap. 33.

[76] Cap. 3: "Non est legum officium ut tu scribis servili metu solum ad virtutes cogere atque a vitiis deterere quod ipsum tamen divinum est, sed ab iniustis iusta distinguere, naturam sequi . . ."

[77] Cap. 30.

[78] Cap. 36.

[79] Cap. 32.

[80] Poggio, *Opera,* 1513, fol. 16r.

ophy, since it deals both with the internal and essential and with the external and accidental passions of man, while moral philosophy deals only with externals.[81] Salutati, on the contrary, had affirmed that moral goodness was superior to any good in medicine.[82]

Closely akin is the question whether the reason is superior to the will, the latter being especially associated with the law and the reason with medicine. The law commands, says John of Arezzo; medicine persuades. Even Salutati practically accepts this distinction, since he is at pains to argue that the will is nobler than the intellect, and prudence than speculation, although in other chapters he claims for the law lofty speculative flights concerning the powers, virtues, and passions of the soul, while he contends that speculation could dispense with the results of medicine.[83] John Baldus, in his discussion of the compatibility of profane science with the Catholic faith, identifies medicine itself with the intellect and law with will. He notes that *intellectus* is of masculine gender, *voluntas*, feminine. The intellect cannot be deceived, while the will often errs. No holy religion ever commanded one to deny his own understanding — surely a remarkable utterance for the so-called ages of faith and pre-Reformation period, though representing an attitude by no means so unusual as has been assumed — whereas the first precept of any religion is negation of one's own will.[84] Therefore medicine is above law.

Medicine, Salutati is fond of repeating, seeks an end common to us with the beasts, deals only with the body, or at best with the vegetative and sensitive soul.[85] The treatise of 1415 repeats his contention that the law is superior in that it is concerned with the rational soul, while, as Galen says, the medical man's

[81] Laurent. Plut. 77, cod. 22, fol. 41r: "Sed morali philosophia dignior medicina est cum circa intraneas et essentiales atque extraneas et accidentales hominis passiones versetur, moralis vero duntaxat circa extraneas."

[82] Salutati, cap. 25.

[83] *Ibid.*, caps. 22, 23, 3, and 26.

[84] Laurent. Plut. 19, cod. 30, fol. 27r: ". . . nulla sancta religio vult proprium intellectum debere negari sed cuiuslibet talis primum preceptum est negatio proprie voluntatis."

[85] Cap. 27.

point of view does not go beyond the senses ("consideratio medici non transit sensum").[86] But the treatise of 1415 also notes that Aristotle said that health is the *summum bonum* in the life of the living.[87] Salutati, however, held that the conservation of human society by law was a higher good than the preservation of the human body by medicine, and that *honestas* was superior to *sanitas*, or honesty to health.[88] Poggio and John of Arezzo both note the argument that the law deals with a higher side of human life than the body, but also the counter-argument that medicine is concerned with man's very being (*esse*), the law mainly with mere property rights and "other things alien to man."

An argument of which the advocates of medicine make a great deal is that medicine is based upon immutable nature and not, like the law, upon the fluctuating human will and the variable decrees of pontiffs, kings, and emperors. No human power can change the principles of nature, affirms the treatise of 1415,[89] while in his other work John Baldus goes even further, asserting that no human power can upset the canons of medicine — an ill-advised confidence in the Galenic tradition![90] Even Salutati has to admit the diversity and contrariety of laws among different peoples, but he submits that often the same reasoning lies behind the existence of different laws for different regions and tribes.[91] When Carlo Marsuppini, in John of Arezzo's dialogue, holds that the laws were made by the Roman jurists (*legum consulti*) for all men, Niccolò Niccoli replies that in practice their laws are now confined to Christendom and even to Italy, and furthermore are constantly being changed and are in conflict with one another, especially at Florence, whereas the

[86] Gaddi reliq. 74, fol. 103r.

[87] *Ibid.*, fol. 102v.

[88] Salutati, cap. 15.

[89] Gaddi reliq. 74, fol. 102v: "Nulla humana potentia possunt nature principia mutari."

[90] Laurent. Plut. 19, cod. 30, fol. 27r: "Nullo autem humano posse possunt canones medicine cum eorum negatione ad oppositas sententias transmutari."

[91] Salutati, cap. 16.

medical art prevails the world over. Moreover, there is scarcely a law upon whose interpretation the jurists agree — *quot capita tot sententiae* — and the net result is chaos and confusion. As we have already suggested in a previous paragraph, these same arguments had also been presented by Poggio.

Salutati attempted to offset the charge of variability brought against the laws by bringing one of uncertainty against medicine. When the mere breath of a toad may change the virtue of a medical herb into a poison, what certainty can there be in medicine? Undoubtedly nature is fixed and immutable, but who can ever learn all its complexities? What physician knows all the specific forms or occult virtues of materia medica? How often medical prognostications are at fault! How greatly human constitutions differ! [92] "By daily experiments you find that the same thing sometimes is helpful, sometimes has no effect, sometimes works the exact opposite." [93] Similarly the treatise of 1415 asks if physicians never make mistakes.[94]

Another moot point was whether medicine or the law involved and called for the more all-round education and exercise of the human faculties. Salutati denied that the physician was better trained in the liberal arts than the lawyer or jurist,[95] but the advocates of medicine asserted that all seven liberal arts serve medicine, which requires as prerequisites moral and natural philosophy and dialectic.[96]

It is further contested which discipline is the superior in their mutual relations. Salutati argues that the laws can forbid impure drugs and malpractitioners, while in legal questions of birth and conception the physician simply testifies to the facts

[92] Salutati, Cap. 16.

[93] *Ibid.*, Cap. 12: "Quotidianis experimentis invenitis rem unam aliquando prodesse, quandoque nichilum, et aliquando totum oppositum operari."

[94] Gaddi reliq. 74, fol. 103v: "Nonne ut legis lator potest medicus non vera precipere et medendi rationem obmittere?"

[95] Salutati, Caps. 28 and 32.

[96] Leonardus says in John of Arezzo's dialogue: "Nam est medicus rectus philosophie moralis et naturalis ac dialectice doctor quas medicina sibi prepostulat." Laurent. Plut. 77, cod. 22, fol. 41v.

For all the seven liberal arts serving medicine, see Gaddi reliq. 74, fol. 102r; Laurent. Plut. 19, cod. 30, fol. 16r–v; Poggio, *Opera*, 1513, fol. 16r.

and does not affect the law in the matter.[97] On the other hand, in the treatise of 1415 it is asserted that medicine does not need the civil law, but that the latter cannot exist without medicine, which ushers all prospective lawyers into this world.[98] The manuscript appears to add that anyone born in the tenth or eleventh month should be dedicated to the legal profession. John of Arezzo does not discuss the legal regulation of medical practice as bearing on the disputed precedence of the two subjects in his second book, but in his first book on the prevalence of quacks in fifteenth-century Florence he laments the lack of municipal medical regulations and legislation there. Niccolò Niccoli is stupefied that peoples and cities of repute, where universities flourish, should tolerate such a criminal state of affairs, when in small towns and meager populations it is enacted by law that only those shall be admitted to medical practice who have a degree from one of the more reputable universities. Thus he incidentally testifies to the careful regulation of the medical profession by many medieval municipalities. Carlo Marsuppini, for his part, cannot understand why even without such explicit statutes the magistrates and senate, who have the power of overseeing occupations in general, allow such charlatans and impostors to practice medicine openly.[99]

Leonardo Aretino, with perhaps a touch of sarcasm, replies, "You now want that sort of laws among free peoples which exist in subject nations." "Let us leave them," he adds, "to live with their doctors as they please. For many of them will pay a capital penalty for their crime." But Carlo protests that if popular liberty is to degenerate into mere license, the life of the dumb animals is the freest, while Niccolò declares that some of the populace already behave in public in a bestial fashion,

[97] Salutati, cap. 21. According to Guido Zaccagnini, *Cino da Pistoia*, 1918, p. 192, citing Hermann U. Kantorowicz, "Cino da Pistoia, e il primo trattato di medicina legale," *Archivio storico italiano*, Vol. XXXVII, 1906, the "first time that jurisprudence had recourse to medicine" was when Cino, in connection with a case of illegitimacy, consulted Gentile da Foligno as to when life began in the foetus.

[98] Gaddi reliq. 74, fol. 102r.

[99] Laurent. Plut. 77, cod. 22, fol. 24r–v.

"eating and purging their bodies in forum, court, or church like brute animals, hallooing like wolves or whinnying like horses or making love like asses." Niccolò thinks that the people are not qualified to regulate medical practice, a matter which should be in the hands of trained physicians and a *protomedicus*.[100] It is granted, however, that the universities are popular institutions, and Carlo does not understand why the people are led astray by ignorant quacks in medical matters, when the same people constitute their university faculty solely of true scholars, whom they strive to attract with such diligence that their own citizens are not enough for them but they add foreign scholars. Niccolò then admits that the medical quacks have their clientele not merely among the populace but too often among the *optimates* (nobility) and magnates. Trying to account for this folly in "those magnates who would surpass the prudence of a Metellus or a Cato," he attributes it to their being so puffed up by honors and pride that, despite their lack of learning, they come to have excessive confidence in their own judgment and presume to crown human donkeys with the poet's laurel as well as to patronize medical nobodies and impostors.[101] So John of Arezzo seems to have little more confidence in the despots and patrons of the Quattrocento than in the populace, and we respect him for boldly saying so at a time when among humanists there was so much toadying to the great. His second book opens with some further discussion which is more directly political, namely, whether the law depends on rulers, or whether rulers depend on the consent of the governed and the law.

Turning back from such social and political questions to the main dispute of medicine versus law, we encounter the question,

[100] Laurent. Plut. 77, cod. 22, fol. 27r–v.

[101] *Ibid.*, fols. 19r–20v, for all the passages quoted since the preceding note. Amusing passages from Henri de Mondeville, writing between 1306 and 1320, describing how unscrupulous second-rate surgeons deceive the rich, have been translated into English by D'Arcy Power in his edition of John Arderne's *Fistula in ano*, 1910, pp. xx–xxi, from E. Nicaise's and A. Bos's editions of Mondeville.

which discipline is the more indispensable? Salutati tries to show that medicine is a useless luxury by pointing to the longevity of the Old Testament patriarchs before the development of the medical art and to the many races of men who have lived without it.[102] In a later chapter he shifts his ground, holding that medicine is not necessary either to eternal life or even to speculation.[103] But according to John of Arezzo the law deals with external goods which are not absolutely essential to human being, whereas medicine is occupied with dispositions of the human body which are absolutely essential to the well-being of both soul and body.

Which subject is of nobler origin? The medical men proudly quote the verse from *Ecclesiasticus*, "The Most High created medicine from the earth," [104] as evidence of divine sanction and auspices for their art, but Salutati turns this line of argument against them, holding that God handed down the law in thunders from the sky, thus demonstrating its higher and more directly divine source.[105] In the treatise of 1415 it is asserted that the promulgators of laws were always men of praiseworthy ends — high priests, kings, and emperors — but the opposing argument points out that Moses never reached the promised land, and that high priests killed Christ by their treachery.[106] Poggio devotes a considerable fraction of his space to debating the question which profession is the more ancient, as this gives him an opportunity to air his humanistic attainments in ancient history and classical mythology. The first practitioners of medicine, Isis and Horus, Mercury and Aesculapius, were deified; Podalirius and Machaon were summoned to the Trojan War on account of their medical skill centuries before Hippocrates.[107] But Phoroneus gave laws to the Argives six hundred

[102] Salutati, cap. 19. [103] *Ibid.*, cap. 26.

[104] This verse occurs in the apocryphal book *Ecclesiasticus*, XXXVIII, 4, but is ascribed to *Ecclesiastes* in the treatise of 1415 (Gaddi reliq. 74, fol. 102r) of which it forms the Incipit. John Baldus also quotes it more than once in his treatise that no science of the Gentiles is contrary to the Catholic faith (Laurent. Plut. 19, cod. 30, fols. 15v and 26v).

[105] Salutati, cap. 9.

[106] Gaddi reliq. 74, fol. 104v. [107] Poggio, *Opera*, 1513, fol. 15v.

years before the Trojan War, and Xenophon says that the ancient Persians needed no medicine.[108] Salutati, in his chapter on the inventors of law and medicine,[109] far from limiting himself to classical examples, gives generous space to medieval and recent names, chiefly Florentine, it is true, but with a few other Italians. In medicine he mentions Thaddeus of Florence, Turisianus, Dino del Garbo and his son Tommaso, Gentile da Foligno, and Christophorus de Honestis of Bologna. "But above all, I firmly believe, should be put Peter of Abano, the Paduan, who published in medicine that book of the greatest divinity known as the *Conciliator* and also expounded the *Problems* of the Philosopher, — a man indeed universal rather than medical, and a true philosopher, than whom you probably have not a more illustrious among medical men." Peter of Abano and his *Conciliator* are also more than once cited in the various treatises of John Baldus.[110] Salutati's list of famous interpreters of the civil law includes Accursius, Franciscus, Dino del Mugello, James d'Arena, the Guidos, Riccardi, Bottrigari, Azo, Cino of Pistoia, and Bartolus of Sassoferrato. Omitting most of the canon lawyers, he names John d'Andrea as the supreme interpreter of the decretals.

Whichever profession was the nobler in its origin, it is generally recognized that at present the lawyers occupy a higher social position.[111] In John of Arezzo's dialogue [112] Carlo states that they are called lords, and their wives are called ladies, whereas medical men are simply designated as masters, a name common to all vile craftsmen, while their wives receive no title whatever. To this Niccolò can only retort that professors of theology, the supreme science, also are called masters, and that the peasant sometimes calls his donkey "lord." Leonardo adds that in some enlightened provinces and cities physicians and

[108] Poggio, *Opera*, 1513, fol. 16v.

[109] Salutati, cap. 9.

[110] Laurent. Plut. 19, cod. 30, fols. 5r, 26v, 41r, etc.

[111] Salutati, cap. 8.

[112] The following discussion occurs towards the close of the dialogue, Laurent. Plut. 77, cod. 22, fol. 42r *et seq.*

their wives are called lords and ladies. He further explains that lawyers impose on the populace by assuming an air of superiority because of their higher birth or wealth, whereas learned physicians are confused in the popular mind with quacks and impostors of low origin. But this seems to be rather a begging of the question.

The question, of which profession is the practice the more agreeable, leads to some interesting revelations. Salutati contends that the law is more agreeable because "doctors of the laws, when they teach and dispute, do not depart from the examination of reason. But yours so teach by reason and disputations that unless many things are present before the eyes of the doctor they cannot fulfill their function. Whence it is that the human frame ought to be shown by dissection (*per anathomiam*) and that you are accustomed to display whatever is especially deserving of knowledge. Yet it is repulsive to inspect and demonstrate by the hands of the one performing that service the viscera of man through veins, arteries, cartilage, bones, medullas, muscles and joints, and the very human intestines, heart, liver, lungs, stomach, ilia, and colon and bladder and whatever diligent nature has no less curiously concealed than constructed, — all which so far departs from humanity that one cannot even hear of it without a certain horror, and I do not see how the caverns of the human body can be viewed without effusion of tears. Why need I mention the impurities, disagreeable to smell, foul to the sight, and unsettling to the stomach, through which your consideration of the human body wends its way, or the examination of urine proceeds, or the judging of corrupted blood, and the inspection you must make of the very excrement." [113] Poggio and John of Arezzo make the same point.

[113] Salutati, cap. 12: "Legum doctores ab examine rationis cum docent et cum disputant non discedunt. Vestri vero sic ratione et disputationibus docent quod nisi multa subiciant oculis doctoris officium nequeant adimplere. Quo fit ut hominis texturam per anathomiam oporteat et soleatis ostendere quelicet dignissima scitu sit; horrendum tamen est hominis viscera per venas arterias cartilagines ossa medullas nervos atque iuncturas et ipsa hominis intestina cor

I have translated this passage *in extenso* as another bit of evidence to add to the ever accumulating mass which is being discovered by students of the history of medieval medicine to show the frequency of dissection of the human body long before the time of Vesalius. But it has further implications. Either Salutati's sensitiveness as to the sight of human viscera is somewhat overdrawn, or physical injuries, weapon wounds, tournaments, duels, street fights, party strife, feudal warfare, and so on and so forth, were probably less common then than we have often been led to believe. And either his sensitiveness as to the inspection of urine and excrement is considerably overdrawn, or else people did not pour slops and pitch offal into the streets at that time to the extent that has often been stated.[114]

Florence, however, claimed to be superior to other cities in the matter of cleanliness. Thus in a dialogue by Leonardo Bruni (1369–1444), Salutati is represented as saying: "In magnificence, indeed, Florence perhaps surpasses those cities which are now in existence, but in cleanliness it surpasses both those that are now in existence and all those that ever were. . . . For neither Rome nor Athens nor Syracuse were, I think, so clean and well kept, but in this respect were far surpassed by our city." [115] Bruni again treated of this theme in his *Eulogy of the City of Florence*, where he remarks that some towns are so dirty that whatever filth is made during the night is placed in the morning before men's eyes and to be trodden underneath their feet, "than which it is impossible to imagine anything fouler. For even if there are thousands there, in-

---

epar pulmonem stomachum ilia atque colum et vesicam, et quicquid diligens natura non minus curiose celavit quam fecit, inspicere et per manus presidentis illi ministerio demonstrare, que quidem adeo ab humanitate dissident, quod sine quodam horrore non possint auribus percepi, nec sentio quomodo possint humani corporis laniena sine lacrimarum effusione videri. Quid referam immundicias, olfactu graves, aspectu fedas, et toleratu stomachosas per quas transit hec vestra consideratio corporis humani, vel urinarum procedit examen, vel sanguinis corrupti iudicium, et ipsius egeriei necessaria vobis inspectio."

[114] But see Andrelini's description of the streets of Paris in note 117 below.

[115] Theodor Klette, *Beiträge zur Geschichte und Litteratur der italienischen Gelehrtenrenaissance*, Vol. II, 1889, "Leonardi Aretini ad Petrum Paulum Istrum dialogus," liber II, pp. 67–68.

exhaustible wealth, infinite multitude of people, yet I will condemn so foul a city nor ever think much of it. For just as there cannot be felicity in a deformed body, although it may possess all other excellencies, so there can be no beauty in cities, if they are filthy, although all other advantages may be present." [116] Similarly the Italian humanist, Andrelini of Forlì, who taught at the University of Paris in the later years of the fifteenth century, addressed a vivid complaint as to the filthy condition of the streets of the French capital in the form of a Latin poem to Budé.[117]

[116] *Ibid.*, "Leonardi Aretini laudatio Florentinae urbis," pp. 87–88. Davidsohn, *Geschichte von Florenz*, IV, iii, 1927, pp. 262–63, gives a much less favorable estimate of the condition of the streets of Florence in the thirteenth and early fourteenth centuries.

[117] *Publii Fausti Andrelini Foroliviensis poete laureati ad Guillermum Budeum Parrhisiensem patricium, graeca et latina litteratura insignitum, de influentia syderum et querela Parrhisiensis pavimenti carmen*, 1496. The poem will hardly bear translation into English, but a few lines of the original may be given to illustrate its character:

Ast ego continuo turbe pede calcor euntis
    Et curru infelix preterunte teror,
Et iactam ex altis urinam poto fenestris,
    Mingit et in media sexus uterque via,
Undique merda fluit puerorum infecta cacantum
    Et ventri pateo [patet?] spurca latrina gravi.
Stercora quinetiam brevibus resoluta cucullis
    In non tergendam deiiciuntur humum.
Suavior ut fiat triplici mixtura sapore
    Immundum effundit lota culina situm.
Principio ignarus solum putat advena cenum
    Et damnat multo sordida strata luto.
Clamat et, O verum sortita Lutetia nomen
    Quambene sunt fame congrua facta tue.

Louis Thuasne called attention to and quoted the passage in his article, "Rabelæsiana," in the *Revue des Bibliothèques*, November–December, 1904. He further noted that Erasmus inveighed against the filthiness of the streets of Paris, which thus appears to have been unusually bad in this respect and so should not be taken as representative either of the fifteenth or earlier medieval centuries. Further details concerning the condition of the streets of Paris in the late fifteenth and sixteenth centuries will be found in the work of Marcel Poëte, *Une vie de cité: Paris de sa naissance à nos jours*, Tome II, *La cité de la Renaissance (1450–1600)*, 1927, pp. 254–58; and for the earlier period, the same work, Tome I, 1924, pp. 613–19. I have discussed the question of "Street-cleaning, Baths, and Sanitation in the Middle Ages and Renaissance" somewhat further in an article of that title in *Speculum*, Vol. III, 1928, pp. 192–203.

Coming back to medical practice, we may note what John of Arezzo says concerning the relations between medicine and surgery. Carlo had suggested that mere manual skill was almost enough to qualify one as a surgeon, an approach to the assertion of many modern writers that surgery was chiefly in the hands of barbers in the middle ages. This Leonardo denied, affirming that surgery requires medicine as a prerequisite, although those who have long consorted with learned medical men and have seen much of their practice may attain some skill in slight and frequently occurring disorders. Carlo had further asserted that a physician was never a surgeon, or a surgeon a physician, but this was denied by Niccolò, who said that such might be the popular notion, but that the ordinary public always got everything mixed up and wrong, and that Hippocrates, Galen, and other makers of medicine were masters of both arts. Whereupon Leonardo chimed in that Carlo's contention was against reason, again asserting that surgery receives its foundation from medicine and that they are never separated any more than are the head and feet of one body or the civil and canon law.[118]

In discussing whether the judge or the doctor is the more cruel, Salutati gives us a glimpse of the cruelty of fourteenth-century justice which is as vivid as his description of medical dissection already noted. "The judge in a thousand ways tortures the criminal and tortures the witnesses in order that he may learn the truth." Salutati, indeed, is inclined to admit that the ministers of the law are more cruel, or at least more needlessly cruel, than the doctors, and that torture is employed more than the laws intend.[119] With this may be compared the attitude of Fortescue in fifteenth-century England: "For my own part, I see not how it is possible for the wound which such a judge (who permits torture to be applied) must give to his own conscience, ever to close up or be healed; so long, at least, as his memory serves him to reflect upon the bitter

[118] Laurent. Plut. 77, cod. 22, fol. 18.
[119] Salutati, *op. cit.*, cap. 12.

torture so unjustly and inhumanly inflicted on the innocent."[120]

In the treatise of 1415 John Baldus states that since the fall of our first parents seven continual wars have gone on within man without hope of peace, but that a remedy has been divinely provided in each case. The first war is between reason and the senses, and its remedy is found in theology, which therefore ranks as first and foremost of the sciences. The second war is caused by conflicting states of the humors and members of the human body, by the influences of the stars and the contrarieties of the elements, the contrary properties of things growing in the earth, and the venomous dispositions of animals; all of which vex the human body continually. For these afflictions the divinely constituted remedy is medicine, which therefore ranks second after theology. The last war, continues John — apparently forgetting that he had said there were seven such wars, or else a portion of his discourse has been omitted in our manuscript — is of man against man and of men against men, and laws were invented as its remedy. "And so in the order of perfection they are of the third grade, and when they sometimes do not suffice, then the Most High wished by persuasions and examples that rhetoric be taken as the remedy, and hence after the laws in the fourth place is located Rhetoric." If it fails, then recourse is had to arms (*militia*).[121] Practically the same passage is found again in John's argument that no science of the Gentiles is contrary to the Catholic faith, except that he there speaks of the warfare as fivefold.[122] He names, however, only three wars as above, although, again as before, we can count up five gradations of remedies, namely, theology, medicine, law, rhetoric and poetry, and last, arms or *militia*.

[120] Quoted by Miss A. E. Levett in *The Social and Political Ideas of Some Great Thinkers of the Renaissance and the Reformation*, edited by F. J. C. Hearnshaw, 1925, p. 74.

[121] Gaddi reliq. 74, fol. 105r–v. Viewed from another angle, however, *militia* is preferred to civil or legal justice, and it in turn to medicine.

[122] Laurent. Plut. 19, cod. 30, fol. 27r: "Est enim homini quincuplex ordine nature bellum sine spe sperande pacis insertum. . . ." The passage extends to fol. 28r.

A faint reflection of this allegorical and Platonic myth, if it may be so called, is perhaps seen in the close of John of Arezzo's dialogue where, the preëminence of medicine over the law having been conceded, Carlo asks which is to be regarded as the worthier, one learned in the laws or a soldier? When Leonardo hesitates to answer lest he incur the disfavor of the *militia*, Carlo himself declares the jurist far superior. Poggio had terminated his dialogue in a different way by an attack on the canon law from the lips of Niccolò da Foligno, and a brief deprecation of such an attitude and defense of the church and papacy from his own mouth.

The prominence of astronomy and astrology in the thought of the time is seen by their obtrusion in three of our treatises. Salutati adduces as a splendid example of the exercise of rational scientific imagination and a beautiful improvement upon the doctrine of Plato and Aristotle concerning the heavens the hypothesis of many astronomers (*astrologi*) that beyond the eighth sphere of the fixed stars exist a ninth sphere which sweeps the lower spheres along with it but is itself moved by none, a tenth sphere which itself moves but neither draws others with it nor is drawn by any other, and a last fixed and immobile seat of the blest.[123] The treatise of 1415 states that children born in the tenth or eleventh month should enter the legal profession.[124] In John of Arezzo's dialogue, when Niccolò seeks an explanation of the jealousy existing between medical men, Leonardo Aretino, after suggesting one or two other possible causes, says that the most potent cause of all is that the science and especially the practice of medicine is under the rule of Mars and Scorpion, which sign and planet are "invidious, malevolent, plotting against and hating all others." [125]

The chief value of our treatises has been their reflection of

[123] Salutati, cap. 16.

[124] Gaddi reliq. 74, fol. 102r.

[125] Laurent. Plut. 77, cod. 22, fol. 44r: "Alia autem reliquis potior causa est quia medicine scientia inspecta presertim practica parte marti et scorpioni subdita est qui planete sunt invidi malivoli omnibusque aliis insidentes atque odentes, quare si illorum naturam medici sapiant, consequens est."

the mental attitude of their period. They have mirrored a tendency to depart from the set form of scholastic disputation to a more informal and discursive dialogue between historic or contemporary personages of note, and in a lighter vein though retaining something of argumentative character. We have had unfavorable glimpses of the intellectual caliber of the people of Florence and of Lorenzo the Magnificent himself, and these have suggested that the intellectual capacity of the Florentines of the Quattrocento has at times been considerably overestimated. We have seen a little of the political and scientific discussion of that period, and more of medical and legal theory and practice. The experimental method is observable in the natural science and medicine of the time, but in essentially the same manner and degree as in the immediately preceding medieval centuries, and is associated with empiricism, magic, and occult sciences, again in much the same way and to the same extent. In connection with the law and politics empiricism and experimentation are not directly mentioned either by way of blame or praise — though the charge of variability perhaps implies their existence — but in at least one passage it is strongly hinted that there is no marvelous virtue in democracy, while Poggio is cynical as to the value of law and holds that political success more often results from the employment of force and individual or national self-interest.[126] The passages which we have noted concerning legal and medical practice, the employment of torture, the legal regulation of the medical profession, the clean or filthy condition of fifteenth-century towns, the relations between surgeons and physicians, the prevalence of dissections, and of popular healers and quackery and superstition, are, of course, as interesting to the student of social customs as to the student of beliefs and thought.

[126] As Walser, *Poggius Florentinus*, etc., 1914, pp. 255–56, has already emphasized this point, I have not dwelt upon it in the foregoing text.

CHAPTER III

THE MANUSCRIPT TEXT OF THE *CIRURGIA* OF LEONARD OF BERTIPAGLIA[1]

Numerous important differences exist between the text of the work on surgery of Leonard of Bertipaglia as given in such printed editions of it as I have been able to see,[2] and the text as presented in several manuscripts of the fifteenth century which I have examined. These manuscripts will now be named in the order in which I happened to see them. In the Laurentian or Medicean Library at Florence is a copy of Leonard's work made in 1471.[3] In the Sloane collection of manuscripts at the British Museum is another manuscript[4] of our work which may possibly date from 1421, although it is probably a somewhat later copy and not Leonard's original. A third copy of the text is found at the Vatican among the manuscripts collected by Christina of Sweden.[5] A fourth manuscript is found in the

[1] Revised and enlarged from *Isis*, Vol. VIII, 1926, pp. 264–84.

[2] Those of 1498, 1499, and 1546; while that of 1519 has been examined for me at the Library of Congress.

[3] Cod. Biscioniani 13, fols. 1–68v: "Hee sunt recepte date per magistrum Leonardum de Bertapalia anno domini millesimo, etc., in studio paduano et hoc[?] super tertiam quartam et quintam fen quarti canonis avicenne. . . / . . . Expletum est hoc opus compositum padue anno 1424 per excellentissimum professorem cirurgie magistrum Leonardum de Bertapalea, qui numquam voluit graduari propter excusare vituperium multorum doctorum ignorantium; nam potius voluit esse bonus scutifer quam malus miles. Scriptum et completum per me Iohannem Andream de Faldis de Mantua anno millesimo CCCC LXXI die III menssis augusti in die sabati ad laudem omnipotentis dei sueque beatissime matris Virginis marie [etc.?] omnisque corie [curie?] sue celestis, etc."

[4] Sloane 3863, fols. 1–110v: "Incipit Cyrurgia magistri Leonardi de Bertepallia 1421 . . . Hec sunt recepte date per magistrum Leonardum de Bertapallia anno domini 1421 suis sociis; qui deputatus fuit ad lecturam cirurgie per rectores ducalis dominii Venetorum in studio Paduano et hoc super terciam et quartam et quintam fen quarti canonis . . . / . . . Explicit ciru[r]gia compilatum per magistrum Leonardum de Bertepalia excellentissimum professorem ciru[r]gie, etc."

[5] Reg. Suev. 1969, fol. 4r, col. 1: "Incipiamus ergo ab tertia fen quarte in primo de flegmone corpore mundo. Hec sunt recepte date per magistrum leo-

library of St. Mark's, Venice.[6] I examined the first two manuscripts named in 1925 and again in 1927, when I saw the other two for the first time.[7] My feeling concerning the first two manuscripts at least was that neither was copied from the other. The other two manuscripts also have some variations of their own, but perhaps the Vatican manuscript more closely resembles the Sloane, and the Venetian the Florentine. Yet they all seem to give essentially the same text. The three printed editions which I have seen also are essentially identical. The striking divergences are between the printed and the manuscript texts. The editors have done much to render Leonard's work colorless and drab by omitting personal remarks and observations and clinical cases, and on the other hand have added much matter that is obviously spurious to his treatise.

Leonardo da Bertapaglia has perhaps been hitherto the most commonly received form for Leonard's name, but Bertapaglia was probably the same as the modern Bertipaglia, a small place a little to the south of Padua. The manuscripts give the name as Leonardus de Bertapallia, Bertepallia, Bertapalia, or Bertapalea. As the Explicits of manuscripts inform us, Leonard was professor of surgery, and as the full form of title or the subtitle near the beginning of the manuscripts informs us, he gave his treatise in the form of lectures on the third, fourth,

---

nardum de berta palea anno domini M° CCCC° XXI° suis sociis qui deputatus fuit ad lecturam per rectores ducalis dominii in studio paduano et hec supra tertiam et quartam et quintam fen quarti canonis Avicenne."

[6] In Valentinelli's catalogue it is described as S. Marco XIV, 28, chart., 15th century, fols. 11–115, Receptae datae per magistrum Leonardum de Bertapalea anno domini millesimo et c. [*sic*] in studio paduano super tertiam, quartam et quintam fen quarti canonis Avicennae. But the library shelf mark is L. VII. LI, while in the manuscript itself I found the designation, "Classis 7, No. 28."

[7] What seems to be a fifth manuscript of portions of the *Cirurgia* is mentioned in Karl Sudhoff's *Beiträge z. Gesch. d. Chirurgie im Mittelalter*, Vol. II, 1918, p. 509. It is a fifteenth-century collection of medical treatises now in the library of the Leipzig Institute for the History of Medicine: Txt. var. 41 (now Cod. A1), fols. 194v–98v, Dicta Leonhardi (de Bertapalia) in chirurgia. It consists of a few extracts from Leonard's *Cirurgia*, beginning with the chapter on medicines which make the flesh grow in wounds, and having to do with wounds and ulcers. Slovenly writing in double columns.

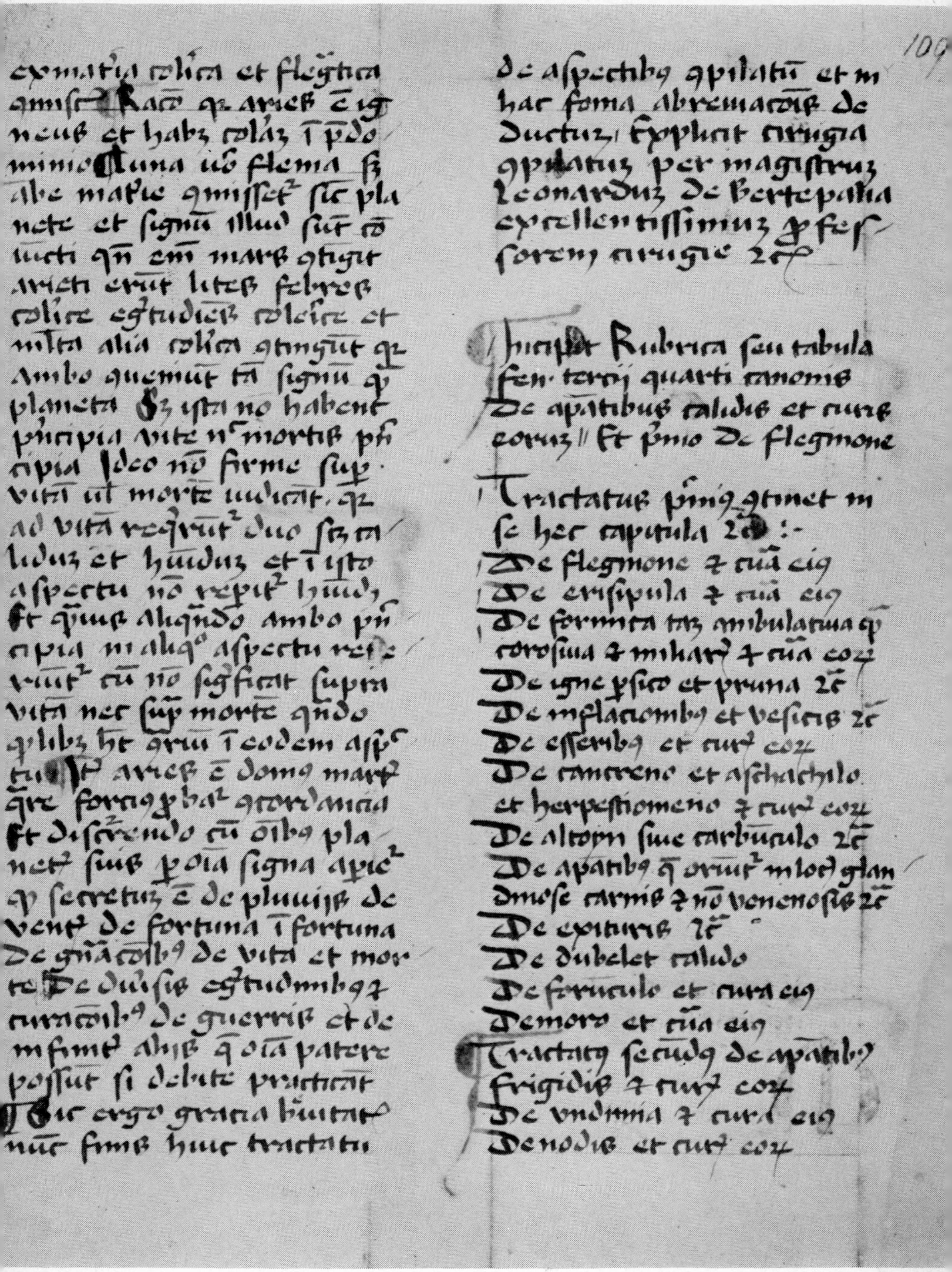

109

exmatia colica et flegmatica
qmisset Racio quia aries est sig
neus et habet colam in pdo
minio luna vero flema sed
alie maxie qmisset sic pla
nete et signum illud sunt co
niuncti quando enim mars qtigit
arieti erunt lites febres
colice egritudines colerice et
multa alia colica qtingunt quia
ambo queniunt tam signum quam
planeta Sed ista non habent
principia vite nec mortis prin
cipia ideo non firme super
vitam vel morte iudicat quia
ad vitam requiruntur duo scilicet ca
lidum et humidum et in isto
aspectu non reperitur humidum
Et quamvis aliquando ambo prin
cipia in aliquo aspectu reper
iuntur tamen non significat super
vitam nec super morte quando
quilibet habet gradum in eodem aspec
tu Et aries est domus martis
quare fortius habet qcordanciam
Et discernendo cum omnibus pla
netis sunt propria signa apparent
ex secretum est de pluuijs de
ventis de fortuna in fortuna
de generacionibus de vita et mor
te De diuersis egritudinibus et
curacionibus de guerris et de
infinitis alijs que omnia patere
possunt si debite practicat
Sic ergo gratia habitam
nunc finis huius tractatum

de aspectibus qpilatum et in
hac forma abreviatorius de
ductum. Explicit cirurgia
qpilatum per magistrum
Leonardum de Bertepalia
excellentissimum profes
sorem cirurgie etc

Incipit Rubrica seu tabula
Sen. tercij quarti canonis
De apatibus calidis et cura
eorum. Et primo de flegmone

Tractatus primus qtinet in
se hec capitula etc :-
De flegmone et cura eius
De erisipula et cura eius
De formica tam ambulativa quam
corosiua et miliaris et cura eorum
De igne persico et pruna etc
De inflacionibus et vesicis etc
De esseribus et cura eorum
De cancreno et aschachilo
et herpestiomeno et cura eorum
De altoym siue carbunculo etc
De apatibus qui oriuntur in locis glan
dulose carnis et non venenosis etc
De exituris etc
De dubelet calido
De furunculo et cura eius
De moro et cura eius
Tractatus secundus de apatibus
frigidis et cura eorum
De undimia et cura eius
De nodis et cura eorum

Plate III
Leonard of Bertipaglia
Sloane MS 3893, fol. 109r

and fifth Fen of the fourth Canon of Avicenna at the University of Padua, where, as the Sloane and Vatican manuscripts further inform us, he was deputed to lecture on surgery by the Venetian government. In the manuscripts, however, he addresses the work to his son. The Sloane and Vatican manuscripts state that the lectures were given or the work published in 1421. The Florentine manuscript gives an illegible date in one place and the year 1424 in its Explicit as the date of composition. It is possible that the date 1421 should apply to the main body of the work, and the date 1424 to the closing *Tractatus de iudiciis* or *De aspectibus*, which appears to bear no relation to the text of Avicenna and to be in the nature of a supplementary and well-nigh separate treatise on the theme of astrological medicine and surgery.[8] In the printed editions a passage which is evidently not by Leonard speaks of him as present at an "anatomy" performed at Padua in 1429 and as then still lecturer in surgery at the university. The assertion of Gurlt [9] that he attended another dissection *de matrice in muliere* in 1440 probably has as its sole basis the mention in the same passage of another "anatomy" (*de matrice in muliere*) in 1430, but nothing is said of Leonard's being present thereat. In addition to the treatise of 1424 just mentioned, in astrological medicine, the Venetian manuscript contains further evidence of Leonard's astrological activity in the form of a prediction for the year 1427, which was apparently composed early in that year.[10] Thus the four dates in Leonard's

[8] In Biscioniani 13, fol. 68v (and in S. Marco L. VII. LI, fol. 122v) the colophon by the copyist John Andrea de Faldis given in note 3 above is immediately preceded by the following Explicit for the astrological treatise, which occurs also in the other MSS:

"Sit ergo gratia brevitatis nunc finis huic tractatui [*huius tractatatus* according to Valentinelli, but I did not so read the MS; *huic tractatu* in Sloane 3863] de aspectibus compillatum [*compilati* in the S. Marco MS] et in hac forma abbreviationis deductum [*deducti* in the S. Marco MS] per Leonardum de Bertapalea paduanum anno mill. CCCC XXIIII de mense martii" [*deo gratias amen*, adds Reg. Suev. 1969].

[9] E. Gurlt, *Gesch. d. Chirurgie*, Berlin, 1898, Vol. I, p. 858.

[10] S. Marco L. VII. LI, fols. 123r–125. The rubric reads, "Iuditium revolutionis anni 1427 incompleti," and the text includes such an expression as

career which our materials supply, 1421, 1424, 1427, and 1429, all fall within the same decade of the fifteenth century. On September 12, 1400, one of the witnesses to a will at Torreglia was a student of medicine named Leonard, son of the late Bartholomew Bufo of Bertapalea.[11] This was presumably our author in his student days. On January 21, 1412, Leonard de Bertepalea of Padua, scholar of medicine, is listed as attending an examination for the licentiate, while on June 22, 1450, occurred the examination in surgery of a master Leonardus de Bertapalea.[12] But this must have been some later bearer of the same name and a member presumably of the same family.

Leonard's work is said to have been printed at Venice in 1490 and 1497 with the title, *Chirurgia sive recollecta super quartum canonis Avicennae*,[13] and again in 1498, 1499, 1519, and 1546, all at Venice — with editions of Guy de Chauliac and other surgical treatises. I have been able to examine the editions of 1498, 1499, and 1546, where the work is headed, "Recollecte habite super quarto Avicenne ab egregio et singulari doctore magistro Leonardo Bertapalia." Of the editions of

---

"in presenti anno." It ends, ". . . Et hec sunt que compre[hen]dere potui iuxta ingenioli mei infelicitatem iudicactione [?] sumpta a revoluptione anni magne [satis] plus tamen et minus secundum deii [or, *dey*] nostri predispositionem qui sit laudatus per infinita secula amen."

[11] "mag Leonardus stud. in medicina fil. q. Bartholamei Bufi de Bertepalea": A. Gloria, *Monumenti della Università di Padova (1318–1405)*, 1888, Vol. I, p. 444; Vol. II, p. 373. Although Leonard is sometimes said to have been professor of surgery at Padua from 1402 to 1429, he is not so mentioned in this work by Gloria which covers to 1405.

[12] For these two events see documents 230 and 2415, *Acta Graduum Academicorum Gymnasii Patavini ab anno MCCCCVI ad annum MCCCCL*, ed. C. Zonta et Ioh. Brotto.

[13] Valentinelli, Vol. V, 1872, p. 100. Gurlt, who repeated this information after Mazzuchelli, *Gli scrittori d'Italia*, II, ii, 1032 (Brescia, 1760), himself used only the edition of 1498 in his analysis of the work's contents. Ludwig Choulant, *Handbuch der Bücherkunde für die ältere Medicin*, 1841, p. 416, includes in the *Collectio chirurgica veneta* of 1497 (impr. per Bonet. Locatellum Bergomensem, octavo kal. Mart.) "Leon. Bertapalia recollectae super IV canonis Avicennae," and states that it was published separately by Octavianus Scotus at Venice in the same year. He further mentions that an earlier edition in 1490 is alleged to have appeared at Venice, *ap. Octav. Scot.*, but that it probably did not have quite the same contents.

1490 and 1497 I have found little trace; they are not contained in the British Museum, Bibliothèque Nationale, or National Library at Florence, and are not recorded in Hain's *Repertorium bibliographicum* and its various supplements or in any other catalogue of incunabula that I have seen. The edition of 1519 is contained in the Library of Congress, where it has been examined for me. The surgical collection of 1546 contains, preceding its tables of contents, an introductory note or advertisement by its editor or publisher which is not found in the editions of 1498, 1499, and 1519. In addition to claiming to have improved the text of Guy of Chauliac over previous editions, to have substituted the *Surgery* of Roger for his *Physica* given in previous editions, and to have added a completer version of William of Saliceto's *Chirurgia*, the note boasts of having made very considerable additions and emendations to the text of Bertapalia from a manuscript.[14] As a matter of fact, in so far as I have compared them, the 1546 text of Leonard's treatise is identical with that contained in the 1498, 1499, and 1519 collections of surgical treatises. This warns us how little faith is to be placed in these advertisements or "blurbs" of the early printers, whose main object was of course to sell copies of their particular editions rather than to contribute accurate data for the history of textual criticism. This note or advertisement is not found in the 1498, 1499, and 1519 editions. Furthermore, the 1498 and 1519 editions (and I think also the 1499 edition) contain Roger's *Physica* rather than his *Surgery*, and do not include William of Saliceto at all. There is therefore a certain amount of truth in the later note or advertisement. Consequently, although its boast of additions to Leonard of Bertipaglia's text does not seem justified so far as the text of the editions of 1498, 1499, and 1519 are concerned, it may have some truth with reference to the earlier editions of 1490 and 1497 (if indeed there were any such editions). Or at

[14] "Idem in Bertapalia fecimus quippe qui integras paginas interdum adiunximus ex manuscripto codice tum simul plurimis in locis non raro quidem quatuor vel quinque versus saepius vero integras sententias ac dictiones addidimus plerunque etiam ipsas emendavimus."

least we seem justified in assuming that it would be very unlikely that the text of the 1490 and 1497 editions (assuming their reality) contained the passages found in our two manuscripts and omitted in the later editions. The later editions from 1498 on may possibly, however, have been the first to add the spurious matter which should not be attributed to Leonard of Bertipaglia.

One of our manuscripts has also undergone certain vicissitudes, not however of its text, but in the matter of binding and pagination. In the old catalogue of the Sloane manuscripts, written out in long hand in several thick volumes, of which the only copy is that preserved in the general reading room of the British Museum, there being no fellow to it in the Manuscript Room for Students, the work of Leonard of Bertipaglia is described as covering only fols. 1–100, and as followed on fol. 100v by an "Aque caustice magistri Petri de Tossignano," and at fols. 101–10 by a fragment of a book on wounds of the head. In reality this third item is a portion of Leonard's own treatment of the fifth Fen of Avicenna, and has, since the time when the old manuscript catalogue was compiled, been rebound and the leaves renumbered so that they now constitute fols. 91–100, while the former fols. 91–100 are now last in the manuscript and numbered 101–10. This brings the conclusion and table of contents of Leonard's work where they belong, at the close of the manuscript, followed only by the brief note concerning the *Caustic Waters* of Peter of Tossignano which someone has added in the blank space on the last leaf. But, whether it be that the recent rebinding merely failed to note and rectify a further misarrangement of the leaves of the codex that was already in existence when the old catalogue was drawn up, or whether in transposing the last two decades of folios the earlier ones were accidentally disturbed from their previous and proper order, at any rate the leaves from fol. 11 to fol. 90 are now bound and numbered in wrong order and should be read in the following sequence: following fols. 1–10 should come fols. 71–90, then fols. 61–70, then fols. 51–60, then fols.

41–50, then fols. 11–40, followed in their turn by fols. 91–110 as now numbered.[15] This Sloane manuscript presents Leonard's text in a double-columned page with ample margins. From the Vatican manuscript, which also is double-columned, a number of leaves are missing. Otherwise it is legible, although it contains many abbreviations, and the text which it presents seems reasonably accurate.

We have already alluded to the relation which the work of Leonard bears to the fourth Canon of Avicenna, but it seems to be less a commentary upon the text of Avicenna than a collection of recipes (as it is described in the subtitles of our manuscripts), cures, unguents, plasters, and some of Leonard's own clinical experiences. He roughly adheres to the order and main topics of the third and fourth Fens, but in the case of the fifth Fen, he seems to pass over Avicenna's first two *Tractatus* and deal only with the subject of the first chapter of Avicenna's third tractate, *De fractura cranei*. Then Leonard's concluding astrological treatise or treatises or chapters seem to have nothing to do with Avicenna whatever.

The division of Leonard's work into treatises and chapters, and the presence or absence of rubrics and headings, vary considerably, as is apt to be the case, in the printed text and our four manuscripts. The Venetian manuscript has very frequent rubrics through its text, practically one for every recipe. In Appendix 2 I reproduce the table of contents given at the close of the Sloane manuscript, with which the headings of the Florentine and Vatican manuscripts are practically identical. Its first treatise under the third Fen deals with hot apostemata, as does the corresponding treatise of Avicenna, but the manuscript has only thirteen chapters where Avicenna has thirty-four.[16] Its second treatise under the third Fen deals with cold apostemata, like Avicenna's second treatise, but has only

[15] I called this to the attention of the librarian in charge, and a note has now been inserted in the MS giving the correct order of folios.

[16] Thus *De formica* is cap. 6 in Avicenna, cap. 3 in Leonard; *De exituris* is cap. 20 in Avicenna, cap. 10 in the Leonard MSS, cap. 12 in the 1498 printed text.

twelve chapters against his twenty-two. The printed text in the 1498 edition combines these two treatises into a single one of twenty-seven chapters. The Vatican manuscript has almost the same chapter headings as the Sloane manuscript but, like the printed editions, does not make the division into two treatises. Avicenna's third tractate under the third Fen, treating *De lepra* in three chapters, finds no parallel in Leonard's text, which, however, divides into the same four treatises under the fourth Fen as does Avicenna, and with but slight variations in the numbers of chapters. Here again the printed text combines the first two of these treatises into a single one of twenty chapters. So far, then, for the third and fourth Fen, we have six treatises indicated in the Sloane manuscript, five in the Vatican manuscript, and four in the printed text. The transition from the third to the fourth Fen had been indicated in our manuscripts but not in the printed text; that from the fourth to the fifth Fen passes unmarked in both manuscripts and printed text. In the printed editions the next treatise that we encounter is headed, *Tractatus quintus de egritudinibus que accidunt in ossibus*, and its first chapter corresponds to that at fol. 35r of the Sloane MS, *De ventositate spine*, etc. But there seems to be no support in the manuscripts for commencing another treatise at this point. They rather point to the heading, *De fractura capitis*, which occurs a few leaves later (fol. 39r in the Sloane MS; fol. 56v in Biscioniani 13) as the opening chapter of a treatise, *De fractura cranei*. The printed editions next distinguish a sixth treatise, *De iudiciis vulnerum*, etc., but the manuscripts appear to divide this astrological matter into two treatises. The printed editions then add a seventh treatise, *De antidotis*, which is not contained in the manuscripts at all and of which we shall say more presently. Leaving it out of account, we find that the Sloane manuscript distinguishes nine treatises, while the printed editions divide the same extent of text into only six treatises. The catalogue of the Biscioniani manuscripts even describes our work as only four treatises in medicine or surgery, perhaps because the only beginnings of treatises that are clearly marked in that manuscript (Biscion. 13) are those of the second, third, and fourth treatises under the fourth Fen, occurring at fols. 27v, 35v, and 49r re-pectively.[17] The two astrological treatises are represented simply as additional "chapters" and not as treatises. In the Venetian manuscript the first astrological treatise is called a *Capitulum*, but the second, a *Tractatus*. On the other hand Valentinelli catalogued the "Capitulum de iudiciis vulnerum, etc." as a separate treatise from the *Cirurgia* of Leonard.[18] But in the Vatican manuscript there is no Explicit or other sign of ending before the astrological portion.

The divergence between the manuscript and the printed text of Leonard's work is noticeable in their very opening words, which introduce two prologues that are quite different both in wording and in length, that of the manuscripts being twice as long as the other. At the same time they express somewhat similar ideas and in part cover the same ground, so that it would seem impossible and inconceivable that they constitute two sections of one prologue. Therefore, either one of them is not genuine but concocted by some editor, or possibly Leonard himself issued two versions of his work, corresponding it might be to the varying manner in which he lectured on the subject in different years at the University of Padua. However, against this hypothesis it may be noted that although our manuscripts seem to suggest two different dates, 1421 and 1424, for Leonard's lectures, they present the same prologue. As for the divergence between this prologue and the shorter one given in

[17] In the descriptive title on the vellum flyleaf preceding fol. 1r — very likely written in by some later hand — "Tractatus chirurgicus seu Recepte date per magistrum Leonardum de Bertapalea Paduano [*sic*] in studio eiusdem civitatis super tertiam, quartam, et quintam Fen quarti canonis Avicenne; necnon Tractatus de signis celestibus et planetis," the last clause would thus seem to apply to the astrological work of the Pseudo-Hippocrates, which follows in the MS at fol. 69, and not to the astrological section of Leonard's work. This Pseudo-Hippocrates and some other brief astrological tracts precede Leonard's *Cirurgia* or *Recepte date* in the Venetian MS. The Pseudo-Hippocrates does not occur in the Sloane MS.

[18] *Op. cit.*, Vol. V, p. 100.

the editions, both implore divine aid, but in quite different terms; and while the printed prologue refers briefly to Leonard's own experiments, the manuscript prologue tells of another man, who was ignorant of the art of surgery but who made much money and reputation as a physician from a single "experiment" or cure of Leonard's, until he became puffed up with vainglory and an object of vituperation for scientific medical men. But the divergence between the two prologues may be best shown by reproducing the Latin text of both in Appendix 3.

The printed editions seem clearly in error in adding a seventh part or treatise, *De antidotis*, which does not appear in any of our manuscripts, and which apparently consists of miscellaneous recipes which some student or practitioner has added at the close of his copy of Leonard's work. This is indicated by several circumstances. In giving the title of the entire work, "These are the *Recollectae* held over the fourth of Avicenna by the outstanding and singular doctor, master Leonard Bertapalia," the heading in the printed editions adds, "and here are marvelous secrets possessed by him and tested (or, experienced) by me." [19] That is to say, some later person has added his own medical experiences to those of Leonard. Secondly, the whole general character of this concluding treatise, *On Antidotes*, is very miscellaneous, suggesting a scrapbook, or occasional jottings and notes, rather than a consecutive treatise. For instance, besides cures by Hugh of Siena [20] for dropsy and a cough, and various other recipes, we find a few notes on the significance of different colors of urine, and eight verses listing a number of surgical instruments. Third, in one particular passage dated 1429, whereas Leonard's work as a whole is dated

[19] ". . . et ibi sunt mirabilia secreta habita ab eo et per me experta."

[20] Hugh was famous as a philosopher as well as "medicorum princeps." Aeneas Sylvius tells (cap. 52, "Europae") how he invited the Greeks at the Council of Ferrara to a banquet and disputation over points on which Aristotle and Plato disagreed. Hugh allowed the Greeks to take either side they pleased and then defeated them. I owe this reference to Theodor Zwinger's *Theatrum vitae humanae*, 1604, V. i. 1209.

1424, we read that on the eighth of February of that year an anatomy was performed on the body of a robber and murderer of Bergamo "by the outstanding and singular doctor, master Hugh of Siena, lecturer here in ordinary,[21] in the morning in a house near St. Luke's in the city of Padua; and I was present at it with master Leonard, lecturer in surgery . . ." The writer, evidently a third person and presumably a pupil or possibly a colleague of Hugh and Leonard, then goes on to record another anatomy held in 1430.[22]

[21] The reference, of course, is to the distinction made in the schedules of classes in the medieval universities between "ordinary" and "extraordinary" lectures.

[22] The Latin of the entire passage, which is picturesquely circumstantial, is as follows in the edition of 1546: "Anno Iesu Christu M. CCCC. XXIX. Octava die mensis Februarii facta fuit anotomia de quodam viro Bergomensi qui quendam ut ei subriperet aurum occiderat per egregium et singularem doctorem Magistrum Ugonem de Senis ibi ordinarie ad lecturam deputatum de mane in quadam domo apud Sanctum Lucam in terra Patavina: et ego huic interfui cum Magistro Leonardo deputato ad lecturam chirurgie, et hoc actum in squadra de Turricellis et inde sepultus fuit ad eandem ecclesiam sancti Lucae qui nos ab hoc tanto casu defendat Rectore M. Marco. M. CCCC. XXX in vigilia Ascensionis Domini facta est anotomia de matrice in muliere de mense Aprilis die quarto Rectore Magistro Marco Fuscari nobili Veneto." (Fol. 299v.)

It may be translated somewhat as follows: In the year of Jesus Christ 1429, the eighth day of the month of February, an anatomy was performed on a certain man of Bergamo, who had killed somebody in order to steal gold from him, by the outstanding and singular doctor, master Hugh of Siena, deputed here to give ordinary lectures, in the morning in a house near St. Luke's in the city of Padua; and I was there with Master Leonard, lecturer in surgery; and this took place in the square of Turricelli; and then he was buried at the same church of St. Luke — may he preserve us from such a fate — during the rectorship of M. Marcus. In 1430 on the eve of the Ascension of our Lord an anatomy was performed on a woman's womb on the fourth day of the month of April during the rectorship of Marcus Fuscari, a noble of Venice."

Possibly "in the morning" should go with "ordinary lectures" rather than indicate the time of the "anatomy."

The mention of the university in each case may be explained by the fact that it was a common provision in the statutes of the Italian universities in the fourteenth and fifteenth centuries that the corpse for the anatomy should be furnished annually by the local Podestà or other official at the request of the rector, and that no doctor or scholar should acquire any body for purposes of dissection except through the rector. The number of persons permitted to attend an anatomy was limited so that all might obtain a good view — for example, in the Statutes of the University of Ferrara of 1444, to fifty: see Borsetti, *Historia almi Ferrariae gymnasii*, Ferrara, 1735, Vol. I, pp. 431–37, Statutum 60 — and it seems to have been a much sought after privilege. At the University of

But the most striking and important discrepancy between the manuscript and the printed texts of Leonard's work is the presence of more personal and clinical material in the manuscripts. Leonard, like so many medieval men who possessed intellectual curiosity and ingenuity or some specialized skill, had a distinct and interesting, albeit somewhat naïve and quaint, personality which he does not hesitate to reveal in his text. He shows a pardonable pride in his own healing powers and surgical skill, a pardonable interest in his own clinical cases, and he has a style of writing of his own, quaint, garrulous, and rather breathless, somewhat defective in point of grammatical correctness and elegance. "Let no one," he remarks in one place, "charge me with prolixity of rude speech because I have said many things complicated by obscurity and confusion." [23] A great deal of unsubstantiated claptrap has been written about the lack of individuality in the middle ages and the development of individuality as a result of the Italian Renaissance. But the humanists objected to anyone's having a style of his own almost as much as to his writing ungrammatically, and strove to write like the ancients in general and Cicero in particular. At any rate in our particular case the editors and printers of the late fifteenth and early sixteenth centuries have ironed out and suppressed, whether intentionally or accidentally, a number of expressions of Leonard's individuality and personal scientific experience, so that the printed text fails to give us a correct and accurate idea of this early fifteenth-century work or of the surgery of that time. It is a

---

Bologna in the fifteenth century twenty students were admitted to see the anatomy of each man, thirty of each woman: ed. C. Malagola, 1888, p. 289. The number admitted was scrupulously apportioned between the several nations making up the university, and it was further ruled that a student who "has seen the anatomy of a man once, cannot see more in the same year. He who has witnessed two may see no more at Bologna, except the anatomy of a woman, which anyone may see once and no more."

[23] "Nemo michi crimen imponat ex prolixitate rudis sermonis cum multa complicata obscuritate et confusione dixerim . . .," Biscion. 13, fol. 27v; Sloane 3863, fol. 51v; Reg. Suev. 1969, fol. 35r; S. Marco L.VII.LI, fol. 56r. I did not find the passage in the printed editions. It occurs at the beginning of the second treatise under the fourth Fen.

good single instance of the general truth that the early modern period failed to appreciate and misunderstood much in the previous medieval civilization, which has thus hitherto suffered in our estimation from this misinterpretation or neglect.

This failure to reflect Leonard's personal remarks and clinical observations is especially noticeable in the portion of his work devoted to fracture of the skull. Here he appears to have added to his university lectures some surgical counsels for the benefit of his eleven-year-old son, Fabricius.[24] In an introductory passage which does not appear in the printed text, he mentions his longing for truth and learning, "being of the opinion that no better thing for men could be perceived in this world. Wherefore before I knew this, I did not know whether it would come from God or from fortune. But in the manual art I never could distinguish a completely unskilled from an unskilled person." Perhaps the writer of the manuscript has by a slip written *unskilled* twice here where one of the words should be *skilled*. Leonard continues, "Since many doctors and skillful persons have been deceived, and especially in wounds of the nerves and fractures of the head, wherefore to rehearse so many and so long statements as have been made by the men of old would be tedious to hear and too confusing and not well adapted . . . to my son Fabricius who is eleven years old. Therefore in this my work . . . I shall follow another method than that followed by my professors, but I shall cite some authorities where they are in my judgment praiseworthy, and I will narrate marvelous works of nature with God's aid and following the method and rules of the ancients. For in this work . . . I intend to make special chapters concerning each disease treated surgically, beginning first with the head, speaking concerning it theoretically. Secondly, treating of it practically and giving the best examples. And this according to my own opinion put in the form of a counsel according to cases I have had under cure and have seen in the city of Padua,

[24] Gurlt, following Mazzuchelli, says that Leonard had a son named Giovanni Michele who lectured on surgery in Padua in 1435–36.

Rome, Verona, Venice, in Alexandria, in that city in which Mohammed is worshipped as a god by the Saracens in Mecca. But I swear by the living God and truly Crucified to make no false statement to you, my son, in this my book to the best of my ability. But first you ought to have these eight notable points ever in mind, if you wish to be a perfect surgeon, and one who so holds them always should be preferred to others.[25]"

At this point the printed text resumes, giving these eight essentials, but in a briefer form than that of the manuscripts. The chief discrepancy is in connection with the third qualification, "You ought to have light hands and expeditious in operating lest you cause the patient pain." Here the manuscripts add, "For, my son, you heard him who said that I had light and expeditious hands when I extracted for him that bit of bone lodged in the hollow of the brain with that instrument

[25] I give the Latin of the passage as it occurs in Sloane MS 3863 at fol. 38v with variations from Biscioniani 13, fol. 56r, and S. Marco L.VII.LI, fol. 104r. Not only this passage but the whole context is missing from Reg. Suev. 1969, where a leaf or so seems to have been lost. Variant readings are put in brackets, but here as elsewhere I have not thought it worth while to note every minor variation in spelling such as *alliquos* for *aliquos* or *narabo* for *narrabo*.

"*Sequitur* [*Capitulum*] *De fractura cranei*. Concupivi veritatem et disciplinam estimans nullam meliorem rem hominibus in hoc mundo posse percipere. Quare [Quia] antequam scirem hoc nescivi [an] si a deo an si a fortuna hoc accessissem [accessisset]. Verum in arte manuali numquam novi plene imperitum ab imperito. Cum multi doctores atque periti decepti fuerant et maxime in vulneribus nervorum et fracturis capitis quare tot et tanta narrare quanta a veteribus narrata sunt esset quid [aliquid] tediosum audire atque perconfusum et non bene capasibile pro tunc Fabricio filio meo qui est xi annorum. Ideo in hoc meo opere ammodo aliud sequar stilum non secutum a meis professoribus [precessoribus] sed alegabo aliquos ubi sunt meo iudicio laude digni et narrabo mirabilia opera nature cum auxilio divino et sequendo modum et regulas antiquorum. Nam in hoc [meo] opere ammodo intendo facere capitula specialia de unaquaque egritudine pertinenti ciroico [cirogico]. Incipiendo primo a capite declarando de ipsa theorice [theorica]. Secundo tractando de ipsa practice [practica] et optima exempla dando. Et hoc [omitted] secundum meam opinionem ponendo in formam consilii secundum quod habui in cura et vidi in civitate paduana rome verone venetiis [et] in alexandria in civitate illa in qua Maumeth a sarracenis in mecha pro deo colitur. Sed iuro per deum vivum et verum crucifixum nullum mendacium fili mi in hoc meo libro tibi facere iuxta meum posse. Sed primo oportet te [te oportet] hec [omitted] octo notabilia bene in [tua] mente habere semper si vis esse perfectus ciroicus et sic habendo semper preferendus eris aliis."

of parchment through a small hole in the broken bone. And you saw that I thrust that instrument to the depth of one finger into the hollow of the brain. And witnesses of this were the most famous monarch of the arts and doctor of medicine, master Galeatus de Sancta Sophia,[26] and master Nicholas the barber, and master Gera Cerdo [or, Geracerdo], and you, my son, who saw all these things."[27]

When I read the following personal passage in the manuscript text of Leonard's work, I wondered whether it would be found in the printed editions. "Note this, dearest son, lest it happen to thee as happened to a certain good man of Padua who had a puncture in the nerve, made by a minute iron in the ring finger of the left hand above the middle joint. And a certain physician, who was wise and famous in his own subject but lacking experience and reason in surgery, yet opinionated

[26] The family of Sancta Sophia included a number of noted medical men in successive generations. This Galeazzo is presumably the one who died of plague in 1427. L. Senfelder published his *Consilium pestilentiae* and another medical advice for a lord about to take a sea voyage, in the Vienna *Klinische Rundschau* of 1888. His works on fevers and the Ninth Book of Rasis to Almansor were printed in editions of the early sixteenth century. He was a nephew of the more famous Marsilius de Sancta Sophia. Tiraboschi, *Storia d. lett. ital.*, Vol. V, 1823, p. 394, however, ascribes a work on fevers, printed at Venice in 1514, and at Lyons in 1517, to this Marsilius de Sancta Sophia the younger, whom Michael Savonarola put first among the physicians of his time. Galeazzo and Marsilius the younger are sometimes incorrectly identified, but there are two works on fevers in the 1517 edition at least, and Savonarola clearly distinguishes between Marsilius Junior (who probably died about 1411) and Galeazzo, who had been his own teacher. Savonarola also mentions Daniel, John, and William of Santa Sofia — *Libellus de magnificis ornamentis regie civitatis Padue Michaelis Savonarole*, Muratori, *Scriptores*, new edition, Vol. XXIV, Part XV, pp. 36–40.

[27] The portion of the passage which I have included in parentheses in the following Latin is found only in Sloane MS 3863 and not in the other three MSS. Variant readings are enclosed in brackets.

"Nam fili mi audivisti illum qui dixit quod habebam [habebat] manus leves et expeditas quando extraxi sibi [sibi extrasi] illud [illum] frustrum ossis existens in concavitate cerebri (cum illo instrumento de carta membrana per parvum foramen ossis fracti. Et vidisti quod fixi illud instrumentum ad quantitatem unius digiti in concavitate cerebri.) Et de hoc esset testis famosissimus monarcha artium et medicine doctor magister Galeatius de Sancta Sophia et magister Nicolaus barbitonsor et magister Geracerdo [*gera cerdo* in the Sloane MS] et tu fili mi qui hec omnia vidisti."

in the matter, ordered mollificative medicines to be applied, namely, a plaster of wheat flour and water and oil and saffron. But at length the hand putrefied, and he died the seventh day, and this for the reason that spasms occurred on account of putrefaction produced by undue application of a bad plaster. So believe that the expert is to be trusted in his own art." The passage does occur in the printed text, but it has been tampered with. Not merely is "dearest son" altered to "friend" and nothing said of Padua, but the whole point of the passage is lost by ascribing the prescription of the plaster to a stupid surgeon instead of physician. Presumably the printed text of 1498 or the manuscript on which it was based had been edited by some medical man who resented Leonard's slur upon one of his profession and turned the criticism back against surgeons.[28]

Finally in illustration of our point may be noted a much longer passage in which Leonard recounts one of his own cases under the caption, *Capitulum quod est exemplum*, in the Florentine manuscript, and *De quodam exemplo*, in the Sloane manuscript, but which is entirely omitted in such printed texts as I have examined.

"There came to me with the help of the divine Trinity a certain rustic named Gazabinus with a nephew of his who once had been wounded with three knife wounds, of which one was in the colon of the intestine, and when I first saw it, the excrement came out through the wound, and it was in that place where the turning of the left reins is. Another wound was in the chest and penetrated it. The sign of this was that the air issuing from that wound exstinguished the flame of a great lighted candle. Another wound was in the spleen, for I saw that black melancholic blood issued from the wound. And this wound was below the false ribs on the left side. All which wounds in that nephew of his I had healed already. And from the intestinal wound came out a great worm just

[28] In Appendix 6, I give the Latin of the passage both from the MSS and from the edition of 1498.

as the wound was closing up, which worm I extracted from the wound with my hands.

"Well, this Gazabinus, whose son I had recently treated for fracture of the skull and cured, said, 'My son Pasqualinus, with the brother of this one whom you saved from death, struck a certain young porter with a boar-spear and drove the ear of the spear into the head a bit to one side and not far from the coronal commissura, — about an inch below it.' But two other men who were with him swore to me that as soon as they applied white of egg, some of the substance of the brain came out together with blood. This I was certainly unwilling to believe. But I bethought me of the words of Galen in the sixth part of the Aphorisms in that aphorism *Vessicam incisam*, etc. In the commentary Galen says of the brain, 'Incision of the brain, too, I have seen healed, for once in Nimba, a city of Samaria,[29] I saw a man have a great concave incision of the brain and yet escape death, which happens rarely.' Also Arnald of Villanova in his *Practica*, the third tractate, says that he has heard the same thing from the most skillful surgeons about the substance of the brain coming out and the patient's escaping death. But this I saw with my own eyes, some of the substance of the medulla again come out in this patient, whom I cured alone without other advice [with a stylus] in the presence of many doctors and scholars of Padua whom I led with me by prayers and charity, that they might see the possibility of nature, namely, manifest and ample separation by two fingers' breadth of the first anterior ventricle in which imagination takes place from the middle ventricle in which cogitation or reason goes on, while the third posterior ventricle where retentive or treasuring virtue acts was unaffected so far as I could see.[30]

[29] In the text of Galen, Smyrna in Ionia is the place referred to: see Kühn, *Medicorum Graecorum Opera quae exstant*, 1829, XVIII, i, 29.

[30] These old views of the activities of the ventricles of the brain seem to have survived until Franz Joseph Gall's *Anatomie et physiologie du système nerveux*, 1810–20, and even later. See G. Elliot Smith's recent address on "The Human Brain," printed in his *The Evolution of Man*, 1924 (reviewed in *Isis*, Vol. VII, pp. 149–52). Smith says of Gall, "It was he who destroyed the

"In such a man living all those three virtues were always as it were healthy and without any accident of all the various accidents accustomed to appear in dispositions of this sort, such as vomiting, syncope, *singultus*, spasm, mental alienation, fevers, and epilepsy. The nutritive, animal, and vital virtues were always those of a healthy person until the thirty-fourth day, on which occurred five attacks of epilepsy and great sweats and continuous fever. And this was from a primitive cause, namely, from drinking mountain wine without my knowledge. But it is true that that day was also a critical day, salubrious and radicative according to my computation of the number of critical days in medicine. But when that day passed, weakness remained in the motive virtue of the opposite parts, foot and hand, but how I proceeded in curing him both practically and theoretically I will tell below."[31] This promised account of his treatment of the case is given in the printed text as well as the manuscripts, although in a somewhat condensed form, and so need not be repeated here.

In the colophon to the Florentine manuscript the copyist of 1471 volunteers a bit of information or gossip, which is not found in the printed editions or in the Sloane manuscript, but which occurs also in the Vatican and Venetian manuscripts. It is to the effect that Leonard, although a most excellent professor of surgery, had never taken his degree, apparently on the ground that there were so many unworthy holders of the doctorate[32] — or else because he feared the criticism of ill-informed

ancient speculations concerning vital spirits dwelling in the ventricles of the brain." And again, "It was not until more than thirty years after Gall's death that the localization of function in the cerebral cortex began to be seriously entertained." Gall died in 1828.

[31] In spots the passage seems a trifle incoherent, and I have had to guess at the text or meaning. But its general trend is clear enough. In the Latin text, which is given in Appendix 5, I have collated our four manuscripts, adopting the more usual spelling or form in each case of variation. Possibly it is just because of the textual difficulties that such passages present that they have been omitted in the printed editions.

[32] It is difficult to construe or translate the words, "propter excusare vituperium multorum doctorum." The complete colophon reads: "Expletum est hoc opus compositum Padue anno 1424 per excellentissimum professorem

doctors—and that "he preferred to be a good squire rather than a poor knight." In the printed editions, however, Leonard is called "doctor" as well as "master," but I think that the Sloane manuscript employs only the latter title and "professor."

In any case Leonard of Bertipaglia is an interesting representative of the relations between medicine and surgery in the fifteenth century, and this is brought out especially by the very passages that have been omitted in the printed editions. We see that the surgeons of that time were not necessarily either mere barbers or bookish theorists. Even the printed editions contain a passage against barbers as surgeons, and it occurs in the spurious seventh treatise *De antidotis*, which we have shown to be by someone else than Leonard, and so may be regarded as additional testimony confirming the impression that we have already received from his work. The aforesaid spurious treatise opens: "These are secrets to be memorized and magnified, and not given into the hands of barbers or of those who through failure to understand them vituperate good authors, as if these seem to have written badly, and yet their sayings are of the best. But those ignorant fellows do not know how to operate, wherefore men ought rather to commit themselves to the hands of skilled surgeons than to those of ignoramuses and barbers, whom we ought utterly to scorn and neglect." [33] This cleavage between surgeons and barbers may be further illustrated from the history of the University of Paris

---

cirurgie magistrum Leonardum de Bertapalea qui numquam voluit graduari propter excusare vituperium multorum doctorum ignorantium; nam [quare] potius voluit esse bonus scutifer quam malus miles."

[33] "Haec sunt secreta commendanda memorie et magnificanda nec danda manibus barbitonsorum nec qui male intelligendo auctores bonos vituperant quasi male videntur scripsisse, et tamen eorum dicta optima sunt. Sed isti ignari nesciunt operari unde potius homines deberent se committere manibus peritorum quam ignorantium et barbitonsorum, quos aspernari et negligere prorsus debemus . . ."

A kindred attitude was displayed earlier in the surgical work of Bongianus de Orto of Arezzo, entitled *Spinea rosa* (*The Thorny Rose*), and contained in a Laurentian MS of the fourteenth century (Plut. 73, cod. 26, fols. 1–74). Another form of the title is *Rosea Spina*. In the preface Bongianus inveighs against "those profane, scurrilous beclouders of science, its detractors rather

where in 1423 when the barbers were trying to be incorporated in the college of surgeons and to conduct anatomical demonstrations, the surgeons secured from the prévôt of Paris an injunction prohibiting the barbers from exercising any of a surgeon's functions.[34] There was a like struggle between the surgeons and barbers of London in the fourteenth and fifteenth centuries.

Leonard was of the class of skilled surgeons and operating practitioners. Yet he was also widely read in medical literature from Galen's *Commentaries on the Aphorisms of Hippocrates* down to the 181st *Differentia* of the *Conciliator* of Peter of Abano,[35] and the books of Bernard Gordon, Arnald of Villanova, William of Saliceto, and William of Varignana, or the still

---

than promoters, who employ "blind remedies" and use no reason in their cures, but merely experiments. They take no account of the differences between species or of places or the constitutions of patients, but think that they can cure all wounds alike with wine and white of egg.

Fol. 1r–v: "Sic et isti profani maledic[t]i nubilatores scientie ob audacie stimulum, dum caducis utuntur remediis. . . . Qui potius detractores cernuntur scientie quam fautores quum in curis nulla ratione utuntur sed experimentis solummodo nulla ratione firmatis. Credentes certissime omnem speciem unitati oppositam quibusdam eorum medicaminibus posse sanari nulla consideratione adhibita specifici[s] unionis solute nec inter differentias specierum ad invicem vel si cum aliis generibus egritudinum componantur . . .," etc. Sudhoff, who printed the entire preface (*Beiträge z. Gesch. d. Chirurgie*, Vol. II, 1918, pp. 418–19) seems to have misread one or two words of this passage.

Concerning Bongioanni dall' Orto, consult further Ugo Viviani, *Medici, fisici e cerusici della Provincia Aretina vissuti dal V al XVII secolo*, 1923, pp. 42–45. Viviani dates him early in the fourteenth century and gives a brief description of the above MS.

[34] L'Abbé Comte de Guasco, *Recherches sur l'état des lettres, des sciences et des arts en France sous les règnes de Charles VI et de Charles VII*, couronné par l'Académie royale des inscriptions et belles-lettres pour le prix de 1746, printed in C. Leber, *Collection des meilleurs dissertations*, etc., 1838, p. 281. As recorded in the *Chartularium Universitatis Parisiensis*, Vol. IV, pp. 442–3, Document 2253, "Lis coram praeposito Paris. et coram parlamento inter chirurgos et barbitonsores Paris., qui praetendebant se, quamvis non approbatos, artem chirurgicam in quibusdam casibus exercere posse," the decision, while maintaining the privileges of the surgeons, allows the barbers certain minor surgical activities.

[35] Sloane 3863, fol. 98r: "Experimentum conciliatoris seu magistri Petri de Abano quod curat fracturas cranei absque elevatione ossis. Unde lege conciliatorem quia dicit de hoc experimento in differentia 181. . . ."

more recent works of Pietro da Tossignano (died about 1411) and Pietro d'Argellata (died 1423). In a sentence which is omitted in the printed text he advises the prospective surgeon to "read and well read through our predecessors, if you would know in what way and how and when these things should be done." [36] He was on good terms and a footing of equality, it would seem, with his medical colleagues of the highest reputation at Padua. He appears at one time to have traveled as far as Alexandria in Egypt, if not to forbidden Mecca itself.[37] A new edition of his text, based on the manuscripts, of which others can probably be found than the four that I have used, would seem to be highly desirable.

The superstitious side of Leonard's works should not, however, be passed over in silence, and I would be the last person to do so. The very fact that his *Cirurgia* is so largely a collection of recipes makes it the more likely to savor of magic. Thus we find a cure for the pest which Peter of Abano is said to have learned from the demons by exorcising them,[38] while the archangel Sathael is said to have taught men astrological medicine after his fall.[39] But this tendency and his penchant for judicial astrology [40] Leonard shared with his age and his more

[36] Sloane 3863, fol. 93r: "Qualiter [quare] lege et bene perlege nostros precessores si vis scire quomodo et qualiter et quando ista debent fieri . . ."

[37] See note 25 above.

[38] It occurs both in the printed text (see edition of 1498, fol. 238r, col. 1) and in the MSS (Sloane 3863, fol. 71v; S. Marco L.VII.LI, fol. 22v; etc.): "Experimentum mirabile et secretum revelatum per exorcizationem a demonibus Magistro Petro de Abano . . ."

[39] Edition of 1498, fol. 263r; Sloane 3863, fol. 101v; Biscioniani 13, fol. 63v; S. Marco L.VII.LI, fol. 115r.

[40] Is our Leonard to be identified with the Bertapalia or Pertapia of Tifi Odasi's *Macharonea* of the fifteenth century?

> "Est etiam astrologus tanquam speciale cusinus
> Quid didicisset dicit celum guardando vel astra
> Utile nil aquam vino missiare fumanti
> Est herbolatus ciroicus et cavadentes
> Est negromantes factis cum cera figuris
> . . . .
> Est etiam medicus facit guarire podagras."

—From p. 70 of "Macaronéana," published by Octave Delepierre in *Miscellanies of the Philobiblon Society*, Vol. VII, 1862–63.

learned contemporaries. Moreover, these frailties appear as plainly in the printed as in the manuscript versions of his works and so do not strictly fall within the scope of this chapter.

His *Judgment of the Revolution of the Year 1427*, however, has not been printed so far as I know, so that it may be well to give some brief account of it. After a devout opening in the manner of the Arabic astrologer, Haly, in his treatise on *Revolutions of Years*,[41] and expression of the hope that what he says may be pleasing to God, Leonard treats, first, of the entry of the Sun into the first minute of the sign Aries and of the lord of the whole year; next, of the state of the Roman church and of prelates; third, of princes and nobles and certain cities; fourth, of war; fifth, of the state of human bodies and of changes in the weather; sixth and last, of want and abundance. A few details from his prognostication may be noted. There will be discord in the church and "all prelates" will try to dominate by force and fraud and secret treachery. Many will be imprisoned. Leonard refers to the planet Jupiter as the general governor of the church, but to Mercury as the protector and defender of our Christian faith. The year will be a bad one for martial surgeons (*cirurgici martiales*) — a phrase which probably indicates surgeons born under the influence of the planet Mars rather than those associated with armies. Leonard cautions "a great woman of royal line" to guard herself diligently lest she be deceived by a magnate. Mortality and famine and mutation from place to place are predicted for the Arabs. The year should be free from pestilence, but Leonard warns men to keep away from places where the pest prevailed last year, since long experience has shown that it spreads by contagion. But shameful deaths are likely to abound in 1427, and there will be many kinds of fevers and sicknesses from catarrh. Leonard's prediction throughout appears to follow the method of Haly in the aforesaid book on revolutions.

[41] S. Marco L.VII.LI, fol. 123r: ". . . quantum ingenioli mei facultas supetit incipiam primo cum alii filio ab curagel tractatu de revolucionibus annorum hec verba prorumpente laus in optimo deo qui est dominus subtilitatum . . ."

CHAPTER IV

A *PRACTICA CIRURGIE* ASCRIBED TO JOHN BRACCIA OF MILAN OR TO PETER OF TOSSIGNANO

Strictly speaking, the work to which the present chapter will be devoted appears to belong to the late fourteenth rather than to the fifteenth century, since its author refers to cases of his when in the employ of members of the Visconti and Gonzaga families who lived in the second half of the fourteenth century. Among these he mentions two sons of Barnabò Visconti — "Macarulus," a name which seems to designate Marco or Carlo, and "Olfus," which is probably short for Rodolfo. He would presumably have been in their service before the overthrow of their father in 1385. In one manuscript of the work, there is also a reference to a Galeazzo Visconti, who is doubtless Barnabò's brother of that name.[1] Of the Gonzaga family there is mentioned a John or a Guido [2] who would appear to belong to the same period. But all four manuscripts of the work that I have seen and know of date well along in the fifteenth century, to which period the treatise may therefore be said in a sense to belong. Indeed, it is not inconceivable that these accounts of earlier cases may have been taken over by the author of a later work. It is also true that the author seems to be writing in his old age, after his days of practice were over, since he refers again and again to the methods he employed and the cures he effected "in my time," as if that anteceded the day of the generation for which he writes. It is not impossible, therefore, that he may have had the aforementioned members of the Visconti and Gonzaga families as employers and yet have lived to write on the verge, or even in the opening years, of the fifteenth century.

[1] Vienna Latin MS 4751, fol. 131v. This and the other passages involving mention of such names will be cited more fully later in other connections.

[2] One Guido of Gonzaga died in 1369; another, in 1382.

The work is concerned with the practice of surgery, and is discussed here for the further reason that it so well complements the impressions which we have just received in the previous chapter from the writings of Leonard of Bertipaglia as to the Italian surgery of the closing middle ages. Although our present treatise may be regarded as certainly earlier than that of Leonard, it has seemed preferable to deal first with the work of fixed date and authorship, and then, in the present chapter, turn back to this somewhat earlier analogous work of more uncertain authorship and date. This procedure furthermore conforms to the course of my investigation, since the initial study of Leonard of Bertipaglia which formed the basis of the preceding chapter was published before I examined the manuscripts of the treatise to which we now turn.

In Karl Sudhoff's *Beiträge zur Geschichte der Chirurgie im Mittelalter* [3] there is a brief section entitled, "Eine Chirurgie Magisters Peter von Tussignano oder Johannis de Mediolano?" [4] This is based upon two manuscripts at Munich in which the same work on surgery is variously ascribed to the two men in question. The work seems never to have been printed and to have been little noticed apart from this brief discussion by Sudhoff and a previous citation by Henschels.[5] In addition to raising the question of authorship, Sudhoff printed the Incipits and Explicits and tables of chapter headings of the treatise, but did not go further into its contents and merits. I may therefore give some further account of it, especially since I have found two other manuscripts of it in the National Library at Vienna. Its general plan is much like that of the work of Leonard of Bertipaglia and those of other commentators or lecturers upon the surgical section of Avicenna's *Canon*. It consists of two books, one devoted to *apostemata*, the other to wounds and ulcers. Again, like

[3] Zweiter Teil, Leipzig, 1918. Heft 11 u. 12, *Studien z. Gesch. d. Medizin.*

[4] *Ibid.*, pp. 421–23. If anyone takes exception to the genitives and nominatives in this heading, I can only say that I have transcribed them exactly as I found them.

[5] A. W. E. Th. Henschels, *Janus*, Vol. II, 1852–53, pp. 419–21.

the manuscript in distinction from the printed text of Leonard of Bertipaglia, it seems of considerable importance for the amount of personal clinical material which it offers and for the apparently independent attitude which its author sometimes assumes.

During the summer of 1927, while still unaware of the aforesaid discussion by Sudhoff, I stumbled within the space of a fortnight upon four different manuscripts of what was apparently one and the same surgical treatise, though existing in them in different versions and with varying inscriptions. The first manuscript that I saw, in the National Library at Vienna,[6] was a copy written in 1436, and was called "The Practice of Surgery of John of Ptraccia." This last information was given in the final rubric.[7] The treatise itself opened without title or other heading,[8] and without proemium or other introductory explanation. In another manuscript of the same library [9] is an anonymous treatise of surgery which seems to be essentially the same work, although differing not a little from the other in wording and fullness.[10]

Moreover, the anonymous version has a proemium. After

[6] Vienna 2358, fols. 124r–149v, double-columned page, 21 x 15, neatly written but with many abbreviations; about 44 lines to the column.

[7] Fol. 149v, col. 2, "Explicit practica Cyrurgie Johannis de ptraccia Anno 1436 feria 2a ante Jocobi a." The last words seem to mean "the Monday before the feast of St. James the Apostle," that is, July 23, 1436.

[8] Fol. 124r, col. 1, Incipit, "Causa antecedens intrinseca flegmonis est ex repletione humorum. Flegmon dicitur apostema . . ."

[9] Vienna 4751, fols. 5v–212r, 19 x 11; coarsely written but with many abbreviations; about twenty lines to a page on the average.

[10] Its text closes at fol. 212r, ". . . fiat pulvis et utatur in omni cibo"; whereas the last sentences in Vienna 2358 at fol. 149v read: "Et comedat poma et pira cocta sub prunis post cibum et cum hoc potest commedere pullos gallinas aves parvos [*sic*] degentes in arboribus et non in vallibus. Vinum si vellet bibere, sit aquosum debile et sit aqua in duplici quantitate respectu vini." The two Munich MSS close in essentially the same way. The first of these two sentences, with the text preceding it, occurs in Vienna 4751 back at fol. 197r.

Again, whereas in Vienna 2358 the first book is slightly longer than the second, in Vienna 4751 the second book is much the longer. This is partly accounted for by the fact that fols. 110r–120r have been recopied out of their place as fols. 182r–193v, which are therefore superfluous.

invoking divine aid, the author states his purpose, lists headings for the thirty-eight chapters [11] of his first book on *apostemata*, and gives the definition and etymology of the word "surgery" (*cyrugia*). He further emphasizes the requirement that the surgeon must employ both reason and experience, must read the books which contain the past acquisitions of the art, and must have a practical experience of his own. "And all scholars of the science of surgery should know that surgery cannot be fully understood except by long time spent on it and by intercourse with old skilled medical men. But I have set down in this little book of mine all that I have experienced and proved in the time in which I have lived. The prohemium being over, with God's aid I come to the main theme." But nothing definite is revealed in this preface concerning the writer's identity or the date of his work. In the colophon at the close of the treatise, however, it is stated that the date of copying it was September 9, 1424, and that this was "by the hand of Mathew Carfem, present head of the diocese." [12] The identity of this person I have been unable to discover. The present manuscript is thus an older copy than Vienna 2358, and its proemium, or preface, is not found in the other manuscripts.

[11] This number does not agree with the other manuscripts. In Vienna 2358 I counted thirty-two chapter headings for the first book; CLM 273 gives twenty-six in its table of contents, which is given on a sheet of paper inserted between fols. 113 and 114. Such variation is not surprising, however, since in a single manuscript there are often headings in the text which are not found in the table of contents and *vice versa*. Indeed this proves to be the case with CLM 273. A table of twenty-one chapter headings for the second book which is found at fols. 93v–94r of Vienna 4751 is in closer agreement with the other MSS, which list twenty chapters for that section.

[12] Vienna 4751, fol. 212r: "Finitum anno domini M°CCCC°XXIIII° die vero nona septembris per manus Mathie carfem presentem culmen diocesis pro quo deus sit benedictus." It seems odd that a bishop should copy so long a work of surgery with his own hand, and especially that he should copy ten leaves of it twice over — a slip which one might rather expect from an unscrupulous hired copyist. However, I have looked through Eubel's *Hierarchia catholica* in hope of finding what diocese Mathew was head of. But while a number of bishops holding office in the year 1424 were named Mathew, there seems to be none who is also distinctly named Carfem. I recognize that the Latin as I have read it parses none too well, but it is difficult to get any other meaning or reading out of it.

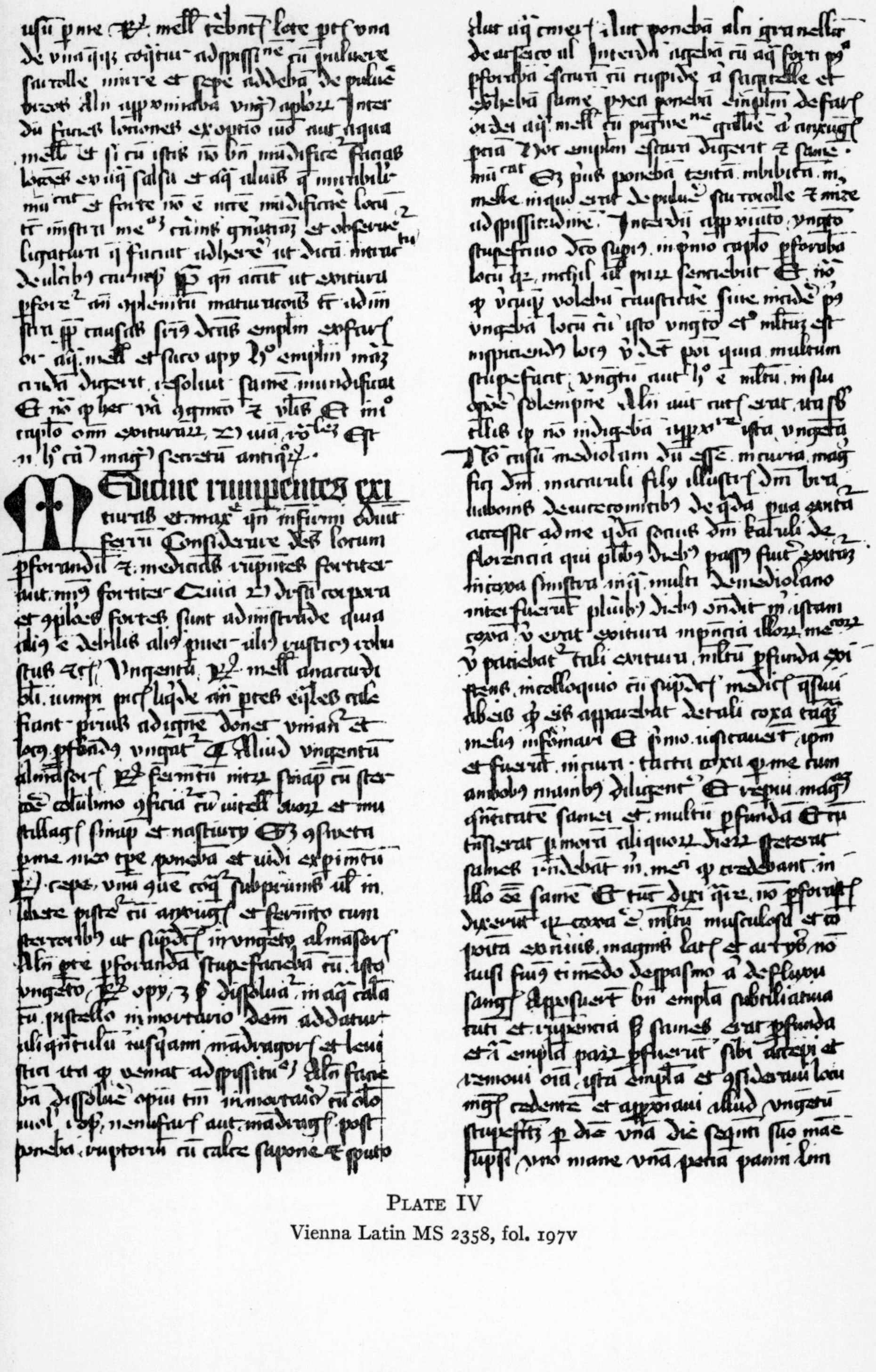

PLATE IV

Vienna Latin MS 2358, fol. 197v

It is somewhat strange that it should occur only in the very manuscript where our treatise is anonymous.

The third manuscript, in the National Library at Munich,[13] is dated A.D. 1453 and once belonged to the German humanist, Hartman Schedel (1440–1514), who presumably brought it back from Italy with him. Our treatise occurs in the manuscript between the thirteenth-century surgery of William of Saliceto of Piacenza and the *Practica in cyrurgia* of William of Brescia (1250–1336). The original scribe had written at the beginning of our treatise, "The Surgery of Master John of Milan,"[14] while on the cover of the manuscript is written, "John of Braccia."[15] But Hartman Schedel wrote in as the title of our treatise, "The Surgery of Master Peter of Tossignano."[16] He also inserted a number of additional passages, both on the margins and on interleaves which differ in size and texture from the manuscript's own leaves.

Pietro da Tossignano might be the author so far as his dates are concerned, since he is mentioned among the salaried professors of Bologna in the later fourteenth century[17] and died about 1407. He was of course a well-known physician and medical writer, whose treatise on the pest is familiar, but no work of surgery is ascribed to him in the recent monograph of Mazzini.[18] Giovanni Garzoni, however, who was himself professor of medicine at Bologna from 1466 to 1506, states that Tossignano professed to be a surgeon.[19] And in one of the manuscripts of Leonard of Bertipaglia's surgical work, there

[13] CLM 273, fols. 113–46, with the same Incipit as Vienna 2358.

[14] "Cyrurgia mag. Iohannis de Mediolano."

[15] "Johannis de Braccia." Sudhoff, *op. cit.*, p. 423, spells it "Brascia."

[16] "Cyrurgia mag. Petri de Tussignano."

[17] His name first appears in the *Rotuli* as published by Dallari under the year 1379–80, but Mazzini dates his teaching at Bologna back as early as 1364. See the following note.

[18] Giuseppe Mazzini, *Vita e opera di Maestro Pietro da Tossignano,* Rome, 1926, 160 pages.

[19] "Petrus Tosignanus etsi chirurgicum se profitetur de moribus tamen particularibus libellum qui saepenumero ad manus meas venit scriptum reliquit": Muratori, *Scriptores,* Vol. XXI, p. 1162; quoted by Mazzini.

are added on the last leaf, by a later hand, "Caustic Waters of Master Peter of Tossignano."[20] Now the use of caustic waters in surgery is one of the specialties of the author of our treatise. But these are the only reasons I have thus far been able to find for accepting Schedel's ascription of the work to Peter of Tossignano instead of to John Braccia or John of Milan. At the close of the treatise in this Munich manuscript the work is again ascribed to John, who is this time called of "Prattia."[21]

Moreover, in another manuscript of our treatise at Munich,[22] which also belonged to Schedel, the work is again ascribed to John of Milan,[23] and in this case Schedel neither altered the ascription nor interpolated additional leaves of text. This second Munich and Schedel manuscript appears to correspond closely to the text of the other before it received Schedel's corrections and interpolations, which must have been drawn from some third source. It may have been this third source which suggested to Schedel the ascription of the treatise to Peter of Tossignano. Our second Munich manuscript also corresponds closely to the text of Vienna 2358, except that it omits some of it.[24]

John of Milan and John de Ptraccia, Prattia, or Braccia might well be alternative appellations for the same person. Indeed, one cannot help thinking that John of Ptraccia, etc., may be a confusion for the *Practica* of John. Such a person seems little known to bibliographers and literary or medical historians. The name, Johannes Braccius, indeed, appears in Argellati's work on writers of Milan, but all the information we

[20] Sloane 3863, fol. 100v: "Aque caustice magistri Petri de tossignano."

[21] "Explicit practica Cyrurgie Johannis de prattia anno domini 1453 in vigilia nativitatis Criste." Thus, except for the date, this rubric is practically identical with that which closed the work in MS Vienna 2358.

[22] CLM 321, 15th century, fols. 207–249v. It has no table of contents for the first book, but gives one for the second.

[23] "Incipit Cyrogia Magistri Iohannis de mediolana [*sic*]."

[24] For example, the rubrics, "Cum numerati sint . . ." (Vienna 2358, fol. 143r) and "Cum nervi sunt instrumenta . . ." (fol. 147v), and the text following under them are not found in CLM 321.

obtain is that Picinelli ascribed a work of surgery to him which no one else apparently had been able to find.[25] In the faculty lists for the University of Bologna we find a John of Milan mentioned as lecturing on medicine in the afternoon and philosophy in the evening at a salary of one hundred and fifty pounds in 1370–71, as lecturing on astrology in 1381–82, and on natural philosophy in 1404–05.[26] Nothing is said to connect him with surgery. Dallari has indexed these items as all having reference to the same individual, but it is a little unlikely that a person who in 1370 had already advanced to a salary as large as anyone in the Faculty of Arts and Medicine for that year received, should still be teaching thirty-five years later. Also it was more usual for a man to advance from teaching natural philosophy to astrology and then to medicine than to recede in the opposite direction. On the other hand, a John de Machariis or Manchariis of Milan who taught astrology in 1380–81 would seem to be identical with the John of Milan who taught the same subject the next year, although they are indexed separately by Dallari. Since John of Milan was apt to be a common name, it is doubtful if we can connect any of these entries with our author. Fabroni in his history of the University of Pisa mentions a Joannes Gittalebraccia who in 1373 was appointed to teach medicine for two hundred ducats and died in 1393,[27] but does not connect him either with surgery or Milan, so that it is doubtful if he can be identified with our John Braccia.

That the author of our treatise had indeed some connection with Milan is indicated by his locating certain of his clinical cases in that city and at the court of the Visconti. At the time of composing our treatise, however, he would appear

[25] Philippi Argellati, *Bibliotheca scriptorum Mediolanensium*, Milan, 1745, I, ii, 221. Nor have I been able to find Argellati's reference to Picinellus.

[26] U. Dallari, *I rotuli dei lettori legisti e artisti dello studio bolognese dal 1384 al 1799*, Bologna, 1888–1924, Vol. IV, pp. 4, 8, 26. The first entry reads, "Magister Iohannes de Mediolano legit medicinam in nonis et phylosophiam in vesperis cum salario in anno librarum CL."

[27] Angelo Fabroni, *Historia Academiae Pisanae*, Pisa, 1791, Vol. I, pp. 72–73.

to have no longer been there, and the passages seem to imply that he was not a native of Milan rather than that he was such. We know that Pietro da Tossignano left Bologna about 1390 to enter the service of Gian Galeazzo Visconti,[28] but he appears to have lived at Pavia rather than Milan.[29] Moreover, the allusions in our surgery are to members of the Visconti family before Gian Galeazzo who were overthrown by him — another indication that its author can scarcely have been Peter of Tossignano.

In our anonymous version of the surgery, instead of the references to Milan we find mentions of Crema and the accompanying allusions to persons are also somewhat different. This may be illustrated most conveniently by the parallel column method. In the left-hand column is the text as found in Vienna 2358, fol. 148r, col. 1, with which the text as contained on a sheet inserted between fols. 144 and 145 of CLM 273 agrees except for minor variations. The passage does not seem to occur in CLM 321 at all. In the right-hand column is the different text of the anonymous version contained in Vienna 4751, fol. 175r.

Mediolano cum essem in cura domini olfi [30] de vicecomitibus qui passus fuit puncturam in nervo manus et in pede, alter

Simile accidit cuidam nobili viro de crema qui patiebatur puncturam nervi in pede qui quasi erat in articulo mortis et dum essem ibi creme propter unum filium domini karoli de vicomitibus fui vocatus ad curam et in-

[28] And not of Francesco di Carrara at Padua as is stated by Mrs. D. W. Singer, "Some Plague Tractates," *Proceedings of the Royal Society of Medicine*, Vol. IX, 1916, Section of the History of Medicine, pp. 159–212. It was, as Mazzini shows, in 1377 that Pietro da Tossignano resided temporarily at Padua and "Francisci Carrariensis auctoritate inter Collegii Doctores sopranumerarius receptus est."

[29] His name appears repeatedly in the *Codice diplomatico dell' Università di Pavia*, from February 5, 1390, to November 16, 1398, and then again on June 6, 1401, and December 20, 1403. Consult Index of Vol. I, ed. R. Maiocchi, Pavia, 1905, and II, i (1913), 4, 37. About 1400 he seems to have gone for a time to Portugal.

[30] Probably short for Rodolfo, one of the sons of Barnabò Visconti.

medicus prefuerat [ante me][31] et apposuit putrefactivam et mollitivam, et ea removi. Et usus fui exsiccativis quia pes erat apostematus apostemate calido. Approximavi emplastrum de farina [*col. 2*] fabarum ordei cum lixivio et aceto cum aliquantulo oleo rose et actu calidum applicabam

veni unum cyroicum litteris carentem apposuisse putreda. Et dei auxilio ablatis putrefactivis [*fol. 175v*] evasit quia pes erat apostematus magno apostemate et calido, et tunc feci emplastrum de farina fabarum et farina ordei cum lixivio et aceto aliquantulo olei rose et actu calidum semper applicabam

TRANSLATION

When I was in Milan on the case of lord Rudolph Visconti who suffered from a puncture in a nerve of the hand and in the foot, another doctor had been before me and had applied putrefying and mollitive medicines, but I removed them. And I used drying ones because the foot was affected with a hot sore. I applied a plaster of bean and barley meal with lye and vinegar and a little oil of rose and I applied it hot.

A similar case was that of a certain noble of Crema who suffered a puncture of the nerve in the foot, who was practically at death's door. And while I was there at Crema on the account of a son of lord Charles Visconti, I was called into the case and I found that a surgeon without education had applied putrid medicines. And the patient escaped by God's aid when these were removed, because the foot was affected with a large hot sore, and then I made a plaster of bean and barley meal with lye and vinegar and a little oil of rose and I always applied it hot.

Another example of such recounting the same case and procedure in almost the same words but with some change in place and personal names will be given later in our author's account of his case before the physicians of Milan. The question arises whether such alterations are due to the desire of someone else than the original author to pass the work

[31] These words occur in CLM 273, but not in Vienna 2358.

off as his own composition and the cases as his own experiences. If so, in the original version were the references to Milan or to Crema? It might be thought that the version which contains the greater number of personal allusions and states them in the more precise and circumstantial manner would be the original. The anonymous version on the whole has more of them, being the longer text anyway, and employs the first person more in its exposition. It also tends to be somewhat more circumstantial in its personal references and at the same time not to connect them quite so directly with great personages as do the other three manuscripts. It is perhaps a suspicious circumstance that they do so. Yet they are three against one; they roughly agree in their ascription of the work to a definite author, John Braccia or John of Milan; and the superior handwriting and neatness of one of them rather prejudices us in its favor as against the anonymous Vienna 4751. But the last seems the earliest manuscript as well as the fullest. Unfortunately its greater fullness in part consists of fulsomeness and wordiness, so that it has something the appearance of being an expansion of, say, the text of Vienna 2358, rather than that the latter is a condensation and abbreviation of it.

The relation of our four manuscripts to one another may be roughly stated as follows. Vienna 4751 is the longest and fullest text. CLM 321 is the shortest. CLM 273 was originally about the same as CLM 321, but the insertions made by Hartman Schedel include both passages which are found in Vienna 2358 and not in CLM 321, and other passages which are found in Vienna 4751 and not in Vienna 2358. With these added, CLM 273 becomes longer than Vienna 2358. But otherwise the wording of Vienna 2358 and the two Munich manuscripts is almost the same and may be regarded as representing one version of the work, while the differently worded Vienna 4751 represents another, as we have already implied.

The difference between CLM 321 and Vienna 2358 may be

illustrated as follows: For the first and most of the chapter headings or rubrics of the first book, they run along essentially the same, with the same opening and closing words for each chapter. But towards the close of the book, CLM 321 omits entirely the short chapter on castration,[32] also the latter half of the chapter on the stone [33] and the closing portion of the chapter *De variciliis*.[34] In the second book CLM 321 more often omits the rubrics of Vienna 2358, and, as we have noted above, in two cases omits also the text that goes with them.[35]

As for Vienna 4751, towards the close of the first book it introduces chapters on the hermaphrodite [36] and dropsy [37] which are not in Vienna 2358 or CLM 321, but have been interpolated in CLM 273 between fols. 128 and 129, and between fols. 130 and 131 respectively. The chapter on the stone is also very different in Vienna 4751 from the text in Vienna 2358 and CLM 321, although they have some things in common. The other manuscripts omit all the first part of the chapter as contained in Vienna 4751 [38] which included long recommendations as to diet. They state that they omit the assigning of a cause for stone and the regimen therefor, and pass at once to the cure of it by the blood of a goat.[39] Again, in Vienna 4751 the author's peculiar method of extracting stone [40] comes four or five pages after the account of the woman of Cremona,[41] whereas in the other manuscripts it immediately precedes it. At the close of the second book the text of Vienna 4751 runs on for some pages [42] beyond the point where that of Vienna 2358 and the two Munich manuscripts terminates. The chapter on cancer in the first book starts alike in both versions, but

[32] Compare CLM 321, fol. 227r with Vienna 2358, fol. 134v, col. 2.

[33] The chapter ends at fol. 229v in CLM 321, omitting the text found in Vienna 2358, fol. 136r, col. 2 — fol. 136v, col. 2.

[34] Compare CLM 321, fol. 229v with Vienna 2358, fol. 136v–137r.

[35] See above, p. 86, note 24.

[36] Vienna 4751, fol. 62v.

[37] *Ibid.*, fols. 69v–77r, "de extraccione aque ydropicorum."

[38] *Ibid.*, fols. 77r–79v.

[39] "De materia vel cura lapidis pretermisso regimine et cause assignatione": Vienna 2358, fol. 135v, col. 1; CLM 321, fol. 228v.

[40] Vienna 4751, fol. 85r.

[41] *Ibid.*, fol. 82v.

[42] Fols. 197r–212r of Vienna 4751 are not found in the other MSS.

in Vienna 4751 in the course of the chapter a number of personal cases are recounted which do not appear in Vienna 2358 or CLM 321.[43] Similarly in the second book Vienna 4751 has an additional page concerning hydrophobia after the corresponding chapter in Vienna 2358 and CLM 321, on wounds made by dog or bird, has come to an end.[44]

Returning to personal allusions and mentions of contemporaries, which seem to offer the most hopeful means of dating the two versions which confront us and identifying their author or respective writers, we may note that once at least the other manuscripts contain something not paralleled in Vienna 4751, namely, an allusion to a Master Nicolaus de Andrio.[45] On the other hand, an account of an illiterate English practitioner, Tonolinus Melegeta — surely a strange name for Briton or Anglo-Saxon! — and his cure of Galeazzo Visconti is confined to the anonymous version: "I saw in my time a certain Tonolinus, an illiterate Englishman, who gave those who suffered from such ulcers as strong wine as could be found. And he gave this reason, for he said that such wine provoked high fever which caused the pus to dry up. I saw one at least, lord Galeazzo Visconti, cured by that method and by this very Master Tonolinus, known also as Melegeta. Or rather, I wasn't present, but I heard the aforesaid Melegeta tell about it." [46] Vienna 4751 also appears the only manuscript

[43] Compare Vienna 4751, fols. 33r–36r, with Vienna 2358, fol. 130r and CLM 321, fols. 218v–219r, CLM 273, fol. 122v.

[44] Compare Vienna 4751, fols. 141v–142r, with Vienna 2358, fol. 143v and CLM 321, fol. 241. CLM 273, fol. 140r, has part of the addition.

[45] Vienna 2358, fol. 142r, col. 1, bottom. In the midst of recounting his own procedure the author remarks, "Et tu hoc vidisti a magistro nicolawo de andrio." See also CLM 321, fol. 239r. The passage does not occur at the corresponding place in Vienna 4751, fol. 130r.

[46] Vienna 4751, fol. 131r: "Vidi meo tempore quendam tonolinum anglicum illiteratum qui dabat pacientibus talia ulcera cassalia meliora iura (corrected to *vina*) quam poterant reperiri et adducebat talem rationem quia dicebat quod talia medicamina erant provocancia magnas [*fol. 131v*] febres que erant causa exicacionis saniei. Vidi unum saltem dominum Galeam vicecomitis curatum per illum modum et per suprascriptum magistrum tonolinum et vocabatur melegeta. Vere tamen non interfui. Vidi tamen suprascriptum melegetam narrantem."

to recount the case of cancer of the citizen of Brescia.[47] Other names and cases are common to both versions, such as that of the German doctor who treated a fellow countryman who had been bitten by a rabid horse,[48] or John of Piacenza who suffered great pain from a corrosive *formica* on his thigh and was treated by our author,[49] or the man of Bologna who was hit by a cannon ball in the left arm [50] — possibly one of the earliest recorded cases of the sort, or the man of Forlì whose left hand was injured by a piece of marble and amputated by our author.[51] But here again there are slight differences between our two versions. The anonymous version gives us concerning John of Piacenza the further particular that he made tarts (*tortas*). The other manuscripts call the man of Bologna John of Bologna, whereas the anonymous manuscript vaguely describes him as a stipendiary of that city. Finally, the similar account of the person from Forlì in both versions is immediately followed by a case of *herpestiomenus* induced by too tight a ligature of a broken arm. In Vienna 4751 this is told of a boy of Castronuovo Buccadine in the diocese of Cremona; in the other manuscripts it is narrated of rustics in Genoa and Milan. These are curious divergences, but we must leave them to treat of other aspects of our surgical treatise. In passing, however, we cannot refrain from the surmise that this altering of personal experiences and tampering with place names, of which we likewise noted evidence in the case of Leonard of Bertipaglia's work as between the manuscripts and editions, may have been a rather widespread — albeit questionable — practice in the surgical literature of the time.[52]

[47] Vienna 4751, fol. 34v.

[48] *Ibid.*, fol. 141r; Vienna 2358, fol. 143v, col. 1–2; CLM 321, fol. 241v.

[49] Vienna 4751, fol. 11r–v; Vienna 2358, fol. 125r–v; CLM 321, fol. 209v.

[50] Vienna 4751, fol. 14r: "qui percussus fuit de una bombarda in brachio sinistro"; Vienna 2358, fol. 126r, col. 2; CLM 321, fol. 211r.

[51] The passage immediately follows that cited in note 50.

[52] Somewhat analogous, but more justifiable, was the revision of dates and alteration of names of persons and places in the salutations of successive redactions of medieval manuals of the art of letter-writing, especially as these passed from one region to another. See C. H. Haskins, "An Italian Bernard,"

These medieval treatises of course copied and repeated one another a great deal, although Guy de Chauliac's reproach that his predecessors "followed one another just like cranes" is now regarded as too harsh.[53] There was naturally a common body of knowledge, and little objection was felt to repeating this in the same words as before, while perhaps adding important new observations, methods, or ideas of one's own. Even as independent a surgeon as Theodoric often copied his predecessor Bruno by the yard. Moreover, one can never be sure that what an author states as his own experience may not have been taken from some previous work. Thus in the chapter on the treatment of those who have been beaten or tortured, our author presents as if it were his own idea the wrapping of the patient in the skin of a sheep which has just been flayed, while the sheepskin is still warm.[54] But his predecessors, William of Brescia [55] and William of Saliceto, both ascribe this treatment to the ancients, and the latter adds that he has not proved it in his time.[56] Indeed, this suggestion that a fresh sheepskin will give relief is found in the text of Avicenna himself. But to represent as one's own experience what has been repeatedly stated by previous authors is after all something of a tribute to experimental method, since the writer apparently feels that it will be more cogent to present the remedy as based on his own experience rather than upon the agreement of authorities.

An interesting disclosure of our author's attitude towards past authorities and present practice in surgery is given in his

---

pp. 211–26 in *Essays in History Presented to Reginald Lane Poole*, 1927, for some specific illustrations of this from the twelfth century.

[53] Walter von Brunn, "Die Stellung des Guy de Chauliac in der Chirurgie des Mittelalters," *Archiv für Geschichte der Medizin*, 1921, p. 103, regards it as unjust.

[54] "Nota quod meo tempore accipiebam pellem ovinam excoriatam subito et calidam applicabam talibus vulneratis que mirabilem in eis includebat effectum. Et expertus fui multociens hoc et vidi in pluribus": Vienna 2358, fol. 143r, col. 2; Vienna 4751, fol. 138r–v; CLM 273, fol. 139v; CLM 321, fol. 240v.

[55] See CLM 273, fol. 155r.

[56] *Chirurgia*, 1546, II, 25: "Sed istud nostro tempore non probavimus."

final chapter on the fracture of the skull. At the beginning of the chapter he cites the previous treatments of the subject by Avicenna, Galen, Bruno, William of Piacenza, "Almansor," Albucasis, Roger, and others, but adds that while following all these authorities he will set forth the method of curing wounds of the head and fracture of the skull "according to modern practitioners."[57] After mentioning procedures which may be found in other earlier medieval surgical authors, such as covering the cranium with encaustic to detect a fissure[58] or inserting a cloth between the *dura mater* and cranium,[59] he adds in some manuscripts: "But note that some modern surgeons place between the cranium and *dura mater* a small piece of red silk dipped in honey of roses and oil of roses, after which they add other pieces, as has been said, of old white cloth. And this they do because they say, and it is true, that kermes[60] possesses the property of comforting the brain and its coverings and parts."[61] Even this passage, however, may be fairly closely matched in an earlier writing than ours.[62]

Like Leonard of Bertipaglia, our present author lays stress

[57] Vienna 2358, fol. 148r, col. 2: " . . . tamen sequendo omnes auctores ponam modum cure cranei secundum modernos practicantes de vulnere capitis cum fractura et sine fractura non removendo me ab opinione auctorum predictorum . . ." See also Vienna 4751, fol. 176r–v; CLM 321, fol. 247r.

[58] Karl Sudhoff, *Beiträge zur Geschichte der Chirurgie im Mittelalter*, Vol. II, 1918, p. 270, gives an earlier passage of this sort.

[59] *Ibid.*, pp. 160–161, 268, for examples.

[60] That is, the red dyestuff similar to cochineal.

[61] Vienna 2358, fol. 149r, col. 2: "nota tamen quod aliqui moderni cyrurgici ponunt inter craneum et duram matrem paucam peciam de serico grane imbibito in melle rosarum et oleo rosarum. Post ponunt alias pecias ut dictum est de panno vetusto albo. Et hoc faciunt quia dicunt, et hoc est verum, quod grana a proprietate artatur [*comfortat* in Vienna 4751] cerebrum [*fol. 149v*] et pellicula eius et eius partes." See also Vienna 4751, fol. 194r–v. The passage does not occur in the corresponding place in CLM 321, fol. 249r.

[62] As in the following extract from marginal notes to the surgery of Roger as contained in an Erfurt manuscript written shortly after 1300 and printed by Sudhoff, *op. cit.*, p. 253: "Nota quod purpura vel samit magis valet in vulnere, spissitudine enim sua resistit putredini et duo panni in vulnere capitis debent immitti, unus supra duram matrem et ex obliquo, alter vero in ore vulneris ad recipiendum putredinem ab exterioribus fluentem."

on the importance of personal experience and skill for the surgeon. He remarks towards the close of his first book: "But take note that this art of incision is never perfectly learned except by the observation and practice of a good and expert medical man in that art. And I have seen masters in that art who could incise marvelously and yet did not know how to grow flesh over the wound. And similarly I have many times seen those who knew how to grow flesh but not to incise." [63] On the other hand, again like Leonard of Bertipaglia and other educated surgeons of the time, our author manifests an unfavorable attitude to the mere empiric or barber-surgeon. In closing the chapter on *sephiros* he tells of a baker who had on his right arm a sephiros of melancholic complexion, hard and large and hairy, in which he felt no pain when it was struck with a stone. Our author was unwilling to accept the case, but "a certain barber undertook to cure it and killed him." [64] Our author in his time has seen many barbers and ignorant surgeons and herbalists who tried to cure warts and *natae* of dark color and black *morphea*, but only succeeded in bringing on cancer and shortening the lives of their

[63] "Tamen nota quod hec ars incisionis numquam perfecte scitur nec apprehenditur nisi per visum et consuetudinem boni et experti medici in arte ista. Et vidi magistros in arte ista qui mirabiliter incidebant et tamen nesciebant vulnus incarnare. Et sic aliquotiens multotiens vidi scientes incarnare et non incidere": Vienna 2358, fol. 136v, col. 1; Vienna 4751, fol. 85v. In CLM 273 the passage occurs on a sheet inserted between fols. 130 and 131. It does not occur at the corresponding place in CLM 321.

[64] "Et quidam barbitonsor accepit ipsum in cura et eum interfecit." The wording of the whole account of this case in Vienna 4751, fol. 32r, differs markedly from that of the other MSS which are in essential agreement: see Vienna 2358, fol. 130r, col. 1; CLM 321, fol. 218v; CLM 273, fol. 122r. In Vienna 4751 we are given the additional information that the baker (or cuirassier? — *clibinarius*) "stood near the Porta Mosa of Cremona through which the road to Parma runs," and the wording of the remainder of the passage is somewhat fuller than in the other MSS.

A similar attitude and incident are found in the treatise, *De fistula in ano* of John Arderne, written in 1376. He tore off the corrosive dressings which an incompetent barber had put on the wound of a rich fishmonger and replaced them by a soothing fomentation which permitted the patient to sleep. See D'Arcy Power's edition for the Early English Text Society, 1910, pp. xix and 100.

patients.[65] He also tells of an old man who had a tiny cancer in one eye. A barber applied a caustic powder which corroded the entire eye and part of the nose. Then our author was called in. He comforted the old man with the hope that he could cure him, but informed his friends privately that the case was incurable.[66] Another man, whose wife had cancer of the breast, declared that he would search the whole world over until he found a physician who would cure it. A barber attempted a cure by incision, but the husband admitted to our author that this attempt had failed.[67] In the second book of the anonymous version, the author states that in his time he has often seen old wives and barbers treat certain wounds with wool and oil, which caused pus to form and prevented the wound from healing as it should. He goes on to say that the way to bind up wounds is learned better by practice and association with a good rational physician who is expert in the art of surgery than from reading books on the subject,[68] which brings us back to his emphasis upon personal experience and practical training.

In yet another passage which seems to occur only in the anonymous version, attention is called to the fact that the science of medicine is too long in comparison with human life and hence cannot be fully mastered. "And therefore the physician who has seen more and is experienced in more matters ought to know more and to understand the properties of medi-

[65] Vienna 4751, fol. 33r–v: "Et meo tempore vidi multos barbitonsores ac quamplures cyrugicos pauca noscentes et herbalaios qui voluerunt curare verucas et natas fusci coloris et morpheam nigram et male successit eis quia disposuerunt ad cancrum et vita eorum abreviata est." I do not find this or the two following cases in the other MSS.

[66] *Ibid.*, fols. 33v–34r.

[67] *Ibid.*, fols. 34r–35r.

[68] Vienna 4751, fol. 102v: "et hoc meo tempore vidi pluribus vicibus quia mulierculas et barbitonsores qui solidabant et que sigillabant talia vulnera cum lana et oleo [*103r*] unde causabatur putredo, et sic cessabat conglutinacio vulnerum que debebat fieri quia tales pacientes ad me veniebant et eos curabam sed non per modum superius scriptum.

Modus autem ligandi vulnera melius apprehenditur per usum et conversationem boni et experti et rationabilis medici in arte cyrugie quam per scripturam . . ."

cines better and how to suit them to the human body, since long time makes expert." Medicines, moreover, sometimes fail to produce their usual effects because both the air and the human body have been altered by the influence of the constellations, whereat the inexperienced and unskilled physician marvels greatly, but the skilled expert understands it and takes the altered conditions into account in applying his remedies.[69] Thus we see experience and astrology, if not experimental method and magic, once again in close association.

That our author was not free from the superstitious theory and magical paraphernalia of his own and preceding times is further shown by his recommending the blood of a goat — which was supposed to break even a diamond — for the cure of stone, and further prescribing that the animal be killed in August when the moon begins to be full, and that the goat be three or four years old and have eaten nothing but diuretic and aperitive herbs for fifteen days before its death. "And the first blood that comes out and the last are not good," but what comes in between should be dried in the sun in a vase of glass made from stone and well stopped up. This dried blood is to be given with water of asparagus or fennel. But this prescription is simply taken from Thaddeus Florentinus; [70] our author adds a powder of his own.[71]

[69] Vienna 4751, fol. 113r: "In conclusione est advertendum quod scientia medicine est nimis longa in comparatione vite humane, et ideo non potest ad plenum comprehendi. Et ideo ille medicus qui plura vidit et in pluribus est expertus plura debet scire et qualitates medicinarum melius cognoscere et corpori humano eas proportionare quia longitudo temporis experientiam facit, et sicut superius est narratum et que sunt magis propinquiora nature demonstrat. Videmus autem disposiciones aeris interdum a constellacionibus mutari et que mutant corpora humana, quibus si applicentur medicine eis conformes non inducunt effectum solitum. Quare medicus inexpertus et imperitus valde admiratur. Sed expers et peritus in mente cognoscit et applicat remedia iuxta posse [*fol. 113v*] oportuna que habent insistere talibus disposicionibus . . ."

[70] Concerning Thaddeus of Florence, who lived from 1223 to 1303, see G. Pinto, *Taddeo da Fiorenza o la medicina in Bologna nel XIII secolo*, Roma, Tip. della R. Accad. dei Lincei, 1888.

[71] Vienna 2358, fol. 135v, col. 2; Vienna 4751, fol. 80r; CLM 273, fol. 130r; CLM 321, fol. 229r. Although the recipe is introduced in Vienna 4751

Both versions of our treatise are emphatic in pronouncing cancer and tuberculosis incurable, if either has reached an at all developed stage. This conclusion seems to rest especially upon the author's own experience, which, as we have seen, is adduced somewhat more at length in Vienna 4751 than in the other manuscripts. In its early stages cancer is with difficulty recognized except by surgeons who are very learned or very expert in their art.[72] "When it begins to appear, it is like a pea or bean of dark color, and when it is confirmed no one can cure it because its roots are fixed in the liver."[73] Or our author remarks anent a particular case, "And I said again to him that no physician in the world save God alone, who heals all languors, can cure confirmed cancer." [74] The most that can be done is to prolong the life of the afflicted person by evacuations and good regimen. The attempt to cut out the cancer or otherwise to eradicate it has always ended in failure, so far as this has come under the author's observation and knowledge.[75]

Nor has our author ever known of anyone recovering from a wound in the substance of the lung, whether produced by an external or internal cause, despite Galen's apparent belief that recent wounds of this sort might be cured. Phthisis or con-

---

with the words, "Sed ultimum experimentum quo valde fui expertus meo tempore," and in the other MSS with the words, "Nota ultimum remedium quod reperui et est mirabile," it concludes in all the MSS except Vienna 4751 with the confession, "Et habui a thadeo."

For similar use of the blood of a goat in the fine arts in the *Mappe Clavicula*, Heraclius, and Theophilus see my *History of Magic and Experimental Science*, 1923, Vol. I, pp. 767–69.

[72] Vienna 2358, fol. 130r, col. 1; CLM 321, fol. 218v: "Cancer a principio cum difficultate cognoscitur nisi cyrurgici multum docti in arte." In Vienna 4751, fol. 33v, the last clause reads: "nisi sint cyrogici valde experti in arte cyrugie."

[73] *Ibid.* (all MSS except Vienna 4751, where the wording is somewhat different): "Ista quando incipit apparere est sicut cicer vel faba fusci coloris et quando est confirmatum nullus potest curare quia radices sue sunt in epate confirmate. Sed ponimus eis prolongare vitam."

[74] Vienna 4751, fol. 35r: "Et ego dixi iterum sibi quod nullus medicus nisi solum deus qui sanat omnes languores possit curare cancrum confirmatum."

[75] I give the text of the two versions in parallel columns: (See page 100.)

sumption or tuberculosis is caused by choleric or other humors, or by blood pressure causing a break in the veins of the lungs and spitting of blood, or by other diseased condition of the substance of the lung itself.[76]

The chief distinguishing feature of our author's surgery is his reluctance to resort either to the knife or cautery. In preference to these he used ruptories, caustic waters, binding with silk thread, and other devices. The growths on the head

---

VIENNA 2358, FOL. 130R, COL. 2	VIENNA 4751, FOL. 36V
Sed meo tempore non inveni cancrum confortatum et curatum nec aliquem scire curare.	Sed meo tempore non inveni aliquem cancrum curatum nec aliquem curantem nec quod posset curari in principio nec in fine.
Et vidi cancrum ut cicer et	Et vidi cancrum ad formam ciceris fabi pomi [?] et in quantitate minori
intromisi me in cura cum incisione totali et eradicatione suarum radicum	et volui me intromittere de curando cum incisione totali ac cum eradicatione suarum radicum i. e. venarum suarum et causticatione
et male mihi successit	et male successit quia cancer augebatur per dolores et debilitatem membri et penitus emisi talem curam
et reversus fui ad curam cum evacuationibus precedentibus et bono regimine . . .	et reversus fui ad blanditiva [fol. 37r] cum evacuationibus precedentibus et bono regimine . . .

[76] The essence of the description of phthisis in the two versions is as follows:

VIENNA 2358, FOL. 138R	VIENNA 4751, FOL. 98R
Item vulnus in pulmone potest dupliciter accidere scilicet ab intrinseco et ab extrinseco. Ab intrinseco ut dicunt phisici aut ex materia [*col. 2*] colerica,	Si vulnus in pulmone fuerit, dupliciter consideratur aut a causa exteriori aut a causa interiori. Si a causa interiori ptisis appellatur et fit tribus modis vel ex humoribus colericis a capite descendentibus sive ex flegmaticis et salsis in substantia pulmonis existentibus cum vulnerantibus et putrefacientibus.
ex inordinatione cibi et potus vel plenitudine venarum in ipso pulmone.	Secundus modus est ex humoribus aliunde ad pulmonem currentibus quam a capite. Tercius modus est in quibusdam passionibus in substantia ipsius pulmonis nascentibus
et scindantur vene et fit sanguinis sputum et materia colligit et putrescit per tempus et causatur empima deinde ptisis.	et hoc cum accidit sanguinis siccitas siccat ex venis a corporis insectione [?] spiritus ruptis vel in pulmonem in qua scissura nascuntur [*fol. 98v*] vulnera empica et ptisis est.

which are vulgarly known as horns he professes to have cured by use of caustic water alone.[77] Having advised the employment of powders to staunch a flow of blood, he says that if they fail to stop it, one may then resort to the cautery. "Yet one must take care lest some nerve be burnt. For myself, I have never ventured to employ actual cautery but only potential with the medicines mentioned above. And it has never failed me, for by means of these and ligature I checked all flux, whether from vein or artery, and this I have tested by experience in my time."[78] In discussing the treatment of stone, one version of our treatise says, "As for cure by incision, I never cared to undertake it, therefore I will pass it over."[79] The other version reads, "Now I intend to set forth the cure by incision according to some of my predecessors, but I never cared to undertake it myself, although I saw many experimenters in that art operate in my time as narrated above in the chapter on cure of rupture." [80] In a third passage our author warns that if the surgeon attempts cure by the knife under certain circumstances, he will be guilty of homicide.[81] In the chapter on scrofula our author states that he is unwilling to discuss the cure of scrofula by incision or excoriation or the use of acute medicaments, although Bruno and many others have included it. His reason is that scrofula is for the most part too closely connected with nerves and arteries. "And in my time I have seen many physicians at Bologna who ventured to attempt to cure scrofula by incision

[77] Vienna 2358, fol. 131v, col. 2; Vienna 4751, fol. 46r; CLM 321, fol. 221v; CLM 273, fol. 124r.

[78] Vienna 2358, fol. 144v, col. 1; CLM 321, fol. 242v; CLM 273, fol. 141r; Vienna 4751, fol. 147r.

[79] Vienna 2358, fol. 136r, col. 2; CLM 321, fol. 229v; CLM 273, fol. 130v.

[80] Vienna 4751, fol. 83r, "Nunc intendo ponere curam per incisionem secundum aliquos meos predecessores sed numquam volui me intromittere, licet viderem multos experimentatores in tali arte operari meo tempore prout superius in capitulo de cura rupture narravi." A passage of like tenor but different wording is inserted between fols. 130 and 131 of CLM 273.

[81] Vienna 2358, fol. 134r, col. 1; CLM 273, fol. 127v; CLM 321, fol. 225v. The thought is worded differently and less emphatically in Vienna 4751, fol. 58v.

and excoriation and acute medicaments. But they failed and death followed." [82]

To illustrate the clinical side of late medieval medicine and surgery we may give some further examples of what seems to be our author's own surgical experience. He states that he had employed in his day the following method of removing the stone. "I took a silver stylus dipped in butter or chicken fat and inserted it through the opening of the *virga* until I reached the stone and I gently removed the stone from the neck of the bladder." [83] This method of removal I have failed to find in a number of other medieval surgical works which I examined, whereas the method of extraction by inserting a finger in the *anus*, which is referred to in at least two manuscripts of our treatise,[84] is quite common in other treatises. The use of the catheter is of course found in Guy de Chauliac in 1363. Our author goes on to tell of a woman he saw in Cremona, aged twenty-seven, who suffered from colic and iliac passion for a month and was given the usual medicines by her physicians, such as clysters and draughts, and then voided *per umbilicum* in two or three days no less than twenty-two stones of the size of beans, small nuts, and chick-peas. When he inquired as to her mode of life, he was told that she ate cheese and milk

[82] Vienna 4751, fol. 29v: "Ego autem nolo ponere curam scrofularum hic cum incisione et excoriatione neque cum medicamine acuto licet brunus ponat et quamplures alii. Cum pro maiori parte scrufule sint infiltrate in nervis et artariis et eis annexe. Et meo tempore vidi quamplures medicos bononie qui se voluerunt intromittere de curando scrofulis cum incisione et excoriacione et medicamine acuto et male successit eis quia mors secuta est." See also Vienna 2358, fol. 129v, col. 1; CLM 321, fol. 217v; CLM 273, fol. 121r.

I have given the text from the MS which seemed most nearly correct. CLM 321 has *volo* instead of *nolo* which the sense clearly calls for. Vienna 2358 has *prunus* instead of *brunus*, and adds to *Bononie* the words "and elsewhere" (*et alibi*). So does CLM 273, but it corrects *prunus* to *brunus*.

[83] "Et ad removendum lapidem tenui meo tempore hunc modum. Accipiebam stilum argenteum intinctum butiro aut pinguitudine galline et imponebam per foramen virge donec ad lapidem perveniebam et suaviter lapidem a collo vesice removebam": Vienna 2358, fol. 136r, col. 1; CLM 273, fol. 130r; CLM 321, fol. 229r. In Vienna 4751, fol. 85r, the account is somewhat fuller and differently worded.

[84] Vienna 4751, fol. 83v; CLM 273, on the sheet inserted between fols. 130 and 131.

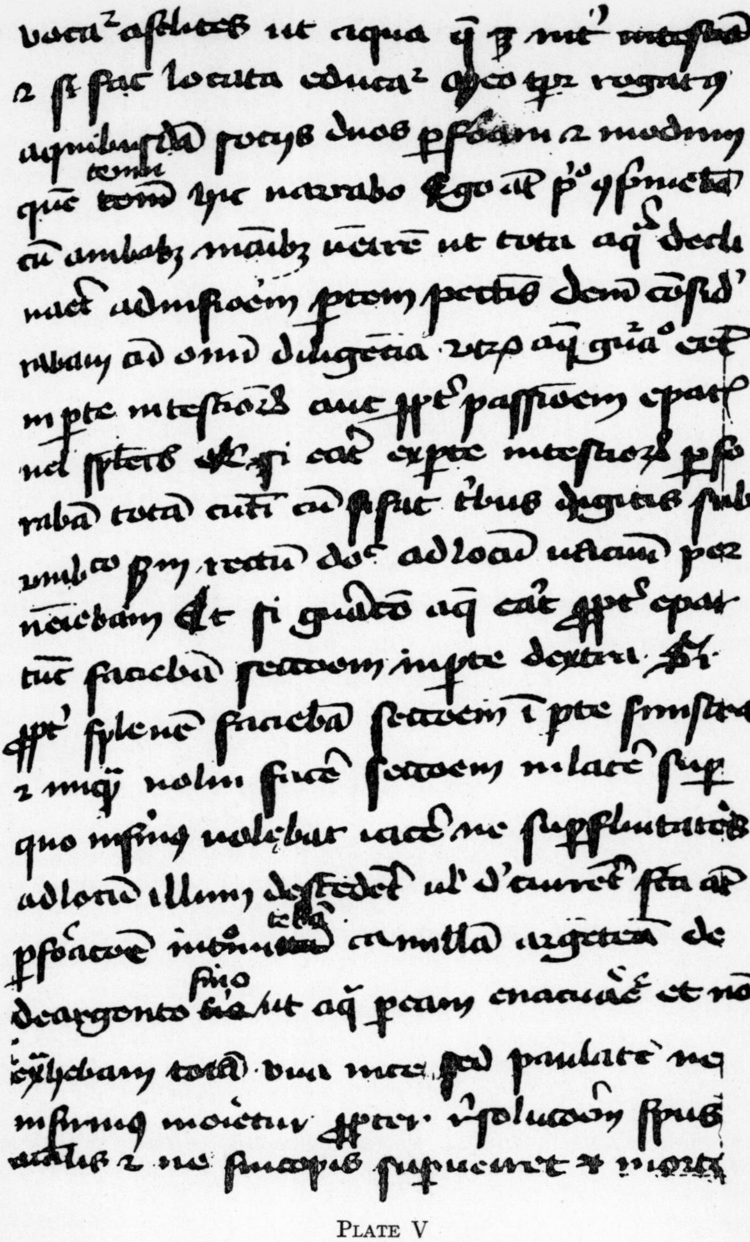

Plate V
Vienna Latin MS 4751, fol. 70r

foods, flatulent vegetables, and coarse meats, such as pork, and lived a gross existence. "And I perceived that such a life would be shortened." [85] Whether this was the same woman of Cremona who is elsewhere described as menstruating through the right breast [86] is not made clear.

The following account of operating in cases of dropsy occurs only in two of our manuscripts and is none too consistent with our author's opposition elsewhere to use of the knife:

In my time, at the request of certain associates, I perforated two, and I will tell how I did it. First I compressed the abdomen with both hands so that all the water would run down to the lower part of the breast. Then I considered with all diligence whether the generation of water took place in the intestines or was because of a diseased condition of liver or spleen. And if it was of the intestines, I cut all the skin with the peritoneum three fingers below the navel straight in until I reached the spot. And if the water was produced because of the liver, then I made a section on the right side. If because of the spleen, I made a section on the left side. And never would I make a section on the side on which the patient liked to lie, lest the superfluities descend or run off to that spot. When the incision was made, I inserted a silver tube of fine silver for the water to run off through. And I didn't draw it all off at one time, but gradually, so that the patient might not die because of loss of animal spirit and so that sincopis might not come on and the patient approach death. But according to his strength I drew it off, and always before I perforated I lifted up the skin, then I perforated and inserted the tube. When I took out the tube I put in the opening a probe covered with decoction,[86a] in the end of which I tied a silk thread or linen twine. Then I let the skin drop down over it with the end of the thread hanging out. Then on the following day I inserted the tube again and drew off the water as the patient's strength would permit, and I did this until none of it was left within, or very little. And if it

[85] Vienna 2358, fol. 136r, col. 2; CLM 321, fol. 229v; CLM 273, fol. 130r. The vegetables and meats are mentioned only in Vienna 4751, fol. 82v. It does not locate the woman in Cremona but at some small place which I could not make out — possibly near Cremona.

[86] Vienna 2358, fol. 135r, col. 2; Vienna 4751, fol. 66r; CLM 321, fol. 227v–228r. [86a] Or *apozima* or *elixatura*.

seemed to me that some water was still left, I made him take artificial salt baths and alum and sulphur ones, and those of lye are quicker than water baths to get rid of the residue of water. But natural mineral baths are best of all, such as those in Tuscany and similar places.

Some tell of burying in hot sand in the sun. I saw a certain doctor who had a sufferer from dropsy put in a furnace after some of the water was extracted. But first he had the patient see if he could stand such a temperature, and he said he could. Then he had a wide seat placed in the furnace and made the patient take off all his clothes except his shirt and enter the furnace and sit on the aforesaid seat. Moreover, I was present and saw the mouth of the furnace closed up, but not wholly, so that the patient might be able to breathe, and so matters stood for half a long hour, and then the patient began to say that he could not stand it longer. And then the aforesaid doctor made the patient take a most copious sweat and get into a bed with hot linen, and then he anointed the patient's abdomen with an unguent of gums which is made thus . . .

After describing the unguent, our author continues:

Moreover, I asked the patient how long he had suffered from this ailment, and he said that it was eight months and more since his belly began to swell. Afterwards I was with the doctor and I told him that he would never cure him, just as I could not cure these two whom I perforated.[87]

As final specimens of our author's personal narrations and clinical method we may note his chapter on *Nata* and his account of the cure he achieved in the presence of various doctors of Milan.[88] Like the doctors whom Leonard of Berti-

[87] For the Latin text, see Appendix 7.

[88] Bonvicino de Ripa, writing towards the end of the thirteenth century, estimated the number of physicians in Milan as about two hundred. Galvaneus Flamma, early in the fourteenth century, estimated the number of physicians and surgeons at over one hundred and eighty, including several municipal physicians who received salaries from the commune and gave free medical service to the poor. "Artis medicine professores et phylosophi nominati computatis cyruicis sunt plures clxxx, inter quos sunt plures sallariati per communitatem qui gratis tenentur pauperes infirmos medicare." — "Chron. Extrav.," ed. A. Ceruti, *Misc. Stor. Ital.*, Vol. VII, p. 489.

There was no university or school of medicine in Milan — the University

paglia invited to witness his operation, their presence suggests that medical consultation and bedside instruction were then by no means unusual. Our author's first paragraph on *Nata* is largely identical with the chapter on it in Bruno and other medieval manuals of surgery, but is reproduced for the sake of clearness. In the rest of his account our author seems to report a personal experience.

There frequently happens in certain men a superfluity which is commonly called *nata*, and it is a fleshy apostema, soft like a fungus, and there is no pain even if there is pus, nor is there heat or pulsation. And sometimes it becomes very large. And it is called *nata* because it swims over the limbs. Brunus says he saw a man who had one on his shoulder so large that he seemed to have a cushion on his shoulder, and [Brunus] was unwilling to treat the case. But a certain uneducated empiric extracted it, and it weighed seven pounds. I never saw or heard of such magnitude in a *nata*. The usual and safe mode of cure of large or small, provided it is not dark-colored or very hard, is to cut in and excoriate it with its sac and take it out. Then let the roots be well cauterized to prevent loss of blood. Yet though they say this cure is possible and secure, one must take care that it is not rooted in limbs, veins, and arteries where it cannot be removed without great risk of death.

Here in truth I will tell the method which I used in my time, and I say this of a *nata* which is not dark-colored or very hard and is not deep rooted in veins and arteries and nerves, as in forehead, hands, and throat and the like, such as I saw in the house of Lord John of Gonzaga,[89] and he [?] had [one] in the upper part of the right hand which was three pounds in my judgment. I would not take the case for the said reasons. If such [a *nata*] was pendant, I proceeded with a silk thread and I made a knot [?] and I bound it tightly, if the root and origin was subtle, until the whole part was eaten away, [and then] I cauterized the entire root with my strong

---

and Faculty of Arts and Medicine being at Pavia — but the practitioners of medicine in Milan formed a gild or College of Physicians. See Argellati, *Bibliotheca Scriptorum Mediolanensium*, Vol. I, 1745, p. xxxi.

[89] This might be either Ioannes Franciscus de Gonzaga, lord of Mantua, or his son Ioannes Lucidus, prince of Mantua, one of Vittorino da Feltre's pupils.

caustic water. But if the *nata* was not pendant and the root broad and not too entangled in nerves and arteries nor of dark color or hard substance, I placed a perforated cloth over the *nata* or part, with stupefying [drugs] steeped in white of egg, stirred often with oil of roses. For a repercussive I placed over the hole some of the stupefactive unguent described in the chapter on the medicines which break *exituras*. Finally I applied a ruptory of lime and soap. When the ruptory was removed, I applied a poultice of barley water, lard and oil of roses. And if it was not cauterized [and] I saw *escara*, I applied powder of white arsenic until it was entirely cauterized. And sometimes I applied the aforesaid water because I did not permit any of its sac to remain until it was cured. And if it was small, I used merely the caustic water until it was all cauterized with its sac. Then I applied the poultice, and having removed the *escara* with medicines, cleansing and consolidating the flesh, I effected a cure. But in my time I cured any number of *natas* with this caustic water. And admitting what is said, that one ought to incise and excoriate, as was said in the case of scrofula, yet, as I have said, I never cared to adopt that method for the aforesaid reasons and dangers of death. But I used caustic water, in which I found wonderful efficacy. And note that the cautery is a noble medicine, aiding in altering the member, and it dissolves corrupt matter existing in the same and checks flow of blood. But the aforesaid powder much mitigates pain [and] breaks up *escara*. And I have applied cautery in my time as cautiously as I could.[90]

Since the account of the case before the doctors of Milan opens in the anonymous version with a noticeably different wording from that of our other three manuscripts, it will be advisable to employ double columns at first, giving the anonymous version in the right-hand column.

[90] Translated from Latin text in MS Vienna 2358, fols. 131r, col. 2,–131v, col. 2; Vienna 4751, fols. 43v–46r; CLM 273, fols. 123v, col. 2,–124r, col. 2; CLM 321, fols. 221r–v. One MS, Vienna 4751, has a sentence in the first paragraph on the danger of operating, which I have omitted. It also begins the Gonzaga case somewhat differently, giving the lord's name as Guido, rather than John, and describing the patient more specifically as "a certain old woman living in the house of Guido of Gonzaga." The Latin text will be found in Appendix 8.

Note a case at Milan while I was at the court of the magnificent Lord Macarulus,[91] son of the illustrious Lord Barnabò Visconti, concerning a certain small *exitura*. There came to me a friend of Lord Karulus from Florence who had suffered for many days from an *exitura* in the left thigh, in which case many [physicians] of Milan were in attendance for many days.

Once when I was at Crema on account of a son of Lord Karolus Visconti, who suffered from an *apostema* in the right thigh, a certain fat [rich?] man of Florence sent for me, and with the permission of Lord Karolus I went to him and I found [there] many medical men of the aforesaid city, and in the presence of the said physicians he showed me his left thigh.

He showed me the thigh where the *exitura* was, in the presence of those physicians, and the *exitura* with which he was afflicted was very deep. Entering into conversation with the aforesaid doctors, I asked them, as if to be better informed, what they thought of such a thigh. And they had visited him before and been engaged in the case. When I touched the thigh carefully with both hands, I found a great quantity of bloody matter and very deep. And after several days had passed, the bloody matter remained, and the physicians replied to me that they believed there was bloody matter in him. Then I said, Why haven't you pierced it? They said, Since the thigh is very muscular and composed of great wide nerves and arteries, we have not dared to do so, fearing spasm and flux of blood. They had indeed applied plasters to penetrate the skin and break it up, but the bloody matter lay deep and the plasters did him little good. I took and removed all those plasters, and I considered a place more yielding, and I applied that stupefying unguent for one day. On the following day, early in the morning, I grasped in one hand a piece of linen cloth folded double and I soaked it in rose water and white of egg and I placed it over the more yielding place I wished to pierce. Next to the hole in the cloth, of the size I wished the rupture to be, I placed a ruptory of lime and soap, and I made the aforesaid ruptory adhere well to

[91] Is Marco or Carlo referred to, of the five legitimate sons of Barnabò? Presumably the former, who was the oldest son, was knighted by Charles IV in 1355, and married in 1365: see Corio, *Storia di Milano*, ed. of 1856, Vol. II, pp. 195, 220. But "Karolus" in the other MS must designate Carlo.

the flesh with bandages of linen cloth and a good ligature, and at six in the evening I visited him and asked if he had pains, and he said not. And then I removed the ruptory and cut the *escara* with the point of a *pilum*. And I washed it with the strong caustic water I carry with me and pierced and cut with the *pilum* so that a basinful of bloody matter came out in the presence of the doctors of Milan. Then I inserted a good long probe covered with the said unguent of honey, and I found a great depth. On the next day I began to make lotions with a syringe, of Malmsey wine and alcohol, since the patient was well-to-do, and then I took salt water and water of alum, since without these the aforesaid bloody matter could not be dried up, there was so much of it both from the past and what had been generated anew during the good treatment. But by reason of the weakness of the place and virtue and some custom of nature, this turned out as I had foreseen, so that with the aforesaid waters and in the way I have written and with the incarnative and consolidative medicines mentioned I cured him, by God's aid, and I gained thereby much honor and profit.[92]

[92] Translated from Latin text in MS Vienna 2358, fols. 127v, col. 2,–128r; MS CLM 273, fol. 118v–119r; MS CLM 321, fol. 214r–215r; MS Vienna 4751, fols. 21r–22r. The Latin text will be found in Appendix 9.

CHAPTER V

SOME MINOR MEDICAL WORKS WRITTEN AT FLORENCE[1]

The purpose of this chapter is to discuss some medical works, written at Florence between 1460 and 1512, which appear to be little known and to have never been printed. They exist in manuscripts of the Laurentian Library at Florence. By John of Arezzo we have a work on the heart in three books or treatises addressed to the studious Piero, son of Cosimo de' Medici and father of Lorenzo the Magnificent.[2] The manuscript is the very copy presented to Piero by the author, since at the close, following the table of contents, is written in capitals, "Liber Petri de Medicis Cos. F." (This book belongs to Piero de' Medici, son of Cosimo.) John of Arezzo says in the dedicatory preface that he is sending another copy to the illustrious knight or soldier, Petrus Borgarinus of Siena. The work is entitled *De procuratione cordis*, or *De valitudinis cordis procuratione* (as it is called in the rubric on an illuminated folio following the dedication), or *Opusculum de curanda cordis valitudine* (as John describes it in the dedication to Piero de' Medici upon the preceding flyleaf). Its third book or treatise deals with the subject of poisons (*De venenis*). John of Arezzo subsequently wrote for Lorenzo de' Medici a dialogue, *De medicina et legum prestantia*, which has been already discussed in Chapter 2.

The second work with which we shall now be concerned is on the preservation of health (*De tuenda sanitate*) by Bernardus

[1] Revised from *Isis*, Vol. IX, 1927, pp. 29–43.

[2] Laurent. Plut. 73, cod. 29, 15th century, membr., 68 fols. Incipit: "Cum sepenumero mecum agerem petre vir spectatissime ut te munusculo aliquo quod tibi gratum esset inferem . . ." The text proper opens on fol. 2r, "Cor est animatum omnium membrorum princeps . . ." Explicit: ". . . quare fertur rutam agricolas prope salviam plantare ne salvie buffones adhereant."

Tornius.[3] Bandini, in cataloguing the manuscript, which is a beautifully written and illuminated codex of the fifteenth century, gives from an epitaph the dates of Bernard's life as 1452–97.[4] The epitaph spoke of Bernard as professor of the arts and medicine, a count, and one "to whom the fatherland owed the safety of many citizens." Tornius was long connected with the University of Pisa, teaching philosophy from 1475 to 1478, during which time the students petitioned that his salary be raised, and medicine from 1478 to 1496, with his salary gradually mounting from 50 to 540 florins. In 1489 Lorenzo de' Medici invited him to dinner with Pico della Mirandola, Ficino, Politian, and Paul e Fosseto to discuss theological topics. In 1494 he printed some notations on the *De motu locali* of Hentisbery.[5] He also wrote a treatise on Lenten food (*De cibis quadragesimalibus*) of which Fabroni gives some account and which was addressed to Lorenzo de' Medici's son, John, the young cardinal, later Leo X.[6] John was also apparently the "most reverend lord" to whom the *De tuenda sanitate* is addressed. But someone has scratched out with a knife the rubric of the Titulus and also the names of Tornius and his dedicatee where they occurred on folio 1 *verso* and at the close of the treatise on folio 90 *recto*. Bandini further notes that in a work on syphilis (*De morbo Gallico*), which a Julian Tanius addressed to Leo X, and which is contained in another Laurentian manuscript,[7] he spoke of our Bernardus Tornius in very compli-

[3] Laurent. Plut. 73, cod. 34, 15th century, 90 fols. "Incipit prologus. Cum iuxta sententiam Aboaly . . ." Explicit: ". . . Legat igitur [*erasure*] libellum nostrum hilari animo [*erasure*] amet. Et [*erasure*] comendet Felixque semper valeat."

[4] Bandinius, A. M. *Catalogus codicum Latinorum biliothecae Mediceae Laurentianae,* 1774–77, Vol. III, p. 65. "In medio Capituli Dominicanorum Prati eius legitur Epitaphium," etc.

[5] For these facts see Angelo Fabroni, *Historia Academiae Pisanae,* Vol. I, 1791, pp. 292–95, 362, 390, 396–98.

[6] *Ibid.*, Vol. I, p. 294.

[7] Laurent. Plut. 73, cod. 38, early 16th century, 131 fols., Julian Tanius de saphati sive de morbo Gallico. The treatise is in four chapters with a proemium to Leo X. The author says that it is his first work, written some years

mentary terms and referred to a brief *Consilium* which Bernard wrote for a doctor of laws, Philip Decius of Padua or Pavia, and which was known to all the medical men of Florence.[8] Julian Tanius further states that he himself saw this same Philip Decius afflicted with syphilis in the summer of 1495 when he was lecturing at Prato, whither the university had been moved during a rebellion at Pisa.[9] Of opuscula by Bernard Tornius, preserved in a manuscript of the Riccardian Library, we shall defer treatment until our next chapter.

The other work which we are to consider is that of John or Giovanni Martellini on critical days (*De decretoriis diebus*).[10] It is dedicated to Petrus Soderinus, patrician and standard bearer of the Republic of Florence, and therefore was written between 1502 and 1512, the term during which he held that office. Bandini supplies the information that Martellini was born in 1464, became a teacher of logic in 1489, a teacher of medicine at Pisa in 1501, and died in 1520. In opening the dedication to Peter, John speaks of "a paraphrase on the soul which we edited in your name last year."[11] Soderinus had participated in the expulsion of the Medici, and in 1502 was made gonfalonier for life, but Julius II forced the Florentines to

---

before. He ascribes syphilis to the extreme rains of 1495 and seems unaware of the way in which it actually spreads. He composed the treatise largely at the urging of the chaste and erudite Vicar General of the Dominicans.

[8] Bandini, *op. cit.*, Vol. III, p. 73, quotes, "Bernardus Tornius medicus nostra aetate quam praeclarissimus in consilio duarum chartarum omnibus medicis Florentinis noto pro domino Philippo Decio Patavino composito . . ."

[9] *Ibid.* "Nos anno MCCCCXCV extrema aestate egregium utriusque iuris doctorem dominum Philippum Decium Papiensem in Florentino Gymnasio Prati, Pisis tunc rebellibus, publice legentem, hac labe affectum ipsi conspeximus."

[10] Laurent. Plut. 73, cod. 35, 16th century, small quarto, 51 fols. "(I) OHANNIS MARTELLINI MEDICI DE DECRETORIIS DIEBUS AD ILLUSTRISSIMUM PRINCIPEM PETRUM SODERINUM PATRICIUM ET R.P.FLO. VEXILLIFERUM PERPETUUM PRAEFATIO."

[11] "Superiori anno paraphrasim de anima tuo nomine edimus, nunc vero de decretoriis diebus syllogen tamquam flosculum hinc inde excerptam tibi dedicamus."

depose him in 1512. The next year, however, Leo X restored his confiscated property.

We now return to a more detailed consideration of John of Arezzo's work on cures for diseases of the heart as the first of our treatises in chronological order. Its dedication to Piero de' Medici is a fair example of the overcomplimentary, curry-favoring addresses of humanists to despots, magnates, and patrons. At the same time John adopts a somewhat paternal tone towards Piero, praising his father Cosimo even more highly, and saying that after much reflection he has decided that a book would be the best and most welcome gift he could make Piero, "for I have been well aware that even in your boyhood dogs and hawks and horses, in which many persons less sound in judgment greatly delight, do not satisfy your free and lofty soul."[12] With a professed modesty which is very possibly really false pride to conceal the fact that he could have done no better, no matter how long he had tried, John speaks of his treatise as a trifle which he has dashed off in the course of a few nights and which he fears may still require much correction. He hopes that sometime when Piero has a few moments free from busy cares, say while he is in his bath, he will glance over "these our first fruits" and give them the benefit of his distinguished correction. John remarks, "I pass over the excellence of your father Cosimo, that most illustrious man of all those of our city. For if you too are prominent in your city, he indeed with one consent of all surpasses others the world over."[13] From this it would seem that Cosimo was still living, and consequently that our treatise was composed before 1464.

[12] Laurent. Plut. 73, cod. 29, fol. 1: "Nam optime novi etiam in tua pueritia canes aut aucipitres vel equos quibus plerique iuditio minus integri summopere delectantur tuo libero ac elevato animo non convenire."

[13] "Prestantiam tamen illustrissimi illius omnium nostre civitatis viri Cosme patris tui pretereo. Nam si tu quoque prestans tua sis in urbe, ille vero uno omnium ore ceteris prestat in orbe."

Throughout the treatise John or his amanuensis is inconsistent and uncertain in the spelling with the dipthong *ae* or the single *e*. He also employs such spellings as "naravimus" rather than "narravimus."

In Appendices 10, 11, and 12, I print the Latin text of the headings of John's various chapters, of the eleventh chapter of his first book *in toto*, and of the account of fungi from the fifth chapter of his third book on poisons. It will be seen from the table of contents that after a few brief chapters on the formation of the heart in the embryo, its anatomy, the instruments with which it performs its actions, its twelve passions, the causes of delight and sadness, the diverse affections of the heart caused by diversity of the blood, and the difference between rancor and hate — after this the first two books are largely occupied with medicines simple and compound and with other modes of cure. In the tenth chapter of the first book on medicinal simples that act as cordials, John distinguishes them as hot, cold, dry, and moist. Hot cordials are amber, agaric, basilicon, behen, citrus, cinamomum, crocus (saffron), caro (meat), dornicus, fisticus (pistachio), iacinta, oosmel (planta cinamomo similis — a plant like cinnamon), kabs, lilium, lignum aloes, melissa, macis (mace), muscus (musk), mumia, menta (mint), malum granatum (pomegranate), malum matianum, ova de volucribus (birds' eggs), olibanum (frankincense), ozimum (clover), polipodum, stricum, sticados arabicus, terra sigillata, usnea, zedoria.[14] On the other hand, silver, gold, vinegar, acetositas citri (citric acid), camphor, coral, coriander, embliricus, endive, lapis armenus, lapis lazuli, mirtus, mirabolani kebuli, macianus, pira pontica, rose, spodium, sandali, and tamarindi are cold. All the dry cordials have already been listed as either hot or cold. Under moist cordials John adds lingua bovis and nenufar or neufar.

[14] Barth. Castelli, *Lexicon medicum*, 1713, p. 751, defined *Usnea* as used by the Arabs of moss in general, but as restricted in his time to moss growing on a dead man's skull, which was supposed to be a specific against hemorrhages. Castelli defined *Zedoaria* as an exotic root which was very good against colic. Sometimes it means camphor root. Of the drugs listed in the next sentence of the text, mirabolani kebuli were in high favor with Roger Bacon. See *Opera hactenus inedita Rogeri Baconi*, Fasc. IX, *De retardatione accidentium senectutis cum aliis opusculis de rebus medicinalibus*, nunc primum ediderunt A. G. Little, E. Withington, Oxford, 1928: pp. 49, lines 25–26; 51, line 16; 128, line 18; and, under "Glossary of Drugs", p. 221, for an explanation of the meaning of the term.

John says that in treating of the virtues of these medicines he has simply followed the past authorities, especially Avicenna. "For in these matters I would not presume to advance anything of my own. Since the richest treasures have been found rather by the opinion of the ancients than by reason, it is better for anyone to acquiesce rather than to attempt something new."[15] Thus in the very center and springtime of the so-called Renaissance we encounter an example of trust in authority and shrinking from any individual expression such as we can no longer ascribe generally to the previous medieval period. As this suggests, there is not much use in looking in John's works for any important contribution to knowledge or advance upon previous medieval collections of medical recipes or works upon the heart, such as that of Alfred of Sarshel (or Anglicus), and upon poisons, such as that of Peter of Abano, whom John quotes more than once.

The usual medieval remedies occur in our author's pages: the employment of parts of animals, of gems, the bezoar, and the other wonted paraphernalia. We are told that the lion cannot endure a cock or a white cat, that many a dangerous beast will flee from the presence of its own canine tooth, that one is also quite safe if one carries the eye of a lion in one's armpit or a magnet bound on one's left arm.[16] The basilisk kills, in John's opinion, by wide dissemination of its vapors rather than by sight or by the sound of its hiss.[17] The substance from the head of a snake known as serpent's horn is one of the surest indicators of the presence of poison. "Human industry, the supreme God ordering, has investigated to such a point that certain natural substances have been found which indicate the presence of poisons and the fraud of the wicked. One of these is serpent's horn. For experience has discovered that in

[15] *De procuratione cordis*, I, 10, *De medicinis frigidis:* "In his namque nil ego a me presumerem. Cum divitissima potius vetustorum sententia quam ratione comperta sint [or *sit*] cui potius acquiescere quam novi quicquam temptare rectius est."

[16] III, 25.

[17] III, 18.

the presence of any poison it pours forth a sort of sweat in the form of moist vapors."[18] John compares this interaction between serpent's horn and poisons to that between the magnet and iron.

John finds amusing Pliny's remedy that the patient whisper in the ear of a donkey that he has been stung by a scorpion and he will be cured, but the modern reader may find still more amusing the treatment prescribed by John to get rid of a frog which has been generated in the human stomach. The patient should be suspended by his feet over a vessel full of cold water and then shaken continually to encourage the frog in what should be its natural inclination to seek its native element. In case a lizard is confined in one's interior, a similar suspension is resorted to, but this time over a vessel filled with milk and wine as being liquids more attractive to a lizard. In the case of the frog, if this procedure fails, the patient should go without drink until he becomes very thirsty, when he should take medicine for worms along with water. The frog, seeking the water, will consume the poison also. Thereupon the medicine against worms should be withdrawn from the stomach. But what becomes of the expiring frog is not definitely stated. Another remedy for those having a frog is the blood of a sea turtle given in drink with the rennet of a hare and of a deer and wine.[19]

The list of narcotics enumerated by John may be worth repeating. Besides opium, he mentions *solater* or quicksilver and "what many call inverted beans" as producing dreams, phantasms, and stolidity. "Nux methel, too, inebriates if one dram is taken, while a greater weight kills." Mandragora is most powerful, but the root and apple and grains induce *subeth* (i.e., a state of coma) and weakness of the stomach. Lettuce,

[18] III, 3. "Humana industria altissimo iubente deo exploratum est adeo ut quedam inventa sint naturalia venenum indicantia et malignorum fraudem quorum alterum est serpentis cornu. Experientia enim compertum est ipsum ad cuiusvis veneni presentiam vapores quosdam humidos sudoris instar effundere."

[19] III, 13.

too, with its syrup taken in large doses does the same. John further names jusquiam, hemlock, and coriander.[20]

Like almost everyone of his time, John of Arezzo was a firm believer in occult virtues, in the influence of the stars, and in the close connection of the two. This fact comes out in his chapter upon specific form or occult virtue.[21] It may originate from nature alone without art, as in the case of the properties possessed by the magnet and rhubarb. Or it may have its first beginning in art and thereafter be increased by the natural influx from the stars, as in the case of the famous antidotes Tyriac and Mithridatic, or other medicines which through fermentation increase in strength with age rather than gradually lose their potency, and hence acquire from the influence of the stars an occult virtue which the simples entering into their composition did not possess. Here, as in earlier medieval writings, we see the conceptions of occult virtue and astral influence associated with chemical change. With this influx of the stars and planets goes, John says, the form of intelligence and of the supreme God. John apparently ascribed a soul or souls to the heavenly bodies, for in his first chapter in describing the formation of the embryo he states that "the formative virtue given by the father" is present in the semen, yet is not in it integrally but in a state of quasi-separation from it, not that mode of separation characteristic of the human mind and body, but just as soul is included in the celestial bodies.[22] Such inclusion would seem a much closer union than the "separate intelligences" of Aquinas, who move the spheres.

John states that other animals than dogs may have rabies and gives the following signs by which they may be distinguished. "If then they do not eat and flee when they see water, or die at the sight of it, and if they foam with open mouth and

[20] III, 6.

[21] I, 12.

[22] I, 1: "Virtus hec a patre data informativa . . . semini presens est, non tamen in eo ut in proprio subiecto inmersa sed quasi separata ab illo non eo separationis modo quo intellectus a corpore sed sicut anima in corporibus celestibus inclusa."

tongue hanging out, and moisture also runs from the nostrils, and the eyes are bloody, and, with head turned to the ground and tail relaxed and between their legs, they run hither and thither like a drunken man, . . . and rush directly into whomsoever they meet and bite him. And if [the rabid animal] is a dog, others flee when they see him, especially when he barks. Moreover, his voice in his barking, although he barks but little, is raucous. And he doesn't recognize his master. Then he should be thought mad."[23]

Bernard Tornius says in the prologue to his work that he will first state as briefly as he can the marks of each natural state of health, so that the most reverend lord to whom he writes will be able to recognize them. "Next I shall explain the universal rules which others speaking of the preservation of health lay down. Finally, running through the six non-natural things, I will bring forward what is good to be done to preserve health."[24] In pursuance of this program he takes up various signs of the state of the brain, heart, liver, and other parts of the body. He also includes some matters noted by Rasis in regard to physiognomy, "in order that your most reverend lordship may be easily able to tell the characters of men at a glance."[25] By folio 17 of the manuscript we meet the universal canons of health, of which some fifteen are listed. Some discussion of tastes, with

[23] III, 15: "Si ergo non comedant et aquam cum vident fugiant vel eius intuitu moriantur oreque aperto lingua exeunte spuma et humiditas effluat etiam a naribus oculis sanguineis capite ad terram propenso caudaque relaxata et coxis vincta incedunt diversis motibus ad hebrii instar vigilantes [vacillantes?] et soli cursitant dirrecti in quemcumque obviant ut mordeant. Et si canis sit alii ipsum videntes fugiunt cum presertim latrat. Vox vero eius in latratu suo quamquam parum latret rauca est nec eius dominum discernit tunc arbitrandum rabiosum esse."

[24] Laurent. Plut. 73, cod. 34, fol. 1v.: "Deinde regulas universales explicabo quas alii de conservatione sanitatis loquentes obnuntiunt. Demum per sex res non naturales discurrendo quid bonum sit fieri pro conservanda sanitate in medium afferam."

[25] *Ibid.*, fol. 13v: "Placet tamen de Fisonomia quedam rasis annotata percurrere ut mores etiam hominum tua Reverendissima D. ex visu possit faciliter cognoscere."

citation of Galen and Rasis, follows. Then are taken up Galen's six non-natural constituents of diet in the broad sense, namely, air, food and drink, movement or quiet, sleep and waking, inanition and repletion, and "accidents of the soul" or mind. In these connections Bernard gives his lordship interesting practical advice and prescriptions. But the last two-thirds of the work treat in roughly alphabetical order of various foods and drinks from almonds to wine and sugar.

Bernard concludes by saying that he thinks many will condemn his book. Some will say that he has not used the right words, to whom his reply is that medical men want facts and the sense. Others will say that he has brought forth nothing new. He admits this, but justifies the making of a brief compilation to save the reverend lord for whom he writes from having to read all the books of the ancients. "Let others write new things and with these make experience, as they are wont to do many times, continually involving healthy persons in new fantasies and bringing them to a state of sickness."[26] After this unfavorable reference to medical empiricism and experimentation, Bernard goes on to say that if he has been brief on many points, it has been in order to avoid boring the lord for whom he writes. Other critics will charge him with having copied the writings of moderns word for word, but he asks them to read his work first and see whether he has been more influenced by the authority of recent or of ancient writers. In his opuscula, however, we find him making excerpts from the *Plusquam commentum* of the fourteenth century.[27] Nevertheless, from these opuscula, as may be seen from our next chapter, we ob-

[26] Laurent. Plut. 73, cod. 34, fol. 90r: "Scribant alii nova et cum illis experientiam faciant ut solent multotiens continue sanos novis fantasiis involventes ad egritudines perducendo."

[27] The work of Turisianus or Pietro Torrigiano de' Torrigiani, a pupil of Taddeo Alderotti, who died about 1350 and is not to be confused with Pietro da Tossignano who lived in the next half century. This title, "More than a Commentary," implied that his work added new matter to Galen's *Ars parva: Trusiani plusquam commentum in librum Galieni qui microtechni intitulatur*, printed Venice, 1504, 1517, 1526, etc.

tain a more vivid and satisfying impression of Tornius as a physician than we do from the somewhat perfunctory and unoriginal *De tuenda sanitate*.

A more consistently favorable attitude to "modern" (i.e., late medieval) authors than was implied in Tornius's above remark is shown in John Martellini's work on critical days. The chief features of this treatise are its explanation of the critical days in diseases on astrological grounds, and its rejection of Galen's medicinal month. Galen had made this month only twenty-six days and twenty-two hours in duration, and in consequence had regarded the twentieth day of the medicinal month as critical, rather than the twenty-first, since the moon would complete one of its quarters in less than seven days. Martellini would take the other planets and signs, as well as the moon, into account in the matter of critical days, and would regard the fourteenth and twenty-first, as well as the seventh, day of the month as critical days. For this view he finds support in such writers of the fourteenth and fifteenth centuries as Peter of Abano, Gentile da Foligno, Augustine of Suessa,[28] Pietro Torrigiano de' Torrigiani, Dino and Tommaso del Garbo, Niccolò Falcucci, and other Florentines. He even cites Pico della Mirandola's work against astrology,[29] but agrees with him only in his criticism of Galen's estimate of the duration of the lunar month.

The problem of critical days continued to call forth treatises and excite controversy in Italy, and more particularly at the papal court, during the first half of the sixteenth century.[30] Indeed already before Martellini, Matthew of Lucca, in a work on critical days printed at Rome in 1493, had laid stress upon

[28] Laurent. Plut. 73, cod. 35, fols. 3r–v and 46v–48r are places where such citations especially occur.

[29] *Ibid.*, fols. 22r–v and 25v.

[30] In fact throughout the century works on critical days formed a large fraction of the astrological medical literature of all lands, as may be seen from the numerous treatises listed by Sudhoff, *Iatromathematiker vornehmlich im 15 u. 16 Jht.*, Breslau, 1902, although it must be added that many such treatises went beyond the strict bounds of their titles to treat of astrological medicine generally.

the influence of the stars and especially the moon.[31] Agostino Nifo, the commentator on Aristotle and Averroës, and author of a treatise on the false prognostication of a flood from a conjunction of the planets to come in 1524,[32] also composed a work on this theme of critical days, which was printed at Venice, first in 1504[33] and again in 1519.[34] Nifo, who taught at Naples, Salerno, Padua, and Cologne, has this connection with the papal court, that Leo X made him a count palatine. At Bologna in 1543 was published a work by the papal physician, Andrea Turino, in which he defended the teaching of Hippocrates and Galen concerning the causes of critical days against the noted Geronimo Fracastoro of Verona who lived 1483–1553.[35] This provoked a reply the following year from Michelangiolo Biondo, who addressed to Paul III a treatise concerning critical days and their real causes, following in the path of Galen against the innovators.[36] In it he held that Turino, instead of defending Galen, had offended against the great master. I have not seen Biondo's treatise but infer from Agostini's notice of it that he regarded the astrological and Galenic interpretations as reconcilable. A pupil of Agostino Nifo, Biondo shows his astrological bent by volunteering the information that he was born under the planet Venus, and he was superstitious in other

[31] Mattheus de Lucha, *De diebus creticis*, Roma, Andreas Freitag, 1493. Sudhoff, 1902, p. 35, ascribed this edition, which he had been unable to find, to Eucharius Silber rather than Andreas Freitag, and was not sure whether it was iatromathematical or no. I, too, have not seen the work itself, but follow a notice of it in a recent sales catalogue.

[32] Augustinus Niphus, *De falsa diluvii prognosticatione*, Florence, 1520.

[33] For this edition see Sudhoff, 1902, p. 36, where is also given a synopsis of the book.

[34] Augustinus Niphus, *De diebus criticis seu decretoriis aureus liber*, Venice, 1519, 10 fols.

[35] *Hippocratis et Galeni defensio de causis dierum criticorum adversus Hieronymum Fracastorium*, Bologna, 1543.

[36] *De diebus decretoriis et crisi eorumque verissimis causis in via Galeni contra Neotericos libellus*, Rome, 1544. Recently there was offered for sale a manuscript of the early sixteenth century and of Italian provenance, written in a humanistic cursive hand, containing a *Compendium de diebus decretoriis* of which the contents were largely astrological.

ways.[37] Tiraquellus, who lived from 1480 to 1558, in his long list of medical men past and present includes Ioannes Quintianus Italus who confuted some of Galen's writings on critical days.[38] Finally may be mentioned Lucas Gauricus, who, in his *Super diebus decretoriis axiomata*, published at Rome in 1546, made the theme of critical days a starting point for a dozen treatises devoted to astrological medicine. After having been for a time professor of mathematics at Ferrara and having served as astrologer of Catherine de' Medici, Gauricus died at Rome in 1558 as bishop of Civitavecchia, to which see papal favor had raised him.[39]

In conclusion, it may be admitted that our three treatises are works of minor importance, yet they probably reflect fairly enough the general character of the ordinary run of medical thought and literature at that time. Although written in the period commonly designated as the High Renaissance, in cultured Florence, and under the Medicean Maecenate, they are in the main compilations and continuations of the medical thinking and literature of the preceding medieval centuries. And a broad streak of what we should today pronounce superstition — occult virtues and bits of sympathetic magic, physiognomy and astrology — runs through all three. They contain nothing to suggest that the members of the Medici family (despite its auspicious name) had an unusual interest in promoting medical knowledge or exercised any enlightened patronage in that direction. Indeed, what John of Arezzo has to say in another treatise of the prevalence of medical quacks and impostors in fifteenth-century Florence and of their acceptability to mag-

[37] P. Giovanni degli Agostini, *Scrittori Veneziani*, Venice, 1752–54, Vol. II, pp. 488–508, where he lists various works by Biondo.

[38] Tiraquellus, *De nobilitate*, cap. 31, ed. of 1574, fol. 136v.

[39] A brief synopsis of the twelve tractates will be found in Sudhoff, 1902, pp. 56–57. Gauricus had edited the Alfonsine Tables with *Theoremata* of his own at Venice in 1521 and 1524.

Sudhoff, 1902, pp. 54–55, has treated of "Der Federkrieg dreier päpstlichen Leibärzte." See also his "Zur Geschichte der Lehre von den kritischen Tagen," in the *Wiener medicinischen Wochenschrift*, 1902, No. 7.

nates as well as populace gives us the impression that its medical standards were, if anything, below the medieval average.[40] Our next chapter, however, may somewhat alter this impression.

[40] See Chapter 2.

CHAPTER VI

A FIFTEENTH-CENTURY AUTOPSY[1]

In the following pages we shall obtain a quite different glimpse of the medicine of the second half of the fifteenth century from that afforded by the preceding chapter. Yet we are about to consider a manuscript by the hand of one of the very authors of whom we there treated, Bernard Tornius. But we shall now see him as a practicing physician, confronted by a definite and specific practical problem, instead of having the task of writing a brief manual upon so general a subject as the preservation of health. Instead of compiling from the ancients he will act, observe, and infer on his own responsibility and with considerable independent acumen. For we now have to do with a first-hand account, by the family physician in charge, of an autopsy and medical inferences therefrom and prescription for others still living and liable to similar disease.

Our present treatise is the fifth of eleven *Opuscula* by Tornius contained in a manuscript of the Riccardian Library at Florence,[2] a small codex of which our treatise covers five pages written in a small and abbreviated but neat and legible hand. The other opuscula are partly medical and partly philosophical in character. The first treats of the nature of the juice of wormwood and whether it is good for quartan fever. Next there are conclusions concerning fevers, then some propositions concerning different constitutions or states of health, and fourth, some charts or outlines connected with the primary qualities in general and heat in particular. Following our treatise, which is described in the table of contents upon the flyleaf of the manuscript as "An Anatomical Relation," there

[1] Revised from *Annals of Medical History*, Vol. X, September, 1928, pp. 270–77.

[2] Riccard. 930, 15th century, paper, 38 fols., "Bernardi Tornii Florentini opuscula medica." Our treatise occupies fols. 17v–19v.

are two letters. The first deals with problems of motion suggested to Bernard's mind by the noted writers on mathematics and physics, John Marlianus of the fifteenth century, and Richard Suiseth of the fourteenth. The second, addressed to Master Franciscus Ninus, deals with bloodletting and pharmacy. In the eighth opusculum Tornius argues against three of the nine hundred theses which Pico della Mirandola, at the age of twenty-one, had offered to defend at Rome against all comers: namely, the twentieth of those taken from the writings of Aquinas, 'That it is not within God's power to have the same body in different places at the same time'; the fortieth of those drawn from the works of Aristotle, 'That difficulty in understanding may come in part from within and in part from the thing to be understood'; the forty-third of the same, 'That it implies a contradiction that matter should exist without form.' In the ninth and tenth items Tornius discusses with Master Franciscus of Siena the thesis: 'No state of health always is health absolutely.' In the last entry, dated 1485, Tornius culls some definitions of bodies from the words of "More than Commentator," that is, from Pietro de' Torrigiani, author of the medieval medical work of that title (*Plusquam commentum*). Tornius might have argued against Pico's theses before 1485, but his sixth opusculum may possibly have been written after the death of Lorenzo the Magnificent in 1492, since in closing it Tornius commends himself to "petro laurentio de medicis domino meo."

In our consideration of Bernard Tornius in the preceding chapter, he appeared as a somewhat bookish individual who contented himself with a compilation from past writings and spoke slightingly of rash medical experimentation. From most of these other opuscula our impression of him would be that of a person much given to the then current scholastic disputation, although with a breadth of interest extending beyond the strict field of medicine into those of physics, philosophy, and even theology. For, however much we may smile at the outworn dogmas and superstitions of medieval and early modern physicians, or at their persistent adhesion to Galen and Avicenna, we cannot deny that a doctor of medicine then was more widely educated and possessed broader intellectual interests than some of our modern specialists. But now we have to view Bernard Tornius in a new aspect as a sympathetic and kindly family physician, and as a medical practitioner acquainted with dissection and the anatomy of the human body.

The post-mortem examination which he recounts shows us more than that. Too often have we been told, with little or no evidence adduced to support the charge, that religious prejudice operated to prevent dissection of the human body in the middle ages. Now it is recognized that "anatomies" or systematic dissections of human bodies for purposes of instruction were held regularly in the schools of medicine of the fourteenth and fifteenth centuries, and the skill of the practicing surgeons of the same period is becoming better known. The bodies used in the university dissections were commonly those of executed criminals or other outcasts; the surgeons usually would treat only those cases where they thought that recovery was likely. In the present autopsy, on the other hand, we find a physician of note recommending, and a high official, presumably of good family, social standing, and considerable property, agreeing to a post-mortem examination of the vital organs of the official's own son, with the aim to discover if the complaint of which he died was of hereditary character and so to prescribe more intelligently for the other children of the same father. No doubt the advancement of science and the promotion of human health in general by investigation of a disease which, as he says, is "not yet fully understood by doctors," were further motives which actuated Bernard Tornius. He does not, however, obtrude these motives upon the afflicted father.

The report of the physician upon the autopsy which he has conducted is marked by two qualities which are far more characteristic of medieval thought and expression than is generally recognized, namely, clearness and directness. After a tactful word of sympathy to the bereaved parent, he concisely reviews the results of the post-mortem examination, then briefly enumerates his five findings as to the nature of the disease. He also explains in clear detail the diagnosis and reasoning by which he reached these conclusions. Finally he suggests a prophylactic treatment for the remaining children, with the intelligent proviso that it may need to be varied according to time and circumstance by the attending physician. He expresses his intention to acquaint himself better with the other children by frequent visitation. He even reveals one modern foible, suggesting the consultation of a specialist, George of Cyprus, at Florence upon a certain point. Some of the details of his report may seem quaint and amusing today, and of course Galen and Avicenna are cited duly. But across the gap of intervening centuries this brief, scientific, human document carries a vivid conviction of reality, transporting us as by some magic carpet back into the very midst of the medical theory and practice of long ago. Expressed in modern medical phraseology, the autopsy seems to have revealed that the boy suffered from multifold metastatic abscesses of the liver, the result of septicemia or pyleophlebitis. But let Bernard Tornius speak for himself in English translation. In Appendices 13 and 14 at the close of the volume I give the Latin text of the "Relatio anatomica" and the table of contents of the *Opuscula* as found in the Riccardian manuscript.

Worshipful Judge, I grieve over thy sad lot, for to lose one's offspring is hard, harder to lose a son, and hardest [to lose him] by a disease not yet fully understood by doctors. But, for the sake of the other children, I think that to have seen his internal organs will be of the greatest utility. Now, therefore, I will not hesitate to state as briefly as I can what we have seen and draw my honest conclusion and adduce the remedies which in my judgment are advantageous.

In the first place, the belly appeared quite swollen, although the abdomen was thin. But after dividing according to rule the abdomen and peritoneum, we saw the intestines and the bladder, which was turgid and full of urine. Removing further the colon and

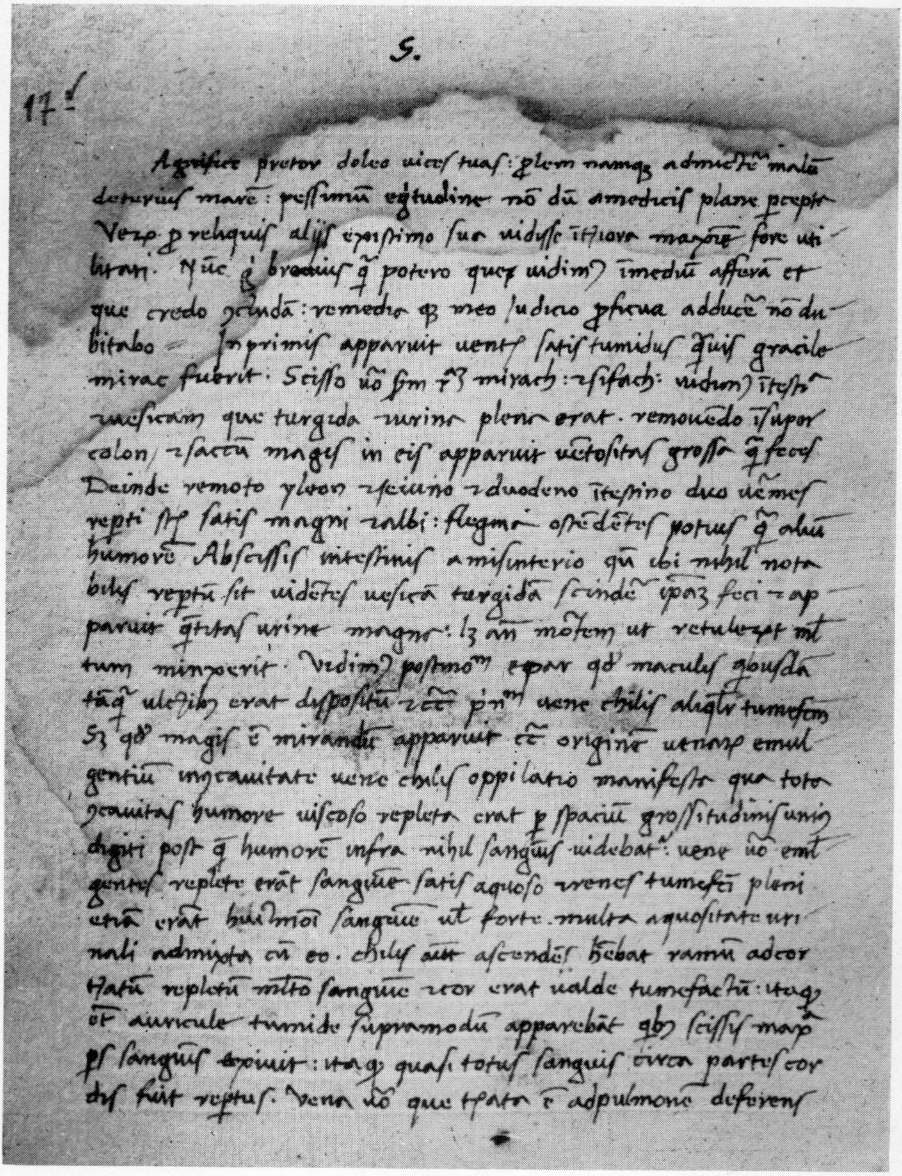

9.

17v

Magnifice pretor doleo vicem tuam: quem namque admiserunt mala
deterius mare: pessimum egritudine non dum a medicis plane percepta
Verum quia reliquis aliis existimo suo vidisse interiora maiorem fore uti
litatem. Nunc quam brevius quam potero que vidimus in medium afferam et
que credo scienda: remedia que meo iudicio proficua adducere non du
bitabo. Inprimis apparuit ventris satis tumidus quamvis gracile
mirac fuerit. Scisso vero secundum totum mirach et sifach: vidimus intestina
vesicam que turgida urine plena erat. removendo insuper
colon et sacrum mages in eis apparuit ventositas grossa quam feces
Deinde remoto yleon et ieiuno et duodeno intestino duos vermes
repperimus satis magnos et albi: flegmatici ostendentes potius quam aliud
humorem. Abscissis intestinis a misenterio quod ibi nihil nota
bile repertum sit videntes vesicam turgidam scindere ipsam feci et ap
paruit quantitas urine magna: licet ante mortem ut retulerat mul
tum minxerit. Vidimus postmodum epar quod maculis quibusdam
tamquam ulceribus erat dispositum et etiam principium vene chilis aliqualiter tumefactum
Sed quod magis est mirandum apparuit circa originem venarum emul
gentium in concavitate vene chilis oppilatio manifesta qua tota
concavitas humore viscoso repleta erat per spatium grossitudinis unius
digiti post quem humorem infra nihil sanguinis videbatur. vene vero emul
gentes replete erant sanguine satis aquoso et renes tumefacti pleni
etiam erant huiusmodi sanguine ut forte multa aquositate uri
nali admixta cum eo. chilis autem ascendens habebat ramum ad cor
tractum repletum multo sanguine et cor erat valde tumefactum: itaque
et auricule tumide supramodum apparebant quibus scissis magna
pars sanguinis exivit: itaque quasi totus sanguis circa partes cor
dis fuit repertus. Vena vero que tracta est ad pulmonem deferens

PLATE VI

AUTOPSY OF BERNARD TORNIUS

Riccardian MS 930, fol. 17v

(Slightly enlarged)

caecum, there appeared in them more gross wind than filth. Then when the ileum and jejunum and duodenum were removed, two worms were found, quite large and white, showing phlegm rather than any other humor. After the intestines had been cut off from the mesentery, since nothing notable was found therein, seeing that the bladder was turgid, I had it cut open and a great quantity of urine appeared, although before he died, as they reported, he discharged a large amount of urine. Afterwards we examined the liver, which was marked with certain spots like ulcers and somewhat swollen about the beginning of the chilic [i.e., portal] vein. But what is more remarkable, there appeared around the source of the emulgent veins in the hollow of the chilic vein an evident obstruction by which the whole cavity was filled with viscous humor for the space of the thickness of a finger, beyond which humor no blood was seen beneath, while the emulgent veins were full of blood, quite watery in character, and the swollen kidneys were also full of this sort of blood, or perhaps of much urinal wateriness admixed with it. Moreover, the ascending chilis [vena cava] had the branch to the heart filled with much blood, and the heart was much swollen, and so the auricles too appeared swollen beyond measure. When these were cut open, a great part of the blood came out, and so almost all the blood was found near the heart. But the vein which carries the nourishing blood to the lungs was also full of similarly viscous humor and seemed wholly free from blood. Having seen this much, I did not examine further concerning anything else, since the cause of his death was apparent in my judgment.

From these facts I infer, first, that this lad had contracted a great oppilation [obstruction] either from birth or in course of time, and it is safe to assume that matter of this sort was accumulated by gradual congestion rather than brought by a deflux from another member.

Second, I infer that those worms were generated after the beginning of his principal illness and were in no way the cause of his death.

Third, I infer that when transmission of blood through the chilic vein and the pulmonary vein was prevented, ebulition and fever resulted. And because in that blood there was much phlegm, that fever was like a phlegmatic [quotidian] one in many of its accidents, though from the manner of its oncoming and development it seemed like a double tertian. For every third day it came on worse in the night, as those present reported and I infer clearly from his restlessness and perceived from his pulse.

I infer, fourth, that those spots of the liver were generated after the oppilation.

Fifth and last, I infer that any son of yours of the same constitution is to be preserved to his twelfth year with the usual medicines which I will mention in closing.

The first corollary quickly follows from what I saw with my own eyes. For Galen remarks in the sixth book of his *Therapeutic*, first, those matters which require consideration should be considered, and then certified by experience, so that reasoning may be confirmed by experiment. Moreover, before his death there appeared many signs of obstruction of the liver and veins, since the hue of his face while the fever slackened was discolored, and he had difficulty in breathing, and lassitude of the body, and slowness in his motions, and sometimes I had seen egestion partly chimosic and partly chilosic. So I was assured on seeing the chilic vein that there was an obstruction in it as I had suspected. Moreover, his pulse, since it appeared to vary greatly, indicated obstruction in the veins adjoining the heart, especially those serving the lungs, according to the example in Galen's fourth book on internal members, of the physician whose pulse displayed diversities of all sorts, who afterwards died like those who die of cardiac complaint. But Your Worship is witness that that lad had the greatest diversity of pulse, and to such a degree, as I reported, that I was always in much perplexity because I could not administer the requisite medicines.

The first part of the second corollary seems clear, for while long worms, according to the opinion of Avicenna in the chapter "De speciebus vermium," are generated from humidity over which division and separation do not prevail apart from the attraction of the liver and force of putrefaction, and are more harmful than small worms and harder to get rid of, yet it does not seem likely that they would have remained in the duodenum for so many days while medicines were being taken which are good against worms, both to expel and to kill them. And the second part of the corollary is manifest from the opinion of Lord Avicenna, first chapter concerning worms, where he says, "And on this account are produced worms and flies and crawling things from humid putrid substances, since that which is taken away from that matter in order to receive form, when it is rectified becomes a worm-like or fly-like animal, for this is better than that it should remain pure putrefaction."[3] By which words Lord Avicenna seems to suggest that a few worms found in the intestines are not harmful, since, as he says, the worms spring from putrefactions and feed on them because of their homogeneity and take them from the body. While that may be the case, yet I do not assert that, as many believe, worms in our body are a good thing, since, again from the authority of the prince of medicine, it is not their nature to help without harm, since from worms are generated epilepsy and canine hunger and *bolismus* and putrefaction which is the cause of fever. Nay more, as some have reported, worms sometimes have bored holes in the belly and come out, as Lord Avicenna testifies in the aforesaid chapter.

The third corollary is patent from the proof there given, for the fever was without chill and burning, although at the beginning, because of a great rising of ascending vapors to the head, sleep was produced as if in hectic fever, with some coldness of the extremities while the [diseased] matter was moved about, which perhaps happened, as I have often observed in other cases, from withdrawal of heat to the inner parts when injury is felt about the principal members. Moreover, the fever was continuous, having proportionate exacerbations of cholera, and, since the [diseased] matter was in the parts near the heart, there was a tremulous movement of the heart, where especially was manifested frequent constriction, which, like putrid fever, revealed a great lack of the emission of vapors, nor were the accidents those of *causodes*,[4] since, on account of his humid age and the abundance of phlegm, the impression of cholera was strongly repressed. Nor does it matter that there were two tertians within the veins, with two accumulations in different

[3] The reference is of course to the then accepted belief that worms, flies, and other insects were spontaneously generated from filth and putrefaction. The chapter on worms occurs in Avicenna, III Canon., Fen 16, Tract. 5, cap. 1, and is the same which we shall in a later chapter of the present work hear Niccolò da Foligno cite anent the spontaneous generation from putrefaction of worms and flies. See MSS Vatic. Lat. 3897, fol. 79v, col. 2; Laurent. Plut. 82, cod. 22, fol. 30r–v.

[4] A particular variety of fever.

veins variously moved to putrefaction, as I have shown in other cases, for very likely the matter which was putrefying in the ascending chilic vein [vena cava] made a tertian of greater exacerbation, and that which was in the descending chilic vein made one of lesser exacerbation.

But this is a matter of grave doubt, how the chilic vein, which is so large, especially the descending one, could be so stopped up, for it does not seem that that vein could be clogged unless first the other veins of the liver were clogged with the greatest oppilation, which cannot happen while life lasts. And this is the strongest argument to me for believing that oppilation of this sort was contracted from the disposition of natural principles [i.e., from a fundamental disposition of nature]. Nevertheless it is quite true that the matter which was mixed with urinal aquosity in the bladder may have produced oppilation in the veins of the hump of the liver and been expelled by nature and filled those veins with watery fluid simultaneously with death and produced a cathimic crisis, according to that saying of Galen's in the first book on critical days, "Two sons were gladiators, who, fighting together, killed each other":[5] so nature may have expelled the matter and have been overcome by it. But I am more inclined to think that the matter producing the fever, retained, as I have said, in the vein which leads to the heart, was the cause of that suffocation than was anything else, since neither in the meseraic [veins] nor in the liver was any obstruction apparent, but only, as I have said, in the chilic vein. Unless it is held that the matter in the small veins of the liver is so small that it cannot be seen, as can that which was in the chilic vein — gross and viscous in appearance and adhering to its linings — and that nature expelled the subtle [matter] through the urine but could not expel the gross, and so death resulted. And on that point hangs the whole force of this investigation. So, while you are in Florence, you will consult on this point Georgius Ciprius [George of Cyprus?], an exceedingly learned man.

The fourth corollary follows from what has gone before, for from the heat of the heart and the ebullition of that blood was generated salt phlegm causing mordication [necrosis] and ulceration, as happens to many about the gums from salt phlegm descend-

[5] I fail to find such a passage in Kühn's edition of Galen.

ing from the head. As to why his heart was large, I don't think it came from audacity inborn in him, for he seemed timid, rather, when he was in good health, but the heart was filled with a great quantity of blood, which made it turgid and inflated, but it may be he naturally had a large heart, which in man is a sign of audacity, though in hares it signifies timidity, as may be learned from the statements of Lord Avicenna, eleventh Fen of the third part, first chapter.

The fifth corollary is known [or, noted] because after the twelfth year the natural heat becomes acute, exciting all the virtues strongly to expel superfluities, and humidity is lessened, and hence your sons are less liable after that age to incur such a disease. Therefore they are to be preserved by this preservative, that is, each year in April you ought to administer daily the following syrup: Take a dram each of

Water of Hops
Fumitory
Maidenhair
Agrimony
Betony

Mix in two doses and with each use one dram of pure vinegar and make a potion and spice it with a little cinnamon and give it hot in the morning. But I think that this prescription should be varied according to their years, as the doctors may judge. After this syrup let them take this medicine: Of choice rhubarb take one dram and let it soak in water of milk taken from goats, and water of endive and absinth. Take in equal parts, with the eight grains of spikenard, through the night. Then let it be strained out and give the juice with cassia or with manna or with dyasena or with a dose of trochees of agaric as the doctor in charge judges best. And as I think that the head, because of the rising of vapors, is one cause of trouble, at least to the extent that when heavy vapors rise in the head beyond measure they descend through the nerves and produce softening, as appeared manifestly, therefore at least once a week when they go to bed I would give them one or two pills of aloes soaked in water of endive, but in winter aloes not soaked might be better.

These are briefly what it seems should be prescribed, but I will visit Your Worship often and shall be able to keep you informed concerning the other children. Farewell, Your Worship, to whom I commend myself with all my heart."

It seems unlikely that this autopsy is identifiable with the brief *Consilium*, mentioned in the preceding chapter, which Bernard Tornius wrote for Philip Decius, the doctor of laws of Padua, and which Tanius said was known to all the medical men of Florence. If it were the same, we should identify Philip Decius with the father on whose son's body the autopsy is performed. But a *Consilium*, while likewise concerned with medical practice and a particular case, and constituting further evidence, which we could wish were extant, of Bernard's importance as a practitioner, is not necessarily a *Relatio anatomica* or an account of an autopsy. Indeed, one would rather infer that this particular one dealt with Decius's own state of health and very possibly with syphilis in particular. We therefore seem at present to have no means of telling who the magnificent praetor, judge, or podestà was to whom Tornius addressed his report. Evidently he was not at Florence at the time of writing,[6] and it is not stated where Tornius was.

[6] See Riccard. 930, fol. 19r: "dum eris florentie consultabis," etc.

CHAPTER VII

NICHOLAS OF CUSA AND THE TRIPLE MOTION OF THE EARTH

Histories of modern philosophy have begun with Nicholas of Cusa, as marking the turning point from medieval scholasticism. Histories of physics have dwelt upon him as an early advocate of experimental method and as a precursor of the Copernican theory. For the modern attitude to the middle ages has passed through two stages. For a time the medieval centuries were simply represented as dark and barbarous, with only a few monastic and theological interests to set against the wonderful scientific discoveries, freedom of thought, and general intellectual development of modern times. Then it began to be dimly apprehended that it would not quite do to represent all this modern progress as without any antecedents or as springing full-formed from the classical Renaissance, Protestant Reformation, or brain of Galileo. It began to be realized that there must have been certain men, half medieval and half modern, who marked the turning point from the one period to the other, or even certain rare geniuses who would have been modern had they only lived in modern times but who were so unfortunate as to be born before their time and to have wasted their sweetness upon, or suffered persecution from, an unappreciative age. So a few choice, heroic figures and prophetic minds were resuscitated from the dust and gloom of the border period between medieval and modern times or even from the very heart of the middle ages, to be represented as forerunners, predictors, or martyrs of the glorious age of modern science that was to come. Study centered, then, about a few names, such as Roger Bacon, Nicholas of Cusa, Peurbach and Regiomontanus, Leonardo da Vinci, who were — and still are — written up by enthusiastic admirers, not because they were medieval, for their admirers had no interest in the middle ages, but because they were supposed to be so modern. It is to be hoped that we have now pretty well passed through this stage too, are recognizing that there was no turning point and marked improvement from medieval to modern times, but only the usual historical continuity, and are beginning to study the middle ages for themselves, and their men as their own product. But to come back to Nicholas of Cusa.

It does not lie within my present intention to contest in detail the claim made for Nicholas of Cusa that he "was the first to announce *fundamental principles* of modern philosophy.[1] It may seem strange that this assertion should have been made of a man whose thought was so concerned with religious topics, and so metaphysical and mystical, not to say chimerical. If it was also sometimes mathematical, it is to be remembered that he had studied mathematics in the medieval university of Padua. But the fact seems to be that the name of Nicholas was pushed forward by German investigators in order to antedate the claims made by England for Francis Bacon and by France for Descartes as the founder of modern philosophy. For a more judicious estimate of the German cardinal's thought, the reader may be referred to the recent work of Vansteenberghe.[2]

Our present purpose is limited to some examination of the so-called astronomical system of Nicholas of Cusa, and of the representations of him as an important precursor of the Copernican theory and "a turning point in the History of Astronomy." This last encomium I quote from Heller's *History of Physics*,[3] whose further account of Nicholas's astronomy may be summarized as an example of the exaggerated sort of estimate upon which I wish to comment. Heller, then, affirms that Nicholas marked the turning point from the geocentric to the heliocentric astronomy. That he represented the earth as a

[1] Richard Falckenberg, *History of Modern Philosophy*, English translation, 1897, p. 15. See further his *Grundzüge der philosophie des Nikolaus Cusanus*, 1880.

[2] Edmond Vansteenberghe, *Le Cardinal Nicolas de Cues* (1401–1464), 1920.

[3] August Heller, *Geschichte der Physik*, 1882, Vol. I, p. 214; see also pp. 215–16.

star like other stars, and they like it, thereby dealing a great blow to the Aristotelian view that the heavenly bodies were incorruptible and composed of some fifth and finer element. That the sun's inner core was like the earth, though surrounded by an outer circumference of fire and an inner envelope of clouds and atmosphere. That the stars are inhabitable, and that the earth moves like the other stars. That, more specifically, it has a threefold movement, namely, on its axis, about two poles located on the equator, and a revolution about the poles of the universe.

One other example of overstatement of Nicholas's astronomical and scientific importance, and a rather amusing one, may be cited from such a standard English historical work as that of Rashdall on the medieval universities. Speaking of the University of Bologna, he says: "And the University had already produced in Copernicus' Master, the Cardinal Nicholas of Cusa, one of those anticipators who herald the approach of every great scientific revolution."[4] In a footnote on the same page Rashdall added: "He became a Scholar of Law in 1437 and afterwards expounded an Astronomical system according to which the sun moved." It is quite true that for Nicholas of Cusa, as for Aristotle, Ptolemy and medieval astronomers generally, the sun did move, and about the earth too, but it is difficult to discern in this tenet any anticipation of Copernicus or great scientific revolution!

After reading such statements as this in Heller's work and in other writers in other languages who may have simply followed it, I became curious to examine Nicholas of Cusa's own fuller — or so I supposed it would be — exposition of the subject in his own works and words, and see what it really amounted to. My eagerness to do this was whetted by the considerably different account from Heller contained in the more recent History of Physics by Gerland,[5] who warned that Nicholas

[4] Hastings Rashdall, *The Universities of Europe in the Middle Ages*, 1895, Vol. I, p. 245.

[5] Ernst Gerland, *Geschichte der Physik*, 1913, p. 223.

could not be regarded as a forerunner of Copernicus, since he left the sun its movement, and did not make the earth go round the sun; that the Cusan system can scarcely be regarded as an improvement upon the Ptolemaic, but must be viewed rather as an emendation or further development of the old Aristotelian theory. But Gerland repeated the statement about the triple motion ascribed by Cusa to the earth. Another reason why I wondered what Nicholas's own account would really amount to, was that these second-hand reports of it gave no adequate array of references to his writings in support of their statements.

Indeed, his *De docta ignorantia* appeared to be the only one of his writings that was cited in this connection, and it hardly appeared to be the sort of work where one would look for a full exposition of a new astronomical system. However, to the *De docta ignorantia*[6] I turned, and my worst fears were confirmed. Here was no astronomical system or anything like it, but merely a few brilliant random suggestions, based not upon astronomical observation, but rather having their origin in pious skepticism, with the aim to show that all knowledge is uncertain, that even the learned are ignorant, and that nothing is fixed or centred except in God. Minimum must coincide with maximum, and the center of the universe with its circumference: its center and circumference are God. If this is the foundation of modern philosophy, take me back to Duns Scotus. It may be delightful as devout mysticism, but as a basis for an astronomical system, is confusing, to say the least. But it is enough to convince Nicholas that the earth cannot be the center of the universe, and that since it is not in the center, it cannot be entirely free from motion. It is true that he goes on to explain that the fact that just half of the signs of the zodiac show above the horizon does not demonstrate that the earth is in the center of the eighth sphere. He further asserts that wherever in the heavens anyone might be placed, it would seem to such an one that he was at the center of the universe. But one cannot find

[6] I have used the edition of 1565, where the statements which follow in the above paragraph will be found at page 38 *et seq.*

precise equidistance outside of God, who alone is infinite Equality. The poles of the universe are not fixed except in God, and so every star, however fixed it may seem, moves somewhat, and the earth, too, moves or is moved. This is why we do not find the stars where they ought to be in the heavens according to the rules and astronomical tables of the ancients. None of the planets can describe a true circle as its orbit, since they do not move about a fixed point or axis.

But of the triple motion of the earth which Heller and Gerland credited Cusa with devising, there was no clear mention in the *De docta ignorantia*. Indeed, it is not contained in any of his works, but is briefly suggested in a note which he made upon one of the blank leaves of an astronomical, or rather, astrological manuscript that he purchased at Nürnberg in September, 1444. This brief note was printed in 1847 by Clemens in a footnote to his book on Giordano Bruno and Nicholas of Cusa, where it occupies barely a page.[7] It is this humble jotting which has been elevated by the unbalanced and fantastic judgment of subsequent writers into an astronomical system marking the cleavage between the Ptolemaic and Copernican views and the beginning of modern astronomy. Could anything, even the most childish of medieval superstitions, be more unscientific, unhistorical, and lacking in common sense than this absurd misappreciation and acceptation of inadequate evidence, not to say outright misrepresentation, by modern investigators and historians of science?

When are we ever going to come out of it? To stop approaching the study of medieval science by such occult methods as the scrutiny of a manuscript supposed to have been written by Roger Bacon in cipher, instead of by reading the numerous scientific manuscripts that are expressed in straightforward and coherent, albeit somewhat abbreviated, Latin? To cease jumping to conclusions as to a man's whole philosophy from a few

[7] F. J. Clemens, *Giordano Bruno und Nicolaus von Cusa*, Bonn, 1847, pp. 98–99. Since this work may be hard to procure, I reproduce the Latin of the passage in Appendix 15.

phrases, torn from their context? Why are we so attached to far-fetched and unnatural, as against simple and direct methods? Why do we select as the great names in the history of philosophy and science men whose time was largely occupied by other interests, and whose fame should and does depend mainly upon something else? We smile at antiquity for regarding Homer, or at the middle ages for citing Virgil as a scientific authority, but is our own attitude very different? Is it likely that Nicholas of Cusa, first a law student, then a private secretary and humanist, then absorbed in matters of church and state, engaged in embassies, legations, and missions, first a supporter of the Conciliar movement and then a cardinal, ever preaching sermons and writing works of theology — is it likely that he, rather than someone who gave all his time to scientific studies or philosophic thought, would produce work of lasting importance in science and philosophy? Or is it likely that his scientific and philosophical utterances have received undue attention because his prominence in other connections has called attention to him and his writings? If his scientific and mathematical and philosophical ideas were so important, why did he not devote his time and energies to them more whole-heartedly? Why do we pick out an ex-Lord Chancellor, privy councillor and rival of Coke, as the inspirer of modern experimental method? Or, some of us, insist that he, rather than a man trained in the theater, must have written Shakespeare's plays? Why has so much attention been lavished upon the scientific notions and knowledge of anatomy displayed in the miscellaneous notebooks of a great painter, Leonardo da Vinci, and so little attention been given to the scientific and complete anatomical treatises of his predecessors or contemporaries? To raise such questions is not to deny that these were unusual men, even great geniuses, possessed of more than common energy and versatility. It is true, too, that their times were not marked by anything like such specialization of knowledge as our day. But there were schools and faculties of medicine, there were specially trained surgeons, there were persons who spent most of their time teaching and writing on mathematics and astronomy. Whereas the possessors of the great names to whom we have referred only occasionally occupied themselves with the broad field of knowledge at all, and must be classed as brilliant amateurs, if not triflers. Why, then, so much stress upon their happy guesses, occasional observations, or chance remarks, which they themselves so seldom fully developed or carried through to a convincing conclusion?

But what does this jotting which Nicholas himself seems never to have thought it worth while to develop farther, amount to? The answer is, very little. One could wish that those who have alluded to this note in Cusa's handwriting[8] had given some account of the astronomical manuscript to which it is appended, and had stated what connection, if any, there is between the two. This they have not done, so we must judge the note by itself. It appears to be primarily an attempt upon Nicholas's part to account for the discrepancy between the mobile and immobile zodiacs, or precession of the equinoxes, or motion of the eighth sphere, which had always been a mooted problem with medieval astronomers, by introducing another movement of revolution of the heavens and earth. He repeats some of the ideas which we have already heard him express in the *De docta ignorantia*. The earth is still situated practically at the center of the spheres of the planets and fixed stars which revolve about

[8] Clemens, who discovered it in 1843 in the library of the hospital at Cues, stated that it occurred on the last parchment leaf, which would rather suggest that it had no vital connection with the other contents of the MS. Vansteenberghe (page 245, note 2), on the other hand, gives as a reference for it, "Cod. cusan. 211, fols. 41–54," but it would seem that this must be the foliation of the astronomical treatise which Nicholas purchased in September, 1444, rather than that of the brief note by Cusa himself. Fortunately in the perilous and storm-tossed sea of secondary works there are such havens of refuge as the catalogues of collections of manuscripts. Turning to J. Marx, *Verzeichnis der Handschriften-Sammlung des Hospitals zu Cues bei Bernkastel a. Mosel*, Trier, 1905, we find that fols. 41–54r are occupied by the Alphonsine Tables or some variant of them, and that after two blank pages Cusa's note occupies a part of fol. 55v. The earlier contents of the MS are largely astrological, indicating Nicholas's interest in that field, and that, whether he marked a turning point in the history of astronomy or not, he certainly marked none in the history of astrology.

it. It perhaps moves in a very small orbit as its position varies with that of the poles of the whole, but except for its revolving or spinning in two directions about its own center, it practically remains stationary at or near the center of the universe as in both the Ptolemaic and the Aristotelian hypotheses. In place of the almost inconceivably rapid revolution of the heavens in the space of twenty-four hours according to the Ptolemaic system, Nicholas substitutes a still more inconceivably rapid revolution in the space of twelve hours. But this was essential in view of his making the earth revolve in the same direction once in twenty-four hours. Ptolemy had given the simplest possible hypothesis to explain the appearances; Nicholas substitutes a complex and clumsier theory. It is misleading in describing Nicholas's theories to speak of a movement of the earth on its axis and another about the poles of the universe, since in his thought the earth's axis is the poles of the universe. There is, then, only a double motion of the earth, except in so far as the earth is affected by the lack of fixity in the position of the poles of the universe. The sun, like the other planets and heavens, goes round the earth, but does not quite get back to the same place in twenty-four hours. That is, it loses one day a year. The statement that the position of the fixed stars varies from the fixed pole about one degree in a hundred years was a commonplace of medieval astronomers. As for the sentence of which so much has been made by Cusa's eulogists, "I considered that the earth can not be fixed, but is moved, like the other stars," it evidently does not mean that the earth moves in every respect like the other stars — for fixed stars and planets themselves do not have a like motion — but only that the earth, as well as the stars, has a movement, or, more specifically, that, while the earth does *not* move as a planet, its position does vary a little like that of the fixed stars.

Vansteenberghe has already remarked that the explanations of astronomical phenomena given in this marginal note of Cusa's "are notoriously insufficient," and are in part a resuscitation of the Pythagorean astronomy. He thinks it possible that Nicholas may have rectified them in a treatise entitled *De figura mundi*, which was written at Orvieto towards the end of his life, but which does not seem to be extant and so presumably had little future influence, not to say little contemporary or intrinsic importance. Vansteenberghe also tells us where Nicholas's views as to the composition of the sun, to which Heller referred, are expressed.[9] They are set forth in a sermon of March 26, 1456! One has heard of sermons in stones, but to find the enunciation of a new astronomical doctrine in a sermon is a trifle startling. One does not quite know whether to recommend to investigators of the history of astronomy in the fifteenth century that they read all the sermons preserved from that period or not. It is even more startling to find that Nicholas of Cusa's so-called astronomical system has been constructed for him by his modern friends from the three quite incidental and scattered passages which we have indicated: namely, a few skeptical observations in his work, *On Learned Ignorance*, a few sentences scribbled on the flyleaf of a work by someone else which he had purchased, and the aforesaid sermon. It is by such faint suggestion that he has been represented as dealing a blow to the Ptolemaic and Aristotelian conceptions of the universe which made them reel on their foundations. It is by such slight leverage that he has been supposed to have effected a turning point in the history of astronomy. There is just one more thing to be said. At least three writers in the fourteenth century before Nicholas of Cusa was born — Franciscus de Mayronis, Albert of Saxony, and Nicolas Oresme — had suggested that it might be better to regard the eighth sphere of the fixed stars as immobile, and the earth as in motion.[10]

[9] *Op. cit.*, p. 246.

[10] Pierre Duhem, *Études sur Léonard de Vinci, ceux qu'il a lus et ceux qui l'ont lu*, Paris, Vol. III, 1913, pp. iii–xi, 29–43, 263, etc.

CHAPTER VIII

PEURBACH AND REGIOMONTANUS: THEIR GREAT REPUTATION RE-EXAMINED

Two mathematicians of the mid-fifteenth century, Georg von Peurbach (1423–61) and Regiomontanus (1436–76), have often been represented as reviving the study of mathematics after the dark ages or as marking the transition from medieval to modern mathematics and astronomy. The number of other prominent mathematicians and astronomers in the fourteenth and fifteenth centuries inclines us to question this old estimate, born of the old conception of a great contrast between middle ages and Renaissance. Let us examine briefly the careers and scientific accomplishments of the two men in order to see how they compare with their predecessors and contemporaries.

Both Peurbach and Regiomontanus died in the prime of life — the former at thirty-eight, the latter at forty years of age. Both came from German-speaking countries. Peurbach was an Austrian; Johann Müller derived his Latin name, Regiomontanus, from his native town of Königsberg in Franconia. They are to be further associated as master and disciple, and both lectured on various familiar Latin classics at about the same time in the University of Vienna. There Peurbach lectured on the *Aeneid* in 1454, Juvenal in 1456, Horace in 1458, and again on the *Aeneid* in 1460. Regiomontanus, who received his master's degree in 1457, lectured the year following on the subject of perspective and in 1460 on Euclid, but in 1461 discussed the *Bucolics* of Vergil.[1]

Besides being a professor at Vienna, Peurbach became astronomer, that is to say, astrologer, to King Ladislas of Hun-

[1] For these facts see Rudolf Kink, *Geschichte der Universität zu Wien*, 1854.

gary. He was also fortunate or attractive enough to become the protégé of two noted men of his time, Nicholas of Cusa and Bessarion. Peurbach's treatises were on familiar fields and subjects: another Theory of the Planets (*Theoricae novae planetarum*), an introductory work in trigonometry, an *Algorismus*. It is not surprising that none of them was printed until after his death, since during his brief lifetime the art of printing was still in its infancy. His works were not without their merits, but were the productions of a good teacher and popularizer rather than of an innovator, although we may think of him perhaps as introducing in Austria what had been public property in Italy, France, and England for a century past. Thus his trigonometry was based largely upon Ptolemy and an Arabic writer of the eleventh century; and he was not even reviving these authorities from medieval neglect, since Jean Fusoris, who died when Peurbach was only thirteen, had already drawn up similar tables of sines and chords,[2] to say nothing of the treatise of Richard of Wallingford almost a century earlier.[3] It very likely never occurred to Peurbach that his name would go down to posterity as the reviver of the mathematics of classical antiquity or as the reformer of the mathematics of his own time, since he had great esteem for his Italian contemporary in that field, Giovanni Bianchini (Ioannes Blanchinus) of Ferrara, who flourished from about 1436 to 1469.

In astronomy Peurbach attempted to reconcile the homocentric spheres of Aristotle with the epicycles and eccentrics of the Ptolemaic system by making them thick enough — for he appears to have thought of them as solid, as did many men of the fifteenth century — to include both the epicycles and eccentric orbits of their respective planets, and yet themselves

[2] P. Gassendi, *Tychonis Brahei equitis Dani astronomorum coryphaei vita. Accessit Nicolai Copernici, Georgii Peurbachii et Joannis Regiomontani astronomorum celebrium vita,* Parisiis, 1654, pp. 340–42.

[3] See the papers by J. D. Bond in *Isis,* Vol. IV, 1922, pp. 295–323, 459–65; and his edition of the Latin text with English translation in *Isis,* Vol. V, 1923, pp. 99–115, 339–63.

be concentric with respect to their inner and outer surfaces.[4] It does not seem that very much can be said for this "new theory of the planets." Peurbach further devised an astronomical or surveying instrument known as the *quadratum geometricum.*

Cardinal Bessarion had planned to translate anew directly from the Greek the *Almagest* of Ptolemy, not indeed for the first time,[5] but with the humanistic idea of avoiding medieval barbarisms and errors.[6] When the press of ecclesiastical and public business prevented him from pursuing this task, he turned the undertaking over to Peurbach. Therewith, however, was also introduced the idea of trying to improve upon the original Greek by making Ptolemy "briefer and clearer" (*breviorem lucidioremque*) in the new Latin version. Peurbach was able to finish only six books of the *Almagest* before his death and left the completion of the undertaking to Regiomontanus, who added seven more books, making thirteen in all. When this translation appeared in print in 1496, twenty years after the death of Regiomontanus, a contemporary, named Abiosus,[7] in an accompanying *Letter to the Investigators of the True Sciences*, also expressed the opinion that it was superior to

[4] Gassendi, *op. cit.*, pp. 343–44. In Appendix 16, I have discussed the similar theory of a John Tolhopf.

[5] The *Almagest* had been translated from the Arabic by Gerard of Cremona in 1175 and from the Greek in Sicily by an anonymous translator a little earlier.

[6] In the 1496 edition Regiomontanus complains of the previous translations of Ptolemy and of the "scabrositas librorum qui ex peregrinis linguis in latinum conversi . . . ," etc.

[7] Johannes Baptista Abiosus was a native of the Kingdom of Naples, a professor of mathematics, and a doctor of arts and medicine. He seems to have been much addicted to judicial astrology, and in 1492 addressed a dialogue in defense of it to Alfonso, King of Sicily, with predictions coming down as far as 1702: *Dialogus in defensionem astrologiae cum vaticinis a diluvio usque ad Christi annos 1702*, Venice, 1494. In the letter of 1496, which is referred to in our text, he expresses gratitude to the German people not only for its services to astronomy in the persons of Peurbach and Regiomontanus, but also for the invention of printing, which he hopes will preserve their works during a period of decline in the sciences which the stars decree for the years 1503 and 1524, so that they may not be lost to posterity.

Ptolemy "in clarity of the Latin tongue," that it covered all that Ptolemy had dealt with and further profited by later experience, and that in consequence one no longer needed to read Greek in order to understand astronomy or astrology. Such praises fail, however, to obscure the fact that the version of Peurbach and Regiomontanus was not a complete and exact translation of the Greek text but an epitome of it, the sort of work that has commonly been held a reproach to the early middle ages, but which we here find the classical renaissance glorying in.

After the early teaching at Vienna of which we have already spoken, Regiomontanus spent a few years in Italy, where he sometimes signed himself John the German (*Iohannes Germanus*). There he studied Greek, at first we are told with George of Trebizond,[8] whom he was later to criticize so violently. At Ferrara he profited by association with the Italian astronomer, Giovanni Bianchini, and the Greek scholars, Theodore Gaza and Guarino of Verona. In 1462 he made astronomical observations at Viterbo. In 1463 he accompanied Bessarion, who was on his way to Greece, as far as Venice. He remained some time in the north of Italy,[9] completing his work on triangles at Venice, lecturing on Alfraganus at Padua with an introductory oration on the history of mathematics,[10] and observing a total eclipse of the moon there on April 2, 1464. In the autumn of that year he returned to Rome just as the papal conclave was about to meet to elect a successor to Pius II, as he tells us in the preface to his *Tractatus contra Cremonensia*. At Rome he worked on the Epitome of the *Almagest* and published an abusive criticism of the commentaries upon Ptolemy and Theon by George of Trebizond, who had taken

[8] Moritz Cantor, *Vorlesungen über Geschichte der Mathematik*, Vol. II, 1892, p. 234.

[9] Among the letters of Regiomontanus published by Christopher Theophilus Murr, *Memorabilia bibliothecarum publicarum Norimbergensium et universitatis Altfordianae*, 1786, are some dated at Ferrara and Venice in 1463. There are others dated at Venice in 1464.

[10] It is summarized by Cantor, *op. cit.*, Vol. II, pp. 238–40.

opposite sides from Bessarion in the Plato-Aristotle controversy.

In 1467 we find Regiomontanus, as a professor of the recently authorized University of Pressburg, selecting a favorable astrological moment for its actual foundation.[11] In the same year was printed an astronomical and astrological work which he had dedicated to the archbishop of Strigonia or Gran.[12] Despite the astrological precautions which had been taken and the glorious future which the astrologers had promised, the university was not a lasting success. In 1468 Regiomontanus returned to Vienna, whence, however, he was soon summoned to the humanistic court of Matthias Corvinus of Hungary to arrange that monarch's collection of Greek manuscripts. In 1471 he took up his residence in Nürnberg, where a wealthy burgher, Bernhard Walther, became his pupil and patron and built a sort of laboratory for him. In 1475 he returned to Rome, whither Pope Sixtus IV had called him to advise him in regard to reform of the calendar. He was made bishop of Regensburg, but died at Rome on July 6, 1476, probably from a pestilence then raging in that city, although some said that he had been poisoned by the sons of George of Trebizond.[13]

[11] See the article on Hungarian universities in the middle ages by H. Schönebaum in *Archiv für Kulturgeschichte*, Vol. XVI, 1925, pp. 41–59. At page 55 we read, "In Gran versammelte er die Erwählten, liess dort von den Professoren Regiomontanus und Martin von Ilkusz der Neugründung das Horoskop stellen, das eine glänzende Zukunft weissagte. Wiener Stadtbibliothek, Pliniuskodex, beendet am 7. III. 1467: Figura coeli hora institutionis Universitatis Histropolitani."

Rashdall, *Universities of Europe in the Middle Ages*, Vol. II, p. 290, says: "Both the King and the Archbishop, who concurred in its foundation, were much given to judicial astrology, and such fame as the University acquired was due to the Astrological eminence of its masters."

[12] *Joannis de Monte Regio Tabulae directionum profectionumque tabulis instrumentisque innumeris fabricandis utiles ac necessariae.* J. B. J. Delambre, *Histoire de l'astronomie du moyen âge*, 1819, pp. 288–9, says of Regiomontanus's dedication to the archbishop, "Il le prie d'agréer ces prémices de ses travaux; il paraît donc que c'était son premier ouvrage." It would seem, however, that it was merely the first to be printed.

[13] Giuseppe Caraffa, *De gymnasio romano*, Rome, 1751, p. 277.

At his death Regiomontanus left a long list of books which he had already completed or was at work upon or intended to write, or to print for the first time.[14] These included editions or new translations of various mathematical classics, such as the works of Ptolemy, Euclid, Apollonius of Perga, Hyginus, and Theon, but likewise important medieval writings in mathematics and physics, such as the *Perspective* of Witelo, the *Arithmetic* of Jordanus, and the *Quadripartitum numerorum* of John of Meurs. Astrological treatises, both ancient and medieval, are also prominent in the list: for example, Ptolemy's *Quadripartitum* and the *Centiloquium* incorrectly ascribed to him, Julius Firmicus Maternus, and Leopold of Austria, who compiled an astrological collection before 1300. Regiomontanus's own writings were for the most part printed only after his death, when the aforesaid Walther kept his instruments and manuscripts, and were perhaps in some instances completed, added to, or otherwise altered by their later editors.[15] Johann Schoner (1477–1547) printed a number of them, notably his work on triangles or trigonometry in 1533, and Schoner's son, Andreas, continued to publish others as Regiomontanus's. His pupil and patron, Walther, made astronomical observations of his own which were utilized later by Copernicus and were spoken of highly by Tycho Brahe. He is also said to have been the first to take atmospheric refraction successfully into account, the first to use clocks worked by weights for scientific purposes, and the first to divide the day into equal hours (in 1488). But these assertions, particularly the last, sound rather dubious.

Meanwhile a Regiomontanus legend had been growing up. In the sixteenth century we find Peter Ramus, the celebrated adversary of Aristotle at Paris, ascribing even the invention of printing to him, and the construction of a mechanical fly which

[14] The list is reproduced by Gassendi, *op. cit.*, pp. 362–64.

[15] I have not had access to the article of H. Petz, "Urkundliche Nachrichten über den literarischen Nachlass Regiomontans und B. Walthers," *Mitteilungen des Vereins für Geschichte der Stadt Nürnberg*, Vol. VII, 1888, pp. 237–62.

would flutter about a banqueting hall and then return to the host's hand, and of a mechanical eagle which would fly to meet the emperor as he approached the city and accompany him back to its gates.[16] Ramus further asserted that the *Ephemerides* of Regiomontanus, first printed in 1474 during his lifetime, was something "new and hitherto unknown," but Cardan in the same century correctly noted that Regiomontanus was not the first to issue such almanacs. He also pointed out that the *Tabulae directionum* of Regiomontanus were largely drawn from Giovanni Bianchini, that the Epitome of the *Almagest* was indebted to a Milanese writer who lived before the birth of Peurbach, and that the work on plane and spherical triangles owed much to a Hebrew writer of Spain.

In more recent years Regiomontanus has been rather fancifully represented by an enthusiastic German admirer as a forerunner of Columbus.[17] It used to be stated that the Portuguese, in first venturing south of the equator along the coast of Africa, followed the tables of solar declination in the *Ephemerides* of Regiomontanus, until it was pointed out that the first editions thereof contained no such tables, for which the Portuguese would have looked rather to the *Almanach perpetuum* of Abraham Zacuto, composed first in Hebrew at Salamanca between 1473 and 1478.[18]

Over a century ago Delambre, in his *History of Astronomy in the Middle Ages*, as a result of a long, detailed examination of the mathematical writings of Regiomontanus, made decided strictures upon his importance as an original contributor in that field. While repeating without much enthusiasm the traditional estimate that Regiomontanus was "the most learned astronomer that Europe had yet produced," Delambre went on to say: "But if we except some observations and his trigonometrical works, we may say that he hardly had time to do more

[16] Gassendi, *op. cit.*, pp. 364–65.

[17] A. Ziegler, *Regiomontanus . . . Vorläufer des Columbus*, Dresden, 1874.

[18] Joaquim Bensaude, *Les légendes allemandes sur l'histoire des découvertes portugaises*, Geneva, 1920.

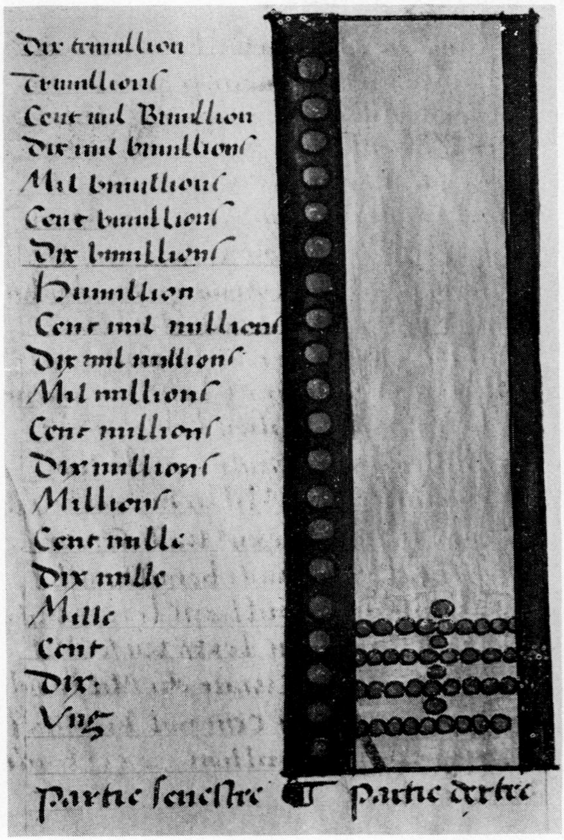

PLATE VII

RECKONING BY JETONS

From the Arithmetic of Jehan Adam, Ste Geneviève MS français 3143, fol. 7v

than show his good intentions. As an observer, he was certainly not superior to Albategni; as a calculator he was less advanced than Ibn Junis, still less than Abul Wefa. He did a useful thing in substituting a radius of 60,000 for the radius 60° 0′0″; he would have done still better to take one of 100,000."[19] Delambre further pointed out that, while Regiomontanus had the reputation of having introduced the use of tangents into astronomical calculations, he had merely recognized their utility as a subsidiary method in certain cases, but had failed to mention them in his work on plane and spherical triangles, and had employed neither tangents nor secants in solving any of the problems in his various works, but only sines and cosines like his predecessors.[20] Delambre also noted that it was surprising that the work on triangles was not printed until fifty-seven years after its author's death, if it was really so important.[21]

Braunmühl, in his more recent *History of Trigonometry*, grants that there is almost nothing original in the work on triangles, but maintains that it had the greatest influence upon the subsequent literature of the subject because by the time it was printed its sources and forerunners had been forgotten.[22] If this be the case, it would seem that Braunmühl should not have headed this section of his *History* "Die Wiedergeburt der Wissenschaften in Europa," but rather, "Die Vergessenheit der Wissenschaften in Europa."

It is not to be denied that Peurbach and Regiomontanus were active, distinguished, and influential mathematicians and astronomers, especially in view of the short spans of their lives, but it certainly seems that their importance has been exaggerated at the expense of the preceding period and their own contemporaries. For this several explanations may be offered. One is the ignorance or underestimate of the learning

[19] J. B. J. Delambre, *Histoire de l'astronomie au moyen âge*, 1819, p. 365.

[20] *Ibid.*, p. 292, *et seq.*

[21] *Ibid.*, p. 347.

[22] A. von Braunmühl, *Vorlesungen über Geschichte der Trigonometrie*, 2 vols., 1900, 1903; see Vol. I, pp. 124–25.

of the preceding medieval period which has hitherto been too prevalent, and the ignorance more particularly of their debt to and use of preceding medieval authors, although this becomes clear enough upon examination. Their fame may further be ascribed to their connection with cardinals like Cusa and Bessarion, and to Regiomontanus's rich patron, Bernhard Walther, who continued his work at Nürnberg; to their alliance of mathematics with the humanistic movement and especially with the revival of Greek, which made their work more acceptable to subsequent generations accustomed to measure everything by the hypothesis of an Italian Renaissance and revival of learning; and to their coming at just the right moment to take advantage of the printing press and to be practically the first published contemporary mathematicians. Indeed, Regiomontanus and his successors were more than this: they were mathematical publishers. Finally, since Peurbach and Regiomontanus were Austrian and German, their work has received rather undue emphasis from modern German historical scholarship, whereas until recent years the English, French, Italian and Spanish mathematicians of the fourteenth and fifteenth centuries have been less studied and written about.

CHAPTER IX

THE ARITHMETIC OF JEHAN ADAM, A.D. 1475 [1]

In a manuscript of the later fifteenth century in the Bibliothèque Sainte Geneviève, Paris, is an arithmetic in French.[2]

[1] Revised and enlarged from *The American Mathematical Monthly*, Vol. XXXIII, 1926, pp. 24–28.

[2] Ste Geneviève MS français 3143. It consists of seventy-five small leaves of membrane, preceded and followed by two flyleaves of paper. At the top of fol. 1r is written, "Ex libris S. Seuourin Parisiensi, 1753," and at the bottom of the same page, "Des livres de Nicolas Moreau s' D'auteuil a Lami Son Coeur." On fol. 75r, below the last six lines of text, is written vertically across the rest of the page, "De M. Moreau Sr. D'auteuil . . ." and another word which I could not decipher. From this we may infer that before 1753 the MS was in the possession of the church of St. Séverin, and that it then passed into the hands of Jacob Nicolas Moreau, Seigneur d'Auteuil (1717–1805), author and historiographer of France, who gave it to Giovanni Lami, librarian of the Riccardian library in Florence, author of a catalogue of its manuscript collection published in 1756, and of *Lezioni di antichità*, 1766.

An item in the 1898 sales catalogue of the library of Prince Boncompagni indicates that he had somehow come into possession of a recent copy or facsimile of the work of Jehan Adam. This copy was apparently made from our Sainte Geneviève MS, but the sales catalogue states that Boncompagni had asked Marre to search for the original MS in the Bibliothèque Nationale and other libraries of Paris, and that he had failed to locate it. It is nevertheless duly listed in Ch. Kohler's *Catalogue des manuscrits de la Bibliothèque de Ste Geneviève*, published in 1893. The following is the notice in the *Catalogo della Biblioteca Boncompagni*, Parte Prima, Roma, 1898, p. 94: "499. Adam Iehan. Traicté d'arismetique pour la pratique par gectouers [*sic*] faite et compillé a Paris en lan mil 475, della Biobl. [*sic*] di 79 carte membranacee, salvo le prime due e le due ultime che sono cartacee. Scritto nel sec. xix. Facsimile, con grande accuratezza eseguito, con iniziali e figure a oro e colori e titoli rubricati. Il Princ. Boncompagni, avendo pregato il Sig. Marre di ricercare se l'originale del detto trattato di Jehan Adam si trovasse nella biblioteca Nazionale od in altra di Parigi, egli gli fece sapere che ogni ricerca in proposito riuscì infruttuosa."

Louis Thuasne, *Roberti Gaguini Epistole et Orationes*, Vol. I, 1904, pp. 215–16, note 11, knew of this MS in the Boncompagni collection, apparently through the second edition of Enrico Narducci, *Catalogo di manoscritti ora posseduti da*

Both its text and its author appear to have passed hitherto unnoted in works upon the history of mathematics. Yet it seems to contain an earlier example of numeration carried as far as trillions than has hitherto been recorded.[3] It was composed in the year 1475. As the introductory epistle at the beginning of the manuscript states, the author is Jehan Adam, who was secretary to Nicolle Tilhart,[4] who in his turn was notary, secretary, and auditor of accounts [5] to Louis XI, king of France from 1461 to 1483. That monarch more than once figures in the examples given in our text. Thus under "Addition" we are told, "le Roy donne a mons^{r} Lepaunetier IIII^{m}V^{c}XXIII, a mons^{r} Leschaconn II^{m}III^{c}XLI l't', a mons^{r} Lesciuer III^{m}II^{c}XXIII l'r', a mons^{r} le maître doustel XIII^{c}XLII l't' . . ." ("The king gives Monsieur Lepaunetier 4,523 livres, M. Leschaconn 2,341, M. Lesciver 3,223, Master Doustel

B. Boncompagni, Rome, 1892, numero 603, which he cites. I do not understand why he says further: "C'est un *Traicté d'Arismetrique pour la pratique par gectouers faite et compillé a Paris en l'an mil* 475, en 1484, selon Aristide Marre, *Bullettino di Bibliografia e di Storia delle scienze matematiche e fisiche, pubblicato da B. Boncompagni*, Rome, XIII (1880), 363." This page reference does not apply to Marre's article, which occurs at pp. 555–92 and mentions neither Jehan Adam nor our MS. As Carrière (see note 4 below), who accepted Thuasne's assertion that Marre dated Jehan Adam's treatise in 1484, has pointed out, that date is inadmissible, since Tilhart, to whom the work is addressed, was then no longer living.

[3] The earliest example hitherto known appears to have been in the *Triparty* of Nicolas Chuquet, a bachelor of medicine in Paris, dated 1484 at Lyons.

See Aristide Marre, "Notice sur Nicolas Chuquet et son Triparty en la science des nombres" in Boncompagni's *Bullettino di bibliografia e di storia delle scienze matematiche e fisiche*, Tomo XIII, 1880, pp. 555–92, followed at p. 593 *et seq.* by Chuquet's text. I owe this reference and other helpful suggestions to the kindness of Professor David Eugene Smith. Chuquet carried the nomenclature on beyond trillion and quadrillion to *nonyllion*, as the form is given in the printed text, or *nouyllion* (or, *novyllion*) as I read it in the facsimile of the manuscript (Paris, Bibliothèque Nationale, MS Français 1346; once Codex Colbert 2170, Regius 7483) in Professor Smith's library. Neither Chuquet nor his modern editor mentions the arithmetic of our Jehan Adam, which is earlier by nine years.

[4] On the career and upright character of Tilhart see V. Carrière, "Nicole Tilhart," *Le moyen âge*, 1905, p. 175 *et seq.*

[5] These offices are ascribed to him at the beginning of our MS.

1,342").[6] Or in the first example of halving (*Mediacion*) we read, "The king gives the half of 51,607 livres to Monsieur de Bourbon, that is, 25,803 livres, 10 sous."[7] Thuasne suggested the possible identity of our Jehan Adam with one of the secretaries, in 1467–68, of Charles, duke of Normandy, brother of Louis XI.[8]

Our arithmetic is of the abacus type, reckoning by *jetons* or counters.[9] This word is variously spelled in our manuscript, and it is sometimes difficult to distinguish letters. Besides *gecton*, *gectoners* or *gectouers*,[10] such forms as *gect*,[11] *greton*,[12]

[6] Ste Geneviève MS français 3143, fol. 9v. Henceforth I shall cite this MS simply by folio. The abbreviations probably stand for "livres tournois."

[7] Fol. 5r: "Mediacion est assavoir combien monte la moictie dun nombir proposi Exemple Le Roy donne la moitie de li^m^vi^c^vii l. [i.e., the sign for livres] a mons^r^ de Bourbon cest xxv^m^ huic cens troys livres dix sols. . . ."

[8] Thuasne, *op. cit.*, Vol. I, p. 216: "J'ignore si Jehan Adam est le même qui figure parmi les secrétaires de Charles, duc de Normandie, frère de Louis XI, sur le registre des comptes de son hôtel. Bibl. nat. fr. 21477, fol. 28, 36, 48 (années 1467–1468)."

[9] See E. Littré, *Dictionnaire*, 1869: "Les jetons se réduisent à une échelle dont les puissances successives au lieu de se placer de droite à gauche comme dans l'arithmétique ordinaire se mettent du bas en haut chacune dans une ligne où il faut autant de jetons qu'il y a d'unités dans les coefficients." Littré cites Buffon, *Ess. arithm.* (*Œuvres*, Vol. X, p. 178).

More recently the whole matter of these *jetons* or *jettons* has been the subject of elaborate treatment with handsome plates by Francis Pierrepont Barnard, *The Casting-Counter and the Counter-Board*, Oxford, Clarendon Press, 1916, 358 pp., lxiii Pl. For briefer accounts, with especial reference to early printed arithmetics and the history of mathematics, see David Eugene Smith, *Computing Jetons*, The American Numismatic Society, New York, 1921; and the same author's recent *History of Mathematics*, 1924, Vol. II, Chapter 3.

[10] See the rubrics at fol. 4r and fol. 20v: fol. 4r, "arismeticque pour la praticque par gectoners"; fol. 20v, "Septiesme et darnier espece darismeticque par gectoners." Littré, *op. cit.*, cites De Laborde, *Emaux*, p. 328, for the form *gectons* in the fourteenth century, "Gectons de la chambre des comptes de Monseigneur le duc d'Orléans." *Gecton* also occurs among some fifty forms of the word in French which Professor Barnard lists at pp. 26–27, but neither of our forms, *gectoners* or *greton*, is among them. Possibly in the two passages quoted *gectoners* may denote those who make use of the counters or *gectons*.

[11] Fol. 8v: "Touteffois deves savoir que ung gect mis en lespace . . ."

[12] Fol. 7r: "Item noctes que le premier greton [or perhaps, *gecton*] dembas vault ung."

gectoer,[13] and *gretouer*[14] also occur. Jehan Adam, however, although he still usually employs the Roman numerals, was acquainted with the Hindu-Arabic numerals. At fol. 9r he writes them out as far as 100, then by hundreds up to one thousand,[15] "2000, 8000,[16] etc. Et ainsi jusques infini en assemblent les nombres digitz articulz."

Our arithmetic is the only, or at least the chief, treatise in the manuscript, which is a small illuminated codex with seventy-five leaves of text in all. The writing is in a fairly large hand, so that there is not very much text per page. The spelling of the Old French is at times difficult to decipher. Illuminated figures to illustrate graphically the sums and calculations of the text also occupy some of the space. None occurs, however, between fol. 33r and fol. 60r inclusive, although connecting colored lines are drawn to indicate the division of a sum into different portions, while at fols. 41v, 42v, 43v, 47v, 48v and 58v there are rude diagrams. The manuscript has been incorrectly bound so that the leaf now numbered fol. 5r–v and devoted to the topics of "Halving" and "Doubling" should be transposed with the leaf now numbered fol. 13r–v, which continues the opening chapter of the text proper begun on fol. 4v. Furthermore the present fols. 10 and 18 should be similarly interchanged. At fol. 63r this main body of text proper ends after three lines at the top of the page. Most of the page is then left blank until, near the bottom of the page, comes the rubric, "Conclusion et fin de ce present traicte en continuant lespitre escripte au commencement dicelluy." That is to say, the author here resumes the epistle with which he opened his work at fols. 1–4. His devout conclusion terminates at fol. 66r with the words, " . . . . a laquelle nous puissons tous venir a la reste de nos jours. Amen." This Explicit, as it would seem, is

[13] Fol. 8v: "... cinq gectoers en la ligne de dessoubz soy"; fol. 9v: "... se abrege lesd' gectoers."

[14] Fol. 35r, lines 8–9.

[15] By a slip 600 is written twice.

[16] Our author employs the old characters, 8, ҷ, and ʌ, for four, five, and seven respectively.

then followed at fols. 66v–69v by a table of contents. The manuscript, however, does not end there, but, with a "Regle pour faire une taille de Monnoye," and further text and headings dealing with the minting of coins,[17] goes on to fol. 75r. If these additions are not by Jehan Adam, they are very similar in character to his work.

Jehan Adam divides arithmetic into nine parts: numeration, addition, subtraction, halving, duplication, multiplication, division, progression, and extraction of roots.[18] He states, however, that in this present treatise he will treat of only seven of these parts, leaving progressions and the extraction of square and cube roots to another treatise.[19] Whether it is in existence or was ever written by him I do not know. He is aware, moreover, that arithmetic may be subdivided differently. Thus Master Bartholomew of Roumanis (or Romains?), professor of Holy Scripture, makes but five parts of arithmetic, namely, addition, subtraction, multiplication, division, and extraction of roots. And it is true that halving is simply dividing by two, and that doubling is simply multiplying by two, while progression may be explained as addition. Division is of two sorts, "*simple et miste.*"[20]

The most interesting and novel feature of Jehan Adam's work is the paragraph and the illuminated figure in his section on "Numeration" which he devotes to the twenty decimal numbers from one to ten trillions (*dix trimillions*).[21] These are

[17] Fol. 71r: "Le Regisme de faire ung deneral"; fol. 72r: "Le Regisme que enseigne de faire une loy"; fol. 72v: "La seconde Regle"; fol. 73r: "Le Regisme qui enseigne de faire une mise de Monnoye"; fol. 73v: "Le 2° Regle"; fol. 74v: "Regime pour sauoir que le seigneur tire de sol de fin ou de march dargent."

[18] Fol. 13r: "Et est assavoir que en arismeticque sont ix especes Numeracion Addiction Substraction meditacion dupplacion Multiplicacion division progression Extraction de Radices.

[19] Fol. 4r.

[20] Fol. 21v. The treatment of simple division continues to fol. 28v; then follow mixed division and the rule of three. "En division mixte la regle de trois est la forme a laquelle toute subtille question se doit reduire tant per nombre roupt que autier (or, *aultre*)."

[21] The text occurs at fol. 7r; the illumination on fol. 7v.

represented in the figure by as many counters (*jetons*), balls, or circles, superimposed one above another as if on an abacus, and with only one ball or counter for each denomination. Instead of "billion" Jehan writes *bymillion*, and instead of "trillion," *trimillion*.[22] He quotes the Latin verses of Alexander of Villa Dei[23] which enumerate up to ten figures (1,000,000,000), but then he goes on by himself to the twentieth figure or *dix trimillions* (10,000,000,000,000,000,000). Explaining the illumination, he says: "Also note that the first counter from the bottom stands for one, the second stands for ten, the third above the second stands for one hundred, the fourth stands for one thousand, the fifth stands for ten thousand, the sixth stands for one hundred thousand, the seventh stands for a million, the eighth stands for ten millions, the ninth stands for one hundred millions, the tenth stands for one thousand millions, the eleventh for ten thousand millions, the twelfth for one hundred thousand millions, the thirteenth for a billion, the fourteenth for ten billions, the fifteenth for a hundred (thousand) [24]

[22] Chuquet, on the other hand, spells the words in question "byllion" and tryllion."

[23] Fol. 8v: Unum prima, secunda decem, dat tercia centum,
Quarta dabit mille, millia quinta decem,
Centum mille sexta dat, septima millia mille,
Mille dat octava millesies decies,
Centesies nova dat millesies quoque mille,
Millesies mille millesies decima,
Sic per millarium centenum denariumque.

These lines do not occur, however, in the version of the *Carmen de Algorismo* of Alexander of Villa Dei published in J. O. Halliwell's *Rara Mathematica*, 1841, pp. 73–83.

[24] "cent mil bymillions" is evidently a slip for "cent bymillions." The French text of the passage reads: "Item noctes que le premier greton dembas vault Ung, Le second vault dix. Le tiers dessus le second vault cent, le quart vault mille, le Ve vault dix M, le VIe vault cent M, le VIIe vault Milion, Le VIIIe vault dix Million, Le IXe vault cent Millions, Le Xe vault Mil Millions, Le XIe vault dix mil Millions, Le XIIe vault Cent mil Millions, Le XIIIe vault bymillion, Le XIIIIe vault dix bymillions, Le XVe vault cent [mil] bymillions, Le XVIe vault mil bymillions, Le XVIIe vault dix Mil bymillions, Le XVIIIe vault cent mil bymillions, Le XIXe vault trimillion, Le XXe vault dix trimillions."

billions, the sixteenth for a thousand billions, the seventeenth for ten thousand billions, the eighteenth for a hundred thousand billions, the nineteenth stands for a trillion, the twentieth for ten trillions."

Jehan Adam makes one or two brief incursions into the history of arithmetic. He has several suggestions to make as to the etymology of the word.[25] Arithmetic he derives from the Greek, *Ares*, meaning virtue, and from the Greek word for number. But the art is also called "Algorismus," from the Arabic, meaning an introduction to numbers, and this word may come from *Algos*, the name of the Arabic inventor of the art, and *richmos*, a Chaldean word for number, or perhaps from the Greek *al*, equivalent to the Latin *in*, and *gogos*, equivalent to *dictio*. In another passage, besides "the noble philosopher, Algus" (Jehan seems to have no preference as between the Latin and Greek forms of proper names), "the inventor and first compiler" of arithmetic, are listed Aristotle, Plato, Pythagoras, Isidore, Boethius, Albert, Alexander of Villa Dei, Masters Bartholomew des Roumanis, John of Sacrobosco, Johannes de Lineriis, Jean de Meun,[26] and Jehan Loquemeren, as past masters of the art.[27]

The problems of our arithmetic range from such simple ones as to multiply 2,321 by xxiiii,[28] or, "If 12 ells of cloth are worth 34 livres, how much will 26 ells be worth,"[29] to more complicated problems concerning the division of profits among merchants forming a partnership or company and contributing different amounts of capital,[30] or even investing different sums for different periods of time,[31] or "touching a serpentine con-

[25] Fol. 4v. These suggestions were not original with him.

[26] One might expect mention of John of Meurs (Johannes de Muris) rather than of the second author of *The Romance of the Rose* in a list of arithmeticians, but Iehan de Mehung seems unmistakably to denote the latter.

[27] Fols. 2v–3r: "Et depuis Aristote platon pitagoras ysodore Boisse Alebert Alixandre de Villedieu Maistres bartholomieux des Roumanis Iehan de sacro bosco Iehan de Ligneriis Iehan de Mehung et Iehan Loquemeren en ont si bien et souverament traicte que nulle Reprehencion ny doit estre faicte."

[28] Fol. 16v. [29] Fol. 30v. [30] Fol. 33v. [31] Fol. 42v.

cerning which the King wants to know the quantity of each metal that will be in one of the broken pieces."[32] We also have "Rules" for overcharge and annulments (? *recindemens*),[33] for recovery of annulments,[34] for equal and mixed proportion,[35] for fractions[36] — as to divide a sum in ratios of 1/2, 1/3, and 1/4, or 1/3, 1/4, 1/5, and 1/6 — and for alloying money.[37]

One problem is concerned with a point of Roman law. A dying man, whose wife is about to lie in, makes a will[38] to this effect: If the child is a boy, he shall receive two-thirds of the property and the mother one-third. If the child is a girl, she shall have one-third and the mother receive two-thirds. The posthumous birth turns out to be twins, a son and a daughter, and the problem is to divide an estate of one thousand crowns between them and the mother. According to the rubric in the Digest beginning, *De liberis et postumis*, near the law *Gallus*,[39] the daughter receives one part, the mother two parts, and the son four parts.

Jehan Adam has ten "general rules" for fractions, namely: (1) to reduce two fractions to a common denominator; (2) to reduce three or more fractions to a common demoninator;

[32] Fol. 41r.

[33] Fol. 36r, rubric: "Regle de trop charge et Recindemens."

[34] Fol. 38v, rubric: "Aultre Regle et maniere de Repprendre les Recindemens."

[35] Fols. 44v–45r.

[36] Fol. 46r *et seq.*

[37] Fol. 59v, rubric: "Regle pour aloyer monnoye avecques aultre monnoye."

[38] Fol. 44r: "Regle ung homme gisant en larticle de mort fait son testament et cognoist que sa femme est preste a coucher. Parquoy il ordonne que se ainsi . . ."

[39] *Idem.* ". . . livre de digestis en la Rubrique qui commence de liberis et postumis pres de la loy gallus." The same problem, but without allusion to works of Roman law and with the sum to be divided 100 florins, occurs in a lecture on arithmetic or, more particularly, the rule of three, delivered by Gottfried Wolack at Erfurt in 1467–68, contained in a Dresden MS (C. 80, fols. 301–3) and published by E. Wappler in *Zeitschrift für Mathematik und Physik*, Vol. XLV, 1900, Historisch-litterarische Abteilung, pp. 47–56.

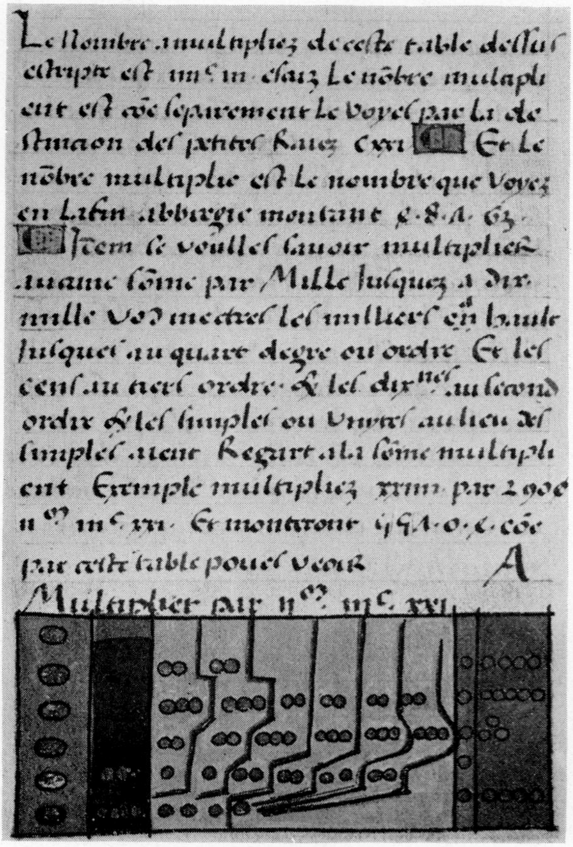
Le nombre a multipliez de ceste table dessus
escripte est iiiᶜ iii escuz Le nõbre multipli
ant est cõe separement le voyes par la de
stinacion des petites barres cxvi Et le
nõbre multiplie est le nombre que voyez
en latin abbregie montant [illegible]
Item se voulles savoir multiplier
aucune sõme par Mille jusquez a dix
mille vous mectrez les milliers en haulte
jusques au quart degre ou ordre Et les
cens au tiers ordre & les dixaines au second
ordre & les simples ou unites au lieu des
simples avent Regart a la sõme multipli
ent Exemple multipliez xxiiii par 2906
iiᵐ iiiᶜ xvi Et montront [illegible] cõe
par ceste table povez veoir
A
Multiplier par iiᵐ iiiᶜ xvi

Plate VIII

Multiplication

From the Arithmetic of Jehan Adam, Ste Geneviève MS français 3143, fol. 16v

(3) to reduce a whole number and a fraction to a common denominator; (4) to reduce a number over one to a whole number and a fraction; (5) to subtract one fraction from another; (6) to halve a fraction; (7) to double a fraction; (8) to multiply fractions; (9) to divide fractions; (10) to divide a whole number and a fraction by another whole number and a fraction.[40] In order to provide the reader with a completer survey of what is in the book, I reproduce in Appendix 17 its table of contents in the original French with an English translation.

It is interesting to associate this arithmetic of Jehan Adam, composed in 1475, with the important *Triparty* of Nicolas Chuquet, finished in 1484. Both works were thus composed within a decade of each other, both were written in French and by authors intimately connected with Paris, and they are the first two works known to employ the terms, billion and trillion. There is another similarity and sign of close connection between them. The master Bartholomew "des Romanis" or "des Roumanis," whom Jehan Adam mentioned at least twice, is also cited and a passage from his work criticized in the appendix to Chuquet's *Triparty*, where he is called '*maistre berthelemy de rōmans*, formerly of the Order of Friars Preachers at Valence and doctor in theology.'[41] Similarly Jehan Adam spoke of him as "*professeur en la saincte escripture*." What was the debt of our two authors to this Bartholomew, and can his own work be recovered?

Poinsignon in his *History of Champagne* has noted that arithmetic was still taught by the method of counters in the schools there in the late sixteenth century.[42] A manuscript at Arras in Artois contains an arithmetic "par l'arbre de grand gect" from St. Vaast, composed by Maistre Jacques de Cœulle

[40] These "rules" for fractions occupy fols. 47v–50v.

[41] Aristide Marre, "Appendice au Triparty en la science des nombres de Nicolas Chuquet Parisien," in Boncompagni's *Bulletino di bibliografia e di storia delle scienze matematiche e fisiche*, Tomo XIV, 1881, pp. 415–16 and 442.

[42] Maurice Poinsignon, *Histoire générale de la Champagne et de la Brie*, Vol. II, 1885, p. 396.

of Hesdin and copied in 1601 by Maximilian de Citey.[43] It opens:

> Lire convient et en lisant entendre,
> Et de faisant par les getz praticquier;
> Par ce moyen porez le tout comprendre,
> Aux ignorans après communiquer.

[43] Arras 145, 34 fols.

CHAPTER X

NICCOLÒ DA FOLIGNO'S TREATISES ON IDEAS: A STUDY OF SCHOLASTICISM AND PLATONISM IN THE FIFTEENTH CENTURY

Niccolò da Foligno or Nicholas of Foligno (Nicolaus Fulginas or, de Fulgineo) has been a fairly well known personage of the fifteenth century, mentioned by such historians of literature and learning as Fabruccius,[1] Fabroni,[2] Vermiglioli,[3] Fiorentino,[4] Della Torre,[5] and Viviani,[6] although not sufficiently well known to have been included in Fabricius's eighteenth-century bibliography of medieval Latin literature. He is commonly referred to in such accounts under the name Nicolaus Tignosius Fulginas, although this middle or family name is not used in the manuscripts of works by him which I have examined. But an inscription on marble placed by his son, Cyrus Marius, in the pavement of a Franciscan monastery outside one of the gates of the city of Pisa to a person of that name describes him as a noted physician, philosopher, and commentator on Aristotle, who had been given the citizenship of Arezzo, and states that he died on September 14, 1474, at the age of

[1] *Opuscula collecta ab Angelo Calogerà* (or, *Raccolta d'opuscoli*, etc.), 1741, Tom. XXXVII, Opusc. vi, p. 54, Stephanus Fabruccius, "Recensio notabilium conductionum."

[2] Angelo Fabroni, *Historia Academiae Pisanae*, Vol. I, 1791, pp. 285–86.

[3] G. B. Vermiglioli, *Bibliografia storico-perugina*, 1823. But he is not mentioned in the same author's later *Biografia degli scrittori perugini e notizie delle opere loro*, 2 vols., 1828–29.

[4] Francesco Fiorentino, *Il risorgimento filosofico nel Quattrocento*, Naples, 1885, p. 250, note 28, where he refers to one of the MSS we are to consider, namely, Laurent. Plut. 82, cod. 22.

[5] Arnaldo Della Torre, *Storia dell' Accademia Platonica di Firenze*, Florence, Carnesecchi, 1902; see pp. 495–500.

[6] Ugo Viviani, *Medici fisici e cerusici della provincia Aretina vissuti dal V al XVII secolo*, 1923, pp. 86–88.

seventy-two while lecturing at the University of Pisa.[7] This description seems to fit our man, and indicates that he was born in 1402. He is to be distinguished from the artist, Alunno, also called Niccolò de Foligno, who was born somewhat later.

The faculty lists or rolls of the University of Bologna attest that a master Nicholas, son of James of Foligno, was appointed to teach logic during the academic year 1426–27.[8] He is not called Tignosius in the *Rotuli*, but inasmuch as young men commonly taught logic at Bologna soon after receiving their degree in arts, this date would fit well with 1402 as his year of birth. Accordingly Della Torre and Viviani identify Niccolò de Giacomo and Tignosi, as did Fabroni in 1791,[9] and Bandini in 1775.[10] Niccolò Tignosi would appear next in Perugia, if Vermiglioli were correct in dating not later than 1429 a work which Niccolò wrote from Perugia "To the most illustrious Giovanni de' Medici concerning the praises of his father, Cosimo . . ."[11] But I suspect that Vermiglioli thoughtlessly confused Giovanni, the father of Cosimo, with Giovanni, the son of Cosimo, and hence concluded that the

[7] The Latin text of the inscription is reproduced as follows by A. M. Bandini, *Catalogus codicum Latinorum bibliothecae Laurentianae*, Vol. II, 1775, p. 460; Fabroni, Vol. I, p. 286; etc.: "D. Nicolao Tignosio Fulginati medico insigni, omniumque sui temporis philosophorum inter clariores enumerando, ac multorum Aristotelis librorum commentatori acutissimo, Cyrus Marius pientissimus filius patri optimo, et suis miris virtutibus civitate Arretina donato posuit. Vix. an. lxxii, mens. v, d. xv. Decessit cum Pisis legeret xviii kal. octob. MCCCCLXXIIII."

Iacobilli, *Bibliotheca Umbriae*, Foligno, 1658, incorrectly gave the date of Niccolò's death as 1484.

[8] Umberto Dallari, *I rotuli dei lettori legisti e artisti dello Studio bolognese dal* 1384 *al* 1799, Bologna, Vol. IV, 1919, p. 53.

[9] Page 285: ". . . Nicolaum Tignosium Jacobi Fulginatis eximia virtute et doctrina viri filium."

[10] Vol. II, p. 460.

[11] There are two MSS of it in the Laurentian Library: Plut. 53, cod. 11, fols. 42–60; and Plut. 54, cod. 10, fols. 60v–73. For fuller description of them see Bandini, *op. cit.*, Vol. II, pp. 607, 646. Vermiglioli noted only the second, of which he gave a somewhat fuller description than Bandini had done. Both MSS were noted earlier by L. Mehus, *Ambrosii Traversarii vita*, Florence, 1759, p. lxxiii.

treatise must have been written before the death of the elder Giovanni in 1429. Since John, the son of Cosimo, did not die until 1461,[12] we have a much greater latitude for dating the work, while, since John was born in 1419, it is hardly probable that Niccolò would have addressed such a work to him until considerably later than 1429, when John would have been only ten years old and his father would have been less likely to be the recipient of praises than later when in full power. Indeed, the Monastery of San Marco with its library, which is one of the things for which Cosimo is praised in the eulogy, was not built until 1437–43. A manuscript of Lactantius in the Medicean Library is a copy made for John in 1458.[13]

Whenever it was that Niccolò da Foligno was at Perugia, he is further said to have taught there and to have been sent as ambassador for that city to Florence. The memorial inscription concerning him, it will be recalled, stated that he had been given the citizenship at Arezzo, which Fabroni says he won by his successful practice of medicine there. This residence would presumably come between his teaching logic at Bologna and writing his eulogy of Cosimo de' Medici at Perugia. Bandini stated that he began in 1451 to teach medicine publicly in Florence, but the university's records show that he was engaged in 1439 to teach the theory of medicine there.[14] He is one of the interlocutors in Poggio's *Historia tripartita*,[15] written in 1450, which would suggest that he was well known in humanist circles, and is represented as physician to Pope Nicholas V. Niccolò, as the inscription informed us, was a philosopher and commentator on Aristotle as well as a medical man. Della Torre even went so far as to call him "aristotelico intransigente,"[16] but this appears inaccurate in view of his favorable attitude to the Platonic ideas. He had already written commentaries on the *Ethics* of Aristotle under Cosimo, since he

[12] Wm. Roscoe, *Life of Lorenzo de' Medici*, London, 1846, p. 23.

[13] Laurent. Plut. 21, cod. 2: see Bandini, Vol. I, p. 663.

[14] A. Gherardi, *Statuti della università e studio fiorentino*, 1881, p. 444.

[15] Poggio Bracciolini, *Opera*, 1513, fol. 14r.

[16] *Op. cit.*, p. 499.

addressed to him a reply to those who had criticized these commentaries.[17] But the two copies of Niccolò's commentaries on the *Ethics* which are preserved in the Laurentian Library are both addressed to Piero de' Medici.[18] Possibly they represent a later recension. When Piero was succeeded by his son, Lorenzo the Magnificent, in 1469, Niccolò was already well along in years. Three years later, however, when Lorenzo restored the University of Pisa, he made Niccolò one of the professors there, and was thanked by him for this in a commentary on Aristotle's *De anima* which Niccolò addressed to Lorenzo.[19] It was probably previous to this that he dedicated to Lorenzo a discussion of Platonic ideas of which we shall have more to say presently.[20] Niccolò was furthermore something of a historian, penning an account of the origins of his native town, Foligno, if Viviani is correct in ascribing such a work to him.[21]

All the works by Niccolò thus far mentioned, except the last, are preserved in the Medicean-Laurentian Library, were listed in the eighteenth-century manuscript catalogues of Montfaucon [22] and Bandini, and have been occasionally referred to by authors since, although few or none have probably really read any of them, and only one of them appears ever to have been printed. But in the manuscript collections of the Vatican Library is preserved another discussion of Platonic ideas which is not identical with that addressed to Lorenzo de' Medici and

[17] Laurent. Plut. 48, cod. 37 (Montfaucon 31), 15th century; Bandini, Vol. II, p. 459, gives the headings of the twelve chapters. Viviani notes the treatise, but incorrectly lists it as Plut. 76, cod. 43.

[18] Laurent. Plut. 76, cod. 43 (Montfaucon 38), 15th century, 233 fols.; Plut. 76, cod. 44 (Montfaucon 39), 198 fols; see Bandini, Vol. III, pp. 118–19.

[19] Laurent. Plut. 82, cod. 17 (Montfaucon 11), 15th century, 253 fols. It was printed in 1551 by Laurentius Torrentinus, the ducal typographer.

[20] Laurent. Plut. 82, cod. 22 (Montfaucon 14), 15th century, 47 fols.

[21] *De origine Fulginatium:* Bibl. Vittorio Emanuele, Roma, cod. II; Bibl. Sem. Foligno, cod. A. II. 5. Viviani also attributes a treatise on those who are born in the eighth month to Niccolò, citing Vatic. Lat. 3897, "De illis qui octavo mense nascentur." But as we shall see, while that MS does contain a treatise by Niccolò da Foligno, it is on quite a different subject.

[22] Bernard de Montfaucon, *Bibliotheca bibliothecarum manuscriptorum nova*, Paris, 1739.

was not addressed to any member of the Medici family. It seems not to have been noticed by those who have treated of or touched upon Niccolò and his works heretofore, except that Della Torre briefly alluded to it, giving an imperfect form of its title,[23] while Viviani gave the number of the manuscript but represented it as containing a treatise by Niccolò on another subject, the astrological-medical theme of babes born in the eighth month. It is this treatise on ideas, together with that to Lorenzo on the same subject, which will occupy our attention in the present chapter, and of which I publish in appendices the Latin texts as specimens of the scholastic Platonism or Platonic, or pseudo-Platonic, scholasticism of the Italy of the Quattrocento and so-called Renaissance, of the Medicean milieu, of Umbria and Tuscany — "that province," as Fabroni pretentiously termed it, "in which philosophy itself seemed to have set up its tabernacle."[24]

This new or second treatise on ideas, if I may so call it in distinction from the work on the same theme to Lorenzo, occupies a little over seven double-columned leaves in the Vatican manuscript.[25] Each column averages about forty lines in length. It was originally an independent manuscript numbered 377, but has been bound up with other works, chiefly of the sixteenth century, with which it has no connection, and of which the first was formerly numbered 895.[26] Our treatise is

[23] At p. 497, note 3, Della Torre (1902) says, "Nella Vaticana, Fondo Vaticano lat., vediamo segnato nel cod. 3897 una *Nicolai Fulginatis quaestio an ad generationem* [*sic*], ma non ne sappiamo altro."

[24] *Op. cit.*, Vol. I, p. 285. This is the reason he gives why Niccolò left Bologna, "a quo, hortantibus amicis, discessit, ut ea in provincia maneret, in qua tabernaculum ipsa philosophia posuisse videbatur."

[25] Vatic. Lat. 3897, 15th century, fols. 79r–86r.

[26] Monsignore Mercati has very kindly supplied me with the following description of the other treatises now composing MS Vatic. Lat. 3897: fols. 1–31, 16th century, formerly numbered 895, "Ubaldini in Periermenias," or "Ubaldini in Antonii Bernardi Commentarium logices"; fols. 32–65, early 16th century, "Epistola expeditionis Avempace interprete Abramo de Balneis," with a preceding dedication to "Dominico Grimando tituli Sti. Marci Episcopo Cardinali dignissimo"; fols. 66–78v, 15th–16th century, "de eccentricis," with mathematical figures; fols. 87–88r, 15th century, "Quaestio quaedam

of the fifteenth century and is presumably in the author's own hand, since it is in the form of a letter written by him from Todi on January 10, 1470,[27] to a correspondent, also named Nicolaus, whom the author calls his *compater* (i.e., one of them had stood godfather to the other's child) and a most famous doctor of arts and medicine. At the close the author signs himself in the same hand as the text, "Nicolaus Fulginas, compater tuus." The writing is very abbreviated and neither neat nor regular, but not especially difficult to read after one has become accustomed to it.

Who the other Niccolò was I am unable to say. Evidently he was, like our author, interested in medicine and philosophy, and one might infer that it was he who had written from Perugia[28] asking Niccolò da Foligno whether this conclusion could be defended, that ideas concur in generation, as Plato thought. In this case he might be one of the faculty at the University of Perugia, where Niccolò da Foligno himself is said to have taught for a time. At any rate, the author asks him for criticism and further suggestion in connection with his discussion of ideas. This other Niccolò was apparently married and had children, since our author sends greetings to "commatrem et cetero[s] tuos",[29] words which would seem to apply to the other's wife and children. It is noteworthy that no reference is made to Florence or the Medici family in this letter. The author expresses a desire to procure the work which he hears had been written in defense of Plato by "the reverend lord cardinal." This appears to be a reference to Bessarion's *Adversus calumniatorem Platonis*, which was printed with a

---

logicalis, in qua de tribus quaeritur. Primo, utrum ens esset unius rationis ad decem praedicamenta vel non. Secundo, utrum relatio esset genus distinctum contra alia praedicamenta. Ultimo, utrum relatio esset unum genus praedicabile. Anon." Incomplete. Fols. 86v and 88v are blank.

[27] Vatic. Lat. 3897, fol. 86r, Explicit, "Ex tuderto die Xa Ian. 1470. Nicolaus fulginas, compater tuus."

[28] The expression in the letter is, however, vague, reading (fol. 79r, col. 1), "Ex perusia ad me scriptum," rather than "scripsisti."

[29] *Ibid.*, fol. 86r.

Latin translation in 1469, the year immediately preceding that in which our letter was written.

The other discussion of ideas by Niccolò da Foligno forms a separate manuscript in the Laurentian Library at Florence. It covers forty-seven leaves, but since they are small, single-columned, and average only about twenty-one lines to the page, and since the writing is much less abbreviated than in the Vatican manuscript, the text is only slightly longer. Lines have been ruled for the writing to follow, which was not the case in the letter, and the hand is more printlike and regular. Very possibly it is that of a scribe, being also a different hand from that of the letter, whereas some marginal corrections and additions are very similar to the hand of the Vatican autograph. The copyist has done his work none too well, since in addition to these marginal corrections a number of repeated or superfluous words have been underlined for omission. The codex has chains attached, like so many of the Laurentian manuscripts. The treatise was presumably addressed to Lorenzo after his accession to power in 1469 and before he named Niccolò professor at Pisa in 1472. It alludes to Donato Acciaiuoli in such a way that he might either be living or dead,[30] but we know that he did not die until four years after Niccolò da Foligno. The work to Lorenzo appears to have made use of the letter which Niccolò wrote on ideas, as we shall presently see, and so to have been composed later than January 10, 1470.

Of our two treatises the letter to Nicholas seems distinctly superior to the work addressed to Lorenzo de' Medici. It seems better thought out, better arranged, more forcefully put and presented, more succinct, continuous, and cogent. The other is more discursive, and, perhaps in an attempt to avoid the appearance of a formal scholastic arrangement of the argumentation, seems to have mixed things up in a rather aimless way and to abound in casual transitions. Is this an effort to write like the dialogues of Poggio or the philosophical essays of Cicero and so make the production more acceptable to

[30] Laurent. Plut. 82, cod. 22, fol. 1r–v and fol. 47r.

Lorenzo and his literary advisers, much as one would employ free verse at the present day in submitting a poem to a magazine for publication? Or may it be because the author is making constant use of the other treatise and wishes to conceal the fact by confusing the arrangement? Except for its brief opening and closing epistolary amenities, which are somewhat in the classical or humanistic manner and in sharp contrast to the text, the letter of Nicholas to Nicholas is a strictly scholastic treatise. So at bottom and in substance is the other, and its author excuses himself for not employing humanistic diction. But his preface to Lorenzo is in the humanist manner, and the very fact that he defends his use of scholastic terminology makes it not improbable that he may introduce something of humanistic lack of order as a compensation. There can be no doubt, I think, that in his text itself as well as the preface to Lorenzo, he attempts a sonorous Latin style with some approach at least to Ciceronian periods and classical word order. He tends, for instance, to place a verb, and especially an infinitive, between an accusative of the noun and its modifying adjective, as in the expressions, "Scientiam esse perpetuam,"[31] "nullam posse perfectam,"[32] "parvum adesse patrem,"[33] "activam continet potestatem,"[34] "formam esse dixerunt principaliter operantem,"[35] "formas esse generationis activas,"[36] "formas substantiales immediate non esse activas,[37] "triplicem esse substantiam,"[38] "qualitatem esse tangibilem,"[39] "nullas formas esse activas,"[40] "suas imprimunt vires,"[41] etc.

There is a marked similarity between our two treatises not merely in subject matter and the arguments employed and in the passages cited from authorities, but to some extent in the wording. I have indicated these parallel passages, which altogether involve about one-half of the entire text of either

[31] Laur. Plut. 82, cod. 22, fol. 4v.

[32] *Ibid.*, fol. 5r.

[33] *Ibid.*, fol. 11r.

[34] *Idem.*

[35] *Ibid.*, fol. 14r.

[36] *Ibid.*, fol. 15r.

[37] *Ibid.*, fol. 15v.

[38] *Ibid.*, fol. 16r.

[39] *Ibid.*, fol. 16v.

[40] *Idem.*

[41] *Ibid.*, fol. 17r.

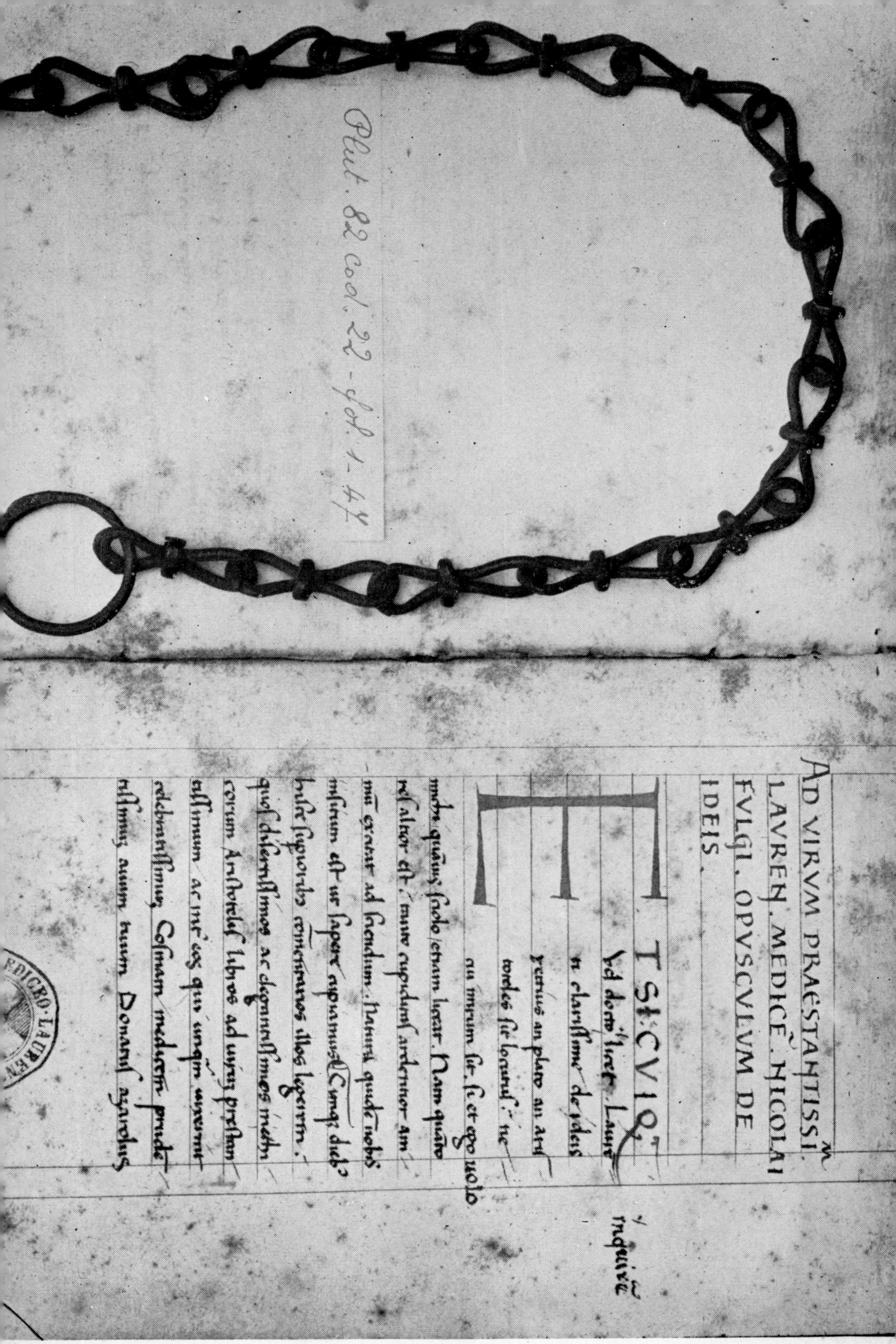
Plut. 82 Cod. 22 - fol. 1-47
AD VIRVM PRAESTANTISSI
LAVREN. MEDICE. NICOLAI
FVLGI. OPVSCVLVM DE
IDEIS

PLATE IX

treatise, in a chart or table among the appendices at the close of this volume. From this outline of correspondences between the two discussions of ideas, it will be seen that the order of presentation varies a great deal in the two treatises. It seems reasonably certain that liberal use has been made of one of the treatises in writing the other, and that the work which was so used and was written first is the letter from one Nicholas to another. It is true that the subject appears to have been a favorite one for scholastic discussion,[42] and that many of the passages listed from authorities were stock citations. Nevertheless, the correspondences between our two treatises seem too numerous and close, and the divergences of one from the other too slight for them to have been written independently. This may be brought out and at the same time the general character of the two treatises indicated by a consecutive summary and comparison of their content. This will not duplicate the table of parallel passages in the two works, to which reference was made above, as much as might be thought, since that will follow the order of the letter to Nicholas, making it its norm of comparison and noting how far the treatise to Lorenzo corresponds to it, whereas we shall now rather make the treatise to Lorenzo our point of departure. The two modes of comparison will thus complement each other.

But first may be noted certain similarities in details of phraseology which are presumably unconscious and tend to convince one that both treatises are by the same author. Thus the letter to Nicholas opens with the words, "Diebus hisce superioribus," an expression which is repeated in the middle of the first page of the preface to Lorenzo in the other treatise.

[42] For the treatment of it by Duns Scotus, see C. R. S. Harris, *Duns Scotus*, Oxford, 1927, Vol. I, pp. 235–37. Duns held that the Platonic ideas were not needed to explain the processes of generation. One particular phase of the discussion, namely, whether animals generated spontaneously from putrefaction were of the same genus as those generated from seed, was treated by Marcus Antonius Janua, a professor of Padua, in a manuscript formerly in the monastery of St. Michael at Murano near Venice: — S. Michael de Muriano 595, cum operibus Francisci Piccolominei, Quaestio an genita ex putredine sint eiusdem generis cum genitis ex semine.

The opening paragraph of the letter to Nicholas also contains the rather unusual phrase, "nauci pendam." The same turn is employed in another context in the next to last sentence of the preface to Lorenzo, where we read, "vel nauci faciunt vel contempnunt."[43] Both treatises in opening further use the words, "fundamenta Platonis,"[44] with reference to the basic propositions or hypotheses which they suppose to underlie his doctrine of ideas.

The preface of the treatise to Lorenzo, besides the verbal coincidences which we have already noted with the opening of the letter to Nicholas, much resembles it in the discussion of what Avicenna called *colcodrea*. Both refer in this connection to "the giver" of forms or life, to the conception of divine emanation, and to the "ymago paterna."[45] The passages of this preface having reference to Lorenzo himself or the Medici family of course are not found in the letter, nor is the allusion to Donato Acciaiuoli's commentary on the *Ethics* of Aristotle[46] as what inspired the writing of the work. If the author of the letter to Nicholas is indeed also the author of the treatise to Lorenzo, it would scarcely seem as if this account of how he was led to write the work could be strictly true, unless he wrote it first and the letter to Nicholas subsequently, which seems unlikely. The chief difference between the preface, with its following treatise, and the letter is that the former emphasizes the opposition between Aristotle and Plato, although holding that we can accept Aristotle's account of the Platonic ideas as accurate, while the letter bases its discussion of the Platonic ideas especially upon the commentaries of Averroës — which is

[43] Laurent. Plut. 82, cod. 22, fol. 4v.

[44] These words constitute the Incipit of the text proper in the letter (Vatic. 3897, fol. 79r, col. 1) and occur early in the preface to Lorenzo in the other MS (Laurent. Plut. 82, cod. 22, fol. 1v).

[45] Compare Vatic. 3897, fol. 79r, col. 2, with Laur. Plut. 82, cod. 22, fol. 2r.

[46] In the seventeenth century Gabriel Naudé accused Acciaiuoli of having plagiarized the lectures of Argyropoulos at Florence in this commentary. *Bibliographie politique*, p. 21: "Argyrophilus Bisantinus cuius praelectiones Florentiae habitas non absque manifesto plagii crimine sibi postea vendicavit Donatus Acciaiolus."

perhaps at bottom the same thing. In this connection, both text and preface of the treatise addressed to Lorenzo further lay more stress than does the letter on the point that the Platonic ideas were regarded by Aristotle as superfluous.[47] The treatise to Lorenzo also concerns itself somewhat more generally with the Platonic ideas than the letter to Nicholas, which limits itself to the particular question whether they concur in the generation of things of nature. The text proper of the Laurentian manuscript accordingly opens with some verbiage — concerning the eternity of science and its need of dealing with lasting matters such as the Platonic ideas — which is not paralleled in the letter to Nicholas. Nor is the following comparison of the essence or idea to the center of a circle in which all lines radiating from it to the circumference participate[48] — an illustration which is again employed towards the close of the Laurentian manuscript.[49] Both treatises then deal with the postulate that anything produced or generated must be produced or generated by something like itself, and that, since this is apparently not the case in animals born of putrefaction or in fire generated by striking stones and iron together, therefore Platonic ideas are required in generation. The same instances of spontaneous generation are adduced, and both treatises argue that a mouse born of putrefaction is of the same species as other mice.

But next in the letter to Nicholas is considered the question whether such spontaneous generation may not be satisfactorily explained by the influence of the heavenly bodies, without recourse to ideas. This involves a discussion whether the stars act necessarily or contingently and whether animals generated from putrefaction by the stars would not be incorruptible which is introduced at a much later point in the treatise to Lorenzo. Meanwhile the letter to Nicholas discusses instances of the properties of animals surviving after death,[50] a subject not

[47] See Laur. Plut. 82, cod. 22, fols. 2v and 46r–v.

[48] *Ibid.*, fol. 5v.

[49] *Ibid.*, fols. 41v–42r.

[50] Vatic. 3897, fol. 80v, col. 1.

touched on in the treatise to Lorenzo. Aside from this displacement and divergence, both treatises go on to deal with the objection that this similitude between the generating force and the thing generated need be only virtual, and the assertion that substantial forms are active, and not neither active nor passive as posited by Plato. In the treatise to Lorenzo, however, Alexander is given first place as the supporter of these objections to the Platonic position, rather than Averroës, although the same citations are made from both authors as in the letter to Nicholas.

The treatise to Lorenzo then launches forth for several pages [51] upon a discussion of the question whether any form, substantial or accidental, can be the principle of any operation. Most of this discussion seems not to be paralleled in the other manuscript. Especially is this the case with the argument from consideration of the smallest particle in which the form of the species is present, [52] the illustration of one's teeth being set on edge by seeing another person eating something bitter,[53] the passages concerning the intellect [54] and the relation of soul to body.[55]

Both treatises then coincide in discussing the question whether form or composite is generated. After this discussion has proceeded a certain way, the letter of Nicholas lists thirteen arguments against form being generated rather than the composite. Having done this, it replies to each of the thirteen in turn. The treatise to Lorenzo on the other hand makes use only of the arguments numbered from 2 to 6 inclusive, which, however, it does not distinguish by any numeration. It then jumps to the introductory considerations which the letter prefixes to its rebuttal seriatim of the thirteen points.[56] But after

[51] Laur. Plut. 82, cod. 22, fols. 13r–18v.

[52] *Ibid.*, fols. 14r, 18r–v.

[53] *Ibid.*, fol. 16v.

[54] *Ibid.*, fols. 13r, 17r.

[55] *Ibid.*, fols. 17r, 18r.

[56] Vatic. 3897, fol. 82r, col. 2: "Pro responsione ad prima sex argumenta notandum primo quod forma est duplex . . ."; whereas Laur. Plut. 82, cod. 22, fol. 28v: "Quo istud clarius habeatur prorsus est advertendum formam esse duplicem . . ." Were the treatises by different authors, it might be the fact

noting two of these preliminary considerations, it fails to include the third, which distinguishes three different senses in which generation may be understood.[57] It then turns to the question whether generation from putrefaction is explainable simply by the influence of the heavenly bodies, which had been taken up earlier in the other manuscript. After repeating, apparently needlessly, the argument that an animal so produced would be incorruptible, the treatise to Lorenzo says: "These remarks are enough for now. This matter requires a longer investigation which, God granting, I will not shun in another place."[58] But this can scarcely be regarded as pointing towards our other treatise and hence as an indication that it was written subsequently, since its discussion of this question of the influence of the heavenly bodies on animals born of putrefaction is more concise rather than fuller.

The treatise to Lorenzo then makes use of much the same material as is introduced in the letter to Nicholas in rebutting the second to sixth arguments, but in a different order. One noticeable point in the treatise to Lorenzo which is not in the letter is a reference to the word "this-y-ness" (*haecaitas*) as a term of the Scotists.[59] Finally, the two treatises diverge in their concluding pages. While the letter to Nicholas is rebutting the last seven arguments listed and setting forth three meanings of matter, the treatise to Lorenzo gives and criticizes Franciscus de Mayronis's summary under four heads of Aristotle's criticism of the Platonic ideas. The seven arguments and the replies to them may, like most of the scholastic content of our treatises, be best appreciated in its original Latin form and phraseology, but we may perhaps note now what the treatise to Lorenzo says of Franciscus de Mayronis. He had

---

that the writer of the letter thus distinguishes the first six arguments from the other seven of the thirteen, that led the writer to Lorenzo to omit these last and pass at once to the reply to the first six.

[57] Vatic. 3897, fol. 82v, col. 1: "Tertio nota quod aliquid generare intelligitur tribus modis . . ."

[58] Laurent. Plut. 82, cod. 22, fol. 36r.

[59] Laur. Plut. 82, cod. 22, fol. 37v.

already been twice cited in this treatise.[60] He is now described as "most acute and most hostile to Aristotle, as if he would prefer himself to Aristotle,"[61] and as one "who although, as I think, he understood the meaning of the Philosopher (i.e., Aristotle), yet as a man of original but sometimes perverse genius wished to take ground opposite to so great a philosopher."[62] Franciscus represented Aristotle as having criticized the Platonic ideas for singularity, the idea being a single individual which was to be common to many; for actuality, although having a separate existence apart from individuals; for being locally separate; and for being measured in time. Niccolò seems to feel that Aristotle would not have raised such objections and that it is derogatory to attribute them to him.

The author of the treatise to Lorenzo then repeats his own view of Aristotle's criticism of Plato. It is that Aristotle regarded the virtue of the heavenly bodies and the disposition of matter to receive it as an adequate explanation of generation, and hence considered the Platonic ideas as unnecessary and superfluous. Aristotle did not doubt that in the divine mind there are ideas of all things,[63] but was concerned with more proximate natural causes. Macrobius and Servius were perhaps right in suggesting that *yle* was full of ideas, or that these were forms latent in matter, which Plato made the source of all forms except the human soul, which is implanted by divine creation. Or perhaps, as Eusebius says many held, the ideas were the virtues of the heavens diffused to the intelligences that move the orbs.

The letter to Nicholas concludes somewhat differently that ideas participate in natural generation and are not to be rejected, as many think, from the system of the Philosopher and the Commentator — that is, of Aristotle and Averroës. The letter uses the same phrase for the creation of the human soul,[64]

[60] Fols. 27r and 36r. [61] Fol. 44v. [62] Fol. 45v.

[63] This had been accepted by both Aquinas and Scotus.

[64] Vatic. 3897, fol. 85v, col. 2: "forma humana . . . per creationem infunditur." See Laurent. Plut. 82, cod. 22, fol. 46v: "forma humana . . . per creationem infundi."

and grants that "all natural forms except it are drawn from the potentiality of matter."

The question remains whether both treatises are by the same author. It would be natural enough for Nicholas of Foligno, after having written out his argument at Todi for the eye of his *compater*, to have made use of it again in a treatise on the same theme to Lorenzo de' Medici. It would also not be strange for him to try to express it in a form more in accord with humanist ideals and practice. But it is not easy to understand why he should have altered it for the worse in so doing, and turned a well knit piece of argumentation and exposition into a discursive essay with a flavor of dilettantism about it. It is also puzzling why he should have ruthlessly omitted a large section of his previous line of argument. On the other hand, if his *compater*, also named Nicholas, is the author of the work addressed to Lorenzo and has procured the letter — written apparently at his solicitation — for that purpose, then it is not difficult to see why he has so changed the order as well as form of presentation, whether of set purpose to disguise his use of his *compater's* work or in a more commendable effort to be original at least in arrangement. This would further explain why he has omitted a considerable portion of the argument of the other work, and why he has made certain additions to it of his own or from other sources. His inferior mind would account for his having developed the whole subject less logically, forcefully, and effectively. It may be also wondered what Niccolò was doing at Todi in 1470, if he is the Nicolaus Tignosius Fulginas of Arezzo, Perugia, Florence, and Pisa.

For such reasons I have been strongly tempted to ascribe the work which is addressed to Lorenzo to another author than the writer of the letter, and in particular to that other Nicholas whom the writer of the letter calls his *compater* and most famous doctor of arts and medicine.[65] But against this is the fact that both treatises are unmistakably indicated as the work

[65] It is perhaps worth observing that citations of medical writings are somewhat more numerous in the work addressed to Lorenzo.

of Niccolò da Foligno, the letter being signed by that name, and the Titulus of the work to Lorenzo containing it. Moreover, the handwriting of the marginal notes in the latter manuscript seems closely to resemble the probable autograph letter of Niccolò. We have also noted identical uses of words and phrases which seemed mannerisms of the same author rather than consciously copied by one treatise from the other. We have no proof that the other *Nicolaus compater*, although his interest in medicine and philosophy appears to have closely corresponded to that of the writer of the letter, was also from Foligno, and it is not even certain that he was at Perugia or connected with its university. I therefore somewhat reluctantly conclude that we must for the present simply leave this mysterious *Nicolaus compater* out of account, ascribe both our treatises to Niccolò da Foligno, and identify him with the person already known under that name who seems to have lived from about 1402 to 1474.

We shall then have to admit that in trying to write on philosophy for Lorenzo de' Medici in somewhat humanistic style, he produced a treatise inferior to that which he dashed off for his *compater* and intellectual peer in scholastic style. This in its turn suggests the inference that the supposed stimulating and beneficial effect of patronage by courts or individual great men in public life upon literary and learned men and works, and that of Lorenzo de' Medici in particular, has been too often overestimated and overstated, and that a scholar was more likely to be influenced to fertile thought and literary productivity by the demand of a fellow doctor and philosopher than by the effort to please a great man prominent in public affairs and to create a demand from that direction. Like is generated by like, as Niccolò makes Plato say in our very treatises. Indeed, this inference will follow from the character of the two works themselves and the persons to whom they are addressed, regardless of their authorship, except that, if we held that one Nicholas asked the other to write in order that he in turn might write more effectively for Lorenzo, we should have the Medicean Maecenate indirectly responsible for the letter as well as more directly for the treatise. On the other hand, it must be admitted that all of Niccolò's Aristotelian commentaries which have been preserved were addressed to members of the Medici house.

Although both treatises discuss the subject of the Platonic ideas with much assurance and are distinctly favorable to them — the work addressed to Lorenzo is, however, the more favorable of the two — it is a noteworthy fact that neither treatise among its many citations includes a single specific reference to any work by Plato. Nor are Platonists and Neo-Platonists cited directly and individually, with the exception of Porphyry [66] and Macrobius. They are mentioned only in the treatise to Lorenzo, and of course had long been familiar medieval reading. There is no evidence that the author of either of our treatises had ever read a word of Plato, either in the original or in translation. Indeed, everything seems to indicate that he had not. The writer of the letter to Nicholas makes no attempt to disguise the fact, since his opening statement indicates that he approaches the subject by way of the commentary of Averroës on the *Metaphysics* of Aristotle: "Plato's fundamental propositions for the ideas are these according to Averroës' thirtieth and thirty-first comments on the seventh book of the *Metaphysics*." Yet if we accept him as the author of the other treatise, he has no hesitation about addressing the patron of the Platonic Academy at Florence and friend of Ficino on such a subject. This suggests what a shallow pretense most of the so-called Platonism of fifteenth-century Italians and the Mediceans must have been.

What our author has read is Aristotle and his commentators, especially Alexander and Averroës, Albert and Aquinas, and such medical authorities as Avicenna, Galen, Hippocrates, and John Mesue. He is an exponent of scholasticism, in both form

[66] Laurent. Plut. 82, cod. 22, fol. 5r, "ut dixit porphyrius" is written in the margin; fol. 6r, "que porphirii perstat sententia"; fol. 45r, "porphirius in libro predicabilium."

and content, and, at least in the treatise to Lorenzo, mentions schoolmen who lived into the early fourteenth century, such as Duns Scotus and Franciscus de Mayronis, and so recent a commentator on Aristotle as his contemporary, Donato Acciaiuoli. However, he names no scholastic writer between the death of Franciscus de Mayronis in 1325 and Acciaiuoli. He is critical of the former's views and attitude and interpretation of Aristotle. Niccolò takes his stand rather on the old text of Aristotle and the commentaries of Averroës. If he occasionally refers respectfully to Albertus Magnus and Thomas Aquinas, he does not always find them in agreement.

Such then is the scholastic, Aristotelian, Averroistic, material, and astrological interpretation and discussion of the Platonic ideas which, in the second half of the Quattrocento, in the height of the so-called Italian Renaissance, was directed by Niccolò da Foligno, whose name graces the humanistic dialogues of Poggio, not merely to his *compater*, the most famous doctor of arts and medicine, but to Lorenzo the Magnificent, for whom *la giovanezza* was *bella*. It is indeed a revelation to see so stiff a dose of scholasticism administered to the patron of the Platonic Academy, however gilded the pill may be with humanistic mannerisms. In closing Niccolò expresses his gratitude to Donato Acciaiuoli for having kept him from wasting the past few days by turning his attention to this problem. Far greater will his thanks be to Lorenzo, if the Magnificent looks benignly on these lucubrations, and Niccolò will demonstrate his gratitude in greater things. Shall we go too far in hazarding the guess that the presentation of this treatise helped to win Niccolò his appointment as professor at the University of Pisa in 1472?

Lorenzo de' Medici was to have his attention again called to Aristotle and the Platonic ideas by Lorenzo Buonincontri di San Miniato, the astrologer and poet, in the commentary [67]

[67] I have examined it in a manuscript at the Vatican (Vatic. Lat. 2845, paper, 142 fols.): "Laur. Bonincontr. commentaria in suos libros rerum divinarum et naturalium ad Laurentium Medicem." It opens (fol. 1r): "Plato tria

to his poem on "Things Divine and Natural," of which the several parts were respectively dedicated to the Magnificent, Ferrante, and Ferdinand of Aragon.

---

arbitratur esse rerum initia: deum, materiam, rerumque formas quas ideas appellat." See also fol. 66r: "hoc est quod fecit Aristotelem errare cum diceret deum non intelligere hec mundana . . . ," etc.; fol. 66v: ". . . nam in deo sunt omnia que sunt et ipsius nutu reguntur. *Ante creando:* mentis sue idea in qua erant omnium rerum forme simplices et eterne ex qua Idea Plato autumnat deum sumpsisse omnium rerum que sunt exemplaria, sed initium omnium corporum materiam esse quam signari formarum impressione commemorat, de qua et nos in anterioribus libris cum de phisicis disseruimus ad Laurentium Medicem plene diximus."

CHAPTER XI

SOME RENAISSANCE MORALISTS AND PHILOSOPHERS [1]

In this chapter some account will be given of four treatises from as many different manuscripts of the Laurentian or Medicean Library at Florence. So far as I have been able to ascertain, only one of them has yet been printed. Not only are these treatises housed in the same historic collection, they were written during the same period, from about the middle to about the close of the fifteenth century. Furthermore, they are treatises of much the same sort so far as subject matter and method of treatment are concerned, dealing with moral and philosophical questions in somewhat cursory fashion. They illustrate the interest of the humanists in moral philosophy and verbose moralizing, and, taken together with the treatises of Niccolò da Foligno discussed in the preceding chapter, afford us an opportunity to compare the metaphysics and natural philosophy of the time of the Renaissance with that of the preceding medieval period. Undoubtedly they must rank as minor treatises, *opuscula* rather than *magna opera.* Yet they were written for persons of great distinction, in the Medicean family or otherwise, and by well educated authors. They may not be dismissed as mere deadwood and rubbish, unworthy of the spirit of the Renaissance, but must be accepted as, in their small way, representative of the thought, interests, and manner of the period. We shall not consider our treatises in quite their chronological order of composition but rather according to a certain sequence of their subject matter.

The treatise to which we shall first give our attention is

[1] Revised from *The Romanic Review,* Vol. XVIII, No. 2, April–June, 1927, pp. 114–33.

dedicated by Gregorius Chrispus or Crispus, a savant of Toulouse, "a student of good arts and all philosophy, and in especial a musician," to Peter of Foix, Infante of Navarre, and Protonotary of the Apostolic See.[2] This appears to have been the Peter of Foix who was born in 1449 and died in 1490, since Gregory speaks of another Peter of Foix, now deceased, who was this Peter's paternal granduncle and a distinguished cardinal and died in 1464, aged seventy-eight.[3] The younger Peter also was created a cardinal in 1476 by Sixtus IV, which makes it appear that Gregory dedicated his work between the years 1464 and 1476. Therefore either Bandini was mistaken in dating our manuscript as late as the beginning of the sixteenth century or it is not Gregory's original but a later copy. The treatise in which we are now interested comes first in the manuscript and is immediately followed by two other brief treatises by Gregory of only a few pages each. One is a defense of astrology against its detractors;[4] the other is a lament over the menacing advance of the Turks and the failure of Christian princes to unite against them.[5] It would seem to have been written after the Turks had overrun central Greece and the Morea, and shortly before their landing in southern Italy at Otranto in 1480. Gregory laments that no image of Christ is left in Greece and that there is no temple of Christ in Greece which has not been profaned, and he

[2] MS Laurent. Plut. 77, cod. 17, beginning of the sixteenth century according to Bandini's catalogue, 121 fols. I have printed the full Latin text of the rubric and dedicatory preface in Appendix 21. The text proper opens at fol. 7r as follows: "Quoniam igitur hominis natura ita ex corpore et animo constat ut homo sine utroque esse non possit . . ."

[3] For the two Peters de Foix, see Michaud's *Biographie universelle*. Other authorities do not agree with Michaud as to the bishoprics held by the two Peters respectively before they were made cardinals.

[4] *Op. cit.*, fol. 110v: "Gregorii Chrispi sapientis tholosani bonarum artium et utriusque philosophie studiosi Invectiva in eos insulsos homines qui astronomie arti quidem prestantissime dictis mordacibus ac salibus detrahunt feliciter incipit."

[5] Fol. 116v: "Gregorii Chryspi sapientis tholosani bonarum artium ac utriusque philosophie studiosi commiseratio lachrymabilis super rem Christianam feritate teucrorum et infidelium Chrystianorum desidiosa somnolentia propemodum profligatam meste incipit."

states that the Turks have just decided to invade Italy and are constructing a huge fleet.[6]

The work of Gregory Crispus has an attractive title, *De cultu humanitatis et honestatis libellus* ("On the Cultivation of Humanism and Right Living"), which seems to promise an alliance between the study of the humanities and moral philosophy against the more purely scholastic interests of the medieval period. But for Gregory *humanitas* is not the study of Latin and Greek, although he interlards his work with classical citations and allusions in the usual manner of the humanists, but rather the proper cultivation of the mind and body. His real antithesis turns out to be between a virtuous Christian life and the mere pursuit of learning, and his attitude is quite as much that of a church father or a sermon as it is that of either a classical moralist or a scholar. His interest is in those studies or pursuits which can make man happy, and he decides that without *humanitas* and *honestas* no one can ever be happy. To know all the liberal arts and the natures of all things may confer some advantage in this life, but little towards the eternal felicity of the soul in heaven. It is true that he begins by identifying the proper cultivation of the mind or soul with moral philosophy, and the care of the body with medicine or hygiene. But he soon dismisses the latter as sufficiently well known[7] and the affair of medical men. Turning to ills of the mind, he draws many analogies and antitheses between bodily and mental ills and cures. He seems to flatter himself that these comparisons are quite smart and ingenious, but to anyone else they would probably sound very flat and commonplace. The final one is

[6] Fols. 117v and 119v: "Nullum in grecia christi simulacrum relinquitur nullumque signum. . . . Nullum in grecia christi templum est quid prophanatum non sit. Omnia sacra polluta sunt. . . . Italiam invadere Turcha brevi statuit, classem ingentem construit. . . ."

Another treatise of the same sort evoked by the fall of Otranto was Vespasiano da Bisticci's last work, the *Lamento d'Italia per la presa d'Otranto fatta nel* 1480.

[7] "Sed quia corporis egritudines satis note sunt que ex virtutum primarum intemperie proveniunt quom simplices virtutum qualitates abundant aut deficiunt, parum quidem de illis disserere institimus."

that as all philosophers agree that cures are by contraries, so it is clear that vices are healed by virtues.[8]

Gregory then turns to the thought that in order for man to live aright, which is the aim of the free man and humanist (*homini libero et perhumano*), he must know what the object and end of life is, in other words the *summum bonum.* The love of God is the true *summum bonum,* and if our life starts from it, we do not need to know what Zeno, Epicurus, Aristippus, Socrates, and Aristotle thought about the *summum bonum.* "Lest nevertheless we seem ignorant of their disputations, we have deemed it not unfitting to run over them briefly."[9] After wallowing about for a time in ancient ethics, quoting Cicero frequently, and concluding among other things that there is nothing diviner in man than voluntary virtues, Gregory returns to a consideration of God as the source of all virtues. As it is impossible to please God without faith, he begins with that virtue and cites the treatise of Aquinas on divine grace.[10] Defining faith, Gregory holds that it does not require physical or mathematical demonstrations, that there is no merit in believing what has been proved by experiment, and that faith is versed in believing the most difficult matters, such as the doctrine of the Trinity or the virgin birth.[11] He also discusses the other two "theological virtues" — hope and charity.

[8] Fol. 13v: "Et postquam philosophorum omnium sententia contraria contrariis curantur perspicuum est virtutes esse vitiorum medelam."

[9] Fol. 22r: "Nam super eo cognoscendo multi veterum philosophorum falsi fuere, et licet parum nobis referat quid Citticus Zeno quid Epicurus et Aristippus quid Socrates quid Aristoteles de summo bono senserunt modo nos recte vereque sentiamus, ne tamen eorum disputationes ignorasse videamur breviter eas percurrere haud indignum putavimus."

[10] Fol. 44v: "quod recte divus ille Thomas in eo quem de divina gratia edidit libello probare videtur."

[11] Fols. 45v–46r: "Fides igitur ipsa non phisicas non mathematicas demonstrationes exquirit, sola simplici credulitate meritum consequitur . . . quod experimento probamus nullum meritum est. . . . Quamobrem fides ipsa circa difficillima creditu versatur. Eternum enim deum trinum et unum esse, tres personas realiter distinctas unam essentiam, natum Christum de virgine conceptum sine semine, hominem et deum una esse, sub eucharistie accidentibus Christum deum et hominem contineri, esse eum filium et patrem, et cetera articulorum fidei miracula credere difficillimum est."

With Gregory's second chapter,[12] however, he turns to moral virtues and philosophy, following especially the authority of Aristotle, whom he prefers as a guide in the active life and intercourse of men, although he does not disapprove of the firmness and severity of Zeno and Diogenes in the contemplative life.[13] As a matter of fact, he cites Cicero more often than Aristotle. He also cites Christian writers like Augustine and Isidore, as well as classical authors like Terence and Seneca. Again he manifests an unfavorable attitude towards mere learning, stating that there are many disciplines which delight, but few which are useful, and that to study obscure and difficult and unnecessary matters is to yield to the vice of curiosity, as those do who neglect moral philosophy to read mathematics. Yet the very next treatise by him in the manuscript which we are following is "an invective against those benighted men who detract from the most excellent art of astronomy (including astrology) by sharp and bitter sayings." This shows that the apparent opposition to mere learning is only a relative matter, or at most a phase or mood of his total intellectual attitude. Petrarch and many other humanists displayed similar qualms at times. Modern historians have erred in representing this unfavorable attitude to learning in general or pagan learning in particular as more characteristic of the medieval period. It was perhaps stronger in Augustine or Petrarch than in the average writer of the twelfth or thirteenth century, although then too it was an attitude very likely to be found in anyone writing a distinctly theological or moral work or who happened to be in an ascetic mood or temporarily sated with secular learning.

But to return to Gregory. He indulges in numerous highly moral commonplaces, such as that "Where the soul is subject

[12] It begins at fol. 48r. ". . . His enim tribus quas nostri virtutes theologales appellant pro fundamento iactis, iam ad morales descendamus. Quanquam autem virtutes morales invicem esse conexas sciamus . . ."

[13] "Et licet nos Zenonis et Diogenis firmitatem et severitatem in contemplativa vita non improbemus, in activa tamen et in hominum conversatione Aristotelem libenter sequimur."

to the pleasures of the body, it is a slave."[14] He upholds freedom of the will, asserting that man is not so dragged by necessity that it is impossible for him, if he wills it, to be changed from evil to good. It is not impossible, but merely difficult.[15]

As for the number of moral virtues, Apollophanes mentioned but one, Panaetius mentioned two, the active and contemplative. Posidonius named four, the cardinal virtues of prudence, justice, fortitude, and temperance. Aristotle added liberality, mercy, right ambition, and others. Apollophanes made prudence the form, parent, and chief of all other virtues, and Cicero in the *Tusculan Disputations* seems to agree with him in this.[16] Gregory then devotes successive chapters to justice, which he divides into severity and liberality; to fortitude; temperance; human affections and modesty; ambition or right appetite for honors; mercy; liberality; integrity in deeds and business; "and sociability in words, that we do not speak like rustics."[17] These chapters are much shorter than his first and include citations of such authors as Euripides, Chrysippus, Horace, and Ambrose.

The closing chapter[18] is a longer one, exhorting to the practice of virtue, with many Biblical citations and examples and much concerning endurance of death by torture or martyrdom, such as the deaths of Regulus, Scaevola, Horatius Cocles, the affair of Antiochus and the seven brothers, and Christian martyrs.

The treatise by Gregory Crispus which we have just considered bears a certain resemblance to a dialogue "On the

[14] "Ubi ergo animus subicitur corporis voluptatibus servus est."

[15] "At non ita trahitur necessitate ut sit ei impossibile si velit ex malo bonus fieri sed difficile quidem quia voluntate semper libera. . . ."

[16] Fol. 60r–v, "Recte igitur Apollophanes ipse, cum Panetius duas tantum virtutes posuisset activam scilicet et contemplativam, Posidonius autem quatuor ut prudentiam justiciam fortitudinem temperantiam, alii plures ut Aristoteles qui adiunxit liberalitatem mansuetudinem honorisque rectam cupidinem et alias ad mores honestos pertinentes, unam tamen dixit esse virtutem prudentiam propterea quod eam omnium aliarum virtutum formam parentem et ducem existimaret. Quod etiam Cicero in tusculanis confirmare videtur."

[17] Fol. 84r, "et comitatem in verbis ne rusticorum more loquamur."

[18] It begins at fol. 87r.

Happiness of Human Life" (*De humane vite felicitate dialogus*) which Bartholomew Facius or Fazio had addressed to Alfonso, king of Aragon and Sicily.[19] Facius is better known as author of *De viris illustribus*, written in 1456, an important though brief source for the lives of men of the fourteenth and early fifteenth centuries. Returning to the works of Bartholomew and Crispus which at present concern us, we have to note that the very opening words of the two treatises are strikingly similar. Gregory begins, "As I often cogitated, most illustrious prince. . . ." Bartholomew opens, "As I often pondered on the condition of human life, most wise king. . . ."[20] Moreover, both were pondering over the problem of human felicity. Both took up the question of the *summum bonum*, to which the second of the three parts of Bartholomew's work is devoted and concerning which he says there was great disagreement among the philosophers. Nevertheless he will confirm all his opinion from the utterances of the wisest men and the tradition of divine inspiration. The names of the classical and other authors whom he cites are repeated in red in the side margins of the manuscript, which is elegantly written. But the contents are rather insipid. The dialogue is represented as taking place between Antonio of Palermo, who had been crowned poet by the emperor Sigismund, Guarino of Verona, the famous humanist educator, and John Lamola. Taking each a day in turn, Lamola is to defend the active, and Antonio the contemplative life against the contention of Guarino that neither leads to felicity. Fazio gave as a reason for composing his dialogue that he found nothing previously written on the theme which

[19] MS Strozzianae 109, 15th century, elegantly written: "Barptolomei Facii de humane vite felicitate dialogus inter Antonium Panormitam, Guarinum Veronensem et Ioannem Lamolam ad Alphonsum Aragonum et Siciliae regem. . . ." It also occurs in two MSS at the Escorial: f. IV. 13, and s. III. 17, both of the fifteenth century. It was printed in *Dialogi decem variorum auctorum*, 1473, in folio (Pellechet, 4212), and separately at Antwerp, 1556.

[20] "Humanae vitae conditionem saepius reputanti mihi rex sapientissime. . . ." In MSS of this period it is not unusual to find both the spelling *ae* and *e* in the same work. The change from the medieval *e* to the humanistic *ae* was just coming in.

satisfied him, but the reader may detect a considerable likeness between it and Lorenzo Valla's *De voluptate* or Petrarch's *De remediis utriusque fortunae.* The particular aspect of the problem of human felicity which Facius was pondering at the start was why man, when he is God's noblest creation, is so seldom happy all his life through — a thought which of course had occurred to Solon and many others many centuries before. Bartholomew suggests that very likely it is to make men turn to heaven for their felicity. The third part of his treatise opens with the statement, "The blessed life, as indeed it seems to me, is all placed in the enjoyment of God."[21] He then proceeds to enlarge upon how fine the future life will be, when we shall be able to know and explore all the stars,[22] and so on. Thus we have much the same combination of classical citation, ancient moral philosophy, and Christian faith and moralizing as in the work of Gregory. To show that happiness here below is not distributed according to deserts, Bartholomew points out that one may see many men of genius and preëminent learning suffering for lack of daily bread, lying on the ground, neglected by the rich, despised by princes. "There is almost no prince in our time who favors literary genius except King Alfonso."[23] Bartholomew recognizes, however, that this fault is not confined to his own age, since Juvenal complained of the same thing.

A third work of much the same order as the two foregoing is the treatise of John or Ioannes Nesius, *De moribus* ("On Morals"), addressed to Piero de' Medici, the son of Lorenzo, in the form of four dialogues.[24] John Nesius is described by

[21] "Beata vita ut mihi quidem videtur tota est posita in dei fruitione."

[22] "Erunt nobis notae et exploratae omnes stellae."

[23] "Vides enim multos viros ingenio ac doctrina prestanti rei familiaris inopia laborare, iacere humi, neglegi a locupletibus, a principibus contemni. Quorum fere nullus est hac nostra tempestate qui litteratorum ingeniis faveat preter Alfonsum regem."

[24] MS Laurent. Plut. 77, cod. 24, 15th century, 169 fols., Ioannis Nesii de moribus ad Petrum Medicem Laurentii filium Dialogi IV. The first dialogue starts on fol. 7r, the second at fol. 63r (66r), the third at fol. 109v (112v), the fourth at fol. 136v (137v). Della Torre, *Storia dell'Accademia Platoniac di Firenze*, Florence, 1902, pp. 422–25, 692–701, touches on Nesius and our manuscript.

Bandini as a Platonist and rhetorician who flourished about 1485, and who finished his *Oraculum de novo saeculo* in 1496 and dedicated it to Giovanni Francesco Pico della Mirandola. This latter work was printed in 1497,[25] but our treatise seems not to have been published except that Bandini printed the prefaces to the several dialogues and a few further extracts. In it Nesius looks back on Cosimo de' Medici — "your great-grandfather," as he says to Piero — as not only the "father of his country" but as, without controversy, the wisest man of his age. He also praises the elder Piero de' Medici and further speaks highly of Lorenzo as a boy. The four dialogues are put in the mouths of the now deceased Donato Acciaiuoli (1428–78),[26] whom Nesius eulogizes,[27] and several younger men, including Nesius himself, Bernardo de' Medici, Antonio Lanfredini, and Jacopo Salviati, who, as Nesius reminds Piero, had married his sister the preceding year.[28] Fabroni [29] gives the date of Lucrezia de' Medici's marriage as 1481, which would make the date of Nesius' treatise 1482.[30]

[25] Hain, *11693. The autograph copy of the manuscript addressed to Giovanni Francesco Pico is preserved in MS 384 of the Riccardian Library. Riccard. 383 is another 15th-century manuscript of the work. In Riccard. 1449 is "Iohannes Nesius adolescens Braccio Martello viro clarissimo," a letter of consolation written in September, 1476.

[26] Donato Acciaiuoli commented on the Politics and Ethics of Aristotle, translated Plutarch's *Alcibiades* and *Demetrius*, and apparently himself composed the lives of Hannibal and Scipio falsely ascribed to Plutarch. He also wrote a life of Charlemagne and translated Leonardo Bruni's *History of the Florentine People* from Latin into Italian. He died at Milan while on his third embassy to the king of France.

[27] In the preface to the second dialogue.

[28] "Instituit autem eo sermone Donatus non quosvis adolescentes sed e multis delectos Philippum Valorium, Bernardum Medicem Alamanni filium propinquum tuum, Antonium praeter Lanfridium ac Iacobum Salviatum cui superiore anno soror tua matrimonio locata est." — From the preface to the first dialogue. From this marriage came the cardinals Salviati and Maria Salviati, mother of Cosimo, the first Grand Duke of Tuscany.

[29] *Laurentii Medicis Magnifici vita auctore Angelo Fabronio Academiae Pisanae curatore*, Pisa, 1784, Vol. I, p. 76.

[30] If these dates are correct, Lucrezia de' Medici married very young, and Piero would have been rather youthful to be the recipient of such a treatise as the *De moribus*. The *Nuova enciclopedia italiana*, Vol. XIX, p. 1147, gives the

Nesius writes in a very monotonously flowing style. He loves to string along proper names from Greek and Roman history or mythology. He is full of classical examples and allusions, and is prone to ask rhetorical questions, such as, "What shall I say of the senses?" or "What shall I say of Hercules, to whom, because of this divine virtue, Pallas gave the peplos, Vulcan the club and breastplate, Neptune his horses, Mercury his sword, Apollo his bow, and finally Ceres, to expiate the slaughter of the centaurs, gave certain mysteries?" Or he calls history to witness, as when he exclaims, "Witness are the Lacedaemonians, who, when oppressed by the Thebans in war. . . ." To this repetitious and oratorical mode of utterance Gregory Crispus was likewise much given; indeed, his fulsomeness often approached very close to that of Dickens' Mr. Chadband.

Like Gregory again, Nesius cites Apollophanes and Aquinas, and follows by preference Aristotle and the Peripatetic philosophy concerning the institution of moral standards and the problem of human felicity. He makes, however, many flattering references to Plato and his *Republic*, and also refers to Marsilius Ficinus's *Theology*.[31] Nor are medieval writers like Egidius Romanus slighted.

The quest for the *summum bonum* for some time commands Nesius's attention. He calls the perfect life that "in which, after we have accomplished many things prudently and wisely, we finally have attained a certain constant and lasting affection for all the virtues." He adds, repeating a proverb which we have already heard John of Arezzo use,[32] that one swallow does not make a spring nor one fine day a summer.[33] Later he de-

---

year 1486 as the date of the marriage, but I do not know on what authority. Nesius mentions the fact that Politian, whom he praises highly, had been selected by Piero's parents as his tutor.

[31] Fol. 11r: ". . . et Marsilius Ficinus summus nostris temporibus iacentis iampridem acchademie excitator atque illustrator in sua theologia apertissime obtestatur . . ."

[32] See Chapter 2, page 40.

[33] Fol. 15r–v: "Vitam autem perfectam appello in qua cum multa pru-

fines happiness as "the best activity flowing from the soul joined in perfect life with good health and fortune." It is acquired by gift of God and our own effort.[34]

Turning to virtue, Nesius defines it as a habit having its starting point in our choice and marked by observance of the golden mean and prudence.[35] After some discussion of actions against the will,[36] he proceeds to the four cardinal virtues of fortitude, justice, prudence, and temperance, and others. He discusses more virtues than Gregory did, including magnificence and magnanimity as well as temperance, liberality, and mercy. He adds three other virtues from Aristotle: mediocrity in social intercourse — which comes close to friendship — truth, and urbanity or sociability. Of these Gregory mentioned only the last. Nesius, like Gregory, includes modesty among human affections that come close to virtues. He also marvels to Piero de' Medici, as Gregory did to Peter of Foix, that men give so much attention to medicines of the body and pay so little heed to those of the mind and soul.

With his third dialogue Nesius embarks on the subject of justice and law, discussing distributive justice and commutative and corrective justice. He then turns to such intellectual virtues as science, wisdom, art, prudence, and *sententia* or *gnome*. Continence and incontinence are then discussed; next, unnatural pleasures and heroic virtue, which rises as far above ordinary human nature as they fall below it. Something is also said of friendship. Finally, our author comes to the discussion of Christian felicity. Though he still draws not a little from Greek philosophy, classical names and allusions now become

---

denter sapienterque gesserimus tandem permanentem quandam constantem perpetuamque virtutum omnium affectionem contraxerimus quemadmodum enim nec unius hirundinis adventu ver nec unius diei serenitate estas adventat."

[34] Fol. 26v: "Diximus foelicitatem esse optimam actionem ab animo profluentem in vita perfecta cum corporis et fortune bonis coniunctam. Diximus eam divino beneficio nostraque simul opera comparari . . ."

[35] Fol. 35r: "Virtus igitur est habitus ab electione profectus in ea que a nobis emanat mediocritate locatus prudentieque examine definitus."

[36] Fol. 41r: "Hactenus de actionibus contra voluntatem."

fewer, and we hear also of Moses, Melchisedek, David, and Paul; or of Albertus, Aquinas, Scotus, Occam, and Nicholas of Lyra. Nesius, who had digressed earlier from his theme in order to flatter the Medici family, now closes with a glowing passage in which Acciaiuoli looks forward to meeting Cosimo and Piero in that happy land where they have won the immortal rewards of their labors and virtues. He then invites his young interlocutors to dinner.

The last work we have to note possesses the most inclusive title, namely, "Of God and the Principles of Natural Things and Supreme Beatitude."[37] It is by Oliver of Siena, doctor of arts and medicine. In 1497 he succeeded another Oliver, further named Arduinius, who had been receiving five hundred florins for teaching physics at the University of Pisa. But our Oliver's humble stipend was forty florins. In 1498 and 1499 he lectured on the *Ethics* and *De coelo et mundo* for eighty florins.[38] Presumably he is the same Oliver as the master of arts and doctor of medicine whose *Opus tripartitum rationalis scientiae* was printed at Siena in 1491[39] and dedicated to the cardinal of Florence, Giovanni de' Medici, son of Lorenzo the Magnificent, and the future Pope Leo X. In this work Oliver is spoken of as the private physician of Francesco, cardinal deacon of Siena.[40] The treatise which at present concerns us was dated by Bandini as a manuscript of the fifteenth century, and is dedicated at the close to the most worthy knight and jurisconsult, Dominicus de Martellis.[41]

[37] Laurent. Plut. 82, cod. 21, 15th century, 30 fols. Rubric, "Incipit tractatus editus ab Oliverio senense de deo et rerum naturalium principiis et summa beatitudine." Incipit, "Omnis mortalium cura quam multiplicium studiorum labor exercet . . ."

[38] Fabroni, *Hist. Univ. Pisa*, Vol. I, 1791, pp. 391–92. [39] Hain, * 12007.

[40] "Prohemium tractatus rationalis scientie Olivieri medici familiaris reverendissimi domini sancti Eustachii domini Francisci dyaconi Cardinalis Senensis ad Reverendissimum dominum dominum Iohannem magnifici viri filium Laurentii Medices Cardinalem Florentinum."

[41] "Oliverius senensis artium et medicine doctor dignissimo equiti iurisconsulto preclarissimo domino Dominico de Martellis tractatum hunc tradidit. . . ."

There are two somewhat different tables of contents,[42] one at the front and one at the close of the manuscript, which, despite its pretentious title, consists of only thirty small leaves of text. In the opening table of contents the author proposes to treat of six matters: (1) definition of God himself according to the more famous positions and truth of theologians; (2) of the making of spiritual creatures; (3) of the principles of natural things; (4) of the creation of the world; (5) what is the *summum bonum?* (6) of rational science and natural philosophy, of medicine, too, and of the end of each, briefly. In the closing table of contents, which is longer, these additional topics appear: of the eternity of the world and its creation, of ideas and forms, of moral wisdom and moral virtues, "finally of one sole God and triune by whom all things were made, from whom depends the sky and all nature, who lives and reigns through all ages, Amen." It will be seen that the majority of the topics treated coincide with those discussed in our other treatises. Also they were all topics commonly and repeatedly treated in the thirteenth century. The discussion is necessarily so brief that there is not much to note. Theologians define God as that than which nothing better can be conceived.[43] Oliver attempts to reconcile the eternity and creation of the world by arguing that God could have created the world from eternity.[44] A familiar spirit is Oliver's source of information for the following

[42] I reproduce these two tables of contents in Appendix 22.

[43] Fol. 3r: "Theologi enim diffiniunt deum esse id quo melius cogitari non potest."

[44] Some of his chief arguments in this connection are: fol. 17r: "Quare cum sapientissimis theologis dicendum est deum potuisse ab eterno producere mundum et quod possibile est ipsum a deo esse eternaliter productum"; "... Beatus quidem Thomas arguit sic mundum esse productum ab eterno non implicat contradictionem nec in deo imperfectionem ..."; fol. 17v: "... quare tales incorporales creature possunt deo condurare ita quod poterant esse ex quo altissimus fuit deus ab eterno. Motus preterea celi circularis potuit ab eterno fuisse quum talis non requirit primum"; fol. 18r: "... Quare et omnia quecumque possunt ab eterno fuisse et generabilia atque corruptibilia et mundus cum omnibus creatis creandis corruptis atque corrumpendis potuerunt ab eterno a deo fuisse creata."

data concerning the orders of fallen angels. Nine orders fell, while eighteen remained in heaven. A third of them are confined in the pit of hell with Lucifer. A second group assist in this lower air. The last third, situated in the upper atmosphere, are those who are invoked in magic art by the virtue of words. They do not suffer so great torments as their inferior and infernal associates, since they did not follow Lucifer but hesitated, vacillated, and showed ingratitude towards their Creator. Of moral virtues Oliver esteems friendship the most highly, devoting an entire page to it. Under the topic of natural philosophy he gives nearly another page to praise of Aristotle. He also accepts the Aristotelian dictum that the three principles of natural things are matter, form, and privation. Considering medicine, he briefly sings its praises, states its utility, and gives an account of its origin "from famous authors." Indeed, he cites a rather large number of authors, considering the brevity of his work: for morals, Seneca, Augustine, Gregory, Bernard, Jerome, Cassiodorus, Isidore, Ambrose, Cicero, and Hugo; on logic, Galen, Avicenna, Boethius, and others; on natural science, Boethius, Seneca, Augustine, Aristotle; on medicine, Galen, Averroës, Serapion, Hippocrates, Asclepiades, Esculapius, Celsus; on the principles of natural things, Dionysius the Areopagite, Avicenna, Averroës, Albertus Magnus, Gilbertus Porretanus; on God, Ovid, Orpheus, Hermes Trismegistus, and others. But of course all these were well known names; in fact, they had all been equally well known to Latin writers of the thirteenth century.

For all-inclusiveness and extreme brevity and superficiality Oliver's little treatise must be regarded as outdistancing any medieval compendium, epitome, or *vade mecum*. To attempt to cover theology, natural science, and morals in thirty brief leaves is something of an undertaking. It slightly reminds one of the "Pedagogue" (*Paedagogus*) of John Thomas Freigius, a work written to familiarize his sons with the common Latin words in all the arts and sciences. But they add in the edition of it which they published in 1582 after their father's death that he was not so foolish as to imagine that by study of this manual anyone could become a lawyer or doctor or philosopher. This work of Freigius, which consisted of simple questions and answers, covered 356 printed pages. Our work, which is more mature in tone and method, was probably intended to give some busy — or lazy — prince or noble a handy smattering of names, ideas, and citations on some of the leading topics of the learning of the time.

To sum up the total effect produced by the treatises which have been considered in this chapter, it has to be said that they display almost no new ideas or advance over the thirteenth century, that they are largely tiresome and insipid reading, sometimes affected. No pagan revival in morals or philosophy is manifested in them; there is merely a slight classical coloring in nonessentials. Classical allusions and citations are multiplied, but the Christian and Aristotelian points of view are intermingled much as in the preceding medieval period. We meet the same virtues as were personified in medieval allegory, drama, and art; we encounter such familiar themes as spontaneous generation and the orders of fallen angels. We fail to detect in our treatises any of that "awakening of the human spirit" which has been so often and so vaguely ascribed to an Italian Renaissance. Their stilted discussion of human felicity strikes no modern note to our ears. In fine, they show a certain amount of humanism — or perhaps better, classicism — of a diluted and restricted kind, but likewise a continuation of scholasticism. They suggest no new movement in human thought, no new period in history.

CHAPTER XII

THE *DE CONSTITUTIONE MUNDI* OF JOHN MICHAEL ALBERT OF CARRARA AND ITS RELATION TO SIMILAR TREATISES[1]

A scientific treatise of the second half of the fifteenth century which has hitherto passed well-nigh unnoticed is the *De constitutione mundi* of John Michael Albert of Carrara.[2] The work is of interest not merely as another specimen of fairly ample proportions — for it covers some 146 leaves in manuscript — of the scientific, or the would-be scientific, thought of that time, but on account of its particularly close relations to the earlier works of Ristoro d'Arezzo and Paul of Venice on the same subject. It further contains some valuable allusions to, and citations of, other authors of the preceding medieval centuries. Indeed, it is not of importance for new ideas or scientific progress, but rather for its backwardness and apparent failure to keep *au courant* with practical advance that was being made in scientific knowledge. On the other hand, it discusses such matters as demons, incantations, magic images, astrology, and alchemy with considerable fulness. Its attitude to religion and theology is also very suggestive as to the state of opinion in the closing fifteenth century.

Apostolo Zeno in his *Dissertazioni Vossiane*,[3] nearly two centuries ago, mentioned a fifteenth-century manuscript of our

[1] Revised and enlarged from *The Romanic Review*, Vol. XVII, No. 3, July–September, 1926, pp. 193–216.

[2] His life, however, has received recent treatment by A. Mazzi, *Sulla biografia di G. Michele Alberto Carrara*, Bergamo, 1901, 8vo, 221 pp. Mazzi made use especially of John Michael's autobiographical poem, *Commemoratio aerumnarum suarum a vigesimo anno usque ad trigesimum*.

[3] Apostolus Zeno, *Additiones ad historicos Latinos Vossii*, or, *Dissertazioni Vossiane*, Venezia, 1752, 2 vols. His account of Giovanni Michele Alberto da Carrara occurs in Vol. II, pp. 27–31.

treatise in 129 leaves at Turin,[4] but did not refer to the manuscript in which I have read the work at the Laurentian Library in Florence, Ashburnham 198.[5] The work is dedicated in both manuscripts to Boniface, marquis of Montferrat,[6] and hence appears to have been completed between 1483, when Bonifazio Paleologo became marquis, and 1488[7] or 1490, when John Michael Albert himself died. His *De constitutione mundi* was

[4] "Cod. cart. in fol. di pag. 129, in Bibl. Reg. Ducal. di Torino," is Zeno's designation of the MS. This was presumably the same as Codex CDI. i. II. 14, chart. fifteenth century, 129 fols., listed in Pasini's catalogue of 1749: J. Pasini, *Codd. MSS. Bibl. Regii Taurinensis Athenaei*, Vol. II. This MS probably was destroyed in the fire of January 26, 1904.

[5] Ashburnham 198 (formerly 130), 15th century, cod. cart. autografo, folio: "Johannes Michael Albertus Carrariensis ad praestantissimum principem Bonifacium Marchionem Montis Ferrati, De constitutione mundi."

In reading the manuscript I did not notice any decisive evidence either for or against the assertion that it is the original copy in the author's own handwriting. It is fairly legible. On the old cover, now bound inside, is written, "Originale manuscriptum."

[6] In Ashburnham 198: "Joannis Michaelis Alberti Carariensis excellentissimi philosophi ad praestantissimum principem Bonifacium Marchionem montis ferati opus inclytum de constitutione mundi feliciter incipit."

In the Turin MS, as reported by Zeno: "Michaelis Alberti de Carraria Guidonis filii ad Bonifacium Montisferrati illustrissimum principem de constitutione mundi." Pasini's description, presumably more accurate, has a "Joannis" prefixed and the word "tractatus" before the title "de constitutione mundi." The opening sentence of the text itself in the Ashburnham MS at Florence reads: "Inter gravissimos ac flagitiosissimos errores quos mortale genus cotidiano lapsu frequenter admittit, Magnificentissime vir Bonifaci . . ." In the Turin MS some scribe had deleted the name of Boniface and substituted "Bernarde Bembe," to whom also he had prefixed some Latin verses which Pasini quotes in his catalogue.

Pasini seems to have known nothing of Zeno's preparation of an account of John Albert Michael which was published three years after his own catalogue, since he says that he could find nothing in any writer about this Albert Michael of Carrara, son of Guido. He cannot be said to have done much towards spreading his fame himself, for although he gives us a short notice of the manuscript, one fails to find any mention of the man in his index under Albert, Carrara, John, or Michael.

Perhaps this is the reason why Zeno, although publishing his *Dissertazioni vossiane* three years after the appearance of Pasini's catalogue, gives us no shelfmark for the MS.

[7] Mazzi gives 1488 as the year; older accounts favored 1490.

never printed; indeed, the only one of his varied works which seems to have been put in type was a treatise on improving the memory published at Bologna in 1491, after his death.[8]

As John Michael Albert himself tells us in still another of his works, he was born in 1438, at Bergamo. He was one of four brothers who all achieved the baccalaureate in arts and medicine. He went to the University of Padua in 1454, lost his lady-love in 1457 by death, returned himself to Bergamo for a time to avoid the pest, and in 1458 took his baccalaureate in arts and began to study medicine.[9] His father, Guido of Carrara, who died in 1457 or 1459, was a learned physician who had written on celestial phenomena and whose views his son cites more than once in the *De constitutione mundi.*[10] John Michael practiced medicine at Rovato, Brescia, Chiari; was private physician to Roberto di Sanseverino and Prior of the College of Physicians in Bergamo.[11] Zeno gives us the titles of a number of John Michael's other works, and was him-

[8] "Liber Johannis Michaelis Alberti Carrariensis de omnibus ingeniis augendae memoriae . . . / . . . impressus per me Platonem de Benedictis civem Bonon. . . . 1491." Hain-Copinger 426; Proctor 6591; Pellechet 270.

Zeno, who reports this title, had not seen the work itself, but there is a copy in the Laurentian Library at Florence and there is one at Venice appended to MS S. Marco, X, 26 (Valentinelli), with other tracts on the same theme. A copy was recently offered for sale by Weiss & Co. of Munich.

[9] For these details see Mazzi, 1901.

[10] In the title of one of his son's works quoted below in note 14 Guido is described as "a great philosopher." In the *De constitutione mundi* John Michael Albert ventures the assertion that his father was "the most eminent man of our times in every variety of letters," and cites his opinions on such matters as sun spots, the creation of mountains, and the division of the earth's surface into climes.

Ashburnham 198, fol. 14v (II, 7): "Quadam tempestate vise sunt due gutte sanguinis in sole et vulgus terrefactum est. . . . Guido autem charrariensis genitor meus quem unum nostre etatis in omni genere litterarum prestantissimum audeo dicere planetas consideravit et adequavit et invenit venerem et mercurium esse causam." Fol. 113v (XI, 8): "Et ipse Guido multos montes in principio orbis creatos a deo credit non omnes postea natos." Fol. 116r (XII, 4): "Guido pater meus aliter et clarius de climatibus in metauris suis disseruit." Guido was also cited in caps. 5–6 of Tract. XI, at fols. 111r–112v; in Tract. VIII, cap. 7, fol. 71v; etc.

[11] See Mazzi, 1901.

self the owner of a manuscript of one of them, namely, *De choreis musarum* or *De origine omnium scientiarum.* It was completed between 1477 and 1487, since it is dedicated to Gabriel Rangonus, bishop of Agria (Erlau) and cardinal.[12] He was bishop of Agria from 1475 to 1487, and became a cardinal in 1477. The composition of this treatise was suggested to John Michael Albert by reading the work of Alfarabi on the origin of the sciences.[13] He also wrote a work in Italian in imitation of the *Divine Comedy* of Dante,[14] and various orations and histories, such as *De bello Veneto* and *Historiarum Italicarum libri XL.* Zeno notes that John listed some of his own works in the forty-ninth chapter of his *De choreis musarum.* In the *De constitutione mundi,* too, he occasionally cites other writings of his, such as his *Commentary on the Aphorisms of Hippocrates*[15] and single book *De fato.*[16] In 1488, John Michael Albert was given the title of Count Palatine by the emperor, Frederick III. In a manuscript of the fifteenth century at Padua an account of the mansions of the Jews in the desert is ascribed to a Franciscan friar, John Michael, of the province of Provence. Sbaraglia reports that some have dated this friar

[12] "... et beatorum Sergii et Bachi presbiterum card."

[13] The treatise opens: "Alpharabii librum cum illum legissem, Rev'issime G. Rangone, in quo de scientiarum origine mira ingenii celebratione disputavit." The work closes with the words: "... ad sibillinos annos summa cum gloria et sanitate perducat. Amen." It divides into six tractates. In treating of each science John Michael Albert not only mentions the chief ancient authorities in it, but also more recent ones and those of his own time. Zeno, *op. cit.*, Vol. II, p. 30, says of the work: "L'argomento è curioso ma meriterebbe di esser posto in miglior lume." A MS of it is S. Marco, X, 228 (Valentinelli), 15th century, 60 fols.

[14] "Comincia la Comoedia di Giohanne Michele Alberto figlio del grande phylosopho D. Guido da Carrara, ne la quale se canta Madonna Ursola in tri libri (anzi quattro) chiamati Cupido, Venus, et Dyana (e Coelum). Capitolo primo ne lo quale Cupido apparve a Pamphilo cum gran Triumpho de Poete e di Signori tra chi era Marrone:" Zeno, *op. cit.*, Vol. II, p. 27.

[15] Ashburnham 198, fol. 71v: "... ut bene notavimus in scripto nostro in 3° afforismo."

[16] Ashburnham 198, fol. 67r: "Nam extat Senece liber de providentia dei et nos de fato librum unum alio quoque tempore scripsimus."

about 1490, but there seems to be no reason for identifying him with our author.[17]

At first glance the work of John Michael Albert on the constitution of the universe seems to contain a number of striking ideas, but then practically all of these are found to go back to the earlier works of the same title by Paul of Venice,[18] who died in 1429, and Ristoro d'Arezzo,[19] who wrote in 1282. Duhem has already charged Paul of Venice with plagiarism on a large scale from Ristoro,[20] but Duhem was unacquainted with our

[17] MS Antoniana XX, 465, 15th century: "Circa quadraginta duas mansiones . . . / . . . Explicit opus de mansionibus editum a Fr. Joanne Michaele ord. minorum de provincia Provinciae."

[18] I have examined the work of Paul of Venice in the edition of 1498, where it occupies fols. 103r–117v, following his commentary on Aristotle's *De generatione et corruptione.* "Divi Pauli Veneti Theologi clarissimi philosophi summi ac astronomi maximi libellus quem inscripsit de compositione mundi Aureus incipit . . . / . . . Pauli Veneti Theologi clarissimi ac philosophi summi liber aureus quem de compositione mundi edidit feliciter explicit. Correctus a proprio originali per venerabilem virum fratrem Jacobum Baptistam Aloyxium de Ravenna lectorem in conventu Venetiarum sancti Stephani. Impressus Venetiis mandato et expensis nobilis Viri domini Octaviani Scoti Civis Modoetiensis duodecimo kalendas Juniae 1498. Per Bonetum Locatellum Bergomensin. Finis."

For the life and bibliography of Paul see Felice Momigliano, *Paolo Veneto e le correnti del pensiero religioso e filosofico nel suo tempo*, Udine, 1907.

Most of Paul's works were printed, and he seems to have enjoyed in the fifteenth century a reputation as both a philosopher and an astronomer which was far above his true worth. The study of his *Logica*, printed at Venice in 1474, was made compulsory at Padua in 1496 (see Vansteenberghe, *Le Cardinal Nicolas de Cues (1401–1464)*, Paris, 1920, p. 12), and in the sixteenth and seventeenth centuries found a last refuge in the schools of the Jesuits (Momigliano, 1907, p. 125).

[19] The treatise of Ristoro d'Arezzo was published in the nineteenth century by Narducci: *La composizione del mondo di Ristoro d'Arezzo testo italiano del 1282 pubblicato da Enrico Narducci*, Roma, 1859; 2d ed., Milan, 1864, with a different pagination. I shall therefore cite it by book and chapter. Although Narducci knew of five MSS of the work, of which at least two were older than the fifteenth century MS on which he based his version, he reproduced its text without giving variant readings from the other MSS. Yet he criticized Gori and Nannucci, who had printed the text of a single chapter on Arezzo vases, for erroneous readings by giving in parallel columns the wording of one of these MSS for that particular passage.

[20] Ristoro d'Arezzo and Paul of Venice are treated by Duhem (Pierre) in

treatise by John Michael Albert. A favorite theory of Ristoro, which he often repeats, is that everything in nature has its opposite or contrary, that our knowledge of things is enhanced by this contrast, and that their operation is somehow increased in potency by this relationship existing between them. Ristoro employs this axiom to arrive at the most varied conclusions, as Duhem has noted. For instance, to give a further example not mentioned by Duhem, he uses it to prove the existence of demons. For if we have animals that are visible, with gross bodies, that cannot pass through mountains or alter their shapes, by this law of contraries we should also have invisible animals with exceedingly refined bodies that can tunnel through mountains and change their forms at will.[21] This same law of opposites is frequently invoked by both Paul of Venice and our John Michael Albert, but the latter alone has a distinct chapter devoted to the topic, "That Nature delights in the production of pairs."[22]

Duhem has devoted several pages[23] to an exposition of Ristoro's account of the generation or formation of mountains, which he thinks was for the most part put together from Avicenna, Albertus Magnus, and Vincent of Beauvais. Paul of Venice simply reproduced it, except that he omitted the important mention of fossils of sea life found high up on mountains, and the inference therefrom that the deluge was one of the causes of mountain formation. John Michael Albert does not make this omission.[24] Moreover, he cites Albert, who seems to have been Ristoro's source for the fossils on mountains, and instead of ascribing the formation of mountains to the particular deluge of the Bible, as Ristoro did, he speaks of great

Études sur Léonard de Vinci, ceux qu'il a lus et ceux qui l'ont lu, Vol. II, 1909, pp. 319–25; and in *Le système du monde: histoire des doctrines cosmologiques de Platon à Copernic,* Vol. IV, 1916, pp. 199–210.

[21] *La composizione del mondo di Ristoro d'Arezzo,* VIII, 3.

[22] Ashburnham 198, VII, 4 (fol. 57v), "Quod natura delectata est in productione rerum parium."

[23] Already cited in note 20.

[24] XI, 8, "de causa generationis montium"; Ashburnham 198, fol. 113r.

floods in a general way. Since Duhem does not mention it, we may note another point, that Ristoro among his further causes of mountain formation suggested the petrifying action of water, narrating the following personal experience. Bathing in a hot spring on a mountain top, he found that stone from the water adhered to his hair as wax does to the wick of a candle.[25] John Michael Albert repeats this, and while he has cited Albert for the fossils found on mountains, he cites "Aretinus" (i.e., Ristoro d'Arezzo) for this personal experience.[26] Paul of Venice, on the other hand, did not include such petrifaction or calcareous deposit at all among his four causes of the formation of mountains.[27]

Closely connected with these three authors' accounts of the causes and process of mountain formation are two other matters which they treat in almost identical fashion. The first is the belief that rivers cannot be explained as the result of mere rainfall and precipitation, but that they are fed from the sea and that the water found on the mountain tops has come up through the pores of the earth and subterranean channels and reservoirs from the sea.[28] This view, indeed, did not originate with Ristoro but is found in earlier medieval authors. Aristotle probably lent encouragement to it by such statements as the following from the *Meteorologica* (I, 14): "We have seen [in *De caelo et mundo*] that some say that the size of the subterranean cavities is what makes some rivers perennial and others not, whereas we maintain that the size of the mountains is the cause, and their density and coldness; for great, dense, and cold

[25] VI, 8. "E nella sommitade d'uno di quelli monti era uno bagno d'acqua calda: nella quale noi ne bagnammo, e nostri capelli, i quali stavano nell'acqua, vi si poneva pietra d'attorno, come la cera allo stoppino per fare candela."

[26] Ashburnham 198, fol. 113r–v: "Tertia causa potest esse aqua cuius natura sit ut saxificetur et sic inducatur lapidi crusta supra crustam et crescat in montem. Refert Aretinus se fuisse in balneo in sumitate montis et illam aquam adhesisse capillis sicut ceram et in saxum conversam esse."

[27] Cap. 18 (1498), fol. 112v.

[28] Ristoro, VI, 5 and 7; Paul of Venice, caps. 18–19; John Michael Albert, XI, 5 and 7.

mountains catch and keep and create most water."[29] Ristoro accepted the ancient theory sanctioned by Aristotle, that earth was the heaviest of the four elements, and that therefore the sphere of water was above the sphere of earth which it circumscribed just as it in turn was surrounded by the concentric spheres of air, fire, the moon, the other six planets, and the eighth sphere of the fixed stars. But in order that the heavenly bodies might exercise their generative force upon the earth, a portion of its surface was uncovered by the waters. In Ristoro's opinion this dry land was about one quarter of the total surface of our globe. It formed the habitable world and was entirely comprised within the northern hemisphere. The waters displaced from this portion of the earth's surface were thought of by Ristoro as piled up elsewhere, where they were held in place and check by the virtue of the stars, but rose higher towards the sky than the tops of the highest mountains in the dry portion of the globe.[30] If once the stars relaxed their hold on these huge piles of water, a universal deluge of the habitable world would naturally result. It was the downward pressure of this great mass of accumulated water which, according to Ristoro, forced water up through the spongy and perforated substance of the mountains to issue forth from their very tops. It certainly seems odd that a learned writer like John Michael Albert should still hold this theory of water ascending to mountain tops in the late fifteenth century, when a mere layman and apothecary like Luca Landucci, in his diary[31] twenty years or so before, had correctly ascribed a sudden flood of the Arno in 1465 to the melting of snow on the mountains.

[29] Translation of E. W. Webster, 1923; see pp. 352b16, 353b10, 356b10; and 279b12, *De caelo*, translation of J. L. Stocks, 1922.

[30] This astrological explanation goes back to Averroës. Another medieval explanation for the emergence of so much dry land above the circumscribing sphere of water was that the spheres of earth and water had different centers, so that a section of the earth projected beyond the circumference of the sphere of water.

[31] Edited by Iodoco del Badia, 1882; English translation, 1927. That rivers were increased by the melting of snow in the Alps was suggested also in the *Opus maius* of Roger Bacon.

Nevertheless, this same theory was still accepted by many at the close of the seventeenth century, when the defenders of the ancients in the struggle with the moderns held that the circulation of the blood had been already known to men like Hippocrates and Plato, who were familiar with the analogous circulation of waters from the ocean by subterranean channels to the mountain tops, and then back to the sea by streams and rivers, just as the blood returns to the heart by the veins which seam the body.[32] This attitude may be more particularly illustrated from the work of Philip Jacob Sachs, published at Breslau in 1664, on the analogy between the movement of waters to and from the ocean and that of blood from and to the heart.[33] In a paragraph on "Why water ascends mountains,"[34] he repeats the reasoning of Ristoro [35] that in correspondence to the diversified positions of the stars more water is heaped up in one place than another and that this piled-up mass of water by its downward pressure forces other water up through subterranean canals to the mountain tops. He also makes the second suggestion, which we shall presently hear from the lips of Galateo writing about 1500, but for which Sachs cites Panarolus, *Arcan. fascic.*, Vol. II, p. 221, that the internal heat of the earth turns the water in its caverns into vapor which ascends by the same subterranean passages.[36]

[32] Francesco Bertini, *La medicina difesa dalle calunnie degli uomini volgari e dalle opposizioni de' dotti, divisa in due dialoghi*, Lucca, 1699, p. 79: cited by Gabriel Maugain, *Étude sur l'évolution intellectuelle de l'Italie de 1657 à 1750 environ*, Paris, 1909, pp. 70–71.

[33] Philippi Jacobi Sachs à Lewenheimb, Phil. & Med. D. & Collegii Naturae Curiosorum Collegae, *Oceanus Macro-Microcosmicus seu Dissertatio Epistolica de analogo motu aquarum ex & ad Oceanum, sanguinis ex & ad cor, ad magnif. nobiliss. excell. experientiss. Dn. Thomam Bartholinum, medicum & anatomicum incomparabilem professorem regium honorarium, & decanum fac. in regia Hafnensi perpetuum*, Vratislaviae, sumtibus Esaiae Fellgiebelii, MDCLXIV, 152 pp.

[34] *Ibid.*, pp. 73–74.

[35] Whom, however, he does not cite.

[36] In this connection he still speaks of nature's abhorring a vacuum, despite Torricelli's recent experiment (1644), to say nothing of medieval theories of the continuity of nature. *Ibid.*, p. 74: "Accedit quod ad evitandum vacuum

The other matter in this connection which our three authors treat similarly is the origin of the Mediterranean Sea.[37] Ristoro makes the point that if the dry portion of the earth's surface is to be habitable, it should be watered in the middle by a great arm of the ocean, into which should flow all the streams that run towards the middle of the earth, of which the Nile is the greatest. The virtue of the sky, working for generation on earth, drives the Mediterranean like a big irrigation ditch into the heart of the habitable earth. Paul of Venice and John Michael Albert repeat these same ideas, although — writing after Marco Polo, John of Monte Corvino, Jordanus Catalanus, John of Florence, and Jacobus Angelus's translation of the *Geography* of Ptolemy as they do — we might expect them in the fifteenth century to have outgrown Ristoro's restricted conception of the habitable world as centering about the Mediterranean and of that sea as the reservoir from which most inland waters are drawn and to which they return.

Indeed, John Michael Albert, although completing his work in the last quarter of the fifteenth century, has not a word to say of the Portuguese navigation which had been making progress down the coast of Africa for some time past. Although the equator, to say nothing of the tropic of Cancer, had been crossed in 1472–73, he still holds, writing between 1483 and 1490, that there is a torrid zone which is arid, sterile, and uninhabited.[38] Ristoro,[39] two centuries before had adopted a view which was common then, to the effect that it is hotter at the tropics than at the equator, where the equal duration of day and night, and the fact that the sun is directly overhead only

ad continuationem fluxus una pars alteram trahat." Yet at p. 112 Sachs cites an experiment of Robert Boyle.

[37] Ristoro, VI, 6; Paul of Venice, caps. 18–19; John Michael Albert, XI, 6.

[38] (Tract, III, cap. 4) Ashburnham 198, fol. 24r: "Comburit igitur terra illa et fit sterilis sine fructu et incolis caret. Et hic locus proprie torrida zona." Paul of Venice, cap. 6, also speaks of a "zona adusta" which is uninhabitable.

[39] Ristoro, I, 23: "Delle cose c'addivengono per lo movimento del sole; . . . e della zona perusta"; VIII, 12: "Da riprovare l'opinione di coloro che vollero dire che la terra fusse discoperta dell'acqua, e abitata nella parte del mezzodì, secondo ch'ella è nella parte di settentrione."

twice a year, were supposed to produce a temperate clime. In fact, Ristoro calls the equatorial region the noblest and most temperate, where the earth yields fruit twice a year.[40] But under the tropics or extremities of the circle of the zodiac, in the signs where the sun tarries longest, was a *zona perusta* or torrid zone, the most intemperate of regions, uninhabitable and yielding no crops. Albertus Magnus in his *De natura locorum* and Roger Bacon in the *Opus maius* had discussed the matter with much more discretion. John Michael Albert cites the treatise of Albert but on the whole he follows Ristoro. He also repeats Ristoro's astrological argument against the existence of the Antipodes or land in the southern hemisphere, that there are more stars in the north, and that the heads of the animals in the zodiac are turned northward while their feet point to the south.[41] He further adds, in almost the same words as Ristoro, that if there were land far to the south beyond the sea, men would have navigated the sea and crossed to the southland, and we should know the customs of those localities. But this has not happened; therefore the southern hemisphere is entirely covered by water.[42] Such medieval views, it may be added,

[40] Ristoro, VIII, 12: "... e noi troviamo, secondo che pongono li savi e spezialmente l'Alfragano nell'ottavo capitolo, che'l mare comprende lo primo clima, lo quale confina collo 'ncominciamento della parte del mezzodì da oriente a occidente; e quello luogo, secondo ragione, è lo più nobile e lo più temperato che sia in tutta la parte del mezzodì; imperciò ch'egli è d'ogni tempo quasi iguale il dì colla notte, e sarebbevi due volte l'anno lo frutto della terra."

[41] Compare Ristoro, VIII, 12 (pp. 273–74 in ed. of 1864), with Ashburnham 198, fol. 72r (VIII, 8).

[42] Ristoro's words are: "E potrebbesi dire, che quello mare fusse uno braccio di mare, lo quale fusse mestieri in quello luogo, e da indi in là fusse abitato; e se lì fusse uno braccio di mare, quello mare sarebbe navicato; si che la gente della parte di settentrione saprebbe la condizione di quella del mezzodì, e econtra: la qual cosa non si truova; e questo è segno, che quella parte sia disabitata e coperta dall'acqua."

John Michael Albert says: "Et si aliquis diceret illud mare esse mediterraneum et ultra illud esse habitationes, tunc profecto navigassent homines et transfretassent in meridiem et scirent mores illorum locorum, quod non adhuc contigit, igitur illa pars aquis submersa est. . . ."

On the more general question of the ratio of land to water on the earth's surface see, Arnold Norlind, "Das Problem des gegenseitigen Verhältnisses von

were not in accord with Aristotle, in whose *Meteorologica* (II, 5) it is stated that there are habitable sections of the earth in both the southern and northern hemispheres, whereas between the tropics life is everywhere impossible.

It should of course be distinctly understood that the most enlightened and best informed opinion of both the thirteenth and fifteenth centuries was in advance of the views either of Aristotle or of Ristoro and John Michael Albert. Albertus Magnus had argued that the southern hemisphere was inhabited and against the existence of an uninhabitable torrid zone.[43] Peter of Abano had learned by inquiry from Marco Polo that the Antipodes were inhabited.[44] Poggio, in his account of the fifteenth-century travels of Niccolò Conti, even affirmed that the mariners of India steer for the most part by the stars of the southern hemisphere, "as they rarely see those of the north."[45]

Ludovicus de Angulo, a Spaniard, in 1456 addressed to René of Provence, titular king of Sicily, a treatise in three books *De figura seu imagine mundi*, which appears not to have been printed [46] and which I should perhaps note in this connection.

Land und Wasser und seine Behandlung im Mittelalter," in *Acta Universitatis Lundensis*, nova series, Vol. XIV, 1918, 57 pp.

[43] *De natura locorum*, I, vii: "Utrum habitabilis sit quarta terrae quae est ab aequinoctiali usque in polum Australem?"

[44] See my *History of Magic and Experimental Science*, Vol. II, p. 885.

[45] "The Travels of Nicolò Conti in the East in the Early Part of the Fifteenth Century, translated from the origina' of Poggio Bracciolini," by J. W. Jones, in *India in the Fifteenth Century*, edited by R. H. Major, London, 1857, pp. 26–27. Poggio goes on to remark rather carelessly that the Indians, being ignorant of the compass, determine their position at sea by the elevation and depression of the pole (i.e., the polar star), which hardly agrees with his previous statement, unless he means the south pole or some star marking it.

[46] I have examined it in a manuscript at Paris, BN 6561, where it covers fols. 1r–152r, opening, "Cum secundum philosophum primo de anima omnium rerum notitiam seu scientiam habere certitudinaliter debemus . . ." and closing, ". . . huius libri qui perfectus fuit divina gratia auxiliante anno domini millesimo quadringentesimo quinquagesimo sexto xviii mensis decembris in civitate Lugdunensi. Deo gratias Amen." The colophon has been cut out. The spaces left blank for figures have sometimes not been filled in.

It divides into three parts, of which the first deals with the creation of the world, the second with the division of the earth and its parts, and the third with the sphere of the sky and the planets and fixed stars. But there seems to be some confusion of arrangement and needless repetition of matter.[47] Despite its author's provenance from the Iberian peninsula, it is perhaps not to be expected that at the date at which he writes he should make any allusion to the work of Prince Henry the Navigator. But he does show some acquaintance with the Far East and with the work of Marco Polo.[48] In general, however, the work shows no particular merit or distinction. To demonstrate the rotundity and center of gravity of our earth the author employs the familiar example of the stone or other object dropped in a hole running through the earth which would stop in its fall when it reached the earth's center.[49] He grants

[47] To give some idea of the contents and arrangement I may note some of the headings: fol. 3r, "de creatione hominis"; fol. 4v, "de initio mundi et fine eius"; fol. 5r, "de mundo si finem habiturus sit"; fol. 6v, "quo tempore mundus principium habuerit"; fol. 7v, "de figura mundi"; fol. 8v, "de numero et situatione elementorum"; fol. 9v, "de parte mundi etherea"; fol. 11r, "de rotunditate terre et qualiter est in medio firmamenti"; fol. 13v, "de motu impetuoso firmamenti"; fol. 14v, "de quantitate terre." At fol. 15v begins "Secunda pars de divisione terre et partibus eiusdem continet"; at fol. 17v comes a T-map; at fol. 28v, "de diversitate serpentum et aliorum animalium que sint in India"; on fol. 29v, we read of the beaver and his testicles and the mice as large as cats; at fol. 32r, of the magnet; at fol. 39r, of Prester John; fol. 40r, "de valle tenebrosa"; fol. 41r, of the land of giants from twenty-eight to thirty feet tall; fol. 41v, "de insulis maris tam in Asia quam in Europa et Africa"; fol. 42v, "de diversitate viarum in peregrinatione terre sancte"; at fol. 45, of Rhodes and Cyprus; fol. 46v, "et si aliquis vult ire per terram in babiloniam"; fol. 51v, "de sepultura Gaufridi de Bullon" (i.e., Godfrey of Bouillon, the crusader); fols. 57v–71v deal with the Great Khan and Marco Polo's account of his empire (67v, Tibet); fol. 72v is blank; fol. 73 is missing; with fol. 74r we come to the division of the earth's surface into seven climes and the influence of the stars thereon; at fol. 81v, the parts of Europe and Africa are taken up for the second or third time. The third part of the work opens on fol. 87v, its second section at fol. 112v, and its third section at fol. 131v. The first section contains many figures of the constellations, etc. The second and third sections are largely concerned with astrological relations and influences.

[48] *Ibid.*, fol. 62v: ". . . dicit marchus pauli in sua hystoria orientali"; fol. 64r: "Et dicit marchus pauli."

[49] *Ibid.*, fol. 13r (cap. 10 of the first book). Actually if there were no fric-

that in some cases it might continue its course a way beyond the center but that it would then fall back again towards it. The author still believes in uninhabitable parts of the earth [50] and states that Ethiopia is situated at the end of Africa and that beyond it there is no habitation on account of the excessive heat of the torrid zone, "and there is nothing there except deserts and wild animals and serpents until you come to the great sea."[51]

The same total ignorance of equatorial regions and the southern hemisphere that Ludovicus de Angulo and John Michael Albert displayed continued to be manifest in the works of the somewhat later, and much better known and more celebrated scientific writer, Alessandro Achillini (1463–1512), the anatomist and Peripatetic or Averroistic philosopher. In his treatise on the elements, as printed in his *Opera* first in 1508 and then again in 1545,[52] the question whether the torrid zone is inhabitable and most temperate is discussed theoretically with citations from Aristotle, Avicenna, and Peter of Abano, but without any allusion to recent actual contact with those regions, the only reference to practical experience being the

tion or atmospheric resistance, the stone would acquire sufficient momentum to carry it on to the opposite side of the earth, when it would swing back again like a pendulum to its starting point, and so on. For the use of this illustration by Adelard of Bath in the early twelfth century, see my *History of Magic and Experimental Science*, Vol. II, pp. 35–36.

[50] BN 6561, fols. 79r–80r.

[51] *Ibid.*, fol. 27v: "Et ethiopia est sita in fine affrice et ultra ethiopiam non est habitacio propter maximum calorem torride zone et nichil ibi est nisi loca deserta et animalia bruta ut serpentes usque ad mare magnum."

[52] Both of these editions were at Venice. There were others of 1551, 1568, and 1608. The 1508 edition was by Octavianus Scotus and Bonetus de Locatellis, in 120 fols., and the *De elementis* is the fourth treatise in it. The 1545 edition was printed by Hieronymus Scotus and is full of misprints. The following citations will be to this edition, in which the three books of the *De elementis* occupy fols. 90v–149r. Just when Achillini composed the *De elementis* I have not discovered. He seems to have published some treatises on physics and motion at Bologna in 1494; *Quatuor libri de orbibus*, which constitute the second item in the 1508 edition, also at Bologna in 1498; and his treatises on chiromancy and physiognomy, in 1503; but there appears to have been no edition of the *De elementis* before that of 1508.

author's own observation of the time of the sun's greatest heat at Bologna. Astrological considerations are also again present in the discussion. Turning from the torrid to the temperate zones, Achillini states that experience shows that the northern one is inhabited, but "not so concerning the southern one."[53] He then continues, "Moreoever, that at the equator figs grow the year round, or that the air there is most temperate, or that the animals living there have temperate constitutions, or that the terrestrial paradise is there — are things which natural experience does not reveal to us."[54]

On the other hand, John of Glogau, a professor of mathematics and philosophy at the University of Cracow, who died in 1507, in a commentary published the previous year on the *Sphere* of Sacrobosco, adduced the existence of the rich and populous island of Taprobane (Ceylon) at the equator in refutation of Sacrobosco's assertion of an uninhabitable torrid zone. He also stated that Portuguese voyages of 1501 and 1504 had crossed the equator to the new world, and that geographers of the fifteenth century had shown that the frigid zone to the north of the arctic circle was inhabited.[55]

By the time of Cardinal Contarini (1483–1542) old views as to the extent of the habitable world had been definitely altered as a result of the maritime discoveries. In his five books on the elements, which were published posthumously in 1548,[56] he notes that Aristotle and the older authors all thought that

[53] Ed. of 1545, fol. 149r: "non sic de meridionali."

[54] *Ibid.*: "Quod autem sub aequinoctiali continue habeantur ficus aut quod aer sit ibi temperatissimae dispositionis aut quod animalia ibi habitantia temperatam habeant complexionem aut quod paradisus terrestris ibi sit sunt res quas experientia naturalis nobis non ostendit."

[55] Johannes Glogoviensis, *Introductorium compendiosum in tractatum spere materialis magistri Joannis de Sacrobusto . . .*, Cracovie, 1506, cap. 2.

[56] *Gasparis Contareni Cardinalis ampliss. philosophi sua aetate praestantissimi de elementis et eorum mixtionibus libri quinque*, Paris, 1548. The work is dedicated by "Ioannes Gaignaeus ecclesiae atque academiae Parisiens. Cancellarius et doctor theologus" to Cardinal Marcellus Cervinus, and was printed by Nicolaus Dives. There is a manuscript of it at the Vatican: Vatic. Lat. 3165, Gaspar Contarenus de elementis eorumque mixtionibus, "Nullum est omnium . . ."

the polar and torrid zones were uninhabitable because too near or too far from the sun, whose rays fell either too obliquely or too perpendicularly to support life. Avicenna, however, held that the heat was due to long presence of the sun rather than to its rays falling directly, and that consequently only the tropics were uninhabitable, while the equinoctial circle was very fit for human habitation.[57] Averroës in turn attacked this view in his *Paraphrase* on Aristotle's *Meteorology*, holding that the heat was intolerable at the equator. Having thus rehearsed the old views, Contarini continues: "This question, which for many years was disputed between the greatest philosophers, experience has solved in our times. For from this new navigation of the Spaniards and especially of the Portuguese it has been discovered that there is habitation under the equinoctial circle and between the tropics, and that innumerable peoples dwell in those regions who are dark brown, not entirely black as the Ethiopians are. . . . Under the tropics, indeed, there are hotter regions than under the equinox, yet they are not uninhabitable except the African deserts filled with sand. And even there, that they may not be wholly vacant, dwell the Ethiopians and Troglodytes."[58] According to Contarini, the voyages of the Spaniards had led to the further discovery that the ocean was surrounded on all sides by land, and that consequently the surface of the land was not less than the sea but perhaps of greater extent.[59] This opinion, however, simply confirmed

[57] Contarini, *op. cit.* fol. 40r–v. [58] *Ibid.*, fol. 41r–v.

[59] *Ibid.*, fol. 38r. This became the prevailing opinion in the sixteenth and seventeenth centuries and was definitely dispelled only by the voyages of Cook in the eighteenth century. See Roberto Almagià, "Il primo tentativo di misura del rapporto quantitativo fra le terre emerse e i mari," *Archivio di storia della scienza*, Vol. II, 1921, pp. 51–64, and Alessandro Piccolomini, *Trattato della grandezza dell' acque e della terra*, 1557, and other works which Almagià cites. He does not mention the *Tractatus in quo adversus Antiquorum et praecipue Peripateticorum opinionem Terram esse aqua maiorem . . . demonstratur* (Paris, Th. Perier, 1585), of Nonius Marcellus Saya, astrologer to Catherine de' Medici. Mercator (1512–94) held that there should be as much land in the southern as in the northern hemisphere. Riccioli changed from a position of uncertainty in his *Almagestum novum*, 1651, to an estimate of forty parts of land surface for every twenty-five of water in his *Geographia et hydrographia reformata*, 1661.

Contarini in the other old view that a vast amount of water was stored in subterranean caverns. He affirms that the earth is full of water like a sponge and that floods are sometimes produced by the emission of water from these caves of earth.[60] A recent great flood which he witnessed in Spain near Valencia could be accounted for on no other theory, since no one knew whence so much water came so suddenly.[61]

Similar but not identical was the position of Antonio Galateo, or Antonio Ferrari il Galateo (1444–1517),[62] who had been a pupil of Nicolaus Leonicenus at Ferrara, in three dialogues, *De situ elementorum*, *De situ terrarum*, and *De mari et aquis et fluviorum origine*,[63] which were written about the end of

For the earlier medieval attitude to the problem, see E. Wisotzki, *Die Verteilung von Wasser und Land an der Erdoberfläche*, Diss., Königsberg, 1879; Giuseppe Boffito, "Intorno alla 'Quaestio de aqua et terra' attribuita a Dante," *Mem. Accad. Sci. Torino*, Vol. LI, 1902; Arnold Norlind, "Das Problem des gegenseitigen Verhältnisses von Land und Wasser und seine Behandlung im Mittelalter," *Lunds Univers. Arsskript*, NF XIV, 1918. Almagià warns that A. Tulli, "I sistemi geografici medioevali sulla distribuzione delle terre e delle acque nel globo," *Rivista di fis. matem. e sci. nat.*, Pisa, Vol. XIII, 1912, is "privo di valore."

[60] Contarini, *op. cit.*, fols. 31r–v and 38r.

[61] *Ibid.*, fol. 40. As late a work as the Rev. William Whiston's *New Theory of the Earth*, 1696, and other editions to 1755, held that Noah's flood was caused by the escape of waters from within the earth as well as the descent of the waters above the firmament. Burnet's *Sacred Theory of the Earth*, 1681, and John Woodward's *Essay towards a Natural History of the Earth*, 1695, also held that before the Deluge the interior of the earth had been filled with water, while Buffon, in full mid-eighteenth century, held the reverse view, that the earth's surface had originally been entirely under water until land was uncovered by the disappearance of a large amount of the water into the earth's interior. See Archibald Geikie, *The Founders of Geology*, 1905, Chaps. 2 and 3.

[62] For some account of him see Ludwig Geiger, *Renaissance und Humanismus in Italien und Deutschland*, pp. 261–62. After composing the paragraphs which follow independently from a direct examination of his works, I find that his geographical opinions and knowledge have already been the subject of a brief note by Roberto Almagià, "Le opinioni e le conoscenze geografiche di Antonio de Ferrariis," *Rivista Geografica Italiana*, 1905, pp. 333–34.

[63] I have used an edition of 1558, of 143 small octavo pages, where the three dialogues occupy pp. 1–120, while pp. 121–143 are occupied by Sebastianus Foxius Morzillus Hispalensis *De aquarum generibus*.

Concerning Sebastian Fox Morcillo (c. 1528–c. 1560) see Aubrey F. G. Bell,

the fifteenth century, apparently in part before and in part after the Portuguese circumnavigation of Africa. Galateo refers to "rex Federicus,"[64] which seems to mean Federigo, who occupied the throne of Naples for a few years following the battle of Fornovo in 1495. He laughs at Albert of Saxony for holding in the fourteenth century that the ocean was unnavigable, since now the Spaniards sail for thousands of miles on its bosom.[65] The dialogues are dedicated to Accius Syncerus Sannazarius,[66] but this does not serve to date them any more definitely.

Galateo, like our other authors, of whom he cites Paul of Venice but not in this connection,[67] believes that there are great recesses in the earth full of water.[68] He further believes that from these recesses the water ascends to the tops of mountains, but in the form of vapor. The water in these subterranean caves becomes heated and forms vapor, the vapor ascends through pores to the mountain tops, where it turns back into water and is distilled through other pores to the surface to form the sources of rivers.[69] "Moreover, it seemed to Aristotle that from the air [?] which is in the veins of mountains were generated flowing waters."[70]

Concerning the evolution of sea and land and the process of mountain formation, Galateo's position is as follows. He refuses to commit himself as to whether the total amount of water exceeds all the land, but he thinks that if the elements

Luis de Leon, 1925, pp. 30–31. He was invited by Philip II to become tutor to Prince Carlos, but was shipwrecked while returning to Spain from the Netherlands. His chief work was *De naturae philosophia seu de Platonis et Aristotelis consensione libri V*, Louvain, 1555.

64 Edition of 1558, p. 25: "Imprimis affero rationem Achilleam quam ipse rex Federicus pro ingenii sui magnitudine inter disputandum ex tempore assignavit." Elsewhere Galateo alludes to the time "cum essemus apud Federicum."

65 *Ibid.*, p. 58.

66 To whom Pontano also dedicated a poem: see Geiger, *Renaissance und Humanismus*, p. 255.

67 Ed. of 1558, p. 26.

68 *Ibid.*, p. 62.

69 *Ibid.*, p. 115.

70 *Ibid.*, p. 116: "Visum est autem Aristoteli quod ex aere qui est in venis montium generentur aquae fluviales."

exist in the ratio of ten parts of water for one of earth, ten of air for one of water, and ten of fire for one of air, there would be little space left between our world and the heavens.[71] As for the proposition that where there is now sea once was dry land and where there is now dry land once was sea,[72] he thinks it not improbable that if the sea loses ground in one place, it should gain it in another.[73] But that high mountains like the Pyrenees or Alps or Athos or Taurus or the Caucasus ever were or will be submerged, he regards as figments of poets or mere theories of philosophers,[74] especially if we date creation only some seven thousand years ago instead of accepting the eternity of the world. In the latter case he admits that the action of rivers might gradually wash the mountains entirely away, and that vast alterations might have taken place in islands, seas, and rivers.[75] One participant in the dialogue, however, suggests that mountains are replenished from rain or air to compensate for the sands washed off by waters.[76] That the Mediterranean Sea was formed by the Atlantic Ocean breaking through into the interior he doubts, demanding to know where were the numerous rivers that now flow into the Black and Mediterranean Seas before that event took place.[77] A long discussion is required to convince the participants in the dialogue that the habitable land is higher than the surface of the water.[78] In the later treatise *On Kinds of Waters* by Fox Morcillo, bound with Galateo's dialogues, the author expresses agreement with George Agricola as to two main causes of mountain formation, namely, the action of water in excavating a portion of the

[71] Ed. of 1558, p. 62: "Utrum autem tota aqua sit maior aut minor tota terra neque ego mensus sum neque aliquem novi qui mensus fuerit. Praeterea si corpora elementorum ita se haberent ut terra sit I, aqua X, aer C, ignis M, parvum esset inter nos et coelum interstitium."

[72] *Ibid.*, p. 71: "Ubi mare nunc est olim arida, ubi nunc arida olim mare fuit."

[73] *Ibid.*, p. 72: "Non est inconveniens quod si quid hic mare perdit aliunde repetat."

[74] *Ibid.*, p. 73.

[75] *Ibid.*, pp. 76–77.

[76] *Ibid.*, pp. 77–78.

[77] *Ibid.*, p. 74.

[78] It occurs between pages 26 and 37.

terrain and making the rest stand out, and the action of winds in piling up dust and sand.[79]

The three dialogues of Galateo seem not to have been printed until forty-one years after his own death and ten years after the appearance, also posthumous, of Contarini's *De elementis*. But Galateo's work was certainly written earlier, and so really gives us a prior glimpse of the effect of the Spanish and Portuguese voyages of discovery upon the old views as to the torrid zone and southern hemisphere. Indeed, in Galateo's pages we can observe the very transition from the old speculative uncertainty to the new definite experienced knowledge. On pages 19 and 20 of the 1558 edition he writes still in a sceptical tone of the reported circumnavigation of Africa: "Some say that those sent recently by the kings of the Occident on a long navigation to the Indian Ocean steered their way e'en to the Gulf of Colchis [meaning the Caspian Sea?] and thence brought back pepper and cinnamon and ginger and ivory [elephants' teeth], all which I remember to have seen under the elder Ferdinand [Ferrante I of Naples, died 1494?]. This was also the opinion of our George the Italian of Genoa, a man most diligent in scouring the globe and in investigating the sites of countries, who was with us at your house in Naples while we were writing these things. . . . More recent writers perhaps call Ethiopia India. But a certain ambassador of the king of the Portuguese [men of Lisbon or Lusitania], who seemed to me better informed than other men of that nation, told me that none of those who had been sent out by their king had ever penetrated to the equator, which he said had been demonstrated by astronomical instruments . . ." This last statement would seem to indicate that the Portuguese government purposely concealed the extent of the progress of its expeditions down the African coast, and that therefore John Michael Albert in 1483–90 had some excuse for his ignorance of their navigations.

On page 21, however, Galateo entirely changes his tone and

[79] Ed. of 1558, pp. 142–43.

says: "All these matters were not sufficiently certain when we were writing the book. But now as we publish it in the last year of the reign of king Federigo [i.e., 1501] all agree that the Portuguese have circumnavigated the whole of Africa and have reached the Indian Ocean and even the Arabian and Persian Gulfs and there have held their own with the fleet of the king of the Egyptians and of Syria whom they call the Sultan, and finally have reached the Gulf of Colchis, that other emporium of spices, and even the isle of Taprobane (Ceylon)."

Later on, Galateo also discusses the discovery of western islands, remarking in reference to Plato's account of Atlantis: "Some think that those islands which the kings of the West have discovered in our age were the mountains and highest spots of that island. All glory to those valiant men and most deserving of our commemoration and well deserving of posterity who dared to entrust themselves to an unknown and boundless sea, who dared to penetrate that vast void of nature. They have taught us that there is nothing that is impossible for man. So great was the care of Nature, parent of all, concerning us. O, hail again and again to those valiant men who dared that great and memorable deed! But I doubt whether it will be for the good of the races whom you have found — races truly blest, and, as Horace says, 'The Isles of the Blest, content with their own resources live in the golden age.' I fear lest while you think to lead them to a more civilized life, while you take pains to introduce religion, laws, varied arts, elaborate dishes, and other things without which life would be happier, you at the same time inject our vices, tyrannies, honors, offices, ambitions, arms and artillery, servitudes, lawsuits and legal puzzles and inexplicable perplexities and those ready to serve either side for filthy lucre, immense lust of possessing, piratical incursions, hard servitude and bodies condemned for life to the galleys, thefts, peculations, sacrilege, usury, gambling and false dice, false merchandise, gladiatorial arts, cruelty, inhumanity, hands so prompt to slaughter . . ."

It may perhaps be doubted whether these remarkably pat

prophetic fears were present in Galateo's original draft of 1501, although there was already some justification for them by that date. It will be noted that he speaks of the western discoveries merely as islands, not as either the coast of Cathay or a new continent, and that he singles out no one discoverer such as Columbus, but appears to regard the braving of unknown seas as a collective effort. However, the Spaniard, Antonio de Nebrija (1444–1522), who in his later years was the teacher of Vives and restorer of Latin letters in Spain, had already referred to the land opposite the islands of Hispaniola and Isabella as a continent in his *In cosmographiae libros introductorium*, first printed at Salamanca in 1498.[80] But he, too, vaguely ascribed the discoveries to "the men of our time" and "sailors."

Returning to the period before the voyages of discovery, we might go on to indicate other parallel passages in Ristoro, Paul, and John Michael Albert, such as the explanation why the week has seven days and the day has twenty-four hours,[81] the conception of nature rising in an ascending scale from inanimate objects up through plants and various gradations of animal life to man,[82] and the assertion on the other hand of the permanence of species.[83] In this last connection it is further asserted that animals do not increase or decrease in size or duration of life with the passing ages. If they increased, there

[80] Nebrissensis, Ael. Ant., *In cosmographiae libros Introductorium*, Salamanca, 1498, cap. 1: "De reliquo huic nostro hemispherio e regione opposito quod incolunt antichthones nihil certi nobis a maioribus nostris traditum est. Sed ut est nostri temporis hominum audacia, brevi futurum est; ut nobis veram terrae illius descriptionem afferant, tum insularum tum etiam continentis, cuius magnam partem orae maritimae nautae nobis tradiderunt, illam maxime quae ex adverso insularum nuper inventarum (hispanam dico isabelam reliquasque adiacentes) posita est."

[81] Ristoro, VIII, 6; Paul of Venice, cap. 27; Ashburnham 198, fol. 48v (VI, 8).

[82] Ristoro, I, 20; Paul of Venice, cap. 19 (fol. 113v); Ashburnham 198, fol. 66r–v (VIII, 2).

[83] Ristoro, VIII, 20; Ashburnham 198, fol. 70v (VIII, 7): "Quod species create nec plures neque pauciores esse debuerunt et quod individua debuerunt neque maiora nec minora.

would no longer be enough fodder for them, unless the herbs increased in size too. Or if the wolf decreased in size, while the sheep remained of the same stature, what would the poor wolf do for food? Moreover, if the number of species of animals on earth increased, this would necessitate an increase in the number of animal signs and constellations in the sky which govern these terrestrial animals.

But we have perhaps sufficiently indicated the indebtedness of John Michael Albert in the last quarter, as well as of Paul of Venice in the first quarter, of the fifteenth century to a vernacular writer of the thirteenth century. This fact leaves a strong impression that in Italy scientific thought had stagnated in the interim, and that the Quattrocento was scarcely a time of scientific originality or progress. As Duhem has well remarked, "In the fifteenth century and in the sixteenth century more than one pretended savant was an author of this sort."[84] Our two fifteenth-century men have not merely borrowed most of their ideas, they have taken these from one and the same book. On the other hand, it is much more difficult to trace the ideas expressed by Ristoro d'Arezzo to their source or sources.[85] It is possible, however, to contend that Paul and John Michael Albert represent a decadent scholasticism rather than the new tendencies of the Italian Renaissance, although that course will still leave the smirch of their decadence upon the fifteenth century. Paul was among other things an Augustinian friar and a theologian. John Michael Albert in the work before us aims to speak truly rather than elegantly and gives little sign of humanistic influence.[86] But Galateo, Achillini, and Contarini, who must certainly be classed as well-known men of the Renaissance, mark little advance or improvement upon the views of Paul and John Michael Albert.

[84] P. Duhem, *Le système du monde,* Vol. IV, p. 210: "Au XVe siècle et au XVIe siècle plus d'un prétendu savant fut auteur de cette façon-là."

[85] Those passages where Ristoro cites his authorities by name — they are not many — have been discussed by H. D. Austin, *Accredited Citations in Ristoro d'Arezzo's Composizione del Mondo,* 1911.

[86] Ashburnham 198, fol. 2v.

Let us now note those respects in which John Michael Albert seems to differ from his two predecessors and to offer some individual interest. In general plan, arrangement, and division into books, tractates, or chapters, there is much divergence between the three works of Ristoro, Paul of Venice, and John Michael Albert, especially considering that they have identical titles and perforce deal with much the same matters, namely, the general constitution of heavens and earth and elements, with some attention to the generation of particular things. Ristoro has an uncertain and complicated arrangement of some two, seven, eight, or nine books,[87] which not only divide into chapters but in at least one case into four distinctions, each with several chapters.[88] Paul's work divides simply into twenty-nine chapters. That of John Michael Albert consists of fourteen tractates, each containing from two to ten chapters. It is true that a number of his chapter headings are similar in theme or wording to those of Ristoro. The closest resemblance of this sort is in his eleventh tractate, "On the Elevation of the Habitable Quarter of the Earth," whose eight chapter headings are practically identical with the first eight of the thirteen in Ristoro's sixth book. Often, however, similar chapters are not in the same position in the two works, and there are sections of either which are hardly paralleled in the other.

Even in those chapters or passages where John Michael Albert's treatment appears to have been suggested by the ideas contained in the work of Ristoro d'Arezzo, his discussion is apt to be fuller, and in general he has added to the sources and authorities which were available for Ristoro a considerable

[87] The Incipit states that the work is divided into two books, but in the printed editions the divisions of the second book have been treated as distinct books. What is printed as Book VIII is headed in the text, "Distinzione ovvero particola ottava del libro secondo" (Eighth Distinction or Particular of the Second Book). "Libro VII" occurs twice in the printed edition; in the second instance there is the additional heading, "Seventh Distinction or Particular of the Second Book."

[88] This is the first of the two seventh books of the printed edition.

amount of citation of writers in the two intervening centuries. These citations include some little known personages such as his father, Guido of Carrara, whom he praises so highly, and Candianus Bollano, a patrician of Venice who wrote a work on the soul, *De anima*. Of two of his teachers whose books he cites, Cajetan and Apollinaris,[89] the former is presumably the famous philosopher, Gaietanus de Thienis (1387–1465), who taught at Padua from 1423 till his death. John also cites well-known names of the fourteenth and fifteenth centuries: — Petrus Crescentius,[90] Peter of Abano,[91] Cecco d'Ascoli,[92] Marsilius d'Inghen who died in 1396, Thaddeus of Florence who died in 1303, Duns Scotus who passed away five years later,[93] and Jean de Jandun. Antonio Averlino Filarete (1410–70), who is commonly thought of as an architect and sculptor, is listed by John Michael Albert among writers on plants as having treated that subject "elegantly in the vernacular tongue."[94] Jean de Jandun, according to our author, became so addicted to the Averroistic doctrine of the unity of the intellect that he manifestly strayed from the Christian faith, and, if he had not feared the argument of fire (i.e., burning at the stake through the Inquisition), would have unblushingly

[89] Ashburnham 198, fol. 97v (IX, 8): "Ex modernis et temporaneis nostris Candianus Bollano patricius venetus in scriptu suo de anima . . . in duorum meorum libris preceptorum Gaietani et Apolinaris facile comperientur."

[90] Ashburnham 198, fol. 78r. Pietro dei Crescenzi (c. 1233–1320) is shown to have had a great influence upon modern agriculture by Luigi Savastano, "Contributo allo studio critico degli scrittori agrari italici. Pietro dei Crescenzi," in *Annali della R. Stazione Sperimentale di Agrumicoltura*, Vol. V, 1922, 132 pp.

[91] Peter of Abano is cited a number of times, and from his *Lucidator* as well as the *Conciliator:* see Ashburnham 198, fols. 2r, 57v, 71v, 74v, 121v.

[92] *Ibid.*, fol. 33v.

[93] Thaddeus and d'Inghen are cited at fol. 74r; Scotus at fol. 74v and fols. 67r and 69r.

[94] *Ibid.*, fol. 78r: "Sed et Antonius Averlinus Philaretus lingua vernacula scripsit eleganter." The work of Filarete on architecture was first printed only in 1890 (ed. W. von Oettingen). In it he alludes to his work on agriculture, which is probably what John Michael Albert has in mind. See M. Lazzaroni and A. Munoz, *Filarete, scultore e architetto del sec. XV*, 1908, p. 281.

professed Averroism.[95] John Michael Albert also cites many names of the period before Ristoro and seems especially acquainted with the works of Albertus Magnus. He further alludes to a number of Arabic authors and to such writers on occult subjects as Hermes Trismegistus, Picatrix, Albumasar *in Sadan*, Belinus, [96] and Alkindi on the theory of the magic arts.[97] Some of his citations are very likely indirect, and it is more than doubtful if he had read a long list of Greek authors whom he mentions in one passage,[98] and most of whom are not extant. In citing adversely the opinions of Democritus and Gilgil the Spaniard as to the matter of which the metals are composed, he copies Albertus Magnus almost verbatim.[99] From a criticism which he makes of a passage in the *Conciliator* of Peter of Abano one might infer that he had read that author none too carefully.[100] However, he cites many more authorities by name than did Ristoro d'Arezzo, for example.

Despite this show of broad erudition, John Michael Albert appears rather ignorant of the literature in certain fields. Thus in the dedicatory preface he asserts that few Latins have written on mathematics, and although he then proceeds to men-

[95] Ashburnham 198, fol. 97v: "Quas stultitias ita secutus est Joannes Jandomus ut manifeste exorbitaverit a fide Christiani, et nisi timuisset argumentum ignis sine erubescentia stulticiam Averrois profitebatur . . . ."

[96] *Ibid.*, fols. 21v, 23r, 28v, 32r, 58v, 76v, 124r.

[97] *Ibid.*, fols. 8r and 9v. For the contents of this work and for the previous authors and works in the fields of occult science and astrology, see my *History of Magic and Experimental Science*, 1923.

[98] Ashburnham 198, fol. 78r.

[99] *Ibid.*, fol. 124r; compare Albert, *Mineralium*, III, i, 4.

[100] Ashburnham 198, fol. 71v. He thinks that Abano erred in the Eighth (numbered Ninth in the printed editions) Differentia of the *Conciliator* in holding that men live shorter lives today than formerly and are of weaker constitutions. His argument against Abano is that the heavens are not debilitated. But Abano did not hold that the heavens were debilitated, but that, when the signs of the zodiac return to their original positions directly under the signs of the immobile or imaginary and ideal zodiac, then virtue passes from the First Cause through the heavens or mediate causes in a more perfect manner, and men live longer and are stronger. This theory of the revolution of the eighth sphere Abano set forth in three different treatises: the *Conciliator*, the *Lucidator*, and the *Tractatus motus octave spere*.

tion Michael Scot, Guido Bonatti, "and certain later writers, before whom, however, there were many celebrated ones, such as the blessed Thomas on supercelestial impressions and before him Albertus Magnus," and although a little later he further cites the *Lucidator* of Peter of Abano, still he has given a conflicting and rather scanty estimate, mentioning only astrological works and writers, and naming no one later than the early fourteenth century. He accepts as genuine the works of alchemy ascribed to Raymond Lull, Arnald of Villanova, Aquinas, Albertus Magnus, Brother Elias, and the ancient church fathers and philosophers. He already refers to the alchemistic *Liber turbe*, or *Turba philosophorum*, as it is more commonly called.[101]

Our author not only appears to be ignorant of the French mathematicians of the fourteenth century, such as John of Meurs and Firminus of Bellavalle, but also of the division of the hour into sixty minutes, and each minute into sixty seconds, which was employed by them as customary in 1345.[102] Instead he repeats the earlier medieval division of the hour into four *puncta*, ten minutes, forty moments (*momenta*), or 22,560 atoms. He adds that *punctum* gets its name from punching (*a pungendo*), because artificers puncture the faces of clocks or sundials as many times as they signify *puncta*.[103]

It may be granted that the work of John Michael Albert is itself of little or no importance in the history of experimental science. He is usually very theoretical in his treatment of scientific questions, and is apt further to be theological and

[101] Ashburnham 198, fol. 124r.

[102] This is shown by their treatise, or report to Pope Clement VI, of that year on the subject of the reform of the calendar. In giving the estimates of Ptolemy, Abrachis (Hipparchus), Albategni, and the Alphonsine Tables for the duration of the true solar year, they express the excess of time over 365 days in hours, minutes, and seconds, stating that "in this table the decimal fractions given by these authors have been converted into the customary fractions of the hour." See Duhem, *Le système du monde*, Vol. IV, 1916, pp. 52–54.

[103] Ashburnham 198, fol. 105v–106r (X, 7): "Punctum autem nomen accepit a pungendo quod artifices pungent horologia totiens ut puncta significant."

astrological by turns. Except for some dabbling in alchemy, he appears to have made no scientific observations himself, nor does he match his citations of earlier medieval writers on science by allusion to the practical scientific inventions and instruments of that period. His rôle is that of a compiler, using, as he himself says in his preface, Greek and Latin authorities for matters of physics and theology, Arabic writers for the fields of medicine and astronomy. Occasionally, however, he notes recent natural phenomena, such as earthquakes at Capua and Naples in 1456 and at Brescia in 1470.[104]

Perhaps the most noteworthy feature of the work before us is the deft and clever combination of two attitudes that would commonly be regarded as conflicting, if not diametrically opposing, namely, on the one hand an edifying, orthodox, and conservative religious position, and on the other a bold acceptance of astrology, alchemy, and other occult arts. These two extremes our author makes no great effort to reconcile. He rides his two horses, not with a foot planted on either simultaneously, but by nimbly hopping back and forth from one to the other. This is alike bewildering to the reader — who suddenly finds his author indulging in an occult art that he had roundly condemned a few pages before — amusing, and exciting, since John Michael Albert occasionally reminds us of the peril of his own position by allusion to the fate of past astrologers and heretics.

John opens his work upon the religious note, asserting that among the most serious and shameful sins which mankind daily commits is that of damnable ingratitude towards God.[105] Presently we find him saying with Hugh of St. Victor that God may be known in two ways, through His universe or through Christ. The philosopher learns of God through the universe; the Christian, through Christ. In the present work on the constitution of the universe John will take the path of philosophy. In a later passage he affirms that his work is not controversial,

[104] Ashburnham 198, fol. 66r.

[105] *Ibid.*, fol. 1r: "Inter gravissimos ac flagitiosissimos errores quos mortale genus cotidiano lapsu frequenter admittit . . ."

"but to show to the best of our ability the majesty of God."[106] In other chapters contemplation of the variety of vegetation or the wonderful structure of the human body fills him with admiration of the deity.[107]

From the chapter entitled "In what respect are the elements affected by the heavens?"[108] one might conclude that John meant to minimize even the natural influence of the planets and signs upon the four inferior elements. The chapter is made up almost entirely of repetition of the arguments of Gregory the Great in the homily on the three Magi, of Cicero in *De divinatione*, of Augustine and others against astrology. The case of Jacob and Esau is brought up more than once, and very little space is given to the arguments for astrology compared to the long rehearsal of those against it. Yet elsewhere throughout the work astrological influence is repeatedly adduced — as it had been by Ristoro and Paul of Venice — to explain the constitution and workings of the universe. This we shall illustrate in more detail in a moment. First let us note the equally inconsistent attitude of John Michael Albert towards Hermes Trismegistus. In one passage he informs us that, according to Augustine, Hermes was not a prophet from God but was enlightened by demons.[109] Yet he continues to cite him as an authority in other passages.

Of the prominence and variety of astrological doctrine in John Michael Albert's work it is possible to give many illustrations. Like Ristoro and Paul of Venice he gives the influence of the sky as one of the causes of the formation of mountains,[110] and we have already noted their common astrological argument against the existence of the Antipodes. We further find John

[106] Ashburnham 198, fol. 98r: "Nam hic liber noster non est litigatorius sed ad ostendendam quantum possumus dei maiestatem."

[107] *Ibid.*, Tract. IX, caps. 2 and 7.

[108] *Ibid.*, fols. 66v–68r (VIII, 3): "quid patiantur elementa a celo?"

[109] *Ibid.*, fol. 23r: "Hunc tamen hominem Augustinus de civitate dei capitulo 23 quod fuerit propheta non a deo sed a demonibus illuminatus et capitulo 24 multa de hoc libello *Ad Asclepium* carpit."

[110] *Ibid.*, fol. 113r (XI, 8).

quoting with apparent approval such astrological dicta as the statement of Albumasar *in Sadan* that the sun and moon are, after God, the life of the living,[111] or that of Hermes Trismegistus *ad Asclepium* that the earth is the recipient of all the impressions of the sky, and that whatever descends from above has generative power.[112] He associates the seven metals with the planets, as was common in alchemy, and gems with the fixed stars.[113] Astrologers are quoted as saying that marvelous swords can be made from meteoric iron.[114] In treating of the seven planets in turn, their astrological influences are given as they had been by Ristoro, with additional matter from Belinus, Picatrix, Hermes or Mercurius Trismegistus, and (Pseudo-) Ptolemy as to the figures and forms of the planets for purposes of carving astrological images.[115] In a later passage we are told that the influence of the planet Mars is diversified, and that sometimes philosophers are multiplied under it, sometimes emperors.[116] Plutarch's three one-eyed generals — Philip of Macedon, Pyrrhus of Epirus, and Hannibal — may have been born under the same constellation. In yet another place it is stated that persons born under friendly planets are apt to be in accord.[117]

Our author affirms that floods are due to conjunctions of the planets and vary in extent as the conjunctions are great, medium, or little. He doubts the possibility of a universal deluge, since the law of pairs or contraries would require that if the stars were favorable to a deluge in one region, they should somewhere else be favorable to a drought. So far on this point John has followed the line of thought of one of Ristoro's chapters,[118] but he continues the discussion further, noting that Noah's flood was regarded as universal by "our ancestors," and that the poets similarly represent the deluge under Deucalion

[111] Ashburnham 198, fol. 21v: "Albumasar in sadan dicit quod sol et luna post deum sunt vita viventium."

[112] *Ibid.*, fol. 76v (IX, 1).

[113] *Ibid.*, fol. 125v (XIII, 3).

[114] *Ibid.*, fol. 65v (VIII, 2).

[115] *Ibid.*, fols. 17–34 (Tract. III).

[116] *Ibid.*, fol. 100r (IX, 9).

[117] *Ibid.*, fol. 91v (IX, 5).

[118] Ristoro d'Arezzo, *Della composizione del mondo*, VI, 12.

and Pyrrha. Albert and many others regard the flood as a divine punishment for sin, "but this reason is a theological one and does not inform us as to the immediate efficient causes." Peter of Abano was accused of heresy for holding that the deluge was due to a conjunction of Jupiter and Saturn 1820 years after the creation, and that Noah foresaw the flood by the science of the stars. But Abano contended before a council of ecclesiastics that not the deluge merely but also the division of tongues was signified by the sky. Certain Arabs ascribed the flood not to any constellation but to the force of imagination exercised by the Intelligence that moves the sphere of the moon. William of Auvergne, the thirteenth-century bishop of Paris, in his *De universo* interpreted the biblical passage concerning the cataracts of the sky being opened as having reference to the influence of such constellations as the Pleiades and Orion, which produce rain and humidity and multiply waters. John Michael Albert concludes the discussion of this point by detailing four different astrological causes of deluges, and asserting that just the opposite conditions will produce a widespread conflagration. But these four astrological causes he copies word for word from the *De causis et proprietatibus elementorum* of Albertus Magnus.[119]

In a previous chapter,[120] separated by some fifty leaves of text from the foregoing discussion in his own work, John appears to have reproduced from a chapter which follows it closely in this same work of Albert the opposing arguments of Avicenna and Averroës as to whether all forms of life could be regenerated merely by natural action of the stars, after they had been obliterated by a universal deluge so that there would be no possibility of the ordinary procreation by intercourse between the two sexes. Avicenna maintained the affirmative, adducing four considerations in its favor: 1, the spontaneous

[119] *De causis elementorum*, I, ii, 9 (Vol. IX, p. 621, of Borgnet's edition of the works of Albertus Magnus). John Michael Albert's discussion occurs at fols. 121r–123r of Ashburnham 198 (Tract. XIII, "De impressionibus mirabilibus," cap. 1, "De causis diluviorum et pluviarum").

[120] Ashburnham 198, fol. 73r–v (VIII, 10).

generation of mice on shipboard from putrefaction; 2, the generation of serpents from the hairs of women in water; 3, monstrous births; 4, the fact noted by astrologers that certain constellations impede human generation. Averroës, however, contended that perfect animals, on account of the diversity of their members, could not be generated by the stars. For this and other reasons he argued that the world and species were eternal, and that there had never been a universal deluge.

If, however, John follows the *De causis et proprietatibus elementorum* of Albert in reproducing these arguments of Avicenna and Averroës, he has not done so very exactly, if we may trust on this point the text of Albert's treatise given in Borgnet's too often faulty edition. Where Albert says, "Moreover, there is a great altercation between Avicenna and Averroës in their books (*libellis*) concerning those deluges,"[121] leaving us somewhat in doubt whether he has reference to special monographs on floods ascribed to Avicenna and Averroës respectively, or simply to discussion of that subject in their works generally, John asserts, "Avicenna and Averroës published a single book concerning the deluge in which they contend in turn.[122] Thus he definitely commits the error of making men contemporaries who were separated by a whole century, in addition to creating an apparently fictitious bibliographical reference. Where, however, Avicenna adduces the spontaneous generation of mice, Borgnet's text is probably at fault in making Albert affirm that we see women generated from earth in some places, the abbreviated form for the word *mures* (mice) having probably been mistaken for *mulieres* (women).

Our author even touches on the risky topic of the relation

[121] *De causis elementorum*, I, ii, 13: "Est autem altercatio magna inter Avicennam et Averroem in suis libellis de diluviis istis quid sit reparans terras et animalia quae sunt in ipsis . . . ."

[122] Ashburnham 198, fol. 73r: "Avicenna et Averrois de diluvio singulum ediderunt librum in quo invice pugnent." MS Vatic. Lat. 4426, fol. 1r–v, listed in the old catalogue as "Avicennae capitulum de diluviis," also mentions in its rubric Averroës, and Albert's summary of their arguments.

of the planets to religious changes.[123] Having said, "Finally, when the moon is in conjunction with Jupiter, Antichrist will come, whose sect will soon be dissolved because of the swift course of the moon," he adds, however, that while these views are found in the book *De vetula* ascribed to Ovid, he thinks that they are not approved by the Christian religion except in so far as the stars incline but do not compel us to action. He continues, "Cecco d'Ascoli reached such a point of insanity that he said that it was natural that a virgin (or, the Virgin) should conceive, for which error he was condemned to be burned by fire. And indeed, unless he has changed his opinion for the better, he now also sighs in hell." [124] The information which our author has offered as to the respects in which the teachings of Cecco d'Ascoli and Peter of Abano were considered heretical, is novel and important, if true.[125]

John's chapter, "Why different impressions are generated in various parts of the world at different times, and concerning the impressions and ascendents of certain cities of Italy," [126] bears a general resemblance to Ristoro's chapter, "On finding the reason why winds and rain and hailstorms, and plenty and famine, and peace and war and other accidents, occur in different parts of the world according to the times and the diversity of location." [127] But John adds further astrological detail, stating that we inquire concerning plans of the planet Mercury;

[123] Ashburnham 198, fol. 33v (III, 8).

[124] "... Ultimum cum iovi coniungetur luna aderit Antichristus cuius lex cito dissolvetur propter velocem cursum lune. Scripta sunt hec eadem in libro de vetula que inscribitur Ovidio que parum christiana religio ut opinor approbat nisi de inclinatione aliqua ut sepe repetitum est. Franciscus Esculanus in tantam insaniam crevit ut dixerit naturale fuisse ut virgo conciperet propter quem errorem damnatus est ut igne cremaretur. Et profecto nisi sententiam mutarit in melius nunc et in herebo suspirat."

[125] I treat of it more fully in an article on the relations of these men to the inquisition in *Speculum*, Vol. I, 1926, pp. 338–43.

[126] Ashburnham 198, fols. 138v–141r (XIV, 4): "Cur diverse impressiones in variis mundi partibus diversis temporibus generentur et de impressionibus et de ascendentibus aliquarum civitatum italie."

[127] Ristoro d'Arezzo, *Della composizione del mondo*, VII, 4.

concerning dances and the crimes of adulterers, of Venus; concerning wars and horrors, of Mars. "And I am much afraid that next year it will shake Italy, and that too with foreign soldiery,"[128] continues our author. Ristoro had not developed the theme of the ascendents of Italian cities, but John puts Florence, Imola, and Ferrara under the sign Aries; Bologna, Siena, Mantua, and Verona under Taurus; and so on, sometimes including foreign countries. Gemini, for example, rules England and Sardinia as well as Cesena. Cancer governs Turkey, Barbary, and Constantinople as well as Lucca and Milan. Cecco d'Ascoli in the fourteenth century had somewhat similarly treated of the control exerted by the stars over the fate of cities.[129]

Astrology was by no means the only occult science in which our author took a lively interest. For alchemy,[130] too, he had a high respect, believing not only that many recent men of note such as John of England, Arnald of Villanova, and Raymond Lull had written treatises on it, but also saints like Fulgentius, Thomas, Albert, Elias, and Ambrose, and philosophers such as Avicenna, Hermes, Geber, Haly, Rasis, Plato, Aristotle, and Galen. If their writings on the art had been found impracticable, it was simply because ignoramuses had misunderstood their enigmatic expressions. Alchemy is the science that above all others imitates nature. In certain writings ascribed to Pluto (Plato?) John had read that the form of the metals was the numerical proportion between the quantities of the component elements and the celestial virtue.[131] He believed that all the metals were of a single species, but that precious stones were

[128] Ashburnham 198, fol. 139r: "Multumque ego iam dubito ne proximo anno quatiat Italiam et proprie milite externo."

[129] See my *History of Magic and Experimental Science,* Vol. II, p. 955.

[130] Ashburnham 198, fols. 123v–126r (XIII, 3), deals with alchemy, the heading being "De generatione minerarum et de alchemia."

[131] I am not sure that I have correctly rendered the meaning. The Latin of the passage is: "In quibusdam alchimicis que Plutoni inscribuntur dicitur quod forma metallorum est proportio numeri que consurgit ex dosibus elementorum proportionatorum cum virtute celesti." — *Ibid.*, fol. 125r.

not, and that this explained why alchemists had more difficulty in transmuting gems than metals. Following the doctrine of Albert in the *Semita recta*, he had tinctured silver in the acid of silversmiths and made gold that endured all tests, but it was produced with so great labor that there was more loss sustained in the process than gain from the gold. But he believed that the following recipe for making gold was supported by the experience of the alchemists. "Of purest quicksilver and a twelfth the amount of natural incombustible sulphur they make an amalgam which they seal up in a glass vase so that the spirits may not evaporate, and with a measured, slow fire they convert the whole substance into natural sulphur, of which one part to a thousand of the quicksilver that they call 'fugitive serf' converts into pure and veritable gold."[132]

Like Ristoro, our author believes in the existence of demons who inhabit the spheres of the planets and are the intelligences that move the orbs. He also holds that there are spirits without bodies on earth, as the marvelous results produced by exorcisms prove. He further affirms that disembodied spirits have been heard to speak in his time in many places, which no one will deny who does not wish to admit that he is mad or insane. Consequently Aristotle and Averroës gravely erred in asserting that an immaterial force such as an angel could not move a material body.[133]

John also treats of dreams.[134] He divides them into four categories: natural, caused by the humors predominating in the human body; animal, which word he here employs in the sense of connected with the soul (*anima*), such dreams resulting

[132] Ashburnham 198, fol. 124r: "... ex purissima enim substantia argenti vivi et parteduodecima sulphuris physici incremabilis conficiunt amalgamam quam includunt in vitreum vas ut evaporare spiritus nequeant et cum igne proportionali lento totam substantiam in physicum sulphur convertunt, cuius una pars supra mille argenti vivi quod vocant servum fugitivum convertit[ur] in merum et verum aurum."

[133] For the contents of this paragraph see Tract. VII, cap. 5, "probans quod dentur substantie incorporee et spiritus qui in singulis speris reperiantur," at fols. 57v–61r, but especially fol. 59.

[134] *Ibid.*, fol. 89r–v.

from mental worry; celestial, which come from God like the dreams of Joseph, or, as Galen suggests in the second book of his work on the treatment of acute diseases, may be due to the relation of the human soul to the heavenly bodies; and last, diabolical, such as the dreams of the wives of Pilate and Caesar, which were suggested by demons. There seem to John to be six essentials for a true dream. First, the mind or soul should be noble and not obfuscated by vice and gluttony; second, it should be sincere and unaccustomed to lie; third, the physical constitution should be temperate; fourth, the mind should not be affected; fifth, the dream should come in the morning; sixth, it should not occur soon after eating. These requirements somewhat correspond to Aristotle's conditions for true dreams.

Marvel-working images and incantations were other occult matters of interest to our author.[135] He lists various works concerning the former, and notes that Albertus Magnus says that they cannot be understood without knowledge of the magical sciences of astronomy, magic, and nigromancy. He cites medical authorities — Walter, Gordon, Gilbert, Haly Abbas, Avicenna — as to cures wrought by use of incantations, and he mentions two cases known to him personally during the past year in which persons had been cured of wounds within eight days by mere repetition of such words as "In the name of the Father and of the Son and of the Holy Ghost. Christ was anointed and pierced (*unctus et punctus*), so you too shall be healed even as He was healed." The second formula was, "Christ was born, Christ died, Christ rose again. As these words are three, so shall this wound be healed without pus." John argues that the mere words could not have so stupendous an effect, and that the cure must be due to the invisible operations of spirits. He is confirmed in this view by the assertion of Plato that incantations are the illusion of demons, and the dictum of Jerome that they are a sin, even if good words are employed, because of their suspicious circumstances which the devil uses like a poison. Nor could anyone become invisible,

[135] Ashburnham 198, fol. 58.

a thing contrary to nature, unless by the aid of spirits. Yet John does not seem to disapprove of the recent cures which were effected by such means. Along with such medicinal incantations, which seem to him to involve demon aid, John mentions the method of curing warts by touching them with chick-peas and then throwing the peas away behind one's back. He ascribes this procedure to Serapion; really it goes back to Pliny.[136]

Such are some features of a work written in Italy as the period commonly known as "The High Renaissance" was beginning. Yet it serves chiefly to illustrate the weakness of natural science in Italy of the fifteenth century, and to support Duhem's conclusion that in physics and astronomy Italy of that time had fallen off from the standards set by the University of Paris in the first half of the fourteenth century. As John Michael Albert's treatise remained in manuscript, though composed almost a half century after the invention of printing with movable types, so his ideas remained those of the thirteenth century — of Albertus Magnus, Ristoro d'Arezzo, and Peter of Abano. Indeed, he only partially absorbed the ideas of Albert and Abano and sometimes fails to do justice to their thought or fund of information. Moreover, he remained in ignorance alike of a changing world forecast by the portentous progress of Portuguese mariners down the coast of Africa and out into the islands of the Atlantic, and of changing times marked by the division of the hour into sixty minutes each of sixty seconds. Yet his work is interesting reading. And he was by no means the last to repeat the contents of the works of Albert and Abano, whose authority was to be long continued.

If anything, John does not keep the fields of science and religion as distinct as did the greater thirteenth-century writers, although he makes some effort in that direction. But he introduces into a work of natural philosophy the kind of adverse criticism of astrology and favoring argument for the existence of demons that in the thirteenth century had been characteristic

[136] Pliny, *Hist. nat.*, XXII, 72; Lynn Thorndike, *History of Magic and Experimental Science*, Vol. I, p. 88.

rather of the *Summa* of theology. The supernatural and the superstitious receive no scientific or critical check at his hands. But of the barriers raised by orthodoxy we are more than once reminded. Our attention is especially arrested by John's playing with the fire that had consumed Cecco d'Ascoli and threatened Peter of Abano and Jean de Jandun. What had been the influence upon freedom of thought of those still remembered incidents — though very likely none too accurately remembered — of almost two centuries ago? Were they isolated, sensational occurrences, and for that reason celebrated in history and legend? Or were they typical of other happenings that have been forgotten? Did our author feel quite secure in his own day? Or did the danger signal of heresy, instead of intimidating the expression of thought, act sometimes as an incentive to venturesomeness and lead men to skate as near the hole as they thought the thin ice would bear, and their own speed and cleverness would permit? If we take our author's three past examples at his own evaluation, we find that Jean de Jandun alone was deterred by fear of the Inquisition. Cecco went to the stake; Peter of Abano successfully defended and boldly amplified his teaching. Moreover, even Jean de Jandun seems to have made it clear enough what his real views were.

CHAPTER XIII

LIPPUS BRANDOLINUS DE COMPARATIONE REIPUBLICAE ET REGNI A TREATISE IN COMPARATIVE POLITICAL SCIENCE[1]

The treatise of Lippus Brandolinus, or Lippo Brandolini, comparing a republic with a monarchy, appears to have hitherto attracted little attention either in works dealing with the political thought of the late fifteenth century or elsewhere. It was first printed in 1890 in the publications of a Hungarian Academy which are somewhat inaccessible to English readers,[2] along with other treatises by humanists who enjoyed the patronage of King Matthias Corvinus (or *Corvus*, as he is called in our treatise) the Great, the famous warrior son of John Hunyadi and king of Hungary and Bohemia. This sovereign had summoned Brandolini[3] from Rome to his court, and our treatise was there begun in the winter of 1489–90, but was interrupted by the king's death and later finished at Florence

[1] Revised from *Political Science Quarterly*, Vol. XLI, 1926, pp. 413–35.

[2] *Magyar Tudományos Akedémia. Irodalomtortêneti emlêkek. II. kötet: Olaszországi XV. századbeli rôknak Mátyás királyt dicsôitö müoei. Közrebocsátja Abel Jenö* (*Aurelius Brandolinus — Ludovicus Carbo — Galeotus Martius — Naldus Naldius — T. Alexander Cortesius — Ugolinus Verinus — Jo. Franc. Marlianus*), xv és 384 lap., Pest, 1890. This publication will hereafter be cited as Jenö (1890). The text of the *De comparatione reipublicae et regni* occupies pp. 79–188. Jenö seems to have used only the Laurentian manuscript in this edition and not to have known of the Riccardian manuscript.

I was thus mistaken in describing the treatise as unpublished in the article in the *Political Science Quarterly* cited in the previous note. Mr. Lester K. Born first put me on the track of this publication, which I was unable to procure in this country and examined at the British Museum. Returning from London, I found a note from Professor Enrico Rostagno, librarian of the Bibliotheca Medicea Laurenziana, also calling to my attention this Hungarian publication.

[3] Crusenius, *Monasticon Augustinianum*, 1623, p. 182, states that Corvinus employed Lippo in his council and as orator to the estates of the realm: "quemque et sibi a consiliis et suum oratorem ad diversos imperii status esse voluit."

as the author's domestic occupations would permit. It was then dedicated by him to Lorenzo de' Medici, the Magnificent, instead of to Corvinus as had doubtless originally been intended. Finally, following the deaths of both Lorenzo and its author, it was presented by the latter's brother, Raphael Brandolinus Junior Lippus, to Cardinal Giovanni de' Medici, the future pope, Leo X. In these respects there is a similarity to the history of *The Prince* of Machiavelli in the next generation, which was written in 1513, which Machiavelli in 1515 was thinking of dedicating to Giuliano de' Medici, which he addressed to Lorenzo de' Medici after Giuliano's death in 1516, and which was not printed until after Machiavelli's death.[4]

There are two fine manuscripts of our treatise at Florence, one in the Laurentian,[5] the other in the Riccardian Library.[6] The Laurentian manuscript is almost certainly the very copy presented by Raphael Brandolinus Junior to Giovanni de' Medici.[7] It contains his preface as well as that of his brother to Lorenzo, and opens the two prefaces and likewise each of the three books into which the text divides with heavily illuminated title pages. On these are found marginal miniatures of both Lorenzo the Magnificent and his son, the cardinal and future pope. They seem to be fairly faithful and realistic, rather than flattering or idealized, portraits, the one depicting

[4] But there seems to be no reference to Brandolini's treatise in works on Machiavelli.

[5] Laurent. Plut. 77, cod. 11, membr. Most of its 164 leaves are unnumbered, though there are some signatures. See Bandini's catalogue for further description. He dates the MS as fifteenth century, but it must have been written after 1497 or 1498, the date of Lippo's death. Jenö's edition was made from this manuscript.

[6] Riccard. 672, cod. membr. in quarto, venutissimus, 112 fols., with a somewhat larger page as well as more words to a page than the Laurentian MS. For further description of it see G. Lami, *Catalogus codicum manuscriptorum qui in bibliotheca Riccardiana Florentiae adservantur*, Leghorn, 1756; S. Morpurgo, *I manoscritti della bibl. Riccardiana di Firenze*, Vol. I, Roma, 1900 ("Indici e Cataloghi," Vol. XV); and a catalogue printed in 1810 with the view of selling the collection. Jenö seems not to have known of this Riccardian manuscript.

[7] A letter of 1567, which is bound in the back of the manuscript, so states.

Lorenzo with an ugly lower jaw, the other showing Giovanni with his usual full-moon countenance. The Riccardian manuscript lacks the preface of Raphael Brandolinus Junior to Giovanni [8] and opens at once with that of Lippus Brandolinus to Lorenzo. It also lacks the illuminated title pages, contenting itself with attractively illuminated initials. The first of these [9] shows a profile bust of a man with a book in his right hand and a red cap on his long hair. The delicate, sensitive face bears no resemblance to the faces of Giovanni and Lorenzo in the other manuscript and probably represents Lippo Brandolini himself as the catalogue suggests.[10] This Riccardian manuscript was at the time of my examination in 1927 in a better state of preservation than the Laurentian, since the binding of the latter was broken, while the leaves of the Riccardian copy were more immaculate. It was written with equal neatness and elegance to the other copy, and had in its margins headings in red indicative of the text's content which were lacking in the Laurentian copy.

The text itself is practically identical in both manuscripts. A chief difference is the greater use in the Laurentian of the humanistic diphthong, *ae,* in such words as *quae* and *prae* and in the genitive feminine singular, while the Riccardian copy usually retains the medieval *e.* We find the spelling *caeteris* in the Laurentian, *coeteris* in the Riccardian. The Laurentian generally uses *quum;* the Riccardian often has *cum* instead. The Riccardian is apt to prefix an *h* to certain words which begin with a vowel in the Laurentian. Perhaps we may regard the Riccardian manuscript as slightly the older, or even as Lippo's original text, which Raphael very likely followed in the copy prepared for Cardinal Giovanni de' Medici.

Since Jenö's edition and Bandini's catalogue and those of the Riccardian manuscripts may not be accessible to the

[8] Bandini printed it entire and part of the preface to Lorenzo.

[9] That is, the C of the Incipit to the preface to Lorenzo: "Cum animalia omnia sui generis societatem appetunt . . ."

[10] " . . . et cum imagine Lippi elegantissime in littera initiali depicta."

reader, I reproduce here the rubrics and Incipits of the two prefaces and text proper. Those for the first preface of Raphael to the future Leo X are found only in the Laurentian manuscript. The rubrics are in illuminated capitals.

RAPHAEL BRANDOLINUS IUNIOR LIPPVS IOANNI MEDICI DIACONO CAR. S. MARIE IN NAVI. NUNCU.[11] S.D. Quum nullum maius atque praeclarius defunctorum memoriae conferri beneficium possit . . . — Laur. Plut. 77, cod. 11, fol. 1r.

LIPPI BRANDOLINI IN LIBROS DE COMPARATIONE REIPUBLICAE [*REIPUBLICE* in the Riccardian MS] ET REGNI AD PRESTANTISSIMUM VIRUM LAVRENTIVM MEDICEM FLORE. REI PU. [*FLORENTINE PUBLICE* in the Riccardian MS] PRINCIPEM PROHEMIUM. Cum [*Quum* in the Laurentian MS] animalia omnia sui generis societatem appetunt . . .

LIPPI BRANDOLINI DE COMPARATIONE REIP. ET REGNI AD PRESTANTISSIMVM VIRUM LAVRENTIVM MEDICEM FLO. REI P. PRINCIPEM LIBER I [the longer rubric of the Riccardian MS continues, *in quo Matthias pannoniorum rex, Ioannes filius & Dominicus iunius eques florentinus loquentes introducuntur. MATTHIAS*]. Gaudeo quidem omni tempore tua presentia fili . . .

Gandolfo, in his work on celebrated writers of the Augustinian Order,[12] gives the name of the author of our treatise as Aurelius Brandolinus, a form also employed in the catalogue of printed books of the Bibliothèque Nationale of Paris. In our manuscripts, however, he is simply called Lippus Brandolinus, but Crusenius in the early seventeenth century called him Aurelius Lippus Brandolinus.[13] According to Gandolfo, our author received the epithet Lippus because he was almost blind

[11] The abbreviated words are presumably, "cardinali Sancte Marie in navicula nuncupate," and at any rate refer to the fact that Giovanni de' Medici was cardinal deacon of the church of Santa Maria in Domnica, also known as "Navicella" from a small marble boat which he placed in front of it.

[12] Le P. Domenico Antonio Gandolfo, *Dissertatio historica de ducentis celeberrimis augustinianis scriptoribus ex illis qui obierunt post magnam unionem ordinis eremetici usque ad finem tridentini concilii*, Rome, 1704, 4to, 407 pp. Pages 85–89 are devoted to Brandolinus, and two columns to his *De comparatione reipublicae et regni* in the Laurentian MS.

[13] *Monasticon Augustinianum*, 1623, p. 182.

from birth. His brother, Raphael Brandolinus Junior, is also called Lippus in the Laurentian manuscript, and refers in his preface to the cardinal to the "wretched blindness which I have in common with him." [14]

In his preface to Lorenzo, Brandolini states that he had left Florence when a mere boy and had been absent therefrom for over twenty years because of loss of his property.[15] His brother Raphael also refers to his straitened circumstances.[16] He was noted for his great memory and could repeat by heart all the thirty-seven books of Pliny's *Natural History*, or at least all the chapter heads, noteworthy passages, and every fact of importance.[17] While in Hungary he taught oratory at Buda and Strigonia (Gran). Jenö prints an interesting extract in Latin from the *Acta* of the Faculty of Arts at Vienna concerning Brandolini's efforts to draw books from the university library without giving any surety for them and further to procure a key to the library for his private use. Finally he was allowed to give a written receipt (*caucionem literatoriam*) instead of furnishing surety, but the faculty refused him a key, ordering the bedell to open the library for the poet but also to be careful "to close it after him." [18]

On Brandolini's return from Hungary to Florence he became a member of the Augustinian Order and a preacher of renown. Matteo Bossi, a canon at the Lateran, wrote to Geronimo Campagnola in a letter quoted by Gandolfo, that when Lippo

[14] Edition of 1890, p. 79. Laur. Plut. 77, cod. 11, fol. 1v: ". . . et miserabili quae mihi cum illo communis est caecitate."

[15] Riccard. 672, fol. 3v: ". . . . in patriam a qua puer admodum profectus . . ."; fol. 4v: ". . . qui viginti amplius annis a patria ob rei familiaris amissionem abfuerim." The same passages are found in the other MS and printed edition.

[16] Laurent. Plut. 77, cod. 11, fol. 1r: ". . . in summa praesertim rei familiaris angustia."

[17] "Sed illud caetera superat quod omnem Plinianam Naturalem Historiam 37 in vol. discretam per singula cuiusque voluminis capita quam plurimis et praeclarissimis versibus extemporaliter enarravit praetermissa re nulla memorabili ac cognitu digna." Gandolfo, 1704, p. 87.

[18] Jenö (1890), p. viii.

spoke, "we seem to hear not your Burleys,[19] Pauls of Venice,[20] or Strodi,[21] but Plato, Aristotle, and Theophrastus."[22] Speaking extemporaneously, he could produce effects that illustrious poets have achieved only by an immense expenditure of midnight oil.

Lippo Brandolini composed numerous other works besides that with which we are here concerned. The list of them, chiefly religious in character, fills a column in Gandolfo's quarto volume. Several were printed in the course of the sixteenth century: an oration or sermon in favor of Thomas Aquinas delivered at Rome in the church of Santa Maria sopra Minerva to the cardinals and people;[23] another on the Passion delivered before Alexander VI[24] at Rome, and issued in Italian translation in 1596 after earlier editions in Latin;[25] a dialogue addressed to Matthias Corvinus and his queen, Beatrice, on the state of human life and bearing of bodily illness (*De humanae vitae conditione et toleranda corporis aegritudine*), of which Gandolfo mentions the 1543 edition, while in the Bibliothèque Nationale at Paris there are two other editions;[26] the *Christian*

[19] Referring to Walter Burley or Burleigh, the English logician, schoolman, and commentator on Aristotle of the first half of the fourteenth century. The date of his death is disputed.

[20] Paul of Venice, who died in 1429, had a great fifteenth-century reputation in philosophy and astronomy, but was something of a plagiarist.

[21] Strodus was the author of textbooks in logic called *Consequentiae* and *Obligationes*.

[22] ". . . non Burleos, non Paulos Venetos, non Strodos, sed Platonem quidem, Aristotelem, Theophrastum audire videamur."

[23] Oratio pro sancto Thoma Aquinate Romae in templo Sanctae Mariae Minervae ad cardinales et populum habita. Rome, without date, 4to. Copy in the Bibliothèque Nationale, Paris.

[24] F. Nic. Crusenius, *Monasticon Augustinianum*, 1623, p. 182, represents this sermon as delivered before Innocent VIII and the sacred college, but is evidently mistaken, since he makes Lippo die shortly thereafter in 1498, when Innocent VIII would have been dead six years.

[25] *Oratione . . . delle virtù del I. S. Giesu Christo, mostrateci nella sua passione, cent' anni prima recitata in Roma, . . . di latino tradotta in volgare.* In Venetia, al segno del Leone, 1596, 4to, 20 pp. Gandolfo lists a Latin edition at Rome in the same year, 1596.

[26] *De humanae vitae conditione et toleranda corporis aegritudine ad Mathiam*

Paradoxes,[27] and a humanistic treatise in three books on how to write, published first in 1549 with similar works by Vives, Erasmus, Conrad Celtes, and Christopher Hegendorph.[28] A manuscript at the Vatican [29] contains poems by Lippo in praise of Pope Sixtus IV (1471–84), and the above-mentioned sermon before Alexander VI (1492-1503) at Rome makes it evident that he returned to that city again after the death of Lorenzo de' Medici. He is said to have died there in 1498.[30] Raphæl Brandolinus Junior, who presented his dead brother's work to the future Leo X, is represented by one work in print, a dialogue in which that same pope is concerned, but which seems not to have been published until the eighteenth century.[31]

We have already noticed a certain parallelism in external circumstances between the relatively unknown treatise of Lippo Brandolini and the celebrated *Prince* of Machiavelli, both dedicated by Florentines to members of the Medici family within a score or so of years. There is also an internal resemblance. It is notorious that literature is prone to adhere to

---

Corvinum Hungariae et Bohemiae regem et Beatricem reginam dialogus, Basel, 1543, 8vo; Paris, 1562, 8vo, 63 pp.; Basel, no date, 8vo, 115 pp. In this work Brandolinus displays a favorable attitude towards princes in general and Italian despots in particular. Crusenius, *Monasticon Augustinianum*, 1623, p. 182, appears to refer to this work, when, stating that King Matthias often sought Lippo's companionship and consolation in the bitterest woes of human life, he proceeds: "Quos deinde idem Aurelius in compendium redegit suumque moecenatem eorundem tolerantiam docuit vel posteris illos mundi lusus enarrans."

[27] *Paradoxa Christiana*, Basel, 15–3; Rome, 1531; according to Gandolfo. There is no copy in the Bibliothèque Nationale, Paris. A digit is missing in the first date.

[28] *De ratione scribendi libri tres, numquam antea in lucem edita*, Basel, 1549, 8vo; Gandolfo also mentions editions of 1573 and 1585.

[29] Vatic. Latin MS 5008, Lippi Brandolini carmina de laudibus et rebus gestis Sixti papae Quarti. The opening is wanting. In another Vatican manuscript is a commentary by him on the Georgics of Virgil: Vatic. Lat. 2740, Lippi Florentini comentaria in Georgica Virg.

[30] Crusenius (1623), p. 182.

[31] Brandolini (Lippi Raph. iunioris), *Dialogus, Leo nuncupatus, cum notis, auctorii vita et additamentis*, Venice, 1753. There seems to be a list of other works by Raphael in a manuscript at the Vatican: Vatic. Lat. 3590, Raphaelis Lippi Brandolini operum index ad Balduinum de Monte per fratrem Eneam collectus.

tradition and slow to respond to changes in actual life and to reflect faithfully unaccustomed features of the present. The castle flourishes in novels long after it has waned in reality, and the factory and office are long denied in fiction the place that they have in fact. So for two centuries or more before the sixteenth, unscrupulous and daring men had been creating or seizing despotisms for themselves by force and craft regardless of moral principles and Christian ideals. But the world had to wait for a Machiavelli before this fairly obvious situation of fact was adequately presented in words and impressed upon thought. And it has been noted by such modern students of Machiavellianism as Nourrisson and Villari that previous works on the prince by humanists like Poggio and Pontano make no approach to the Machiavellian point of view, but are mere exercises in rhetoric and moralizing, and inferior to the previous political treatises of the scholastics.[32] Yet in their correspondence and travels the humanists occasionally let fall acute observations concerning contemporary political conditions. Poggio in inveighing against law and lawyers in the brief dialogues of his *Historia tripartita* displays a cynical realism which, in the opinion of Walser, foreshadows the attitude of Machiavelli.[33] And Nourrisson has argued from the fact that the extensive plagiarism of Agostino Nifo in his *De regnandi peritia*, printed at Naples in 1523 and dedicated to Charles V, from *The Prince*, which then circulated in manuscript copies, passed unnoticed, that Machiavellian opinions were then more prevalent than has often been thought.[34] But this is saying that the soil was in a general way prepared for Machiavelli, rather than indicating particular works that were forerunners of his own.

Now the treatise of Lippo Brandolini can scarcely be called

[32] Nourrisson, *Machiavel*, Paris, 1875, pp. 186–87; Pasquale Villari, *The Life and Times of Niccolò Machiavelli*, translated by Mme Linda Villari, London, 1898, Vol. II, pp. 69–70.

[33] E. Walser, *Poggius Florentinus' Leben und Werke*, 1914, p. 258. And see Poggio Bracciolini, *Opera*, 1513, fols. 16–19.

[34] Nourrisson, Machiavel, 1875, pp. 227–34.

Machiavellian in tone, and it may be doubted if Machiavelli had ever read it or was much influenced by it if he did read it. But it does discuss the relative merits of a republic and a monarchy; and it does this primarily neither by the scholastic method nor with humanistic accumulation of classical allusions and examples, but by a comparison of the present constitution of Florence with that of the kingdom of Hungary, put into the mouths of a citizen of Florence and King Matthias Corvinus himself. It attempts to examine not merely the forms but the actual working of these two governments. It lies open to the same charge as *The Prince* of favoring one-man rule in order to win the favor of the Medici family. And as a whole it seems an instructive example of the transitional character of political thought in the decades just preceding Machiavelli's great, if not epoch-making, book. Lippo Brandolini is, of course, much less original and much less brilliant than the man who was appointed secretary to The Ten in the year following his death. Much of his dialogue is trite or traditional; often his speakers do argue like the scholastics or, what is worse, orate like the humanists. A secondary feature of his book, like that of Machiavelli, is the appeal made to the history of the ancient Greeks and Romans. On the other hand, he gives both economic and cultural conditions an attention which they do not receive in the one-sided, though powerful, argument of *Il principe*. Argument, I say, but of course Machiavelli presented no argument in favor of one-man rule as against a republic; he simply told a despot how to be a despot. Therein lies a fundamental difference between his book and that of Lippo Brandolini; and, on the other hand, they form natural complements one to the other. Lippo decides in favor of monarchy; Niccolò offers the budding despot a pocket guidebook — in place, some would have it, of the New Testament.

The opening words of our treatise, "I indeed rejoice at your presence at any time, my son," are addressed by King Matthias to his son, John, who, as Lippo has just explained to

Lorenzo in the prohemium, during the three days of carnival[35] spent by the crowd in luxury and license seeks out his father to engage in a learned discussion. As might be inferred from this, John is a bit of a prig, albeit of an inquiring turn of mind. He does not take any large share in the ensuing dialogue. He serves, however, to introduce it and dispenses such moral platitudes as, "for my kingdom can be taken from me, but wisdom cannot," leading his fond parent to exclaim in the words of the poet: "Omnis enim in Ascanio cari stat cura parentis."

Proceeding to more serious discussion, John manifests a pessimism as to his own times which it will be well to note as a corrective to the rosy pictures of the Quattrocento and High Renaissance which have been drawn by more recent writers, though the same note of pessimism may be found in Petrarch, Salutati, and other humanists. John finds that "everything that was greatest and most flourishing among the men of old is now corrupted and almost extinct, so that the world seems to degenerate daily and somehow to be hastening to its end."[36] Passing over the arts, disciplines, and studies which all seem to him so enfeebled and diminished "that we scarcely retain a faint shadow of them," he asks, where are the kings and em-

[35] This was possibly suggested by the allusions made in opening the dialogue in Cicero's *Republic* to "these holidays" (I, 9: "Dabant enim hae feriae tibi opportunam sane facultatem ad explicandas tuas litteras"; I, 20: "Quam ob rem ut hae feriae nobis ad utilissimos rei publicae sermones potissimum conferantur"). In general, however, there does not seem to be any close resemblance between Lippo's dialogue and Cicero's *Republic.*

[36] "quod omnia quae apud veteres maxima et florentissima erant nunc labefacta et prope extincta sint ita ut degenerare ab se quottidie mundus et ad finem quodammodo properare videatur," fol. 6v in Riccard. MS 672; fol. 11v in Laurent. MS; Jenö (1890), p. 85. Since Jenö's edition follows the Laurentian MS and the leaves of the latter are not consecutively numbered, I shall henceforth usually not cite it, although I originally took the Latin of my quotations from it, and later collated them with the printed text and Riccardian manuscript. It does not seem worth while to give the minor variations in spelling and the like between the two manuscripts. In two or three cases where reference either to the Riccardian MS or to the printed text is omitted, this is simply because I failed to note the exact page where the passage in question occurred and should not be taken as a sign that it was omitted.

pires of old: the Assyrian, that of the Medes and Persians, but especially the great Roman Empire, long since "divided among many petty kings and tyrants"?

The discussion then dwells for a moment upon the problem of the reasons for the fall of the ancient Roman Empire. Different causes are assigned by different persons, John observes, some saying that Christianity has made us timid or cowardly. This bold approach to criticism of Christianity is not encouraged by Matthias who, very likely following Augustine in *The City of God*, ascribes the decline of Rome not to its adoption of Christianity but to its loss of its pristine virtues and its misgovernment of subject nations. But Matthias himself strikes a somewhat Machiavellian chord when he affirms that two things essential for empires are military discipline and lust for glory in the field, and justice and continence at home.[37] He enlarges upon the proficiency of the ancient Romans in these respects, such as the tremendous loads their soldiers could carry, while modern soldiers do not even carry all their own arms. He thinks, however, that horses are now overloaded with heavy protective armor, impairing their aggressive efficiency. He laments the present neglect of military training; points out that the Turks, who are accustomed to military exercises from an early age, have succeeded in carving out a great empire, and that his father, John Hunyadi, was able to check them only by restoring very severe military discipline in his army.

After this glorification of military virtue, if not of militarism, John gives the discussion a new turn by asking his father if it "would not be much better, if we all lived under some one republic?"[38] If he was not himself of royal line, he thinks he would prefer to live under a good republic, "because all things are better administered by many than by one."[39] Matthias

[37] "Foris disciplina militaris et gloriae cupiditas, Domi iustitia et continentia," Jenö (1890), p. 86; Riccard. MS, fol. 7v.

[38] "Nonne igitur multo satius esset, pater, si omnes sub una aliqua republica viveremus," Jenö (1890), p. 96; Riccard. 672, fol. 18r.

[39] ". . . Quia omnia melius a pluribus quam ab uno administrantur," Jenö (1890), p. 97; Riccard. 672, fol. 19r.

asks in reply if one leader for an army or one pilot for a vessel is not better than many, but this presentation of stock examples is fortunately cut short by their agreeing to discuss the matter Socratically, and by the introduction of Dominic Junius, a Florentine knight, to uphold the side of republics since he was born in one, although he has long lived in Hungary.[40] He modestly attempts to refer them to the works of the philosophers on the subject. But Matthias will have none of this, being of the opinion that "an experienced citizen can dispute better concerning a republic and a king concerning a kingdom than can a philosopher." [41] Dominic then requests the privilege of speaking his mind freely without giving offense to Matthias's royal prerogative. To this suggestion the Hungarian monarch agrees heartily, saying, "We wish to find out the truth and not to contend for precedence." [42]

These fine words are not, however, any too well observed in the subsequent dialogue, where Matthias too often does the lion's share of the talking, engaging in long harangues, and Dominic seems to yield to his flow of words and royal presence rather than to the force of truth. He remarks, in fact, at the end of the second book, "I have indeed very many other arguments for this which I might advance, but I am so weakened and overcome by your eloquence and your arguments that I dare say nothing further." [43] Again towards the close of the third book Dominic states that at first his arguments seemed invincible to him, but after he has heard the king "discussing the matter gravely and copiously, I seem to have spoken child-

[40] Riccard. 672, fol. 20r: "... qui quum in optima ut existimo rep. natus sit et in ea locum non postremum teneat, in tuo vero regno diu vixerit, poterit utraque de re tibi optime respondere.

[41] "Ego enim exercitatum civem de rep. Regem de Regno multo melius quam philosophum disputare posse existimo." — Jenö (1890), p. 99; Riccard. 672, fol. 22r.

[42] "Verum enim invenire volumus non de dignitate contendimus." — *Idem.*

[43] "Habeo quidem alia permulta quae pro ea re possim dicere. Sed ita sum iam tua eloquentia tuisque rationibus debilitatus ac fractus ut dicere amplius nihil audeam." — Jenö (1890), p. 144; Riccard. 672, fol. 70r.

ishly and foolishly."[44] To this flattery Matthias replies that it is the force of truth and no merit of his that has overcome his opponent in the debate, but really what little Dominic gets a chance to say is apt to be much more to the point and to show more political sagacity and practical insight than the royal eloquence. Furthermore Matthias is made by Lippo to violate their proposed Socratic form of dialogue by embodying in his own speeches brief statements of the opposing arguments which might much better have been put in Dominic's mouth. This is perhaps true to royal psychology; otherwise we should have to say that Lippo has made very poor use of the dialogue form. It must be further noted that Matthias is permitted to catechize, quiz, cross-examine, and browbeat Dominic with the object of showing him inconsistent, while Dominic never exercises the same privilege in the case of his royal majesty. Another unfair advantage taken of Dominic is that when in Book II he has compared the commercial freedom and greatness of Florence with the isolation of Hungary and its inhospitality to foreign trade, Matthias complains that instead of arguing the question of republic against monarchy in general, Dominic is putting Florence against Hungary, whereas that is just what he himself has hitherto repeatedly been doing whenever it was to his advantage. Thus he has blamed all the particular defects of the Florentine constitution upon republics in general, and has treated Hungary as a normal monarchy, obscuring the fact that it really was elective and with an elected assembly which was neither created nor controlled by the king. We may meet with further instances of this furtive tipping of the argumentative scales in the favor of monarchy as we proceed.

Dominic opened with the contention that under a republic there is more liberty, superior justice and better laws, that all the arts and disciplines flourish more, and that the government is more stable than under a monarch. The first of the three books of the dialogue is devoted to this first point, whether

[44] "Quum contra te audio graviter copioseque disserentem, puerilia quaedam et ridicula dixisse videor." — Jenö (1890), p. 171.

there is more liberty under a republic than under a monarchy and, in this connection, to specific criticism of the constitution of Florence. Dominic begins by defining liberty badly as the power of each person to live as he wishes,[45] and is forced to qualify this as not including the right to commit crimes with impunity, and to distinguish between liberty and license — an antithesis as common then as now. He has further to admit that the Florentines cannot clothe themselves, or eat and drink, or celebrate funerals and weddings as they choose, since all these matters are regulated or restricted by sumptuary laws. When he boasts that the citizens of Florence have to pay tribute to no one, he has to admit that they cannot export or import freely, but have customs duties to meet the expenses of government. But he states that they levy these taxes of their own free will.

Matthias then questions if the Florentine method of choosing the magistrates by scrutiny and lot is free, and whether one man would not select them more intelligently. There follow some arguments of a sophistical or humorous turn, such as that if the nine priors are called "lords," all the rest of the citizens must be serfs (*servi*), and that if the priors cannot leave the palazzo of the signory except publicly, they have no liberty. The point is then made that the magistracy at Florence is weakened by too great division of power, and Matthias argues that since the magistrates and senate have not full power, they haven't liberty. The method of secret ballot is also criticized by Matthias. In regard to the voting by black and white beans dropped in an urn he asks, "Can one's opinion be adequately expressed by beans?"[46] He objects that one might have to vote for a measure of which one disliked certain features, and says to Dominic, "I see from your words that the citizens are compelled sometimes to say what they do not want, sometimes to

[45] "... potestatem nimirum unicuique vivendi ut vult." — Jenö (1890), p. 101.

[46] "Potestne animi sententiam satis recte fabis exprimi?" — Jenö (1890), p. 108; Riccard. 672, fol. 31r.

keep silent as to what they do want."[47] He further objects to the secret method of voting in the senate that it enables bad men to conceal their character and prevents the good men from becoming known.

The office of podestà, called by Lippo *praetor peregrinus*[48] in humanist style, is then attacked. Matthias objects to the calling in of a foreigner to administer justice, asking if Florence is so poor in good citizens. Dominic replies with dignity, "We are indeed able and we have the best of men in abundance in the city, but we think it wrong for one citizen to put another to death, nor do we think that any citizen can be immune from love, hate, anger, envy, pity, and other emotions on account of relationships, associations, friendships, clientage, and other bonds. But we think that a foreigner having no acquaintance with us can easily remain free from all passion and render judgment impartially to all."[49] Matthias, however, further objects that he thinks it odd that they entrust all public matters to citizen magistrates but turn over private law to a stranger. "For how can one render justice aright to you who knows not your laws, your customs, your institutions?"[50] Moreover, to obtain the post of podestà one must curry favor with the citizens and especially with the aristocrats.[51] And in a short term of six months the podestà is unable to accomplish any-

[47] "Video ex tuis verbis cogi cives ut nonnumquam quae nolunt dicant, nonnumquam taceant quae volunt." — Jenö (1890), p. 109; Riccard. 672, fol. 32r.

[48] Riccard. 672, fol. 33r: "Pretor peregrinus quem nos nescio quo latino usitato certe vocabulo potestatem appellamus."

[49] "Possumus quidem et habemus optimos viros in civitate permultos sed nephas esse ducimus civem civi mortem afferre neque putamus civem quenquam immunem ab amore odio ira invidia misericordia caeterisque affectibus propter cognationes affinitates familiaritates clientelas et alias necessitudines esse posse. Peregrinum vero hominem ob nullam nostri notitiam facile omni affectu carere et ius aequaliter omnibus dicere existimamus." — Jenö (1890), p. 110; Riccard. 672, fol. 33v.

[50] "Quo vero pacto ius recte dicere vobis potest qui vestras leges vestros mores vestra instituta non novit?" — *Idem.*

[51] I presume that *optimates* refers to the leading merchant families of Florence rather than to the nobility disqualified in 1293.

thing; "he scarcely becomes acquainted with men's faces and the lawsuits."[52]

Matthias then concludes concerning the liberty possible under the constitution of the republic of Florence, "But if you are free neither in ordinary life nor in the matter of taxation nor in magistracies nor in councils nor in the administration of justice, I do not see where that liberty of yours is, unless perhaps you think it consists in this, that you are not subject to foreign nations."[53] Asked how much liberty his people have, Matthias asserts that they possess much more. Not only are they likewise subject to no foreign power, but they pay only a small annual tribute to their own king, they dress themselves and expend as much on weddings and funerals as they please, their assemblies and magistrates are not determined by lot or chance but by the prudence of their prince. The senate is elected by the whole kingdom, "for it is seemly that those who are to take counsel for all should be chosen by all"[54] — the familiar maxim of Justinian, Edward I, *et al.* The judges (*praetores*) are natives responsible to the king. How they are paid is not very clear, as Matthias gives the impression that in paying tribute the people have to satisfy the financial needs of only one person, the king, as against the numerous citizen magistracies of Florence. He charges that all the innumerable citizens of Florence feel free to lord it over and prey upon its subject provinces, while Hungary has but one king to do this, and the provinces count it rather a rare favor when he visits

[52] ". . . vix vultus hominum causasque cognoscat." — Jenö (1890), p. 112; Riccard. 672, fol. 35r.

[53] "Quod si neque in communi vita neque in vectigalibus neque in magistratibus neque consiliis neque in iudiciis liberi estis, ubi sit ista vestra libertas non video, nisi forte in eo contineri arbitramini quod exteris nationibus non serviatis." — Jenö (1890), p. 112; Riccard. 672, fol. 35v.

[54] ". . . senatum e regno universo delectum decet enim ut qui omnibus consulturi sunt ex omnibus eligantur." And in the second book Matthias says: "Nos quoque Senatum habemus et quidem ex universo Regno delectum cui leges quas ipsi sancimus ostendimus eiusque iudicio atque auctoritate comprobandas tradimus. Legum tamen latio ut etiam Plato affirmat ad Regiam dignitatem proprie pertinet." — Jenö (1890), pp. 113, 117; Riccard. 672, fol. 36v.

them. Dominic, however, refutes the former charge, saying that it was true of the ancient Romans but is not of the modern Florentines. As for the possibility of a bad and oppressive monarch, Matthias refuses to consider it, dismissing it with the verbal evasion that kings who rule otherwise than he does are tyrants, not kings. John, who for some time has been maintaining a discreet silence, is now asked by his father which liberty he prefers and says: "That of a kingdom. For a republic, so far as I can see, is not free but serves itself, and is oppressed with the greater servitude and solicitude, the better it is administered. For it is necessary that all be vigilant for the public good. The result is that no one can ever have any solid quiet and tranquillity, if he sets out to be a good citizen."[55]

The second book passes on to discuss Dominic's second point, whether a republic is superior to a monarchy in justice and laws. Matthias points out that the ancient Athenians and Romans had single law-givers, Draco and Solon, Numa Pompilius and Justinian; while the Israelites had their Moses; Crete, its Minos; and Sparta, its Lycurgus. When Dominic declares that it is surely preferable to live under the best law rather than under the best king, Matthias wants to know wherein there is any contradiction between the two, and how anyone can live under abstract law alone. Laws must be made by someone, and, once made, must be frequently modified and interpreted by man, "especially when the intention of the writer seems to conflict with what he has written."[56] . . . "Who can better amend or interpret them [i.e., the laws] than he who made them in the first place. Now that this was a single man, and he

[55] "Regni. Resp. enim quantum intelligo non est libera, sed sibi ipsi servit eoque maiori servitute et sollicitudine premitur quo melius administratur. Omnes enim communi bono invigilare necesse est. Quo fit ut nulli unquam si modo bonus civis velit esse solida quies aut tranquillitas esse possit." — Jenö (1890), p. 115; Riccard. 672, fol. 38v.

[56] "Quid quum voluntas scriptoris cum scripto ipso videtur dissentire . . ." This was, of course, a matter that the great jurists of the Roman Empire took into consideration. — Jenö (1890), p. 121; Riccard. 672, fol. 44v.

a King, is sufficiently and abundantly declared. Therefore it is clear that a King is not the minister or instrument of the laws but is set over and dominates the laws. And since this is so, it is much better to submit to Kings than to laws." [57] It is noteworthy that the word *Rex* or King is capitalized throughout Lippo's treatise,[58] for even the word *deus* or God is often not capitalized in medieval manuscripts. Matthias goes on to contend that the mind of one man cannot be so easily corrupted as can the minds of many persons where the contagion spreads rapidly. After this affirmation of mob psychology, Dominic yields on the second point of justice and the laws in perplexed admiration, and the discussion turns to the subject of commerce.

Let us first note, however, an indication from another source that in point of fact the laws of Hungary in the time of King Matthias were not king-made but popular custom, and that royal interference with these was not likely to be wise. In a passage in the works of the Spanish humanist Vives (1492–1540) he states that the people of Pannonia lived very amicably under their old customs without need of jurists until, as a sequel to the marriage of Beatrice of Naples to King Matthias of Hungary, the jurists who came in her train began to introduce the Roman law. The whole countryside was soon plunged into a turmoil of litigation and red tape until some prudent citizens demonstrated the evil to the king and he expelled the Roman lawyers from the country. Thereupon everything went back to the old state of calm as if a violent wind had suddenly died down.[59]

[57] "Quis eas melius vel emendare vel interpretari potest quam is qui de integro condidit? hunc autem unum fuisse et illum quidem Regem satis abundeque declaratum est. Regem ergo non legum ministrum aut instrumentum esse sed legibus praeesse dominarique perspicuum est. Quod quum ita sit multo satius est Regibus obtemperare quam legibus." — Jenö (1890), p. 121; Riccard. 672, fol. 45r.

[58] This capitalization is, however, more noticeable in the Laurentian than in the Riccardian manuscript.

[59] Vives, *De causis corruptarum artium*, VII, 4.

As we have already noted, Matthias objects that Dominic's favorable comparison of Florence's commercial freedom and greatness with Hungary's isolation and inhospitable attitude to foreign trade does not apply to republics and monarchies in general, contending that the Frenchmen and Spaniards scour the orb in quest of gain as much as the Florentines, while the men of the republics of Siena and Lucca usually do not go outside of Italy. However, Matthias further argues that commerce, cosmopolitanism, and intercourse between nations are bad and corrupting influences, perverting youthful morals, adulterating the language of the fatherland, and introducing lust and luxury.[60] Plato did well to locate his republic far from the sea.[61] Against the plea that trade in foreign commodities not produced at home is necessary for life,[62] Matthias declares that there is no region that does not produce all the real necessities of life in abundance, and that it is an insult to God's providence to hold otherwise. Matthias seems to favor a very simple standard of living indeed, since he bemoans that "we are all so sunk in luxury and incontinence that we seem in no way able to live without the use of bread, wine and oil." [63] "What madness 'tis to sail to the Ethiopic or Indian Ocean to

[60] "Nam si verum ingenue fateri volumus quid obsecro est aliud quod bene institutas civitates corrumpat et ex optimis pessimas reddat nisi peregrini mores mutuaque comercia? Haec enim adolescentium mores pervertunt, haec patriam linguam adulterant, haec bene informatos animos illecebris lascivisque effoeminant et de ipso quasi modestiae et constantiae gradu deturbant. Haec cum peregrinis opibus ac mercibus avaritiam pariter ambitionem gulam libidinem et caetera foeda ac nepharia flagicia invehunt. Adolescentes enim domi pudice parce liberaliterque educati ubi mercaturae gratia ad exteras nationes se conferunt liberius vivendi potestatem nacti patriam sensim continentiam parsimoniam deponunt . . . ," etc., etc. — Jenö (1890), p. 124; Riccard. 672, fol. 48v.

[61] "Plato quidem philosophorum omnium sine controversia princeps cum optimam remp. constituere vellet, hoc in primis cavit ut civitas ea procul a mari sita esset." — Jenö (1890), p. 126; Riccard. 672, fol. 50r.

[62] "At indiget externis rebus vita non enim omnia nasci omnibus locis possunt." — *Idem.*

[63] ". . . prolaxi tam omnes in hunc luxum atque incontinentiam sumus ut sine panis vini et olei usu vivere nullo modo posse videamur." — Jenö (1890), p. 127; Riccard, 672, fol. 51v.

search out there gems and pearls!"[64] He is proud that the Hungarian youth leave their land for others for the sake of letters, not of money. "And than this sort of travel none can be more worthy and honorable."[65] He fails, however, to explain why divine providence has not supplied Hungary with schools of its own. After reproaching the Italians with the sale of arms to the Turks, Matthias makes another right-about face in his argument, contending that Hungary is actually more liberal towards commerce than the Florentines, who place restrictions upon foreign goods and merchants. "You, therefore, are the ones who do not cherish commerce. You are the ones who violate the rights of nations. You are the ones who take away the communion of the human race."[66] Dominic thereupon offers the following very clear and well put explanation and justification of Florentine policy in this respect:

Since we are in so large measure given to mercantile life and profess to supply others with an abundance of garments of every sort, we would surely seem to do ourselves an injury if we permitted others to carry on our own craft in our city, especially since we have in that line not only a large output but also a superiority in quality, so that no one could ask for more or better goods. But if we admitted foreign goods of this sort, we would not only lower our price but also our prestige. For by receiving foreign wares we would seem to argue openly either a scarcity or defects of our own wares. Since the opposite is true, we think that foreign woolens should under no circumstances be admitted, but we do not on that account do injury either to our citizens or to strangers. For since many merchants are citizens, they have themselves sanctioned this law, nor would they suffer anyone to modify it. Foreigners, moreover, among whom the same industry is in honor and esteem, employ the like law against us; and it is so arranged between us by tacit consent of nations

[64] "Quae vero [malum] dementia est ad ethiopicum aut indicum Oceanum ut gemmas inde et margaritas eruamus navigare!" — *Idem.*

[65] "Qua quidem peregrinatione dignior atque honestior esse nulla potest." — Jenö (1890), p. 128; Riccard. 672, fol. 52r.

[66] "Vos igitur estis qui commertia non colitis. Vos estis qui gentium iura perfringitis. Vos estis qui humani generis communionem [or, *communitatem*] tollitis." — Jenö (1890), p. 129; Riccard. 672, fol. 54r.

for common utility that neither should bring to the other those wares from which these make their livelihood. But those who have no goods at all of this kind or only a few and of poor quality, they necessarily take goods from all kinds which are brought to them. And this is the reason why you who are given to warlike pursuits admit all wares of all nations. For you cannot exclude them if you wish to live comfortably. We cannot admit them, if we wish to preserve our state.[67]

We next hear communism preached from the mouth of royalty, Matthias contending that in a republic there ought, logically at least, to be an equal distribution of wealth. Dominic retorts that the arts would decline without the incentive of private gain. Matthias insists that "mutual utility and necessity would retain the arts and all studies in the state." [68] As it is now, he pursues, what equality have you with your extremes of the very rich and very poor, whose whole mode of life is utterly different? How can such two extremes "be

[67] ". . . nos quum magna ex parte mercaturae dediti simus profiteamurque nos aliis vestium omnis generis copiam posse sufficere, iniurii profecto nobis ipsis videremur esse si artis nostrae quaestum in nostra civitate aliis tribueremus: Praesertim quum habeamus in eo genere tantam non modo copiam verum etiam bonitatem atque praestantiam ut nemo neque plura neque praetiosiora possit desiderare. Quod si peregrinas eius generis merces admitteremus, nostris non modo praetium verum etiam auctoritatem minueremus. Videremur enim externis accipiendis nostrarum vel inopiam vel vitia aperte arguere. Quae quum contra sint, nullo modo peregrina lanitia censuimus admittenda neque propterea vel civibus vel peregrinis iniuriam facimus. Nam quum plerique mercatores sint cives ipsi hanc legem sanxerunt neque ei a quoquam derogari patiuntur. Peregrini vero apud quos eadem ars in praetio aut in honore est eodem adversus nos iure utuntur: estque inter nos tacito gentium consensu ita propter communem utilitatem comparatum ut neutri ad alteros ex eo quo illi quaestum faciunt genere merces deferant. Qui autem vel nullas omnino vel admodum paucas eius generis et viles habent nimirum eos ab omnibus quae deferuntur accipere necesse est. Atque haec vobis qui bellicis rebus dediti estis causa est ut omnes omnium gentium merces admittatis. Excludere enim eas, si commode vivere vultis, non potestis. Nos admittere, si modo volumus civitatem nostram conservare, non possumus. . . ." — Jenö (1890), p. 130; Riccard. 672, fols. 54r–55r.

[68] ". . . mutua illa utilitas ac necessitas artes et studia omnia in civitate retineret." — Jenö (1890), p. 133; Riccard. 672, fol. 58r.

bound and united in any bond of virtue and equality?" [69] "But if all fortunes were middling, so that one did not much exceed another, all envies and causes of contention would cease, and that equality which we desire would be preserved." [70] Dominic contends that a common standard of life is maintained by the sumptuary laws (but if so, why do men strive for a wealth which they may not spend?), that all Florentines are equal before the law, and have opportunities to acquire the arts and learning. But Matthias remains convinced that it would be better to have an equal distribution of wealth, and to allow the better citizens distinguishing marks of clothing, funeral monuments, and the like, since if no rewards are offered for virtue and nobility, who will strive for glory and the fatherland?

Is a republic or a monarchical form of government the more favorable to education and culture? Matthias points out that the city of Paris, though subject to the king of a people whom the Florentines call barbarous, far surpasses all the cities of Italy in the studies of the best arts. "For in it are always found about twenty thousand, sometimes even thirty thousand, hearers and students in all disciplines." [71] This is an interesting, though probably exaggerated, bit of testimony as to the size of the University of Paris. Matthias has to admit that Florence leads in painting and sculpture,[72] and Dominic contends that republics are more intent on the education of their citizens. Matthias replies that if Florence has more illustrious citizens than the capitals of monarchies and princedoms, this is due not

[69] ". . . ullo virtutis aut aequalitatis vinculo iungi et connecti queunt?" — Jenö (1890), p. 134; Riccard. 672, fol. 59r.

[70] "Quod si mediocres omnibus opes essent, ita ut alter alterum non multo excederet, omnes invidiae et contentionum causae cessarent et illa quam volumus aequalitas servaretur." — *Idem.*

[71] "Sed una parisiensium civitas Gallorum regi quam gentem vos barbaram appellatis subiecta omnes Italiae civitates optimarum artium studiis longe antecellit. In ea enim semper fere viginti nonnumquam etiam triginta auditorum ac studiosorum in omnibus disciplinis milia reperiuntur." — Jenö (1890), p. 139; Riccard. 672, fol. 64v.

[72] "At pictura, inquis, et sculptura in nostra civitate magis florent." — *Idem.*

to the difference in form of government but to the native genius of the Florentines, and he notes that many of them have left the city because their ability was not adequately rewarded there. He then goes off on a tangent in a set speech on the problem whether more is to be ascribed to education or to natural ability.

Matthias opens the third book, which envinces less plan than the two preceding books, by repeating his previous analogies from the desirability of one pilot for a vessel and an undivided command of an army. From reflections on Cannae and Fabius Maximus he is recalled by Dominic's suggestion, "Let us come to matters that are more related to our debate." [73] Matthias then advances other analogies: Should not the father rule the household, and the headman the village? Dominic, however, objects that a state or city is another matter, larger, more difficult, and too much for any one man to govern. Four eyes see better than two, many hands are stronger than one; a king more readily gives way to passion and becomes a tyrant than does the government by many persons; there is profit in common counsel; the work of a monarch is cut short by death, and if many share in the government, its continuity and stability are better assured. Matthias admits that these are strong arguments and difficult to answer, derived from that very rich source of all disciplines, the genius of Aristotle. Dominic, like the best of generals, has kept his most reliable troops in reserve.[74] Matthias, however, will continue the struggle, relying on the doctrine of divine Plato that the rule of one man is the best. He puts forward such a dubious argument as that one man can find the center of a circle better alone than with aid. A kind of compromise is suggested to the effect that the government

[73] "Veniamus ad ea quae nostrae disputationi propinquiora sunt." — Jenö (1890), p. 149; Riccard. 672, fol. 75v.

[74] "Valide mehercule et efficaces sunt rationes istae dominicae et quibus responderi sine summa doctrina non possit. Quippe quae ex uberrimo illo disciplinarum omnium fonte aristotelis ingenio proficiscantur. Tu enim ut optimus imperator firmissimam aciem in postremis collocasti." — Riccard. 672, fol. 81v.

of the many is perhaps safer because the best men are so few and hard to find, with Dominic agreeing that if one best man could be found, the government of the many would not be needed. He still feels, however, that in any case the rule of one man lacks stability and continuity, while Matthias objects to the rule of more than one man, that in the case of disagreement many heads are worse than one, and contends that under a monarchy there are no civil wars and discords, such as Siena has to contend with at the present moment, and Florence would, too, "if you did not have that best and most preëminent citizen, Lorenzo de' Medici, who by his virtue and authority moderates and rules the minds of the citizens."[75] To this Dominic heartily assents: "He is indeed as you say, King, for whatever concord and happiness we possess we have received from him alone."[76] These compliments, however, might have been made more gracefully a few sentences earlier.[77] Matthias continues with other unconvincing arguments against a republic, such as that a tie vote may result between more than one person, that a single ruler will be above human ambition and passions, that the citizens of a republic may be so many tyrants using the state for their private ends.

Matthias then again returns to his inconsistent statement that he takes the advice of a senate popularly elected from his entire kingdom, which seems a combination of republican with monarchial government. But this now leads to a discussion of the place of a senate in a republic or monarchy. Matthias doubts if men engaged in the wool trade like the Florentines can make good senators, but Dominic assures him that they are the equals of the Roman senators of old. Matthias further holds that while such a senate may give advice, the single head should make the final decisions. Dominic, however, makes the pene-

[75] ". . . nisi optimum illum et praestantissimum civem Laurentium medicem haberetis qui sua virtute atque auctoritate civium animos moderatur ac regit. . . ." — Jenö (1890), p. 158; Riccard. 672, fol. 85v.

[76] "Ita profecto est ut dicis Rex, quicquid enim concordiae foelicitatisque habemus illi uni acceptum ferimus. . . ." — *Idem.*

[77] That is, after the words quoted above, "if one best man could be found."

trating observation that in that case the senators will not have a sufficient sense of responsibility; will be less interested, as if dealing with another person's affairs; will act negligently and remissly, much like mercenary soldiers. Matthias denies this, asserting that patriotism and fear of punishment by the prince or devotion to his person will hold them faithful to their work.

The question is then raised whether republican forms of government really do enjoy a more unbroken continuity than monarchies. Against the regencies and interregnums of the latter are instanced the frequent seditions and civil wars in the republics of ancient Greece and Rome. Moreover, if republics lasted longer, they would be more numerous, but the greatest part of the earth once was and today is ruled by monarchs. Furthermore, a change is a good thing occasionally. As republics grow old, they degenerate, like everything else. It is even admitted that a revolution may sometimes be a good thing in a monarchy in order to eject a tyrant or introduce a worthy prince. Matthias then embarks upon a verbose discourse with many illustrations, including that of the office of dictator in the Roman republic, to prove his point that a single ruler can better promote concord. He concludes this discourse with the argument that inasmuch as tyranny is the worst government, therefore monarchy is the best, and then asks his son, John, what he is laughing at.[78] John, however, was smiling at Dominic's discomfiture and not at the absurdity of his father's argument.

Dominic has one question left, nevertheless, and that is, Why then are there republics at all?[79] Matthias thereupon traces the evolution of Greek governments from monarchy to tyranny to aristocracy to oligarchy to republics, which of course is not the correct sequence historically. Finally the republics degenerated in their turn into democracies, "than which nothing more abject and detestable can exist, nor is any roon left for further degeneration or collapse."[80] But it does not

[78] Jenö (1890), p. 174. [79] *Ibid.*, p. 175; Riccard. 672, fol. 103v.

[80] ". . . quo quidem abiectior ac detestabilior esse nullus potest neque enim locus iam ullus degenerandi aut collabendi relictus est." — Jenö (1890), p. 176; Riccard. 672, fol. 104v.

seem to occur to anyone that if democracy is really worse than tyranny, then a republic must be better than a monarchy, according to Matthias's own recent argument. Instead Matthias finds additional instances of royal rule among the bees, in the rule of the head over the human body, the sun's preëminence among the stars, and the supreme power of one God. Search the pages of history and the whole world over, and you will always find kings flourishing, while republics have been few and brief and far between. A word picture of an ideal king is then sketched for John's edification, but Dominic, despite the criticisms that had earlier been lavished upon his city's government, is told to go on being a good Florentine "because there is both a great dearth of excellent princes, and your republic is governed by excellent laws and institutions." [81]

It is deserving remark that in addition to Plato, whom he once calls "without controversy the chief of all philosophers," [82] and Aristotle, whom he elsewhere without much regard for consistency calls the "greatest of the philosophers," [83] Matthias several times quotes Juvenal, whom, however, he calls Aquinas from his birthplace, and in almost every case for some pithy apothegm such as, "He pardons crows but censures doves," or "A king has more of aloes than honey," or "Every sin increases in enormity with the prominence of the sinner," or "Who will guard the guards themselves?" [84]

[81] "Tu vero Dominice tametsi optimum esse unius principatum tibi persuadere debes, tamen quia et magna nunc optimorum principum inopia est et vestra resp. optimis legibus atque institutis gubernatur habetque aliquam etiam illius regni principatus imaginem, patriam tuam prae ceteris defende ac cole daque operam ut eius leges ac mores et tuearis et serves tibique persuade si in ea optime ac rectissime vixeris te non deteriorem regio nactum esse principatum. Sed iam advesperascit. Surgemus. Satis enim disputatum est. VALETE." This last word does not occur in the Riccardian manuscript. This passage forms the Explicit of the treatise. — Jenö (1890), p. 183; Riccard. 672, fol. 112.

[82] "Plato quidem philosophorum omnium sine controversia princeps. . . ."

[83] "summus philosophorum."

[84] "Nam ut Aquinas ait, 'Dat veniam corvis, vexat censura columbas.'" "Ut breviter Aquinatis verba exprima, 'Plus aloes quam mellis habet Rex.'" "Nam ut Aquinas ait, 'Omne animi vitium tanto conspectius in se crimen habet quanto maior qui peccatur habetur.'" "Et ut Aquinas ait, 'Quis custodiat

One naturally wonders to what extent Lippo's treatise was intended as political propaganda in favor of the aspirations of the Medici family towards a throne, but the problem offers much the same difficulties as does that of how far Machiavelli wrote *The Prince* with the Medici in mind. Lippo's work was professedly begun in Hungary at the suggestion of King Matthias, but in its present form seems more intended for a Florentine audience. Brandolini tells Lorenzo de' Medici that when the idea of composing it occurred to him in Hungary, "I thought I should be doing something neither displeasing to that ruler [King Matthias] *nor unacceptable to my fellow citizens*, if I should institute a comparison of the two governments and bring forward all the arguments with which either was accustomed to defend itself and should explain the customs and institutions of both."[85] But Brandolini is obviously more interested in the constitution of Florence than in that of the Hungarian kingdom, of which we get but a confused idea. Propaganda or not, our treatise may be taken as a prophetic leaf, showing that the political wind was blowing from republican Florence towards the grand duchy of Tuscany, as well as in Europe generally towards monarchical absolutism. Raphael Brandolinus of course dedicated it to Cardinal Giovanni[86] during the expulsion of the Medici from Florence and expressed the hope that the work might prove to be an omen of his restoration. Our author, however, is still very far from the

---

ipsos custodes?'" Yet another example is, "Sed illos, ut Aquinas ait, defendit numerus iunctaeque umbone phalanges." These last two passages occur at fols. g4r and k2v of the Laurentian manuscript.

[85] Riccard. MS., fols. 2v–3r: "... rem neque illi principi iniocundam neque meis civibus ingratam me facturum existimavi si de utriusque principatus comparatione perscriberem rationesque omnes quibus uterque se defendere consuevit in medium afferrem et utriusque mores atque instituta explicarem."

[86] Our treatise, it is perhaps worth noting, was not the only one of the sort which was presented to him, since the national library at Rome contains a manuscript of the *De principatu* of Mario Salomonio, the jurisconsult, with a Prohemium to Leo X. Indeed, this very MS is described by the catalogue as the dedicatory copy and has two pages completely filled with illuminations: Fondo Vittorio Emanuele 427, 16th century, membr.

position represented by the doctrine of the divine right of kings. He prefers monarchy or one-man rule only in a rather vague way; it need not necessarily be hereditary, perhaps better not; his arguments lead us more to the idea of a patriot king, or even simply to the conclusion that a single executive is best.

Lippo possesses none of Machiavelli's power of political generalization, and he repeats many time-worn ideas. But he has approached his subject from a somewhat novel angle, and he occasionally makes an acute observation. In part he has abandoned the method of political philosophy for that of political science, and the realm of the ideal for that of the practical. He also has ventured upon the comparative method, although it is really an ideal monarchy which Matthias represents as superior to the actual republic of Florence. And of course Hungary was not a very good selection to hit upon for political comparison with Florence, owing to their almost antipodal economic and cultural differences, which, as our author seems more or less to suspect, serve to befog the issue. But we could wish that some particular monarchical state of the period had been subjected to the same specific practical criticism as is directed against the institutions of Florence. It will be noted, however, that the author of this specific criticism of the working of the constitution of Florence was a citizen of Florence. Perhaps the subject of a monarchy of that age, or even the ruler of the same, would not have dared to publish such specific criticism of his country's constitution. And that may be a sufficient answer to King Matthias.

APPENDIX 1

OTHER EXAMPLES OF DEBATES: MEDICINE VERSUS LAW

A good example of scholastic disputation as to the relative merits of medicine and law is provided by a manuscript of the fifteenth century in the Library of St. Mark's at Venice.[1] There, in the company of such distinguished medical, physical, mathematical, and scholastic writers of the fourteenth and fifteenth centuries as Dino del Garbo, Hervaeus Natalis, Angelus de Fossanbrono, Johannes Marlianus, and Cajetan de Thienis, we find a discussion whether civil or canon law is a nobler science than medicine by John Antony of Imola, doctor of arts and theology, and an eremite.[2] Since he was not a doctor of laws, he is not the same as the John of Imola, a citizen of Bologna, who died in 1435, whose name appears in the faculty lists from 1410 to 1434, and whose Commentary on the five books of Decretals was printed at Lyons in 1549 (per Ioannem Pullonem). He might better be identified with another John of Imola, who taught logic and moral philosophy at Bologna between 1385 and 1396. But this John is not called Antonius in the *Rotuli*. Our author begins with such arguments as that the intelligence of the planet Saturn is nobler than that of the sun, that astrology is nobler than geometry, and that that science is the nobler which has the nobler subject matter and the nobler mode of procedure. He also cites various works of Aristotle. Apparently he devotes the first half of his discussion to the preliminary problem of what the grounds of comparison are to be. Only when his space is half consumed does he come to the main question, saying, "These things

[1] S. Marco Latin MS VI, 105 (Valentinelli, X, 218), 15th century, chart. — a double-column folio with very small and abbreviated writing which I did not think it worth while to attempt to decipher at all thoroughly.

[2] *Ibid.*, fols. 79v–82r: "Excellentissimi artium et theologie doctoris domini magistri Ioannis Antonii de ymolla heremite [?] questio nobilissima incipit. Utrum scientia civilis vel canonica sit nobillior medicinali. Et videtur quod sic: illa scientia est nobillior alia que facit hominem magis honorabilem . . ./. . . ut dicantur domini cum tamen professores tales dicantur magistri sint professores medicine ut patet in prologo Decretalium. Quare, etc. Finis."

then having been seen, I come to what we are after and I say that medicine absolutely (*simpliciter*) and *per se* is nobler than civil and canon law.[3] He then advances almost the same arguments as the authors considered in our second chapter: that man is more truly the subject of medicine than of law; that medicine is a subdivision of natural philosophy, law of moral philosophy; that medicine proceeds by the method of demonstration while law depends upon past authorities; that law is only an art and not a science, since it deals with contingent matters. Or, on behalf of the law, it is urged that Aristotle declared politics nobler than medicine, that it is a higher goal to make men virtuous than merely to make them healthy, that the law is superior because concerned with voluntary acts. Most of such arguments are then rebutted.

Since the question of the ranking of arms and the military profession was raised by both John Baldus and John of Arezzo, we may note that among various questions disputed by candidates for the licentiate in arts at the University of Vienna,[4] John Hymel in 1406 debated, "Whether the magisterial functions of philosophers are more worthy and perfect than the military arts."

In the closing years of the fifteenth century there was printed at Bologna a Latin "Declamation whether the Orator is to be put before the Philosopher and the Physician," by Philip Beroaldus the Elder.[5] He appears as lecturing at the University of Bologna on rhetoric and poetry in the years 1472–75 and 1479–1505,[6] when he died on July 17, aged 51 years, 8 months, and 9 days.[7] Frati calls him Bologna's leading humanist. During the years 1475 to 1478 he was absent from Bologna, teaching at Parma, Milan, and Paris. His edition of Pliny's *Natural History* was printed at Parma in

[3] S. Marco L. VI. 105., fol. 80v, col. 2: "His ergo visis venio ad id quod queratur et dico quod medicina simpliciter et per se est nobilior lege civili et canonica."

[4] MS Melk 6 (A. 8), 15th century, fols. 403–10.

[5] *Declamatio an orator sit philosopho et medico anteponendus.* Several editions are listed in Hain, Copinger, and Pellechet, but the first with a definite date seems to be that of 1497. Besides these editions at Bologna, it was printed at Venice about 1498 and 1499, and at Paris in 1500–1501. This last is the edition I have used: *Opusculum eruditum quo continetur Declamatio philosophi medici et oratoris de excellentia disceptantium*, 1501.

[6] U. Dallari, *I rotuli dei lettori legisti e artisti dello Studio bolognese dal 1384 al 1799*, 1888, etc., Vol. I, pp. 90, 93, etc., to 188.

[7] L. Frati, "I due Beroaldi," in *Studi e memorie per la storia dell' Università di Bologna*, Vol. II, pp. 210–28.

1476.[8] Later he published some corrections of Pliny,[9] subsequently, however, to the controversy of Leonicenus, Hermolaus Barbarus, and Pandolfo Collenuccio over the errors of Pliny. He also corrected some passages, "in part faulty, in part obscure," in the books of Galen, "the noblest of physicians." [10]

In the aforesaid declamation, which sounds like an imitation of the Pseudo-Quintilian declamations, Beroaldus displays more favor to oratory than to medicine and philosophy. A father whose three sons entered these several professions is represented as having left his property to the son who is most useful to the state. The three sons accordingly state their claims to the award before judges, but the philosopher and the physician are allowed less than two pages each, while the orator consumes thrice this space and wins the decision. He is also given what may seem the unfair advantage of knowing not a little concerning the history of medicine and philosophy, whereas the other two are at the disadvantage of having to maintain their case oratorically. Altogether the declamation is a very flat performance, and the numerous editions of it must be regarded as a sign of the popularity then of *humanitas et eloquentia* and also of such disputes as that between medicine and law or oratory, rather than of any merit in the content of the work.

In an Opusculum concerning earthquake and pestilence,[11] Beroaldus described the earthquake which occurred at Bologna in 1505, the year of his own death. It contains such observations in the field of natural philosophy as that the grunt of a pig terrifies elephants, or that earthquakes are a presage and cause of plague, emitting subterranean vapors which pollute the air. His tendency to adopt the magical viewpoint is further suggested by his having commented upon the *Golden Ass* of Apuleius.[12]

André Tiraqueau, or Tiraquellus (1480–1558), in his *Commentarii de nobilitate*, cap. 31, no. 360 *et seq.* (fol. 150v *et seq.* in the Ven-

[8] Other editions at Treviso, 1479; Paris, 1518.

[9] *Plinianae aliquot castigationes*, Brixiae, 1496; Venetiis, 1508.

[10] Beroaldus (Philippus) the Elder, *Opusculum de terraemotu et pestilentia; cum annotamentis Galeni*, 1505. Fol. Eiiii, verso, "de terremotu et pestilentia hactenus dictum sit. Nunc quoniam Galeni frequens mentio facta est, non erit alienum quedam subtexere que partim mendosa partim obscura in libris nobilissimi medicorum deprehensa . . ."

[11] For its title, see the preceding note.

[12] Printed, Venice, 1501.

ice, 1570, edition), devoted some space to the relative merits and dignity of law and medicine, referring to the works of Bernard, physician of Florence, Salutati, and Poggio upon this theme. He also pointed out that theologians like Antoninus of Florence (1389–1459), "in prima parte 3. partis principalis suae summae," and Augustine of Ancona (1243–1328), *De ecclesiastica potestate*, Titulus 109, had concluded that legal science was the worthier. Petrus Charmensis, the medical writer, in his *Lixoperita* had discussed the matter copiously but held the balances even between the two subjects. Another to treat of it was Bartholomew Chasseneux in his *Catalogus gloriae mundi*,[13] first printed in 1529 at Lyons.[14]

The following notice from Macray's catalogue of the Digby manuscripts in the Bodleian is of a codex written in an Italian hand which I have not yet examined. Digby 131, membr. 15th century, 27 leaves. "Opusculum de medicina ac legali scientia que dignior sit atque de medicine causis cur vilior videatur"; dialogus inter Carolum Ghisilerium, legistam et militem, Petrum Johanenitum, medicum, et Nicolaum de Fabis, in cuius domo conveniunt. The dialogue is dedicated to Andrea Piccolomini (of Siena, 1476–1496?), but the author's name is not given. The work is probably an imitation of those considered in our second chapter.

[13] "In 10 parte, in 25 consideratione."

[14] Some other citations, given by Tiraquellus in abbreviated form, are: "Barb. in c. clerici, de iudi."; "Panorm. in c. clerici col. 2, extrà de iudici & ibi quoque Fran. Are. in 2 not. & Phili. Dec. col. 3. vers. secunda regula, & Lucas Pe. in Rub. C. de profes. & medi. li. 10."

APPENDIX 2

MEDICAL RECIPES OF BISTICHIUS

From S. Marco, Latin MS VI, 282 (Valentinelli, XIV, 39).

[*fol. 77v*] Prima medicina per me bistichium expertissima est contra quartanam et tertianam. Unde in nomine Iesu christi collige per tres dies tria folia salvie, vel si vis omnia tria simul in una die, cum maxima devotione et fide dicendo pater noster et ave maria, credo et salve regina, et collectis his tribus foliis scribe in primo si licet [scilicet?] + pater est pax, in secundo + filius est vita, in tercio + spiritus sanctus est remedium et sanitas. Tamen ego expertus sum scribere omnia ista in omnibus tribus foliis et esse simul ista alia verba subsequentia que sunt et valent ad idem scilicet + christus natus + christus mortuus + christus resurexit, et similiter conscribuntur in foliis de salvia et comeduntur in tribus diebus ieiuno stomaco singulum singulo die.

The following is his chief alchemistical recipe:

Balsami recepta expertissima in multis et maximis rebus. Recipe terbentine libram unam thuris unciae duo aloes citrini [*fol. 78r*] uncia una masticis gariofillorum galange cinamomi nucum muscatarum cubebarum omnium uncia una gummi ellemi que apretitreos sic vocatur unciae sex aque ardentis distillate quater libram unam. Hec omnia terantur terenda et misceantur insimul et pone in elambico et claude ne aliquo modo respiret et tunc pone in furnello adaptato scilicet distillatorio et facias lento igne distillare. Prima aqua erit clara sicut aqua fontis, secundo [*sic*] incipiet colorari et spissari et supernatabit alteri aque et non miscebuntur. Tercia vero aqua magis densatur et inspissatur sicut mel. Aque proprie balsamus dicitur et apparebit in distillatione sua spissa. Et est eius virtus sicut virtus balsami in omni probatione. Tamen nota quod si volueris facere unguentum, pone loco aque vite tantum de de [1] unguento laurino, et ponantur omnia mixta sub fimo in ampulla bene clausa per octo dies et valet ad frigida quocunque modo sint ventosa et aquea. Nota quod ista prima aqua ardet sicut aqua ardens. Secunda coagulet lac, et si in una scutella lactis tepidi unam guttam aque predicte tepidam ponas, statim coagulat lac et sicut virtus balsami stat in fundo cipri et non disolvitur etiam postquam steterit per unam horam ascendet. Prima aqua que abstrahitur vocatur aqua balsami; secunda vocatur ebor balsami; tertia vero balsamus artificiatus nuncupatur. Prima

[1] It would seem that *de* is written twice in the MS where it should occur but once.

bona, secunda melior, tertia vero optima. Prima ardet et non comburit pannum sed dimittit eum siccum. Secunda ardet et [*fol. 78v*] comburit pannum. Tertia erit fortior in centuplo et quanto plus reiteratur et distillatur erit fortior in centuplo. Itaque in distillatione comburit ligna et omnia que ponentur in ea.

Bisticius then expatiates for nearly three pages upon its virtues, medicinal and otherwise.

[*fol. 80v*] Ad frangendum omnem lapidem in vesicca humana et ad proiciendum extra, experientia probatissima pro illis qui non possunt urinare propter lapidem. Recipe leporem unum non decoriatum et pone in olla munda et cooperias: deinde pone in furno quousque comburatur multum et fiat pulvis niger, et da de isto pulvere pacienti modicum in ovo, et sanabitur, et est expertum. Tamen nota quod ponas leporem vivum cum omnibus suis intestinis in olla predicta, et si vis prius disponere pacientem fac sic, videlicet coque petrosillum cum oleo, deinde torque oleum et pone patienti petrosillum ante et retro. Deinde post modicum da sibi de pulvere supradicto leporis combusti et sanabitur statim, et fiat hoc quousque sit sanus.

Ad sanandum nubes que fiunt in oculis bestiarum. Tere fortiter vitrum et cribra bene et pone in oculis bestiarum, et infra quinque dies sanabuntur. Ad idem combure de stercore humano fortiter et pone in oculis bestiarum que habent pannos cum uno canone et sanabuntur.

Two recipes for the memory follow.

TRANSLATION

The first medicine, oft tested by me, Bisticius, is against tertian and quartan fever. So in the name of Jesus Christ collect on three days three leaves of salvia, or, if you wish, all three at once on one day, with the greatest devotion and faith repeating a paternoster, Ave Maria, creed, and Salve Regina, and after collecting these three leaves write on the first thus: "+ The Father is peace"; on the second, "+ The Son is the life"; on the third, "+ The Holy Spirit is the cure and health." But I have tried, too, writing all these on all three leaves, and at the same time those other words which follow and are similiarly efficacious, namely, "+ Christ was born, + Christ died, + Christ rose again," and these are written in the same way on leaves of salvia and are eaten on three days on a fasting stomach, one on each day.

Recipe for a balsam oft tested in many and the greatest emergencies. Take a pound of turpentine; of frankincense, two ounces; of aloes, lemon, one ounce; of mastix, gariofle, galange, cinnamon, nux, must, cubebs, one ounce each; of gum elemni,[2] called apretitreos, six ounces; of ardent water four times distilled, one pound. Grind all of them that can be ground and mix together and put in an alembic and seal it so no vapor can get out and place it in a furnace for the purpose, namely a distillery, and distill it with a slow fire. The first water will be clear as spring water, the next will begin to show color and to thicken and it will float on the other water and they won't mix. But the third water will be still denser and thick like honey. It may fitly be called the balsam of water and will appear thick in its distillation, and in every test its virtue is as the virtue of balsam. But note that in case you wish to make an unguent, you should use in place of *aqua vitae* laurel unguent and put the mixture in a well sealed bottle in a dunghill for eight days, and 'twill be good for colds, no matter how windy and watery they may be. Observe that the first water burns like *aqua ardens*. The second coagulates milk, and if you put one tepid drop of the said water in a saucer of tepid milk, it immediately coagulates the milk. And as the virtue of balsam resides in the base of cyprus and is not dissolved, even after it has stood for hours it will rise. The first water that is drawn off is called water of balsam. The second is called ivory of balsam. The third is called artificial balsam. The first is good, the second better, the third best. The first burns itself without burning a cloth, but leaves it dry. The second is combustible and burns a cloth, too. The third is stronger by a hundredfold, and the more it is worked over and redistilled, the stronger it will be to a hundredfold. Therefore during distillation it burns wood and anything which is put in it. . . .

. . . .

To break any stone in the human bladder and eject it: a most approved experiment for those who cannot urinate because of stone. Take a hare that hasn't been skinned and put it in a clean pot and cover the pot. Then put it in a furnace till it is well burnt and becomes a black powder, and give a little of it to the patient with an egg and he will be cured and there's no doubt of it. But take care that you put the hare in alive with all his intestines in the aforesaid pot. And if you wish to prepare the patient, follow this procedure. Cook rock parsley with oil, then wring out the oil and place the parsley before and behind the patient; then after a bit give him some of the aforesaid powdered hare and he will be cured right away, and let this be done until he is cured.

To cure films in the eyes of beasts, grind glass thoroughly and sift

[2] John Parkinson, *Theatrum botanicum*, London, 1640, p. 1586, writes: "We have not yet attained the knowledge of the tree, from whence this Gum *Elemni* is taken."

it well with a sieve and put it in the beasts' eyes, and within five days they will be cured. For the same: burn well human excrement and put it in the eyes of beasts which have leucoma, using a tube, and they will be cured.

APPENDIX 3

THE TWO PROLOGUES OF THE *CIRURGIA* OF LEONARD OF BERTIPAGLIA

A. Manuscript text from Biscioniani 13, fol. 1; Sloane 3863, fol. 1; Reg. Suev. 1969, fol. 4r; and S. Marco L. VII. LI, fol. 11. Variant readings are noted in brackets.

Incipiamus ergo in nomine domini [nostri] yeshu Christi [Amen] et gloriose virginis marie eius [que] matris qui me et vos [omnes] addiscentes confirmet in via cognoscendi [in] semita veritatis et virtutis et reprimat appetitus bestiales et corroboret cor meum et vestrum ingenium ad suum servitium et honorem ut valeam et possim humilique placentia lingue promere vobis in scriptis hec multa archana [*organa* in Bisc. 13] que nostro pectori non intendimus [nostris] clericis occupare quoniam non laudo hominem hanc artem ignorantem qui cum voluerit prodesse nocebit sicut fuit bonus homo de Andria civitate qui cum [hoc] acquisitus fuisset [fuit] multam pecuniam ex uno solo experimento de nostris se nesciente acquisivit [sibi] nomen optimi medici et in tantum se inanivit [or, *habuit*] quod ex vana [or, *una*] gloria ipse redundatus est ab aliis medicis scientificis in vituperium. Quare fili pro tua vera salute et intellectus tui declaratione labora addiscendo ne ingrediaris esse de secta metoicorum vel stoicorum atque imperitorum ut nobis clare patefacit Galen in tercio de ingenio sanitatis.

In style this prologue seems influenced by the *Medical Experiments* ascribed in the middle ages to Galen or Rasis: see my *History of Magic and Experimental Science*, Chapter 64.

B. Text from the printed editions.

Altitonantis implorabo auxilium quo sine nullum rite fundatur exordium nec ad medii finisque alicuius bonitatem ullam sane quis pervenire poterit, ut intellectus mei dilucidare dignetur ingenium ut valeam [ut] ego Leonardus plura mei canonica chirurgiae experimenta in scriptis ad aeternam memoriam redigere quae vero [*et quae* in the 1546 edition] experimento ac ratione theorica habuerim Avicenne prosequendo vestigia et ordinem 3 super Fen Canonis quarti.

A manuscript of Leonard's work with this form of the prologue was formerly contained in the library of the monastery of St. Michael at Murano near Venice; see Mittarelli, *Bibl. codd. MSS. mon. S. Michaelis.* 1779; MS. 103, chartac., 15th century.

APPENDIX 4

TABLE OF CONTENTS OF THE *CIRURGIA* OF LEONARD OF BERTIPAGLIA

From Sloane MS 3863, fols. 109r–110v

Incipit Rubrica seu tabula fen tercii quarti canonis de apostematibus calidis et curis eorum. Et primo de flegmone.

Tractatus primus continet in se hec capitula, etc.

de flegmone et cura eius
de erisipula et cura eius
de formica tam ambulativa quam corosiva et miliari[s] et cura eorum
de igne persico et pruna etc. [et cura?]
de inflacionibus et vesicis etc.
de esseribus et curis eorum
de cancreno et aschachilo et herpestiomeno et curis eorum
de altoyn sive carbunculo etc.
de apostematibus que oriuntur in locis glandinose carnis et non venenosis etc.
de exituris etc.
de dubelet calido
de forunculo et cura eius
de moro et cura eius

Tractatus secundus de apostematibus frigidis et curis eorum

de undimia et cura eius
de nodis et curis eorum
de nata quod est apostema glandosum
de pustulis glandulosis etc.
de fugille et cura eius
de scrophulis et curis eorum
de sephiros et cura eius
de duricie iuncturarum
de almismar id est callus etc.
de cancro et cura eius
de apostematibus ventosis etc.
de vena medena seu civili etc.

Incipit fen quarta quarti canonis de solucione continuitatis in carne, in nervis et ossis (*sic*) etc.

de diffinicione solucione continuitatis
de iudiciis mortis et periculi in quibus communicant vulnera quorundam membrorum
de sermone universali vulnerum quod incipit vulnus carnosum etc.
de cognitione eius quod facit [?] nasci carnem
de medicinis incarnativis
de perforatione vulneris et aliorum cum oportet quod discooperiantur
de vulneribus habencium apostemata et malam complexionem
de vulnere in ventro [*sic*] et modo suendi
de qualitate modo ligandi
de medicinis incarnantibus vulnera
de medicinis consolidativis et sigillativis
de facientibus nasci carnem in vulneribus
de vulneribus que fiunt in capite absque lesione ossis cum vulnere et contusione

Incipit tractatus secundus de offensione et contusione et actricione et excoriacione et punctura et fluxu sanguinis.

de sermone generali
de contusione et actricione et cura
de casu et offensione
de offensione supra ventrem et viscera
de verberatis et flagellatis
de torsione sive egaumau et quia maxime fit in membris officialibus sicut adiutorium et ancha
de excoriacione que fit a sutilaribus aut a lapide aut ad parietem etc.
de punctura et disrupcione eius quod retinetur in carne ex spinis et sagittis et fuscis et similibus
de combustione ignis quocumque
de fluxu sanguinis a vena vel ab arteria et cura eius

Incipit tractatus tercius de ulceribus et primo de sermone universali de omnibus ulceribus

de diffinicione ulceris
de curacione omnium ulcerum in universali
de ulceribus virulentis
de ulceribus sordidis
de curacione ulcerum profundorum et cavernarum et absconsionum
de curacione vermium in ulceribus
de nascentibus carnis in ulceribus

de curacione ulcerum corodencium se preter putrida
de curacione ulcerum putridorum malorum
de curacione ulcerum que sunt difficilis consolidacionis et dicuntur ambulativa
de curacione fistularum et corosionum que non conglutinantur absque labore
de carne addita super vulnera quomodo et qualiter debent [*sic*] removeri
de regimine ulcerum quando disrumpuntur post consolidacionem
de hiis que habent removere vestigia vulnerum [nervorum] et ulcerum

Incipit tractatus quartus de solucione continuitatis nervorum

de sermone universali
de curacione solucionis continuitatis vulnerum nervorum in universali
de medicinis ipsorum vulnerum et ulcerum
de apostematibus que accidunt nervis vulneratis
de actricione nervorum et eius [*sic*] torsione
de iudiciis et extraccione nervorum coruptorum
de duricie nervorum atque torsione ipsorum
de remocione egritudinum ossium
de ventositate spine et corupcione ossis et curis eorum
de modo secandi os coruptum et qualiter medicus se debet habere
de extraccione frustris ossium et corticum eorum que remanent in ulceribus consolidandis
de medicinis convenientibus in fine fracturarum ossium
de fractura cranei
de fractura capitis in forma consilii in quo continentur xi notabilia [in the text this is marked cap. 1]
de quodam exemplo [cap. 3 in the text; there is no cap. 2]
de fractura capitis in universali et hoc theorice [cap. 4 in the text]
de curacione fracturarum ossis capitis et hoc in universali
de ordine receptorum
de dyeta
de iudiciis et cautelis cirogicorum quod in certis casibus et maxime in fractura cranei necesse prodest uti et sunt decem iudicia sive notabilia

De iudiciis vulnerum significancium mortem per singula membra habencia aspectum secundum xii signa celestium aut salutem et hoc cum maxima difficultate et hoc primo incipienda ab ariete

de vulnere facto in capite quando sol est in ariete cum luna coniunctum [*sic*]
de vulnere in collo quando sol cum luna est in thauro coniunctum

de vulnere in brachiis quando sol cum luna est in geminis coniunctum
de vulnere facto in pulmone vel in casso quando sol cum luna est in cancro coniunctum
de vulnere facto in corde vel circa regionem cordis et hoc quando sol cum luna fuerit in leone coniunctum
de vulneribus factis in naturalibus quando sol cum luna est in virgine coniunctis [*sic*]
de vulnere factis [*sic*] in anchis quando sol cum luna est in libra coniunctis [*sic*]
de vulnere facto in virga quando sol cum luna est in scorpione coniunctis
de vulnere facto in coxa quando sol cum luna est in sagittario coniunctis
de vulneribus factis in genu quando sol cum luna est in capricorno coniunctis
de vulneribus factis in tibiis quando sol cum luna fuerit in aquario
de vulneribus factis in pedibus et hoc quando sol cum luna fuerit coniunctum in piscibus

Tractatus de iudiciis secundum aspectus signorum celestium

de circulo zodiaci considerando
de aspectibus in qualibet egritudine
de nominibus aspectuum
de cognicione concordancie signorum penes eorum complexiones
de signis planetarum
de planetis
de laudibus huius sciencie que pertinet ad medicum de aspectibus tractando

Deo gracias. Explicit tabula sive rubrica.

APPENDIX 5

LEONARD'S SURGICAL PRACTICE WITH THE FAMILY OF GAZABINUS

Capitulum [tertium] quod est exemplum.

Venit ad me cum auxilio divine trinitatis quidam rusticus [et] nomine Gazabinus cum uno suo nepote qui quondam fuit vulneratus tribus vulneribus et cum uno cultello quorum unum vulnus erat [in] intestino colum [or, *colon*] et exivit pro tunc quando primo vidi stercus de vulnere illo et erat in illo situ ubi est revolutio renis sinistri. Aliud vulnus erat in casso et penetrabat signum fuit quod [or, *quia*] aer exiens de illo vulnere extinxit ignem unius magne candelle accense. Aliud vulnus erat in splene quod [or, *quoniam* or *quem*] vidi quod [or, *et*] exibat de vulnere sanguis niger melancolicus. Et tale vulnus erat sub costis mendosis in parte sinistra que omnia vulnera in illo suo nepote iam liberaveram. Et de vulnere intestini exivit magnus lumbricus *quasi in fine consolidationis quem lumbricum* [the words which I have just italicized are omitted in the Sloane MS] extrasi de vulnere cum manibus meis.

Dixit itaque dictus Gazabinus cuius filius adhuc de fractura cranei iam habui in cura et liberavi: Filius meus Pasqualinus percussit [se] cum fratre istius quem tu a morte sanasti quemdam iuvenem portatorem cum uno spito de zinglario et auriculam [or, *virgulam*] spiti fixit in capite modicum laterabiliter [or, *lateraliter*] et parum distans a commissura coronali per unam unguem infra. Sed duo alii homines qui erant secum iuraverunt mihi [quod viderunt] ex illa hora cum sanguine exire de substantia cerebri quando posuerunt albumen ovi hoc non certe volui credere. Sed recordans (me) ex verbis Galieni sexta particula afforismorum anforismo illo *Vessicam incisam etc.* In commento dicit G. de cerebro, Incisionem quoque cerebri [multotiens] vidi sanari semel enim vidi in nimb[i]a [or, *India*] civitate Samar[i]a [or, *Sanari*] quandam magne et concave incisum cerebrum habere et tamen mortem evadere quod contingit rarissime. Item Arnaldus [*Renaldus* or *Arenaldus*] de Villanova in sua practica *et in tertio tractatu* [the words just italicized are omitted in the Sloane MS] dicit hoc [or, *quod*] idem audivisse a peritissimis cirurgicis de substantia cerebri exiri [or, *exire*] et a morte egrotantes evadere. Sed hoc vidi oculis meis de substantia medulari iterum in hoc egro exire quem curavi solus [or, *solum*] sine alio conscilio [in place of this word, MS Biscion. 13 has *cum stillo*] in presentia multorum doctorum et scolarium paduanorum quos precibus meis et caritate mecum ducebam ut viderent possibilitatem nature scilicet separationem manifestam et amplam per duos digitos primi ventriculi anterioris in quo inmaginativa [or, *ymaginativa*] perficitur a separatione medii ventriculi in quo cogitatio sive ratio perficitur [et] tertius ventriculus posterior ubi fiat retentiva sive virtus thesaurizativa [Sloane MS has instead *restaurativa*] non fuit pro tunc ad oculum mihi notum.

In tali homine vivo omnes iste tres virtutes fuerunt semper sicut sane [or, *sani*] et sine [or, *sint*] aliquo accidente omnibus accidentibus numeratis solentibus apparere in huiusmodi dispositionibus sicut vomitus sincopis singultus spasmus alienatio mentis febres et epilensia etc. Virtus nutritiva animalis vitalis semper fuit [or, *fuerunt semper*] sicut sane [sani?] usque ad trigesimum quartum diem in qua die supervenerunt [sibi] quinque parosismi [or, *quinquies parosismus*] epilensie cum [or, *et*] magno sudore et febre [or, *febres*] continua. Et hoc fuit a causa primitiva scilicet a potatione vini montani me nesciente. Sed verum est quod illa dies fuit etiam dies cretica salubris et radicativa secundum quod numeravi per computacionem [compunctionem] dierum medicinalium creticorum. Sed transacta illa die remansit debilitas in virtute motiva ex parte contraria pedis et manus sed modum [or, *modus*] qualiter ego processi ipsum curando tam practice quam theorice inferius narrabo.

Sloane 3863, fols. 91v–92r;
Biscioniani 13, fols. 57v–58r;
Reg. Suev. 1969, fol. 67v;
S. Marco L. VII. LI, fols. 106v–107r.

APPENDIX 6

THE FOOLISH PRESCRIPTION

A. Text from Biscioniani 13, fol. 52r; Sloane 3863, fol. 33r–v; S. Marco L. VII. LI, fol. 98v.

Nota fili carissime ne tibi accidat sicut accidit [or, *accessit*] cuidam bono viro paduano qui habebat puncturam in nervo factam ex ferro minuto in manu sinistra et in digito annulari super mediam iuncturam. Et quidam phisicus sapiens et famosissimus [or, *famosus*] in sua doctrina et carens experimento et ratione in cirurgia sed stolidus in hac re iussit aproximari medicinas mollificativas scilicet emplastrum de farina tritici et aqua et oleo et croco. Sed tandem putrefacta est manus et mortuus est in die septima et quia supervenit spasmus propter putrefactionem factam ex indebita aproximatione emplastri mali. Quare crede [or, *credere*] quod quilibet expertus credendus est in arte.

B. Text from edition of 1498, fol. 264r, col. 1.

Nota amice ne tibi accidat sicut accidit cuidam bono viro qui habebat puncturam in nervo factam ex fero subtili in manu sinistra et in digito annullari super mediam iuncturam. Et ivit quidam stolidus cyroicus et approximavit medicinas mollificativas scilicet emplastrum factum ex farina tritici oleo cum aqua et croco. Sed tandem putrefacta est manus et mortuus est die septima ex hoc quia supervenit spasmus propter putrefactionem factam ex indebita approximatione mali emplastri. Et propter hoc non sunt accipiendi homines imperiti aut ceratani ad tales passiones.

Both passages occur just before the opening of the chapter "De apostematibus que accidunt nervis vulneratis."

APPENDIX 7

A CASE OF DROPSY FROM THE *PRACTICA CIRURGIE* ASCRIBED TO JOHN OF MILAN

[*Vienna 4751, fol. 70r*][1] Meo tempore rogatus a quibusdam sociis duos perforavi et modum quem tenui hic narrabo. Ego autem primo comprimebam cum ambabus manibus ventrem ut tota aqua declinaret ad inferiorem partem pectoris. deinde considerabam cum omni diligentia utrum aque generatio esset in parte intestinorum aut propter passionem epatis vel splenis. Et si erat ex parte intestinorum perforabam totam cutim cum sifac tribus digitis sub umbilico secundum rectum donec ad locum vacuum perveniebam. Et si generatio aque erat propter epar, tunc faciebam sectionem in parte dextra. Si propter splenam, faciebam sectionem in parte sinistra. et numquam volui facere sectionem in latere super quo infirmus volebat iacere ne superfluitates ad locum illum descenderent vel decurrent. facta autem perforatione intromittebam canullam argenteam de [de] argento fino ut aqua per eam evacuaretur. et non extrahebam totam una vice sed paulatim ne infirmus morietur propter resolucionem spiritus animalis et ne sincopis superveniret et morti [*fol. 70v*] appropinquaret, sed secundum virtutem evacuebam [*sic*] et semper antequam perforarem cutim ad superiora elevabam, deinde perforabam et canulam interius inponebam. quando vero extrahebam canulam tentam unam decocto involutam in foramine inponebam in extremitate cuius spagum de serico vel de filis lini ligabam. deinde cutim ad inferiora descendere permittebam cum spagi extremitate exterius eminenti deinde. Sequenti vero die iterabam canellam [*sic*] et aquam extrahebam secundum quod virtus requirebat et faciebam donec interius non remanebat aliquid de ipsa vel parum et si mihi videbatur quod aliquid aque remansisset faciebam fieri balnea artificialia salsa et alumnosa et sulphurea et velocius in lixivio quam in aqua[m] de consumptione residui aque. Sed meliora sunt naturalia omnibus aliis ut illa que sunt in Tuscia et similibus locis.[2]

Aliqui dicunt de sepultura in arena calida ad solem.[3] Vidi quemdam medicum qui fecit ponere unum asclitem in uno furno prius parte extracto. sed prius faciebat egrum temptare si potuit pati talem caliditatem qui respondit quod sic. et tunc fecit ponere unum assidem latam [*fol. 71r*] in furno et egrum spoliatum omnibus pannis excepta intrula[?] sola et intrare furnum et super [supra]scriptam assidem sedere. Ego autem fui presens et vidi obturari os furni sed non totaliter ut eger posset eventare et sic stetit per mediam horam grossam et tunc eger incepit dicere quod non poterat amplius stare. et tunc suprascriptus medicus fecit egrum sugare a sudore copiosissimo et in lecto cum linteaminibus calidis poneri, deinde ungebat ventrem suprascripti egri cum unguento de gumis quod sic fit . . .

Ego autem volui scire ab egro quantum tempus erat quod egrotabat tali egritudine qui respondit 8 menses erant et plus quod eius venter inceperat tumefieri. et tunc fui cum tali medico et ei dixi quod [*fol. 71v*] numquam curaret ipsum prout ego non potui curare illos duos quos perforaveram quia unus longi temporis. . . .[4]

[1] Corrected from CLM 273, interleaf following fol. 129v, where the text varies slightly in wording but is roughly the same.

[2] CLM 273 reads: "Sed meliora sunt naturalia quam artificialia ut balnea de comitatu senarum de corsona. Et alia secundum naturas ut in tractatu Gentilis de balneis."

[3] CLM 273 adds: "Et aliqui in stercore bovis, aliqui in fimo ovino calido." From this point on the two MSS diverge markedly.

[4] This last paragraph is not found in CLM 273.

APPENDIX 8

THE CHAPTER ON *NATA*

[*Vienna 2358, fol. 131r–v*] Plerumque accidit quedam superfluitas aliquibus hominibus que vulgariter appellatur nata et est apostema carnosum molle ut fungus et non est dolor et si est pus nec est calor nec est pulsacio. Et aliquando magnificatur multum. Et dicitur nata quia super membris natat. Brunus dicit se vidisse unum [*fol. 131v*] qui in humero habebat et tam mangnum [*sic*] quod credidit in humero habere pulvinare et noluit se impedire. Tamen quidam empericus sine litteris extraxit ipsam que ponderavit libras vii. nullo modo vidi nec audivi tantam magnitudinem in nata aliqua. Modus curacionis consuetus et securus tam parve quam magne dummodo non sit fusci coloris et magne duriciei est ut incidatur et excorietur cum suo saculo et extrahatur, deinde radices cauterizantur peroptime propter fluxum sanguinis secundum istam curam quia tales dicunt possibilem et securam. Tamen cogitandum est quod est infiltrata in membris venis et arteriis nec extrahi potest sine magno periculo mortis.

Hic nota narrabo modum quem meo tempore tenui et hoc dico circa natam que non erat fusci coloris nec maxime duriciei, si nata non erat multum infiltrata in venis et arteriis et nervis ut in tympore manibus et gula et similibus, prout alias vidi in domo domini Johannis de gonzaga et habebit [*sic*] in superiori parte dextre manus que erat libras iii meo iudicio. nolui me intromittere causis dictis. si talis pendebat proced[eb]am cum filo serico et faciebam spagum unum et firmiter ligabam si radix et origo erat subtilis donec corrodebatur tota. post cauterizabam cum aqua mea forti caustica totam radicem. Si vero nata non erat pendens et radix lata et non nimis infiltrata in nervis et arteriis nec fusci coloris nec dure substantie ponebam desuper peciam perforatam super natam vel partem stupefacientia inbibita in albumine ovi agitando sepe cum oleo rose. Pro repercussivo super foramen ponebam de unguento stupefactivo descriptis [*sic*] in capitulo de medicinis rumpentibus exituras. demum applicabam ruptorium ex calce et sapone. Elevato ruptorio applicabam pulticem ex farina ordei aqua et auxungis [*sic*] cum oleo rose. Et si non erat causticata videbam escaram ponebam de pulvere arsenici albi donec causticabatur tota. Et aliquando applicabam de predicta [*col. 2*] aqua quod non permittebam remanere aliquid de eius foliculo donec curabatur. Et si erat parva agebam tantum cum aqua caustica donec cauterizabatur tota cum folliculo suo. post approximabam pulticem. Et remota escara cum mundificativo et consolidantibus carnem curabam. Sed meo tempore curavi quamplures natas cum aqua caustica supradicta. Et dato quod dicatur quod debeat incidi et excoriari, ut dictum fuit in scrophulis, ut dixi numquam volui me illo modo intromittere causis dictis et periculis mortis. Sed usus fui aqua caustica in qua mirabilem operationem inveni. Et notandum quod cauterium est medicina nobilis iuvans ad alterandum membrum et dissolvit materias corruptas in ipsis existens et stringit fluxum sanguinis. Pulvis vero dicta multum mitigat dolorem digerit escara. Et approximavi cauterium tucius meo tempore quam potui.

APPENDIX 9

THE CASE AT MILAN

Following primarily Vienna 2358, fols. 127v–128r.

Nota casum mediolani dum essem in curia magnifici domini macaruli filii illustris domini bravabonis de vicecomitibus de quadam parva exitura. accessit ad me quidam socius domini karuli de florencia qui pluribus diebus passus fuit exituram in coxa sinistra in qua multi de mediolano interfuerunt pluribus diebus. ostendit mihi istam coxam ubi erat exitura in presencia illorum medicorum ubi patiebatur tali exitura multum profunda. existens in colloquio cum supradictis medicis quesivi ab eis quid eis apparebat de tali coxa tamquam melius informari. Et primo visitaverunt ipsum et fuerunt in cura. tacta coxa per me cum ambobus manibus diligenter et reperui magnam quantitatem saniei et multum profundam. Et cum transierat per moram aliquorum dierum steterat sanies respondebant mihi medici quod credebant in illo esse saniem. Et tunc dixi, quare non perforastis? dixerunt quia coxa est multum musculosa et composita ex nervis magnis latis et arteriis, non ausi fuimus timendo de spasmo aut de fluxu sanguinis. Apposuerunt bene emplastra subtiliativa cutim et rumpencia sed sanies erat profunda et illa emplastra parum profuerunt sibi. accepi et removi omnia ista emplastra et consideravi locum magis cedentem et approximavi illud unguentum stupefactivum per diem unam. die sequenti summo mane sumpsi uno mane [*sic*] unam peciam panni lini [*fol. 128r*] duplicatam et balneavi eam in aqua rose et albumine ovi, et posui super locum quem volebam perforare magis cedentem iuxta foramen pecie quantitatis volebam esse rupturam magnam. posui de ruptorio ex calce et sapone et bene feci adherere supradictum ruptorium cuti cum plumaceolis panni lini et bona ligatura. et hora 22 accessi ipsum et postulavi si haberet dolores qui dixit quod non. Et tunc elevavi ruptorium et scidi escaram cum cuspide pili. Et profundavi cum aqua caustica forti quam mecum portaveram et perforavi et incidi cum pilo ita quod unum bochale saniei exivit in presencia medicorum de mediolano. deinde posui unam bonam tentam longam in supradicto unguento de melle involutam et inveni magnam profunditatem. Sequenti veri die incepi facere lotiones cum syringa quam dives [1] ex vino malvasie aqua vite. Demum accepi aquam salsam et aquam aluminis quoniam sine istis non poteram exsiccare supradictam saniem, tanta erat et habundata tam de preterita quam de illa que de novo generabatur stante bono regimine. Sed ratione debilitatis loci et virtutis et alicuius consuetudinis nature hoc accidebat meo videre. Ita quod cum supradictis aquis et modo scripto [2] et cum incarnativis et cum consolidativis premissis dei auxilio curavi et multum de honore [et utilitate] [3] percepi."

[1] Perhaps instead of *quam dives* one should read *grandines*. Vienna 4751, fol. 22r, however, reads: "Sequenti vero die incepi facere lociones cum siringo ex vino malvasie et aqua vite quia dives erat," i.e. because the patient could afford the use of such washes.

[2] The abbreviated form in Vienna 2358 seems unmistakably to indicate *scriptum*, but this would be ungrammatical. CLM 273 and 321 here read *modis scriptis*.

[3] Added in CLM 273 and 321.

APPENDIX 10

CHAPTER HEADINGS OF JOHN OF AREZZO'S *DE PROCURATIONE CORDIS*

From MS Laurent. Plut. 73, cod. 29.

There is no such table in the MS itself. I have collected the chapter headings scattered through its text. The figure following each head is the number of the folio where it occurs.

Tractatus I

1, de cordis ac etiam reliquorum membrorum creatione (2r)
2, de cordis anothomia (3r)
3, de cordis instrumentis quibus suas perficit actiones (4r)
4, de duodecim animi passionibus que cor afficiunt (5r)
5, de delectationis et tristitie causis (6r)
6, de diversis cordis affectionibus ex sanguinis diversitate causatis (8v)
7, de rancore et eius causis ac eius odio differentia (9v)
8, de delitie ac tristitie exteris causis (10v)
9, de exteris delitie ac tristitie corporeis causis (13r)
10, de medicinis cordialibus simplicibus et primo de calidis (14r)
11, de inmanifestis spirituum qualitatibus inmoderatis et medicinis ipsarum (18r)
12, de forma specifica (18v)
13, de compositis cordis medicinis (20r)

Tractatus II, de invalitudinis cordis cura

1, de universali egritudinum cordis cura (23v)
2, de male cordis complexionis cura (25v)
3, de cordis apostematum cura (27v)
4, de cardiaca egritudine (28r)
5, de cordis tremore (28v)
6, de sincopi et eius cura (32v)

Tractatus III, de venenis

1, de veneni diffinitione et eius generibus (37v)
2, de regulis venena vitandi et medicinis (39r)
3, de rebus que venenum ostendunt atque venenati hominis signis (41r)
4, de generali venenatorum cura (42r)

5, de nocumentis particularibus ex venenosis rebus et cura et primo de cibis venenosis (44v)
6, de nocumentis ex medicinis frigidis venenosis cura (46r)
7, de nocumento et cura calidarum medicinarum que veneno sapiunt (47r)
8, de nocumentis medicinarum que caliditate et corosione corrupti a veneno sapiunt (47v)
9, de nocumento medicinarum solutivarum que veneno sapiunt et cura (48r)
10, de nocumentis medicinarum veneno attinentium cum siccitate et grositie substantie et eorum cura (49r)
11, de nocumento ex animalibus interius sumptis et illorum partibus et cura(50v)
12, de nocumento sanguinis et lactis coagulati et eorum cura (52r)
13, de nocumentis animalium os ingredientium et eorum cura (53r)
14, de nocumento ex animalium morsibus et puncturis et cura in generali (53v)
15, de notitia ac signis animalium rabiosorum atque morsuum ipsorum (54v)
16, de utilibus canonibus curationis morsuum et puncturarum (56v)
17, de rabiosi animalis morsus nocumento et potissimum canis et cura (57r)
18, de serpentum maneriebus (58v)
19, de magne ac parve lacerte morsus nocumento et cura et aliorum vermium (60v)
20, de cura nocumenti ranarum et buffonum (61v)
21, de nocumento et cura animalium parvorum ut sunt vespe scarabei apes musce et formice (61v)
22, de nocumento aranee et rutelle et eius cura (62r)
23, de nocumento et cura puncture scorpionis attarie [?] et tarantelle (62v)
24, de nocumento morsus vel puncture animalium in aqua degentium et draconum (64r)
de fugandis atque necandis animantibus non venenosis hominem ledentibus (64v)
de animantium pungentium non venenosorum fuga et nece (65r)
de venenosorum animantium fuga et nece (66r)
de serpentum ac venenosorum quorundam fuga et nece (66v)

(These last headings are unnumbered.)

APPENDIX 11

TEXT OF THE CHAPTER *DE INMANIFESTIS SPIRITUUM QUALITATIBUS INMODERATIS ET MEDICINIS IPSARUM*

Cum de primis iam dixerimus spirituum inmoderatis qualitatibus, modo de secundis tum manifestist um ocultis agendum est. Primo tamen de manifestis puto de ipsorum claritate vel turbitudine. Tenebrositati itaque spirituum conferunt ambra, argentum, aurum, agaricus, coralus, crocus, canfora, iacintus, carabis, lignum aloes, margarite, siricum, spodium, secacul, terra sigilata. Hec itaque omnia cum spiritibus splendorem afferant ut prenaratum est in earum virtutibus spirituum removent obscuritatem. Oculte vero spirituum qualitates sunt venenose qualitates et ipsorum malignitates. Hec quoque medecinis prohibentur tiriace naturam habentibus quemadmodum ambra, argentum, aurum, agaricus, acetositas citri, citrum, canfora, dornicum, endivia, fisticis, iacintus, iadran, lignum aloes, muscus, olibanum, sticados, terra sigilata, zedoarium, atque medicine plurime composite quas infra paulo post narabimus. Spirituum autem nocumenta que modo substantie attinent ut si inmoderate grosi fuerint spiritus huiusmodi conferunt medicine agaricus, basilicon, been, citri cortex flos et folium, cinamomum, crocus, calamentum, cassia lignea, iacintus, hosmel, lapis armenus, lapis lazuli, melissa, menta, ozimum, polipodium, menta, peonia, siricum, sticados, terra sigilata, zedoarium. Si vero subtilitate precaverint[1] spiritus cibi viscosi et potus sanguinem igrosantes conveniunt. Medicine quoque que ipsos solident ac viscosos reddunt puta ambra, corallus, coriandrum, emblirici [?], fistici, iacintus, rosa, sandali, spoditi, terra sigilata, tamaridi. Si autem inepti sint spiritus sua tenebrositate ac humorum melancholicorum mixtione medicinis abstersivis ac ipsorum mundificativis curandi sunt que presertim vapores educunt melancolicos puta argentum, aurum, agaricus, citrum, coralus, emblirici, iacintus, lingua bovis, lapis lazuli, lapis armenus, mirabolani, melissa, margarite, polipodum, peonia, siricum, sticados, spodium, terra sigilata, tamaridi. — MS Laurent. Plut. 73, cod. 29, fol. 18.

[1] Or *peccaverint?*

APPENDIX 12

A DISCUSSION OF FUNGI

From *De Procuratione Cordis,* III, 5.

Iam ad particularium venenosarum rerum nocumenta et curas accedamus. Initium tamen sit a venenosis cibis cum sepius omni hominum generi occurant. Fungi itaque et tubeara [*sic*] non sua nutrimenti non solum malitia solum [*sic*] sed etiam venenositate quam a tota specie ut forma specifica vel singulariter ab extra adepti sunt sapiunt. Nam a forma specifica quedam sunt malignorum fungorum species que infra tangentur. Ab extra autem acquirunt malitiam cum iuxta ferrum eruginosum aut animal aliquod venenosum ut apud bufonum serpentum aut scorpionum caveam oriuntur aut illorum morsu inficiuntur aut venenosas herbas ut esula vel laureola aut lactitinia alia ut etiam qui super nucis arbore oriuntur venenosi dicantur. Qui enim mali sunt noscuntur si post incisionem cum cultello vel sine statim innigrescunt vel livent aut virides fiunt quare abiciendi sunt ut pestiferum venenum inquit serapio. Noscuntur etiam limatie morsu. Nam de ea dicitur quod bonos elligere scit quare de solis bonis edit. Etiam noscuntur mali humiditate quadam que super eis oritur et fracti cito corumpuntur. Galen autem vult in libro de euchimia et cacochimia a boletis neminem mori. Narat Diescorides quosdam voluisse si cortices populi arboris minutim incise et corio asini mixte per agrum diseminentur in agro fungos oriri ex vi optimos. Fungi etiam qui permittuntur pro multa ipsorum crapula obsunt qui minori quantitate sumpti non lederent. Nam cum sua frigiditate et substantie grositie inferunt nocumentum ut rasis 2° continentis. Mali etiam sunt qui in locis oriuntur malis. Fertur etiam malos esse qui mali sunt odoris et qui iuxta olivam arborem oriuntur. Minus tamen mala sunt tubera fungis nam ipsa quantitate potius quam qualitate maligna nocent. Corriguntur autem fungi ut dixit Ysac [Isaac] in dietis piris, nam eis proprietas inest ut si cum fungis coquantur eorum aufferent lesionem, quod etiam asserit aben mesuai. Serapio vero tam de domesticis quam silvestribus piris hoc voluit qui etiam idem de vino dixit auctoritate Diescorides [*sic*]. Optimi itaque decoquendi fungi sunt et diu cum piris et eorum foliis vel fructibus asperis buliendi post vero cum crudis aliis vel cum eis et nucibus cum pipere et sale cum quibus ipsorum malitia minuitur edendi vel rectius forsan dicam abiciendi. Accidentia autem que ex eis vel malis vel non congrue decoctis aut exuberanti quantitate acceptis eveniunt sunt oris stomachi dolor et gravitas et hanelitus constrictio sincopis sudor frigidus et tumor ventris et singultus et punctura et citrinitas coloris [?] atque etiam parvitas pulsus et oripilatio (or, *oppilatio*) ex indigestione. Qui etiam quantumlibet digesti chimos generant crudos viscosos grossos frigidos. Unde multa surgit ventositas et surgunt inde vapores frigidi grossi spiritus grositie et pigritia afficientes et opilantes non parum que omnia tum frigiditate tum venenositate sua roborantur. Curatur ipsorum nocumentum celeri eorum eductione vel vomitu vel secessu. Post vero aperientibus et incidentibus ac subtiliantibus humores grosos. Unde acetum calidis presertim aromatibus mixtum et sinapis et radix sic proprio vocabulo appelata et rafanus conferunt. Sal etiam mixtum cum calamento optimum est. Vomitu tamen prius provocato. Galen laudat fimum pulorum siccum nam cum vini aceto grosorum humorum [vomitum] facile decitat. — MS Laurent. Plut. 73, cod. 29, fol. 44v.

TRANSLATION

Now we come to the injuries from particular poisonous things and their cure. We may begin with poisonous foods, since they happen to every class of men frequently. Mushrooms and truffles are marked not merely by their harmfulness as food, but also by poisonous qualities which they have derived as specific form of a whole species or in individual cases from outside contact. For from the specific form there are certain species of injurious mushrooms which are discussed below. Moreover, they acquire poison from without when they grow near rusty iron or some venomous animal as the hole of toads, snakes or scorpions, or when they are infected by their bite, or grow near poisonous herbs such as spurge or spurge laurel or other lactiferous plants , as also those that grow on nut trees are called poisonous.

They are known to be bad if after cutting them open with a knife or without they immediately turn black or livid or green, whereupon they are to be thrown away as dangerous poison, Serapion says. They may also be distinguished by snail bite. For the snail knows which are good and eats those alone. The bad are also distinguished from a certain moisture that appears on them, and when broken open they quickly rot. Galen holds in the book on *Euchimia et cacochimia* that no one ever dies from eating boleti. Dioscorides tells that some hold that if the bark of poplar trees is cut up very fine and mixed with the hide of an ass and sown in a field, the finest kind of mushrooms will perforce grow in that field. Edible mushrooms are injurious if eaten in too great excess, but not harmful if taken in smaller quantities. For with their frigidity and grossness they work injury, as Rasis says in the second book of his *Continens*.

Those are bad, too, which grow in bad places. It is said that those are bad which have a bad odor and which grow near an olive tree. Truffles are less injurious than mushrooms, for they harm by their quantity rather than evil quality. Moreover, mushrooms are neutralized by pears, as Isaac has said in his *Diets*. For pears have a property such that, if they are cooked with mushrooms, they take away their harmful character, as Aben Mesuë also asserts. Serapion, however, makes this statement about domestic rather than wild pears, and also asserts it concerning wine on Dioscorides' authority. Therefore mushrooms are best cooked with pears and their leaves and for a good while, or boiled with sour fruits, and afterwards eaten with some raw fruits, or with these and nuts with pepper and salt, with which their harmfulness is lessened. Or, I should say, 'twere perchance better to throw them away.

The effects that come from eating them when bad or not properly cooked or in too large amounts are pain in the mouth of the stomach and heaviness and constricted breathing, syncope, cold sweat, and tumor of the belly and singultus and sharp pain and jaundice and slow pulse and obstruction from indigestion. When digested, they produce cold, raw, gross, viscous chyme. Thence arises much wind and cold vapors, gross spirits, sluggishness, all which are not a little increased by their frigidity and venom. The ills from them are cured by quickly getting rid of them either by vomiting or the stool, and then by uncovering and breaking up and thinning out the gross humors. For this purpose vinegar mixed with hot aromatics and mustard and the root known by the appropriate name of radish are helpful. Salt mixed with catmint is also very good, but first vomiting should be provoked. Galen praises dry dung of chickens, for with wine vinegar it easily produces vomit of gross humors.[1]

[1] I have compared this passage with the discussion of mushrooms, fungi, and truffles in Pliny's *Natural History*, XIX, 11–13; XXII, 46–47, etc. While a number of the statements made seem to go back to Pliny, either directly or indirectly, the resemblance is not at all close even in those portions where John does not cite writers since Pliny.

APPENDIX 13

RELATIO ANATOMICA OF BERNARD TORNIUS

From MS Riccard. 930, fols. 17v–19v.

[M]agnifice pretor, doleo vices tuas, prolem namque admictere malum, deterius marem, pessimum egritudine nondum a medicis plane percepta. Verum pro reliquis aliis existimo sua vidisse interiora maxime fore utilitati[s]. Nunc ergo brevius quam potero quorum vidimus in medium afferam et que credo concludam remediaque meo iudicio proficua adducere non dubitabo.

In primis apparuit venter satis tumidus quamvis gracile mirac fuerit. Scisso vero secundum regulam mirach et sifach vidimus intestina et vesicam que turgida et urina plena erat, removendo insuper colon et saccum magis in eis apparuit ventositas grossa quam feces. Deinde remoto yleon et jeiuno et duodeno intestino duo vermes reperti sunt satis magni et albi flegma ostendentes potius quam alium humorem. Abscissis intestinis a mesenterio,[1] quoniam ibi nihil notabilis repertum sit, videntes vesicam turgidam scindere ipsam feci et apparuit quantitas urine magna licet ante mortem ut retulerunt multum minxerit. Vidimus postmodum epar quod maculis quibusdam tamquam ulceribus erat dispositum et circa principium vene chilis aliqualiter tumefactum. Sed quod magis est mirandum, apparuit circa originem venarum emulgentium in concavitate vene chilis oppilatio manifesta qua tota concavitas humore viscoso repleta erat per spacium grossitudinis unius digiti, post quem humorem infra nihil sanguinis videbatur, vene vero emulgentes replete erant sanguine satis aquoso et renes tumefacti pleni etiam erant huiusmodi sanguine vel forte multa aquositate urinali admixta cum eo. Chilis autem ascendens habebat ramum ad cor tractum [terminatum?] repletum multo sanguine, et cor erat valde tumefactum, itaque etiam auricule tumide supramodum apparebant. Quibis scissis maxima pars sanguinis exivit ita quod quasi totus sanguis circa partes cordis fuit repertus. Vena vero que tracta [terminata?] est ad pulmonem deferens [*fol. 18r*] sanguinem nutrimentalem ei plena etiam erat humore consimili viscoso et tota exanguis videbatur. Quibus visis non amplius quesivi de re alia cum apparuerit meo judicio causa sue mortis.

[1] "Misinterio" is the actual reading of the rotograph, but I do not find such a word in the dictionaries.

Ex his infero primo puerum talem vel a principiis nativitatis vel ex tempore magnam oppilationem contraxisse, probabiliterque tenendum est magis per paulativam congestionem quam per defluxum ab alio membro factum huiusmodi materiam esse cumulatam.

2° infero vermes illos post principium sue egritudinis principalis fuisse genitos neque aliquo pacto fuisse causam sue mortis.

3° infero quod prohibita transmissione sanguinis per venam chilis et per venam pulmonis facta est ebulitio et febris. Et quia in illo sanguine multum erat de flegmate, febris illa in multis accidentibus assimilabatur flegmatice, licet secundum modum invasionis et excrescentie videbatur tertianae due. De tertio enim in tertium magis infestabatur in nocte ut abstantes referebant et ego infero manifeste ex inquietudine sua et pulsu percipiebam.

Infero 4° maculas illas epatis post oppilationem esse generatas.

5° et ultimo infero quod quilibet filius tuus eiusdem complexionis usque ad 12m annum est preservandus cum medicinis usualibus quas in fine afferam.

Primum corollarium breviter patet ex his que oculis vidimus. Inquit enim Galienus 6° terapeutice oportet ut prius consideranda considerentur deinde cum experimento certificentur ut ratio per experimentum confirmetur. Ante mortem autem illius apparuerunt multa signa oppilationis epatis et venarum eius cum color faciei dum febris erat remissa esset discoloratus et haberet difficultatem in anhelitu et lassitudinem corporis et pigritiam in motionibus et quandoque viderim egestionem partim chimosam et partim chilosam. Ideo fuerim certificatus videndo venam chilis quod erat opilatio in ea quemadmodum suspicabatur. Pulsus autem eius cum apparuerit valde diversus oppilationem in venis propinquis cordi maxime deservientibus pulmoni declarabat, iuxta exemplum Galieni 4° interiorum, de illo medico cuius pulsus diversitates omnium generum sensit qui postmodum periit sicut illi qui moriuntur ex cardiaca passione. Tua vero magnificentia testis est quod ille puer maximam diversitatem [*fol. 18v*] in pulsu habebat et ideo quemadmodum retuli semper magno dubio mihi fuit eo maxime quod medicamina oportuna non poterant exhiberi.

Prima pars secundi corollarii videtur clara, licet enim vermes longi iuxta sententiam Avicenne capitulo de speciebus vermium vermes longi sint generati ab humiditate super quam non dominantur divisio et separatio ex parte attractionis epatis et vehementie putrefactionis, et sint magis nocivi quam parvi et sint vehementioris fixionis, tamen non videtur verisimile per tot dies sumptis medicaminibus habentibus respectum ad vermes tum in educendo tum in interficiendo eos in duodeno remansissent. Secunda et pars patet ex sententia Domini Avic. capitulo primo de vermibus dicentis, et propter hoc causati sunt vermes, et musce et que cursu eorum currunt ex materiis putridis humidis quoniam ille materie cum rectificatur illud quod tollerant ut suscipiant de forma est animal vermiculare aut muscale, nam illud melius est quam ut ipse remaneant secundum putrefactionem puram. Ex quibus verbis videtur innuere dominus Avicenna paucos vermes in intestinis repertos non esse nocivos cum ipso testante saliant vermes super putrefactiones et cibentur eis propter comunitatem et assummant eos a corpore. Et licet ita sit, tamen non assero, ut multi credunt, vermes in corpore nostro esse bonos, cum etiam auctoritate principis non sit eorum dispositio faciens iuvamentum sine nocumento, cum ex vermibus generentur epilensia et fames canina et bolismus et putrefactio que est causa febris, immo, ut quidam retulerunt, vermes quandoque perforaverunt ventrem et exiverunt, ut testatur dominus Avicenna allegato capitulo.

3^m corollarium patet ex probatione ibi facta, febris enim erat sine frigore et tipo, licet in principio propter magnam elevationem vaporum ascendentium ad caput fuerit sompnus quasi subeticus cum aliquali extremorum infrigidatione dum scilicet materia movebatur quod forte accidebat, ut alias sepe vidi, ex retractione caloris ad intra nocumento percepto circa membra principalia. Et ideo febris erat continua habens exacerbationes proportionatas colere et cum materia esset in partibus propinquis cordi, erat motus tremulus cordis ubi maxime manifestabatur frequens constrictio, que ut febris putridis [putrida?] magnam indigentiam emissionis vaporum ostendebat, nec erant accidentia causonidis cum propter etatem humidam et flegma multum impressio colere valde reprimeretur. Nec inconvenit duas tertianas esse ad intra venas duobus cumulis [*fol. 19r*] in diversis venis existentibus diversimode motis ad putrefactionem, ut alias ego ostendi, forte enim materia que erat in vena chili ascendente putrescens faciebat tertianam maioris exacerbationis et illa que erat in vena chili descendente faciebat illam que erat minoris exacerbationis. Sed hic magnum est dubium quomodo vena chilis ita magna maxime descendens esset tante oppilationis, non enim videtur posse illam venam oppilari nisi prius cetere vene epatis sint opilate maxima opilatione quod non potest esse stante vita. Et hoc est mihi potissimum argumentum ad credendum huiusmodi oppilationem ex dispositione principiorum naturalium fuisse contractam, bene tamen est verum quod forte materia admixta cum aquositate urinali que erat in vesica oppilationem faciebat in venis gibbi epatis et expulsa est a natura et deopilavit illas venas simul cum morte, et fuit crisis cathimica iuxta illud Galie. primo de creticis, duo enim filii fuerunt cathimi qui invicem pugnantes se interfecerunt, ita forte natura expulit materiam et victa est ab ea. Sed magis existimo materiam facientem febrem retentam ut dixi in vena que vadit ad cor fuisse causam suffocationis illius quam aliquid aliud, cum neque in meseraicis neque in estate [epate?] apparuerit aliqua oppilatio sed solum ut dixi in vena chilis. Nisi dicatur quod materia in venis parvis epatis est ita parva que non potest sensu videri sicut illa que erat in vena chilis apparens grossa et viscosa adherens tunicis eius, et quod natura expulit subtile per urinam, grossum autem non potuit expellere et ideo accidit mors. Et in isto passu pendet tota vis huius inquisitionis. Et ideo Georgium ciprium aprime doctum supra hac re dum eris florentie consultabis etc.

4^{m} corollarium sequitur ex premissis nam ex caliditate cordis et ebulitione illius sanguinis fuit genitum flegma salsum faciens mordicationem et ulcerationem sicut multis accidit quandoque circa gingivas ex flegmate salso descendente a capite. Quare autem cor suum fuerit magnum non existimo quod sit audacia a nativitate illi insita, potius enim timidus videbatur tempore sanitatis, sed erat multo sanguine repletum cor faciente ipsum [*fol. 19v*] turgidum et inflatum. Licet etiam forte naturaliter esset magni cordis quod in homine audaciam significat, licet in leporibus significat timiditatem, ut colligi potest ex dictis domini Avicenne, fen xi tertii, capitulo primo.

5^{m} corollarium notum est quia post duodecimum annum calor naturalis fit acutus virtutes omnes excitans maxime ad expellendas superfluitates et humiditas fit minor et ideo minus sunt apti tui filii post illud tempus talem incurrere egritudinem. Preservandi ergo sunt hac preservatione videlicet quolibet anno de mense aprilis debes dare diebus continuis hunc syrupum videlicet

Recipe Aque lupulorum
Fumiterre
Capilli veneris   Omnium [Accipe?] 3.1.
Eupatrii
Bettonice

Misce pro duabus vicibus et qualibet vice ponatur 3.1. acetosi simplicis et fiat potio et aromatizetur cum modico cinnamomi et detur de mane calida. Hanc tamen exhibitionem variandam duco iuxta annorum varietatem ut medici poterunt iudicare. Post huiusmodi syrup. sumant hanc medicinam. Recipe reubarbari electi 3. i., infundatur in aqua lactis sumpti ex capris et aqua endivie et absinthii. Accipe [Omnium?] secundum partes equales cum granis octo spice per noctem, deinde exprimatur et colatura detur vel cum cassia vel cum manna vel cum dyasena vel cum aliqua dosi trociscorum d'agarico secundum quod iudicat medicus abstans. Et quia caput propter elevationem vaporum existimo esse in causa per accidens adminus cum elevati vapores ingrossati in capite postmodum descendant per nervos et faciant mollificationem ut apparebat manifeste, ideo in ebdomada [2] saltim quando vadunt dormitum darem eis unam vel duas pillulas ex aloe loto in aqua endivie, tamen et in hyeme aloes non lotus forte magis conferret.

Hec sunt breviter que videbantur esse danda, sepius tamen visitabo tuam magnificentiam et de reliquis potero certiorem reddere. Valeat magnificentia tua cui me summopere commendo.

[2] Spelled *ebdomoda* in the manuscript.

APPENDIX 14

CONTENTS OF THE *OPUSCULA* OF BERNARD TORNIUS

The following is a table of contents of Riccardian MS 930 as a whole found on its flyleaf. I have added the references to the leaves where the various items begin.

Bernardi Tornii Florentini Opuscula Medica

1. De natura succus absynthii et an prosit in febribus quartanis
2. Conclusiones circa materiam de febribus (fol. 8v)
3. Propositiones quaedam de mala complexione diversa et equali (fol. 14v)
4. Arbor de qualitatibus ac deinde de calido (fol. 16r)
5. Relatio anatomica (fol. 17v — our treatise)
6. Epistola super quibusdam dubiis circa motum (fol. 20r) [1]
7. Epistola ad Magistrum Franciscum Ninum super quandam quaestionem de Phlebotomia et Pharmacia (fol. 23r)
8. Quaestio de reduplicatione corporum (fol. 26r) [2]
9. Dissertatio super conclusione[m] Nulla sanitas semper est sanitas simpliciter, ad magistrum Franciscum Senensem (fol. 31v)
10. Responsiones ad argumenta eiusdem Francisci contra eandem Dissertationem (fol. 34v)
11. Definitiones corporum recollecte ex verbis Plusquam Comentatoris, anno 1485 (fol. 38v)

[1] This letter, addressed to some anonymous personage, opens, "[C]um his diebus in circulis hec duo argumenta a concurrente meo mihi fuerint formata et alias primum a Iohanne Marliano viro clarissimo et fundamentum secundi a Calculatore descriptum fuerit . . ." It closes: "Valeat dominatio tua cui me summopere commendo et petro laurentio de medicis domino meo . . ."

[2] It opens, "[C]um breviter contra quasdam conclusiones a Iohanne Mirandulano erudito quidem et comite concordie domino meo precipuo positas intendam arguere . . ."

APPENDIX 15

AN ASTRONOMICAL NOTE BY NICHOLAS OF CUSA

Cod. Cusan. 211, fol. 55v., as printed by F. J. Clemens, *Giordano Bruno und Nicolaus von Cusa*, 1847, pp. 98–99.

Consideravi quod non est possibile, quod aliquis motus sit praecise circularis; unde nulla stella describit circulum praecisum ab ortu ad ortum. Necesse est igitur nullum punctum fixum in octava sphaera esse polum; set variabitur continue, ita quod semper alius et alius punctus instabiliter erit in loco poli. Recedunt igitur et appropinquant stellae a polo ad polum motu continuo. 2. Consideravi, quod terra ista [ipsa?] non potest esse fixa, sed movetur, ut aliae stellae. Quare super polis mundi revolvitur, ut ait Pythagoras, quasi semel in die et nocte, sed octava sphaera bis, et sol parum minus quam bis in die et nocte. Item consideravi, quomodo alii poli debent imaginari aeque distantes a polis mundi in aequatore, et super illis revolvitur octava sphaera in die et nocte parum minus quam semel, et solare corpus distat ab uno polorum illorum quasi per quartam partem quadrantis, scilicet per gradus 23 vel prope; et per circumvolutionem mundi etiam circumvolvitur sphaera solis semel in die et nocte parum minus, hoc est per $\frac{1}{364}$ sui circuli, ita quod in anno per motum diei unius est retardatio, et ex illa retardatione oritur Zodiacus. Punctus autem in octava sphaera, qui in loco poli mundi motus ab oriente in occasum visus est, continue parum remanet retro polum, ita quod quum polus videtur circulum complevisse, punctus ille nondum circulum complevit, sed remanet a retro, tantum in proportione ad circulum suum in centum annis, vel quasi, quantum sol remanet retro in die uno. Et sicut punctus unus sphaerae solis semper remanet sub uno et eodem puncto octavae, qui sub polo motus revolutionis ab occidente fixe persistit, ita punctus unus sphaerae terrae et solis remanet cum polo mundi fixe. Imaginor enim me esse in medio mundi sub aequinoctiali; sit terra a b c d, et in hoc a c, b d arcus terrae et pone e in puncto sectionis; dico terram super polis a c fixis in terra moveri, et similiter super polo e et opposito ei, simul et semel; nam super a c movetur de oriente in occidens, et super e et ei opposito movetur in horizonte de occidente in oriens; ita quod quum a pervenit in b, tunc e pervenit in d, et ita consequenter. Octava sphaera eodem modo movetur, sed in duplo velocius super polis suis a, c quam e et opposito, sic, quod cum polus ejus a pervenit ad b, tunc b est in a [d?], et quum pervenit ad c, tunc b pervenit ad primum locum scilicet b; et quum in d, tunc b in a, et quum in a, tunc b in b. Et scias, quod polus octavae sphaerae a et oppositus ei sunt fixi cum polis ejusdem terrae, sed mobiles in ordinem ad stellas fixas, puta quod si aliqua stella jam foret in a polo, illa in revolutione remanebit retro, ita quod a polus fixus in terra eam derelinquit retro et alia succedit in ejus locum, ita quod omnes stellae, quae sunt in horizonte in medio mundi sole existente in ariete aut libra in ortu diei successive polo fixo in terra conjungentur in anno magno; sic quod stella, quae distat per $\frac{1}{360}$ circuli ad orientem ab ea, quae modo est in polo, circa centesimum annum succedit.

APPENDIX 16

THE *DE MOTIBUS CELESTIUM MOBILIUM* OF JOHN TOLHOPF TO SIXTUS IV

In the same year or years, 1475–76, that Regiomontanus returned to Rome at the summons of Sixtus IV and died there, another astronomer, whose surname, Tolhopf, seems to indicate that he was of the same nationality, and who had the same Christian name, John, addressed to the same pontiff a curious work on the movements of the celestial bodies, which is preserved in a Latin manuscript of the Vatican library.[1] This approach to coincidence and the fact that this Tolhopf appears to cite Peurbach [2] have led me to append some account of his treatise in this place, although it would seem impossible that Iohannes Tolhopf, master of arts, is identical with Johann Müller, also master of arts. Who he was or what he wrote apart from this manuscript I cannot say. That he wrote in 1475–76 is indicated by a calculation for Rome, 1475, at the foot of each of several astronomical tables at fols. 29v–31v [3] of the manuscript and by a reference to 1476 as the current year in another passage.[4] It might seem sufficient disproof of any possible identification of John Tolhopf with Johann Müller that this passage mentions October 15 of that year, whereas Regiomontanus died July 6. But the passage does not necessarily imply that

[1] Vatican Latin MS 3103. Following a table of contents, which occupies fol. 1r and part of fol. 1v, comes on fol. 2r the rubric, "Ad sanctissimum in Christo patrem et dominum Dominum Sixtum quartum divina providentia sacrosancte Romane ac universalis ecclesie Pontificem maximum De motibus celestium mobilium Iohannes Tolhopf Artium Magister"; and the Incipit, "Universitatis totius haut partem modicam obmitti S. P. arbitror Si de mundi sensibilis scita parte considerantes . . ."

[2] *Ibid.*, fol. 19r: "Quid enim proderit ut vult campanus et moderni insequentes eum quod testatur Buerbac intra quoslibet ecentricos deferentes orbes duos divisos de natura motus stellarum fixarum similes ponere cum uniformiter perpetuo moverentur . . ."

[3] These tables are for the ninth sphere in years, the eighth sphere also in years (1–10; 20; 40; 50; 100; 200; 400; 500; 1,000; 2,000; 4,000; 7,000; 36,000; and 49,000, when the revolution is completed), for each planet in years, months, and days, and for the moon and the head of the dragon.

[4] *Ibid.*, fol. 26r: "Verbi gratia 15ma die octobris hora tertia post meridiem anni 1476 currentis scire volo in quo signo gradu ac minuto sit sol aut planeta alter."

the fifteenth of October had already arrived at the time it was written.

Our treatise is curious in that the author includes the various Christian, theological or biblical heavens as well as the astronomical spheres. He feels that he would omit no small part of the whole universe should he treat only of the sensible or "less principal" world and say nothing of its eternal archetype in whose likeness it was produced. He also devotes chapters to the essential heaven or that of supreme and divine Unity, to the personal heaven or that of the Trinity, to the ideal heaven or that of immense perfection and causality — homeland and source of the Platonic ideas. Even after we have passed to the sensible world, manifest to sight, touch, and hearing, we have to consider the empyrean, seat of the angels and mansion of the spirits of the blest, as Albertus Magnus says, and the watery or crystalline heaven, corresponding to the waters above the firmament of the book of Genesis, before we come to the starry or physical heaven and spheres. We are assured that the aqueous or crystalline heaven is not so called from the element water, which is wet and cold and moves in a straight line.

The chief object of the more strictly astronomical portion of John Tolhopf's treatise seems to be to simplify and reduce the number of spheres, orbits, and circles required to explain the movements of the heavenly bodies in the Ptolemaic system.[5] The matter, as Vincent of Beauvais says, was not fully understood in Aristotle's or Ptolemy's time. Modern astronomers generally accept Campanus's assignment of thirty-four movements,[6] namely, one for the ninth sphere, one for the eighth sphere, three for the sun, five for the moon, six for Mercury, four for each of the other four planets, and one or two for the dragon. These Tolhopf would reduce to twenty-eight in number. In this connection he resorts to the novel expedient of representing the eighth sphere not merely as existing beyond the spheres of the planets, but also as intervening successively between them. Thus there are seven sections or rings of the eighth sphere alternating with the planetary spheres. The inner

[5] It is discussed in the eleventh chapter of his first book, occupying fols. 18r–21.

[6] Fol. 18r: "Campanus autem quem fere tota comunitas modernorum insequitur 34 assignabat mobilia." Campanus of Novara wrote his influential *Theory of the Planets* in the thirteenth century; he also addressed a work on the astronomical errors of Ptolemy to Pope Urban IV (1261–65).

six of these presumably save as many movements which Campanus made independent. Tolhopf illustrates his scheme by a large figure in colors which is folded into the manuscript.[7] Most of these intervening sections of the eighth sphere are eccentric on both their concave and convex faces, corresponding to the eccentrics of the planetary orbits on which they border. But the outermost is concentric on its convex side touching the ninth sphere, and the innermost is concentric on its concave side contiguous to the orb of the moon.

Tolhopf's treatise consists of two books,[8] but the second is much shorter than the first.[9] Aside from the tables which conclude it, this second book is devoted largely to making clear the distinction between the true and the mean motion of the spheres and stars, and to an account of an instrument called the *stellarium*. The majority of its fifteen chapters are only a few lines each in length.

The following table of contents occurs on the first leaf of the manuscript, being prefixed to the treatise itself:

Libri primi Capitula

Ca'm p'm de duplici mundo architipo scilicet et sensibili vel minus principali ipsorumque partibus
Ca. 2. de diversa celi et terre diversorum acceptione
Ca. 3. de celo essentiali sive summe ac divine unitatis
Ca. 4. de celo personali seu individue trinitatis
Ca. 5. de celo ydeali aut immense perfectionis ac causalitatis
Ca. 6. de mundi sensibilis productione
Ca. 7. de celo empirreo
Ca. 8. de celo cristallino
Ca. 9. de celo sydereo sive phisico
Ca. 10. de numero et multitudine motuum celestium mobilium
Ca. 11. de multitudine celestium mobilium
Ca. 12. de multitudine celestium motorum
Ca. 13. de celestibus circulis et de octave spere motu incidenter

[7] It is numbered as fols. 20–21.

[8] From a sentence in its preface, one might infer that there were three books: fol. 2v, "3° libro demigrationes horum que in 2° libro dicta sunt atque distancias orbium celestium . . ." But chapters are given for only two books in the table of contents, so that it would seem that in the passage just quoted he is thinking of the preface as the first book, and the two books of the table of contents as books two and three.

[9] Book II covers only fols. 25r–32r, of which fols. 29v–31v are occupied by astronomical tables.

Libri secundi Capitula

Ca'm 1. de divisione circuli zodiaci in signa gradus et minuta
Ca. 2. de celestium mobilium medii et veri motus diffinitionibus
Ca. 3. de mediis locis celestium mobilium per tabulas inveniendis
Ca. 4. de stellarii instrumenti nobilis declaratione
Ca. 5. de veri loci solis per hoc stellarium inventione
Ca. 6. de veri loci quatuor planetarum investigatione
Ca. 7. de inventione veri loci lune
Ca. 8. de vero loco mercurii
Ca. 9. de passionibus utilibus ad dicta loca invenienda
Ca. 10. de vero loco octave et none spere inveniendo
Ca. 11. de directione retrogradatione statione duplici velocitate ac tarditate ascensione et descensione duplici planetarum
Ca. 12. de numero et multitudine coniunctionum et mediarum binariarum [coniunctionum] [10] inventione
Ca. 13. de eclipsi solis et lune in genere.
Ca. 14. de motibus celestibus ad universum orbem designandis
Ca. 15. de perpetuitate motuum celestium mobilium inveniendo per stellarium

[10] The word in brackets I supply from the form of the chapter heading as given in the text itself at fol. 28v.

APPENDIX 17

TABLE OF CONTENTS OF THE ARITHMETIC OF JEHAN ADAM

The French text of the table of contents is reproduced from Ste Geneviève MS français 3143, and is followed by an English translation. In the manuscript the numbers of the folios where occurs the text corresponding to the heading of the table have not been written in, so I have supplied them in brackets. As is usual in medieval manuscripts, the headings of the table of contents are not always found in the same form in the text and sometimes are omitted there entirely, while on the other hand the text has a number of additional rubrics not found in the table. As I have already explained, the fols. now numbered 5, 10, 13 and 18 do not occur in their proper positions.

De multiplicacion VIe espece et des tables par lesquelles on peut asseoir en deux manieres ses gecto[n]ers Cest asseoir a dextre et a senestre folio [5v]

De la table pour multiplier au dessoubz de dix et comment le gect se doit asseoir fol. [14v]

Des tables pour multiplier X Et pour multiplier par C folio [15v]

Des tables pour multiplier par M Regle generalle neccessaire sauoir pour multiplicacion folio [16v]

Des tables demonstrans la forme de faire la multiplicacion des onzams [onzains?][1] ou aultres monnoies que peuent estre en escus fo. [17v]

Des tables pour multiplier les solz des francs ou liures folio [10r]

Des tables pour la multiplicacion [*fol. 67v*] des payemens des lances et gens de guerre f. [10v]

Regle et question plaisante par maniere de quolibet pour une femme qui Requiert Justice contre cellui qui lui a casse ses œufs quelle ne sauoir nombrer folio [19v]

Regle generalle pour la probacion de multiplicacion folio [20v]

De diuisions VIIe espece et darrier chappitre et des nombres neccessaires en Icelles folio [20v]

De deux manieres de diuisions Cest assauoir Simple mixte Et des notables a Icelle deus neccessaires a nocter folio [21v]

De iiii notables generaulx a noter Pour diuiser simple et premierement du premier faisant mencion de faire diuision sans multiplier qui est de deniers faire liures folio [22v]

Du second notable de diuision simple pour aualuer promptement monnoie a aultre folio [24r]

Du tiers notable de diuision simple qui est de partir vne somme a certain [*fol. 68r*] nombre de personnes promptement folio [25v]

Du quart notable general est pour sauoir promptement calculler que sommes par an font par jour folio [26v]

Item et quelles sommes par jour font par an [fol. 28r]

Apres sensuit [for *s'ensuit*] la diuision Mixte Et premierement de la premiere Regle de prepourcion aultrement appellee La Regle de trois [fol. 28v]

Par ladite Regle pour sauoir quelz gaiges ung Recepueur doit prendre pour Recepuoir une treue aut solz la liure et selon le feur quil a de Recepuoir lordinaire a coustume Et dont la table est escripte folio [31v]

Regle generale pour monstrer a asseoir la gret [gect?] de nombre quociens

[1] F. Godefroy, *Dictionnaire de l'ancienne langue française et de tous ses dialectes du IXe au XVe siècle*, 1887, Vol. V, defines Onzain as "sorte de monnaie, le grand blanc à la couronne portè de dix deniers à onze par l'ordonnance du 4 janvier 1473."

Cest a dire que fault mectre a senestre pour segniffier combien monte ce que on a party et substraict du nombre a diuiser [fol. 32v]

Regle de compaignie et de marchans que est a la seconde de preporcions [fol. 33v]

La Regle des Recindemens et tropt charg sur ung Recepueur [fol. 36r]

La quarte Regle de preporcion qui est [*fol. 68v*] dune serpentine Rompue pour sauoir combien Il y a destaing ou aultres plusieurs mechaulx en la piesce Rompue apres ce quomodo licet combien Il y auoit dun chascun en toute la serpentine folio [41r]

La Ve Regle de preporcions par $\frac{1}{2}$ $\frac{1}{3}$ $\frac{1}{4}$ en aultre maniere que celle dont apres sera faicte mencion folio [42r]

La VIe Regle subtille de preporcion pour de partir argent sellons le temps [fol. 42v]

La VIIe Regle de langonisant testateur dunt est faicte mencion en linforciat [i.e., *l'Infortiat*] [2] de liberiis et postumis [fol. 44r]

La VIIIe Regle de preporcion egalle pour auoir pour lxiiii blancs du poiure a trois blancs la liure des almondes a deux blancs Et de Raisins a ung blanc autant dun que daultre [fol. 44v]

La IXe Regle de preporcion de mixte egalite que est de vuyder ung estang par porcion en certain temps [fol. 45r]

Des Regles touchant les fractions et mynutez en nombres Roups generalles [*fol. 69r*] et particullies folio [46r]

Des minutez et fractions vulgares et phizicalles [fol. 46r]

Regle de preporcion pour departir aucune somme par moictie tiers et quart [fol. 51v]

Regle XIe de preporcion pour departir sommes par tiers quart et quint [fol. 53r]

Regle 12e de preporcion pour partir par la moytie et tiers [fol. 54v]

Regle 13e pour partir par moitie tiers quart et quint et 6e [fol. 55r]

Regle de poix pour sauoir faire Le sol de fin [fol. 56r]

Regle pour feir [?] le mescle de billon et pour alloier en une maniere et au contraire le sauoir [fol. 58r]

Regle pour faire mescle de billon en fait [fin?] dor [fol. 61r]

Pour alloyer monnoie auec aultre monnoie [fol. 59v]

Regle pour sauoir le fin et le non fin de lor auec la table [fol. 60r]

Aultre Regle subtille pour sauoir et cognoistre poix en mescle en or combien [*fol. 69v*] que par auent nest este sceu ne poise [fol. 61v]

Regle et derreniere question subtille de ce traicte qui le peut faire par la posicion faulte touchant ung Reliquiaire etc. [?] ou quel y a la moitie

[2] Referring to the section of Justinian's Digest known in the middle ages as the "Infortiatum."

argent le tiers cuiure Et vi marchs dor combien pesera le dit Reliquiaire et combien y aura de marchs dargent et de cuiure [fol. 61v][3]

La Regle generalle pour prouuer diuision estre bonne et bien faicte et des aultres deux manieres de preuue apertenens a la chiffre par la plume [fol. 62v]

Conclusion et fin de ce present traicte en continuant lespitre que lacteur mect au commencement dicelluy [63r]

TRANSLATION

[*fol. 66v*] Letter of the author to Monsieur Master Nicolle Tillart, secretary of our lord, the King, the conclusion to which letter is written at the close of the present book

The beginning of the prologue in Latin and afterwards it continues in French

Definition and description of arithmetic with its division into different varieties, by way of prologue to begin this aforesaid present work

Of numeration, the first variety; specification of the parts of the large table for placing the counters

The form and figure of that table, containing as many figures as are needed to enumerate the multiplication of the points of the exchequer

Of addition, the second variety, and of the form of the table for adjusting by articles in shortened form

Tables of the placing of sous and deniers by counters

Of subtraction with its tables [*fol. 67r*] of take, carry, and remainder

Of tables of the way to subtract

Of mediation with these tables and the form of performing it

Of duplication with these tables

Of multiplication, the sixth variety, and of the tables by which one can place his counters in two ways, that is, place them to right and to left

Of the table for multiplying [numbers] below ten, and how the counter should be placed

Of tables for multiplying [by?] ten and for multiplying by one hundred

Of tables for multiplying by one thousand, general rule necessary to know for multiplication

Of tables showing the way to multiply *onzains* or other moneys that they may be in crowns

Of tables for multiplying sous of francs or livres

[3] The text opens, "Le Roy veult faire faire ung Reliquiaire ou quel y ait la moitie de cuivre le tiers dargent et six marchs dor . . ."

Of tables for the multiplication [*fol. 67v*] of the payments of lances and soldiers

Rule and pleasing problem of the Quolibet sort concerning a woman who seeks damages from one who has broken her eggs which she cannot count

General rule for the proof of multiplication

Of division, the seventh variety and last chapter, and of the numbers needed in this

Of two modes of division, that is to say, simple and mixed, and of things necessary to note in both

Of four general points to note in simple division, and first of the first one making mention of dividing without multiplying, which is to make livres from deniers

Of the second point in simple division, to evaluate promptly one kind of money in another

Of the third point in simple division, which is to divide a sum among a certain [*fol. 68r*] number of persons promptly

Of the fourth general point, to know how to calculate quickly what sums by the year make by the day

And likewise what sums by the day make by the year

Then follows mixed division; and first, of the first rule of proportion, otherwise called the rule of three

To know by the said rule what gages a receiver ought to take to receive an impost at sous the livre and according to the straw that he has to receive ordinarily by custom. Of which the table is written.

General rule to show how to place the counter of the quotient, that is to say, what it is necessary to place at the left to signify how much that comes to which one has divided and subtracted from the number to be divided

Rule of [or, example concerning] company and merchants, which is the second of proportion

Rule of annulment and overcharge on a receiver

The fourth rule of proportion, which is [*fol. 68v*] concerning a broken serpentine, to know how much there is of lead or several other metals in the broken piece, and also how much there is of each in the entire serpentine

The fifth rule of proportion by one-half, one-third, one-fourth, in another way than that of which will later be made mention

The sixth subtle rule of proportion, to divide money according to time

The seventh rule of the dying testator, of which mention is made in the *Infortiatum*, "De liberis et posthumis."

The eighth rule of equal proportion, to have for 64 *blancs* pepper at 3 *blancs* the pound, almonds at 2 *blancs*, and raisins at 1 *blanc*, and as much of one as of the other

The ninth rule of proportion of mixed equality, which is to empty a swamp [pond?] by portions in a certain time

Rules touching fractions and "minutes" in broken numbers, general [*fol. 69r*] and particular

Of minutes and fractions, vulgar and physical

Rule of proportion, to divide any sum by half, third, and quarter

Rule 11 of proportion, to divide sums by third, fourth, and fifth

Rule 12 of proportion, to divide by half and third

Rule 13, to divide by half, third, fourth, and fifth and sixth

Rule of weight, to know how to make *le sol de fin*

Rule for mixing base coin and alloying in one way, and on the contrary, how to detect the same

Rule for mixing base coin in making gold

To alloy money with other money

Rule to know fine gold and what isn't with table

Another subtle rule to know and recognize the weight of gold in base coin [*fol. 69v*] and to be able to tell beforehand how much it will come to in crowns

Rule and last subtle question of this treatise, which can be made by the position touching a reliquary which is half silver, one-third copper, and six marks of gold. How much will this reliquary weigh, and how many marks of silver and of copper will there be in it?

General rule to prove that division is right and well done, and two other methods of proof appertaining to ciphering by pen

Conclusion and close of this present treatise, continuing the letter which the author put at the beginning of the same.

APPENDIX 18

THE LETTER OF NICCOLÒ DA FOLIGNO TO HIS *COMPATER* NICOLAUS IN ANSWER TO THE QUERY, ARE IDEAS A FORCE IN NATURAL GENERATION?

In publishing for the first time a medieval text, the question arises how faithful to the original manuscript one's rendering should be. This depends somewhat on the nature of the text itself and on one's purpose in printing it. In the case of manuscripts so full of abbreviations as those I deal with in this and the following appendix, it is obvious that, unless the abbreviations are reproduced, the editor must exercise some latitude of discretion in turning them into full words. In such cases I have aimed to spell the full word as the writer of the manuscript would have spelled it, had he written it out in full. For example, I spell the abbreviated preposition *pre* and not *prae*. But inasmuch as he sometimes spells the same word in different ways, I must sometimes make an arbitrary choice. Since the paragraphing, capitalization, and punctuation — so far as there is any — of our manuscripts are unsystematic and incomprehensible from the modern point of view, and not easy to reproduce, and the text if thus reproduced would not make sentences — to say nothing of sense — it has seemed advisable to modify them somewhat in order to make the meaning of the text clearer to the present-day reader. In the case of *u*'s and *v*'s, too, which were then virtually one letter, I have not followed exactly the MSS, which commonly employ a *v* for the first letter of a word or a capital and a *u* elsewhere, but have used the letter which would be most readily comprehensible to the modern eye. I see no great advantage in spelling Averroës as "Auerroes", or Avicenna as Auicenna, or *universo* as *vniuerso*. I have italicized the citations of authorities in order that the reader may more readily refer to them, while the quotations from authorities which I have enclosed in quotation marks were already underlined as such in the manuscripts themselves. Finally, I have sought to avoid unnecessary pedantry and an excess of variant readings.

Latin text from MS Vatic. Lat. 3897, fols. 79r–86r.

Diebus hisce superioribus, mi Nicolae compater ac medicine artiumque famosissime doctor, ex perusia ad me scriptum si hec conclusio substentari posset, si ad generationem rerum naturalium hydeas concurrere, ut plato sensit, absonum debeat reputari. Circa quam noctibus harum festivitatum evigilans quicquid in re tali perceptum habeo duxi ad te mittendum, quo etiam iuditium tuum reddas corrigas emendasque si quid abs me reperies aberratum. Tanti quidem faciam testimonium ac sententiam tuam ut alias quascumque nauci pendam. Tu vale remque ipsam diligenter existimato precor, et si quid teneas aliud, scio quod ad me mittere non dedignaberis. Vale.

Fundamenta [1] platonis ad ponendas hydeas tria sunt apud *Averoim, commentis 30 et 31, VIImi methaphysice:* primum, omne quod fit, fit a sibi simili genere vel spetie; secundum, forme naturales substantiales nec active sunt neque passive; tertium, principia passionis actionisque rerum naturalium sunt prime qualitates tangibiles. Ex quibus motus, *Avicenna, VI naturalium, tractatu 4°, capitulis 2° et 4°*, dixit causam formarum naturalium esse causam separatam,[2] quoniam actiones naturales fiunt per quatuor qualitates primas tangibiles. Sed cum ab accidentibus non fiat substantia, ut dicitur *primo physicorum*, apparet quod per actiones naturales non potest haberi nisi forma complexionalis. Unde sequitur quod forma substantialis adiuncta forme complexionali non habet nisi causam [*col. 2*] separatam. Quam causam Avicenna quandoque vocavit colcodream, ut patet *2a fen primi canonis, capitulo de signis complexionum sexti generis in fine.* Et per literam chremonensis [3] apparet quod colcodrius est dator vite. Quandoque vocavit illam creatorem, ut *prima fen primi, capitulo de viribus ministratis*, quod virtus informativa habet causam precipientem que est creator, et illa vel deus est vel imago paterna. Aliquando vocat illam intelligentiam et emanationem divinam, ut *in 4° canonis* ac etiam *in 3° fen ibidem*, et *de viribus cordis, capitulo 4°*, ubi dixit exitus eius est ab emanatione divina procedente in omnibus rebus et producente cunctas virtutes de potentia in actum suum, et *VII° et VIII° methaphysice* sue dicit ipsam esse intelligentiam. Unde satis patet in hoc Avicennam platoni consensisse, scilicet debere poni causam separatam que formas naturales producat. Quod vero forma substantialis hominis, scilicet anima intellectiva, fit ab agente separato a materia, concedunt perypathetici omnes excepto alexandro. Et habetur *VII°*

[1] In the MS the word was originally written *fundamentum* and has been illegibly corrected, but it evidently should be *fundamenta*.

[2] *Seperatam* in the MS; and again *seperata* on fol. 80v, col. 2.

[3] Presumably the twelfth-century translator, Gerard of Cremona.

methaphysice ab Averoi, in fine commento 31 dicente unde necesse est illud quod est non mixtum cum materia generetur quoquomodo a non mixto cum materia simpliciter, et certum est quod *aristoteles 3° de anima* similiter et commentator probant animam intellectivam esse materie immixtam. Restat ergo dubium de formis naturalibus aliorum animatorum et etiam inanimatorum, an scilicet bovis et leonis, arborum metalli et lapidis, forme generentur a substantia separata quam hydeam vocavit plato vel educantur in actum ab agente mere naturali, scilicet a virtute sive spiritu existente intrinseco, videlicet in semine aut in alio quod semini possit equiparari, habente in se virtualiter omnem potentiam activam illius agentis a quo deciditur.

Plato dixit formas illas fieri ab hydea, quoniam aliter salvari non posset quomodo quelibet a sibi simili fiant ut dicebat primum fundamentum. Cum videamus ignem [*fol. 79v*] fieri ex collisione duorum corporum durorum, scilicet lapidis et ferri, et tamen nullum eorum est eiusdem speciei aut proximi generis, corpus enim non est proximum genus ignis et ferri quamvis ad ista sit genus. Similiter nos videmus vermes et etiam alia animalia multa per putrefactionem generari. Dixit quidem *philosophus in libro de generatione animalium*, castorem fuisse repertum in loco in quem deportari fuerat impossibile, et *Avicenna in libello de diluviis* dixit *ex thymeo platonis* non repugnari naturalibus principiis post cathaclismum universalem quando animalia cuncta perierint hominem absque procreantibus[4] parentibus generari. Apud platonem itaque videtur fuisse necessarium ponere illam speciem separatam que sit similium in specie causa generationis.

Sed forte quis diceret quod ignis productus ab igne et ignis genitus ex collisione non sunt eiusdem speciei. Ac simile diceret — ut videtur velle *Averois, 2° de anima*, ex intentione aristotelis, *commento 34*, ubi dicit quod generare sibi simile in specie contingit tribus conditionibus etc. — quod animal genitum non concurrente semine particularis agentis non est eiusdem speciei cum animali sic genito. Verum iste nihil diceret, quoniam illa sunt eiusdem speciei quorum non solum accidentia propria sed etiam communia sunt eadem, idem effectus, eedem operationes, idem locus, idem vivendi modus, que videntur omnia reperiri tam in rebus animatis quam in his non animatis isto modo productis propterea dictum opponentis nullum. Uterque ignis calidus est et siccus, uterque urit subtiliat resolvit denigrat et incinerat; et utrumque animal, exempli gratia mus, eandem cum aliis muribus figuram habet et similitudinem, corrodit caseum et pernas, castaneas et nuces, et sibi murilega est insidiosa. Ad averoim dico et ad philosophum quod si is bene legerit nequaquam

[4] *Procreantis* in the MS.

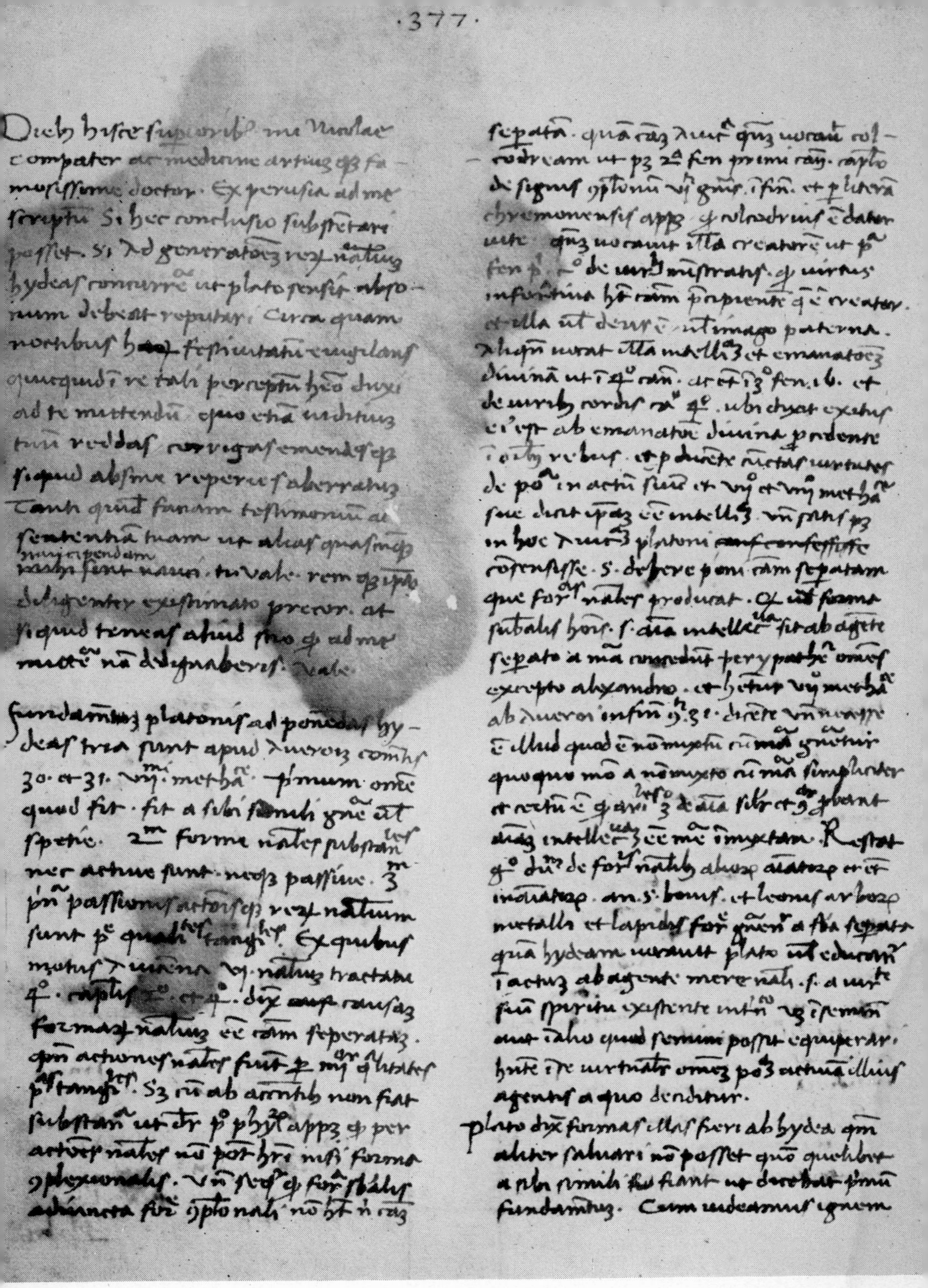

PLATE X

THE LETTER TO NICOLAUS

Vatican Latin MS 3897, fol. 79r

dixisse illa animalia non esse eiusdem speciei, sed quod animal genitum ex putrefactione quod dicitur habere spontaneam generationem non generat, ita quod ex putrefactione [*col. 2*] genita sibi similia non producunt. An istud sit verum alibi videatur, et iuxta intentionem platonis et avicenna negetur quoniam si homo ex non homine particulari generari potest, et is succedentium est generatio ut post diluvium contingere potuit, prorsus et aristotelis et Averois sententia refellatur, nam sic hominum ac cuiuscumque speciei extitisse generata principiis naturalibus non videtur esse contrarium.

Sed fortassis quidam dicet non propterea ponendas esse ydeas, quoniam ad generationem equivocam sufficit agens universale puta celum cum subiecto universali quod est ipsa terra. Nam cum celum sit agens universale, videtur posse disponere ad generationem cuiuscunque animalis et maxime animalis imperfecti. Et ex consequenti dicet sic Averois, scilicet quodlibet agens non esse necessarium ut actualiter sit similis speciei ipsi producendo, sed sufficit habere formam illam sive speciem in potentia: hinc est quod non est opus multiplicare entia separata.

At contra dictum istius presupponatur quod dixit *Averois, VII° methaphysice, commento 31*, videlicet quod actio agentis pendet a subiecto propter hoc quod pendet de forma. 2° presupponatur quod corpora supercelestia non agunt contingenter ut satis ab omnibus conceditur, *2° physicorum, capitulo de casu et fortuna*. Nam si possent agere contingenter, tunc possent etiam non agere et etiam non moveri contra determinata *physicorum VIII°*, et *in libro de celo*, ubi dicitur quod intelligentie movent eternaliter et infatigabiliter. Preterea staret aliqua materia in ultimo preparata [5] ad receptionem forme, et tamen forma non introduceretur, quia posset corpus celeste desinere agere si ageret contingenter, et sic staret ultima dispositio ad formam vermis cum forma terre aut ultima dispositio ignis cum forma lapidis, quorum nullum concedunt aristotelem et Averoim imitantes. Immo ista suppositio est de mente *Averois in libello de substantia orbis* et *in 2° de celo*, et *Avicenne, 3° canonis, fen 16, tractatus Vto, capitulo primo*, dicentis, 'Cum evadit materia et vestitur complexionaliter, necessaria est rectificatio quam tollerant figure et forme,' et subdit, 'Et non prohibetur [*fol. 80r*] eius preparatio a complemento naturali que pertinet ei ex factore potente.' Et *4° canonis, fen prima, tractatus 4°, capitulo primo*, dixit, 'Et cause horum omnium sunt forme ex formis celi facientes esse necessarium illud cuius eventus ignoratur.' Ex quibus habetur corpora celestia agere necessario, scilicet ex necessitate preparationis materie.

[5] The MS reads, "aliquam materiam in ultimo preparatam," which would require an *esse*, expressed or understood, after *staret*.

Tertio presupponatur formas complexionales nec fieri in instanti nec corrumpi. Si quidem hoc non esset, cum accidentium non sit generatio proprie dicta sed alteratio que est vere motus, tunc alteratio fieret in instanti et in hoc non differret a generatione. Et capio hic generationem et alterationem prout invicem distinguntur, quod est falsum quoniam omnis motus tempore mensuratur, *4° physicorum*. Ex quo sequitur quod si forma complexionalis acquireretur in instanti, esset indivisibilis et sic non susciperet magis et minus, contra *Avicennam, primo canonis, capitulo de complexione*. Nam si acquiritur in instanti et est divisibilis, tunc instans in tempore et mutatum esse in motu essent divisibilia contra *Averoim, VIto physicorum, commento 15*, dicentem si in instanti potest fieri alteratio, in eodem potest eadem forma moveri velocius et tardius quoniam etiam illud instans erit divisibile.

Ex his suppositis volo arguere genita que fiunt ex putrefactione non produci in esse a celo tanquam a principali agente, quia dato ipso immediate sequitur tale genitum non posse corrumpi ab extrinseco et quod illius non fieret corruptio in instanti. Immo si corrumperetur esset necessarium ipsum corrumpi in tempore, et sic substantie corruptio fieret in tempore, aut complexionis illius corruptio fieret in instanti, sed hoc dictum est esse falsum. Et quod alia sequantur probo, nam rei illius per putrefactionem a celo producte que ab extrinseco puta gladio vel lapide debet corrumpi, que sit gratia exempli scorpio, complexio que preparabat ad formam scorpionis corrumpitur in eodem instanti sicut forma substantialis illius aut non. Et non primum, quia tunc alteratio fieret in instanti contra secundum [6] suppositum. Si vero non, tunc post corruptionem forme substantialis remanet complexio preparans ad illam formam saltem pro aliquo instanti. Sed cum corpus celeste necessario agat formas stante preparata materia, ut dixit primum [7] suppositum, tunc post corruptionem forme scorpionis instanti sequente aut in eodem in quo illa forma corrumpitur [*col. 2*] corpus celeste reddet formam illi materie preparate per complexionem que remansit, sed stante eadem materia numero et complexione eadem numero stant cetera facientia pro eadem forma numero, sequitur quod redibit aut non separabitur eadem forma numero. Idem ergo numero corruptum non erit corruptum aut idem numero reviviscit, quod naturaliter est impossibile, ut est sententia omnium perypatheticorum, scilicet quod a privatione sequente habitum ad ipsum habitum non est reditus, et istud apertissime declarat *albertus magnus in postpredicamentis, capitulo de habitu*. Si quidem id esset naturale, dominus noster yesus christus nullum fecisset miraculum cum

[6] It would seem that this must be an error and that *tertium* is meant.

[7] This again really was the *secundum suppositum*.

lazarum et alios suscitasset. Ex quibus habetur vel esse necessarium idem corrumpi in tempore, et sic substantia in tempore corrumperetur, aut complexionem corrumpi in instanti, et sic in indivisibili fieret alteratio corruptiva, que omnia sunt contra aristotelem et Averoim, aut quod necesse est concludere alia inconvenientia ad que conducit argumentum que omnis philosophia et cattolica fides aborrent.

Forte diceret Averois quod complexio preparans ad formam substantialem corrumpitur in instanti quantum ad proportionem quam habet ad illam formam sed non quantum ad esse sequens mixtionem. Datur enim ab agente complexio non ut complexio sed quia talis, non enim calidum ut calidum est hoc vel illud agit sed quia tale, nam calidum ignis et solis non in quantum calida sunt differunt sed quia talia, et hinc est quod calor solis preparat ad vermem et non calor ignis. Hec responsio *Averois* colligi potest, *Vto colliget, capitulo de his que operantur a forma specifica, et capitulo de cognoscendo virtutem medicinarum de calore ignis et struetionis in fine.* Et videtur intentio *Iohannis mesuai* dicentis complexionem non agere nisi quia talis est. Scamonea quidem et reubarbarum evacuant coleram rubeam non obstante quod sint calida et sicca sicut et colera. Ex quibus ad propositum dicitur quod non est aliquid agens corpus celeste ad regenerandam formam illam, quia corrupta est complexio preparans ad illam formam quantum ad proportionem quam ad illam habebat.

[*fol. 80v*] Hec responsio est nulla. Nam si propria accidentia a sua specie separari non possunt, ut est sententia eiusdem Averois dicentis quod destructis propriis accidentibus destruuntur essentie, sequitur quod remanentibus illis post corruptionem forme etiam remanet complexio, quoniam propria accidentia sequuntur dispositionem ut umbra corpus, sicut dixit *Galenus, primo de interioribus et questione de accidenti et morbo.* Et quod illa remaneant patet quia post mortem scorpionis remanet venenum contrarium homini et non gallo sicut etiam in vita erat. Item dicit *Albertus, 22° de animalibus, capitulo de lupo,* cordas que fiunt ex visceribus lupi et ovis nequaquam facere armoniam, quoniam odium eorum in vita est radicatum in omni membro quo ad formam mixtionis, et videtur in musca suffocata in aqua quod si inde ad paucum pulvere aspergatur exposita soli reviviscit. Non ergo est corrupta complexio secundum proportionem quam habebat ad illam formam. Rursus *Aristoteles in problematibus* querit propter quid est quod accidit aliquorum morientium corpora quodam spatio post mortem esse calidiora quam dum moriuntur, et respondet quod est propter exalationem caloris naturalis qui movebatur tempore mortis ad centrum, igitur aliquo spatio post mortem remansit complexio naturalis non solum ut complexio sed quia talis, puta decoctio napelli interficit sicut et napellus, et tamen in illa non remansit nisi complexio quia forma est corrupta. Item *Avicenna, 3°*

canonis, fen 14a, capitulo primo, dicit possibile esse ut cause instrumentali currat ex dispositionibus sequentibus causam primam que dispositiones sequuntur naturam ut talis est. Et vidimus ferrum alteratum a magnete etiam attrahere ferrum quemadmodum et magnes. Non est dicendum quod in ferro sit forma magnetis. Ex quibus apparet non esse necessarium ut quando destruitur forma tunc corrumpatur complexio ut talis est.

Quod omnia que ducuntur de potentia ad actum fiant a causa simili sic suadebat plato. Quedam ducuntur de potentia ad actum per motum, ut ignis in motu lapidis et ferri, erat enim lapis potentia ignis et in motu illo fit actu ignis. Quedam [*col. 2*] ducuntur ad actum per putrefactionem ut mus vel vermis. Cum autem motus non sit similis igni nec putrefactio sorici, quoniam non solum sunt diversarum specierum sed nec ipsis unum est commune genus, necessario videtur quod ducens has materias ad actum sit causa separata illius generis propinqua vel eiusdem spetiei. Ignis etiam per motum genitus et qui ab igne productus est sunt eiusdem speciei, patet quoniam accidentia propria et communia sunt eadem et locus etiam qui datur elementis ratione qua est elementum est idem. Igitur causa generans utrumque videtur esse eadem sive generis vel speciei eiusdem, que causa non potest esse nisi separata, ergo etc.

Item forma generatur et non a corpore neque a materia neque a complexione neque ab accidentibus que non sunt complexiones sed addite complexionibus ut sunt gravitas levitas et similes. Relinquitur ergo quod generans formam sit forma, non tamen ipsamet que generatur quia tunc fieret a non faciente [8] quoniam ante actionem quod agitur non est, *Vto physicorum.* Restat ergo quod sit alia forma sibi similis illam agens, et cum illa non sit forma que agitur intrinseca, ut satis patet, clarum est quod sit ab extrinseco sibi similis et illud vel erit individuum eiusdem speciei vel generis in quo est illa forma vel hydea. Sed ignis qui fit a motu et vermis per putrefactionem non fit ab individuo illius speciei vel generis. Igitur necessario a causa separata fiunt que illis est similis. Preterea in semine non est anima in actu sed in potentia. Igitur virtus seminis non est causa agens animam, quoniam quod est in potentia non agit sed agitur. Aut enim anima fetus fieret ab anima patris aut ab anima que est in semine. Non primo, quia cessavit, nec secundo, quoniam illa anima est in potentia et non potest agere. Oportet quidem omne agens ut sit esse in actu. Hec tamen opinio non solum est platonis sed etiam eam videtur sentire themisthius ut asserit Averois.

Averois VII° methaphysice, commento 30, volens his rationibus respondere, dixit duo: primum contra fundamentum positum superius a

[8] It would appear from the context that *existente* must be meant.

platone quod forme substantiales sunt active actione que est mutatio; 2m omne quod fit non fit a sibi simili in actu, sed sufficit quod sit similitudo secundum virtutem, et isto modo in sole est similitudo animalis generandi ex putrefactione et similitudo generandorum ex semine est in ipso semine. [*fol. 81r*] Et in hoc Averois convenit cum *alexandro in libello suo de causis, parte 2a*, ubi voluit duplicem esse actionem, unam que est motus, alteram que est mutatio. Prima actione agunt forme complexionales; secunda actione agunt forme substantiales. Et ideo loco allegato dixit Averois quod forme substantiales sunt forme generantes formas materiales, et sic semina sunt cause dantes formas generatorum ex seminibus per formas quas acceperunt semina ab ipsis generantibus. In his vero que sine semine generantur cause sunt celestia corpora.

Plato ut opinor hec cuncta negaret, et tunc Averois non haberet quo sua dicta probarentur, quamvis cum aristotele convenire videatur. Nec aliquam rationem adduxit sed sole [*sic*] sue autoritati standum esse credidit. Attamen plato tantam autoritatem non admitteret sed potius negaret. Patet igitur dictum platonis quem aristoteles aliquando iuniorem socratem nominat non esse inane.

Conatur tamen Averois, ut patet *VII° methaphysice, commentis 22 et 30*, dicta platonis abicere volens quod forma non generetur sed compositum quod cum substantiis separatis convenientiam non habet. Dixit enim si forma generatur, tunc generatio non est a materia, quia materia habet dimensiones: ex dimensionato autem nequaquam fit non dimensionatum sicut ex corporeo non fit incorporeum. Aut igitur, si forma generatur, generatio esset non a materia, contra *aristotelem, primo physicorum*, aut ex habente dimensionem fieret aliquid non habens dimensionem, scilicet forma, quod est contra philosophum ut clarum est. Non tamen curaret plato an hec esset contra philosophum si alterius est opinionis.

Ad maiorem declarationem predictorum inquirendum est an forma vel compositum principaliter generetur, quo habito fierent que plato voluit clariora. Et ratio dubitationis est, ut paulo ante diximus, quoniam compositum non potest nisi a composito generari nec forma generatur nisi a forma, ex quo generatio est a sibi simili in specie. Secundum opinionem platonis illud generatur quod per generationem acquiritur, et id videtur velle philosophus, *primo physicorum et Vto et primo de generatione*. Sed illud solum est forma, ergo etc. Ex quo videtur sequi quod sola forma generetur principaliter quod videtur sensisse *Averois, 3° celi, commento 52 circa finem*, et *primo physicorum, commentis 58° et 63°*, [*col. 2*] ubi dicit, 'Id quod fit est in subiecto et ex subiecto.' Compositum vero non est in subiecto, *2° de anima*, quare non potest esse ex subiecto in subiecto. Et idem videtur dicere, *primo physicorum, commentis 62 et*

64, ubi dicit, 'Non esse recedit a generato quod est forma.' Et idem consensit *alexander in suo de generatione, parte prima, distinctione sexta.*

Ad idem est ratio sequentium platonem, scilicet quod componentia ex natura rei precedunt compositionem et cause effectum et principia principiatum. Sed materia et forma sunt componentia ipsum singulare sive compositum, ut patet *2° de anima*, et sunt principia ex *primo physicorum*, et sunt cause ex *2° physicorum*, ergo precedunt compositum causatum et principiatum. Et tunc queratur an forma habeatur per motum localem, ut dixerunt ponentes latitationem formarum in materia, sicut asserit Averois, aut per motum alterationis, et tunc forma substantialis esset accidens; aut acquireretur in tempore, et tunc forma substantialis esset partibilis; aut per generationem, et habetur propositum. Item post omnen alterationem previam ad generationem acquiritur forma vel compositum, sed non compositum quia tunc post alterationem fieret aliquid materie, quod est impossibile quia tunc vel fieret aliquid materie per generationem, quod est falsum quoniam materia secundum se totam est ingenerabilis et incorruptibilis, *primo physicorum.* Item quia tunc eiusdem numero essent due generationes diverse numero, quia scilicet generatio materie et generatio forme. Vel fieret aliquid materie per alium motum, quod est falsum per *Averoim, VII° methaphysice, commento 38*, ubi dicit quod materia est de essentia compositi et essentia per nullum motum acquiritur.

Aliqui sequentes Averoim respondent formam et compositum simul generari. Sed istud dictum est falsum patet, quoniam due generationes in materia non continuantur sicut nec due instanti. Igitur inter generationem forme et generationem compositi est tempus modicum et tunc generationem compositi nulla precedit alteratio quoniam habitibus existentibus in materia cessat motus, ac etiam sequeretur quod compositum ex materia et forma substantialibus esset accidens quoniam adveniret enti in actu. Immo forma actuaret materiam et adhuc non extaret compositum; esset igitur compositum et ipsum idem non esset. Item sequeretur quod forma substantialis disponeret ad compositum, [*fol. 81v*] et esset forma de specie qualitatis, et quod habita forma in materia non cessaret motus, et esset aliqua generatio qua natura forma acquireretur, puta generatio compositi que sequitur ex natura generationem forme sicut esse effectus sequitur esse sue cause. Fortassis alii dicerent quod acquiruntur due forme, et primo acquiritur forma simplex que est altera pars compositi, ut gratia exempli anima intellectiva. Deinde acquiritur forma compositi que in suo conceptu includit materiam, que forma gratia exempli est humanitas. Ponimus exempla in aliis sed non sic in illis sunt distincta nomina. Sed contra quoniam ex data responsione sequitur quod iste forme differunt specie, et constat quod tales forme ultime in eodem esse non possunt. Antecedens patet quia conceptus ipsarum differunt specie, et intellectus est verus sic concipiendo; igitur ipse differunt specie. Forte dicitur ambas illas formas non esse ultimas sed quod sola forma compositi est ultima. Et tunc queram an illa forma compositi precedat compositum an sequatur, et erit eadem dubitatio. Quis dubitat secundum *Averoim, VII° methaphysice, commento 42 circa finem,* quod species est ens tale per ultimam formam quia talis forma, puta rationalis que est ultima forma hominis, non est alia a differentia constitutiva cuius oppositum scitur ex data responsione. Preterea, si totum differret a toto per formam qua est totum, sequeretur hominem non differre ab asino per animam intellectivam sed per aliam formam qua esset tale compositum. Item forme substantiales essent forme in potentia quia non ultime, sole quidem ultime sunt forme in actu, ac etiam sequeretur animam intellectivam esse formam compositam quoniam, ut dixit *Averois in prohemio physicorum, commento 3°,* que sunt entes[9] inter primam materiam et ultimam formam sunt materie composite et forme composite. Item materia dependet ad formam et non ad compositum, ergo forma fit et non compositum. Antecedens patet quia materia non est in relatione ad formam nisi per potentiam ex *primo physicorum,* sed potentia sola est in relatione ad actum, actus est forma et non compositum, ergo etc. Item perfectibile dependet ad perfectionem non ad perfectum, quoniam id includit materiam, perfectio autem est ipsa forma, ut habetur *2° de anima.* [*col. 2*] Item generatio naturalis denominatur a forma quoniam ea est natura, *2° physicorum,* et generatio naturalis dicitur quia est in naturam, ut patet ibidem. Dicitur enim naturalis quoniam habet naturam que est forma. Igitur forma per se et principaliter est terminus generationis; ergo principaliter non generatur compositum sed forma. Item generatio fit in instanti, *Vto physicorum;* id quod est quantum in instanti generari non potest; quoniam compositum est quantum, sequitur quod non generabitur in instanti. Aliter sequeretur quod motus augmenti esset in instanti contra ea que determinantur in *2° de generatione,* et ab *alberto in suo tractatu de nutrimento et nutribili,* et ab aliquibus expositoribus *2° de anima.* Ex quibus omnibus recte concluditur quod principaliter generatur forma et non compositum.

Contra istam conclusionem habetur *Averois, primo physicorum, commento 32 in principio et commentis 13 et 18,* et ubi elicitur *ex commentis 51 et 60 in fine,* ubi dicit quod 'in spermate hominis est ratio opposita rationi hominis qui generatur,' et non dixit que.

Item, *VII° methaphysice, commentis 25 expresse et 30,* ubi dixit quod

[9] Or perhaps *existentes?*

si forma generatur et non compositum, tunc aut materia prima non est necessaria in generatione contra *aristotelem*, *primo physicorum*, et *commentatorem*, *commento 51*, nam tunc generatum esset simplex, et *commento 59* dixit quod materia est pars generati, et idem *commento 60*. Aut ex corpore fieret non corpus quoniam ex habente dimensionem fieret aliquid non habens dimensionem. Ideo dixit ibi commentator quod si forma generatur, tunc generatio est non a materia, quod videtur sensisse *12° methaphysice*, *commentis 12 et 18 circa finem*.

Preterea, si forma generaretur, non generaretur nisi a forma patet quia generatio immediate non est nisi a simili sicut corruptio a dissimili, saltem in generationibus que non sunt secundum accidens, generationes enim per se semper fiunt a generante simili, *VII° methaphysice*, *commento 27*.

4°, quod de novo generatur de novo habet quidditatem, sed forma nullam habet quidditatem, ergo etc. Maior patet quia generatio est mutatio de non esse ad esse, *primo de generatione* et *primo physicorum*, sed esse est per quidditatem eius cuius est, ergo etc. Minor etiam patet quia si forma haberet quidditatem, esset [10] processus in infinitum et fieret tunc forma ex aliquo in aliquid, ut arguit *commentator*, *VII° methaphysice*, *commento 26*.

[*fol. 82r*] Quinto, generatio est mutatio entis in potentia ad ens in actu, sed forma non est in actu quoniam est actus, *2° physicorum* et *2° de anima*, ergo non est mutatio ad formam. Antecedens probatur quoniam illud quod mutatur in generatione est materia, et materia est ens in potentia. Ideo dixit *commentator*, *VII methaphysice*, *commento 25*, quod generans non facit in materia formam sed facit ex materia aliquid. Videtur ergo quod ex materia, id est ex ente in potentia, faciat formatum, id est ens in actu. Forma enim non fit ex materia, ut dictum est, quoniam ex dimensionato non fit non dimensionatum.

Sexto, compositum et sua quidditas sunt idem essentialiter, *VII° methaphysice*, *commentis 21 et 27*, sed forma per supradicta generatur, ergo et compositum. Tenet contra quoniam forma est quidditas compositi per *commentatorem*, *VII° methaphysice*, *commentis 7 et 8*.

Septimo, *Aristoteles*, *VII° methaphysice*, facit hanc consequentiam, si forme separate sunt cause generationis, generatum non erit hoc aliquid, quia cause generantes et generatum debent esse similia secundum platonem et fere secundum omnes philosofantes. Sed ille forme non sunt hoc aliquid, ergo nec genita; vel si genita, sunt hoc aliquid et illa similiter quorum utrunque est falsum. Ideo non solum forma generatur sed compositum.

Octavo, agens immateriale, ut ibidem arguit commentator, non de-

[10] *Esse* in the manuscript.

pendet a materia in agendo. Tunc ergo hydea quod est tale agens vel producit omnino sibi simile vel non. Si primum, sequitur ipsam esse hoc aliquid et materiale quia productum est tale. Si non, hoc esset propter defectum materie, nam idem ut sic semper facit idem. Sed materia excluditur a tali actione, igitur si forma est agens, tantum sequitur quod effectus est forma tantum, quod ipse reputat pro inconvenienti.

Nono, quod est hoc aliquid producitur per transmutationem materie. Sed nihil transmutat materiam nisi agens corporeum. Igitur generans est compositum, ergo non forma solum, et isto modo salvatur simile a simili generari.

Decimo, *commentator*, *VIII°* *methaphysice*, dicit quod ex [*col. 2*] actu et potentia non fit unum nisi per agens extrahens actum quod non largitur ei multitudinem sed perfectionem, et ibidem dicit quod existens in actu non est aliud ab eo quod est in potentia, sed illud quod fuit in potentia fit in actu, et non sunt hec duo diversa, quod non contingeret si nihil forme esset in materia, et sic forma educitur de potentia materie per agens quod est in actu, et illud est compositum. Igitur compositum et non forma generatur.

Undecimo, aut forma fit ex nihilo aut fit ex aliquo. Non ex primo, quoniam ex nihilo nihil fit, *primo physicorum*. Ergo relinquitur quod fit ex aliquo et per consequens quod in materia aliquid eius preexistat. Sed tale fieri aliquid ex aliquo naturaliter non contingit nisi per compositum, igitur generatur compositum.

Duodecimo, non potest forma generare quia talis generatio vel esset ab extrinseco passo non conferente vim, et sic esset violenta, vel passo vim conferente, et tunc est opus agente naturali ad eductionem talis generationis. Sed forma non est agens naturale, cum sit actus quidem agi et non agere. Igitur forma non agit. Relinquitur ergo quod compositum agat. Sed simile simile producit, ergo compositum et non forma in actu producitur.

Decimotertio, ex tribus ultimis argumentis potest summi argumentum ad probandum qualiter in materia est incohatio forme, quod etiam posset suaderi per *aristotelem*, *VII°* *methaphysice*, dicentem quod natura fuerit in quorumcumque materia est aliqua pars forme. Et *2°* *physicorum* dicitur quod natura est principium motus et quietis eius in quo est, quoniam tale principium forma non est quia nondum est, nec materia quia pro tunc ipsa est habens tale principium. Relinquitur quod sit agens extrinsecum, vel si ipsum non est, oportet ponere aliquid forme quod sit tale principium, et istud vocant incohationem forme. Sed cum istud sit solum in potentia, relinquitur quod sit opus ponere aliud in actu, et istud, si dabitur, erit agens naturale quod est compositum et intendens compositum.

Pro responsione ad prima sex argumenta notandum primo quod forma est duplex, scilicet universalis et particularis, ut patet et colligitur ab *alberto in principio de sex principiis*. Prima est gratia exempli ut humanitas que dicitur forma [*fol. 82v*] totius compositi, altera particularis altera pars compositi. Prima dicitur quidditativa et ipsa proprie est quidditas compositi, et ista large loquendo appellatur etiam forma. Alia est forma simplex et potior pars compositi et hec proprie loquendo forma dicitur. Secundo, nota quod formam illam universalem significat diffinitio, formam vero particularem vel simplicem non. Hec differentie habentur ab *Averoi, VII° methaphysice, commento 52 in principio*. 3°, nota quod aliquid generare intelligitur tribus modis secundum mentem fere omnium philosophorum. Uno modo subiective et ista generatio non repugnat materie prout ab omnibus expositoribus satis colligitur, *primo physicorum*, qui dicit quod materia prima est que in omni generatione est subiectum determinate forme. Secundo modo terminative et isto modo generatur forma, cum ipsa sit terminus ad quem ipsius generationis et est generationis finis intrinsecus in tantum quod aliqui voluerunt generationem realiter non esse aliud a re generata, quod ego pro nunc non teneo. Tertio modo dicitur aliquid generari quod necessario ex subiecto et termino generationis resultat, et isto modo dicimus compositum generari. Nam ad unionem factam ex materia et forma ex illis tanquam ex partibus in existentibus et essentialibus resultat compositum, ut placet philosopho, *2° de anima*. Et istud compositum ut sic est aliud a suis partibus, cum ipsum nec sit forma nec materia sed ex illis. Ex quibus apertum est quod forma est que principaliter generatur, quoniam ad ipsam tanquam ad terminum intrinsecum stat transmutatio, nam ipsa acquisita transmutatio cessat et omnis actio agentis aut transmutantis vel generantis. Sequitur etiam quod ipsum compositum etiam generatur sed non principaliter nec ut terminus intrinsecus generationis sicut forma, sed consequutive sive resultative, ut sic loquar. Fluit tamen neccessario ex principiis essentialibus agentibus aut intendentibus unionem materie cum forma.

Ad primum, quando Averois dixit quod in spermate est ratio hominis opposita rationi hominis qui generatur et quia non dixit que, videtur de intentione sua compositum esse quod generatur et non forma, dicatur quod quamvis voluit compositum generari, non tamen exclusit generationem forme. Et compositum generari numquam negavit plato sed voluit id generari non principaliter sed consecutive. [*col. 2*] Vel dicas quod per hominem Averois intellexit formam iuxta intentionem *aristotelis, primo celi*, qui dicit celum dixit formam, et qui dicit hoc celum dicit formam in materia.

Ad secundum dico quod commentator tenet esse impossibile solam formam generari in materia propterea est necessarium compositum fieri, et ut videtur non negat immo affirmat formam generari quasi velit esse impossibile formam produci in esse existentie absque materia, quia si agens produceret formam et non in materia vel ex materia, tunc generatum esset simplex, quia simplex forma, et non esset a materia ex quo agens non indigeret materia ad generationem. Et ulterius quando dicit quod ex dimensionato fieret non dimensionatum intelligitur formam generari sed ex unione eius ad materiam necessario resultare compositum. Et quod compositum resultet est sententia philosophi, *2° physicorum* et *2° de anima*. Dixit quidem, *2° physicorum*, quod generatio est in naturam et concludit quod generatio est naturalis ratione nature que generatur, idest forme, et ibidem et *2° de anima* dicit compositum esse ex materia et forma quoniam ex illis resultat. Si ergo compositum est ex materia et forma resultans, et generatio est in naturam et dicitur naturalis ratione forme, clare patet compositum resultare et sic ipsum generari. Et cum putem Averoim a philosopho non esse discordem, credo ipsum idem voluisse in locis dictis.

Iam dictum est quod duplex est forma, scilicet universalis et particularis, et primam significat diffinitio, secunda est terminus intrinsecus generationis. Dictum est etiam quod forma particularis est illa que proprie [11] et principaliter generatur. Unde patet quod quemadmodum ex unione eius ad materiam resultat compositum, ita etiam resultat forma universalis. Ex quibus posset dubium oriri an intelligentia que agit secundum exemplar prius intendat producere formam illam in materia aut intendat producere compositum. Ac si dicamus utrum finis principalis illius intelligentie agentis et generantis sit forma particularis vel ipsum compositum. Pro responsione nota quod aliquid dicitur esse primarie intentum et aliquid secundarie. Prime intentionis est rei quidditas quam supra dixi esse formam universalem quam significat diffinitio, et ideo per quidditatem ego intelligo rem que subicitur [*fol. 83r*] prime intentioni, sicut prima intentio in animali est quod sit substantia animata sensitiva potens per se subsistere. Res ergo que habetur per hunc actum est quidditas quam ego appello formam universalem duobus modis. Uno modo quia complectitur totum esse compositi resultans ex materia et forma, eo enim quod comprehendit omnem partem essentialem compositi et non unam solam dicitur forma universalis. Alio modo dicitur universalis quod in omnibus individuis eternaliter sit una incorruptibilis per se quamvis corrumpatur per accidens. Secunde vero intentionis dicuntur universale et predicabile secundum quod ab intellectu recipiuntur. Et ergo postquam intellectus habuit primam intentionem

[11] At this point *mentiris* is written in the margin between the two columns of text.

statim secundario format in tali intentione sive quidditate intentionem aliam, que accipitur ab ipsa quidditate seu a proprietate reperta in illa quidditate, que est communitas et intelligitur quod illa est forma pluribus communis, et per talem secundam communitatem facit predicabile de pluribus. Et iste due intentiones sunt solum ab intellectu et sunt re ipsa posteriores et secundum intentionem logycam accepte, de quibus in presenti non intendo disserere. Illa vero quidditas que est prime intentionis est illa, ut diximus supra, quam significat diffinitio et est quidditas essentialis sibi et suppositis, propterea ad sortem esse sequitur ipsum esse hominem et animal sed non sequitur ipsum esse universale, scilicet species nec genus, quoniam in ipso sorte tanquam in composito resultante ex materia et forma intrinseca est illa quidditas sive forma essentialis et universalis qua homo est homo et quicquid est per se inferius ad hominem est homo.

Item nota secundum intentionem *Avicenne, VI° naturalium, tractatu 2°, capitulo secundo*, quod esse essentie et esse existentie differunt, nam per essentiam intelligit quidditatem rei intententam [12] que est quidditas prime intentionis, et per existentiam intelligit quidditatem rei productam. Et quia quidditas rei producitur ut hec quia in materia disposita et concurrente agente particulari ad minus dispositive, intelligendo per agens particulare limitatum agens in natura ut hoc subsistens cum [*col. 2*] demonstratis appenditiis materialibus, ideo quidditas producta est quidditas demonstrata et hec et ideo generabilis et corruptibilis. Quidditas vero rei intenta est illa que intenditur sub natura communi et ab agente universali intelligendo per agens universale ut statim dicam non autem ut genus nec species. Ideo quidditas intenta est illa cui ab intellecto imponitur nomen species vel genus, et ista est una quidditas sicut hydea est una illius speciei. Per agens vero universale ego intelligo intelligentiam a qua natura regulatur quemadmodum dicunt Averoiste celum esse agens universale. Sed in hoc differunt quia celum quantum est de se intendit omnem formam cuiuslibet speciei, sicut manus artificis non plus intendit craterem vel vomerem quam aliud quiddam, quoniam instrumentum est activum ut dirigitur ab intentione agentis et potest esse instrumentum diversarum artificum aut eiusdem artificis ad diversa opera non respiciendo quamcumque determinatam materiam. Et ideo secundum ipsum producuntur que sunt a casu et fortuna que non producuntur ratione instrumenti magis limitati et determinati nec ratione exemplaris secundum quod illa intelligentia intendit agere.

3° nota quod quamvis intelligentia habeat exemplar et in esse essentie quidditatem intentam que est forma universalis ut supra diximus, et

[12] Probably *intentam* is intended.

tamen generet aut instanti in esse existentie producat quidditatem particularium quam diximus quidditatem productam, tamen ab illa intelligentia non intenditur hec ut est hec aut sic dearticulata. Et igitur si tale agens esset virtus solis intendens producere rosam, non intendit eam ut est talis nature demonstrate, talis numeri situs qualitatis et similium, et sic patet quod non intendit individuum demonstratum. Sed intendit aliquid producere in quo salvetur in esse existentie determinata species, et hoc non est nisi individuum vagum iuxta intentionem *alberti, primo physicorum*, quia videlicet intendit producere aliquam rosam et non hanc vel illam, quemadmodum artifex puta factor navis non intendit hanc vel illam sic triangulatam [*fol. 83v*] aut contextam sed intendit facere aliquid quo vehantur merces et cum quo possit transfretare. Sed quoniam artifex non potest producere in actu essentiali illam formam hydealem quam habet in mente nisi faciat hanc vel illam, ideo descendit ad factionem istarum particularium sic vel aliter angulatarum aut contextarum et in materiam dispositam inducit formam per cuius inductionem resultat navis, ut videtur clare philosophus dixisse *XVI de animalibus* et sensit *commentator, VII° methaphysice, commento 30 in principio.* Sic intelligentia cum non posset quidditatem illam quam intendit producere in actu existendi nisi per particularia, licet primo intendat nec hoc particulare nec illud sed aliquid, cum istud individuum vagum non possit facere nisi producat individuum demonstratum, ideo facit illud individuum aliquando sic aliquando aliter figuratum non deficientibus tamen que requiruntur ad illam formam recipiendam, nisi forte accidat defectus vel ratione materie vel ratione alterius impedimentis, quem defectum casu vel fortuna dicimus evenire. Et per talia particularia producta sic in esse ille forme hydeales servantur in esse existentie.

Et si aliquis arguat quod dato isto, scilicet intelligentiam intendere tale individuum quod non potest producere nisi per viam generationis, sequitur quod intendat illud generare et sic ipsum est quod generatur et non forma contra superius determinata, respondatur quod intelligentia intendit individuum sed non ut finem intrinsecum generationis, quia sic sola forma generatur, sed ut finem extrinsecum, nam ut diximus ad introductionem forme in naturam resultat hoc compositum et id quod appellamus esse hominem vel equum.

Et si queratur illa hydea aut est hominis similitudo aut forme que in materiam introducitur, dico quod est similitudo hominis que in esse existentie non potest produci nisi per viam huiusmodi generationis nec repugnat generationis esse duas fines, scilicet intrinsecum ut formam et extrinsecum ut compositum, nam si generatio esset motus per quem acquiritur forma, [*col. 2*] certum est quod forma terminaret illum motum principaliter ad cuius terminationem resultaret formatum sive figuratum.

Per albefactionem enim non acquiritur album sed albedo qua acquisita album resultat. Non tamen est omni modo similitudo, quoniam albedo advenit enti in actu et rei perfecte, sed forma substantialis advenit enti in potentia et rei imperfecte. Similibus tamen exemplis utitur philosophus in pluribus locis et maximo *2° physicorum*.

Et si arguitur quod generatio tunc non est a simili quia similitudo in mente intelligentie non est similitudo forme sed hominis ut diximus, respondetur quod quamvis intelligentia intendat producere hominem in esse existentie, intendit etiam producere illud per quod est homo tanquam per partem magis essentialem et ista est forma partis. Habet ergo in se exemplar hominis et omnium que essentialiter concurrunt ad hominis essentiam et existentiam, quemadmodum artifex habet in mente quecumque concurrunt ad esse artificiati quod in esse existentie producitur. Sed quemadmodum artifex intendit compositum et producit formam in materia[m] ~~ut~~ inde resultat compositum tamen illam compositionem est tale per illam formam, ita intelligentia intendit primo hominem et producit animam humanam in naturam ut inde et per suam unionem resultet compositum quod dicitur homo per talem formam. Et sic patet responsio ad dictum de quo principalis questio fiebat, scilicet quod principalius intelligentia illa intendit hominem quam formam intellectivam producere, tamen homo non est homo nec potest esse homo nisi per illam formam et per eam terminantem generationem est in esse productus homo et sua forma universalis que dicitur humanitas, ita quod homo et humanitas tamen sunt in esse essentie antequam producantur in esse existentie quia sunt in mente intelligentie.

Ad tertium dico quod forma non fit nisi a forma, quamvis ad disponendam materiam ut formam suscipiat concurrant agentia corporalia tanquam instrumenta intelligentie hanc generationem intendentis, nec credo quod Averois hoc neget quia nullum sequitur inconveniens. [*fol. 84r*] Et si dicitur quod generatio fit a sibi simili in spetie et illa intelligentia agens et forma inducta non sunt similis speciei, dicatur platonem voluisse rem fieri a sibi simili non quod agens sit simile sed quod sit agens habens hydeam sive illam similitudinem quemadmodum dicunt cattholici deum fecisse hominem ad similitudinem suam, id est, ad exemplar quod erat in mente divina. Ac si in artificialibus diceremus vas sive urceum fieri a sibi simili, id est, illud fecit figulus ad exemplar quod habebat in mente, et istud intendens philosophus, *2° physicorum*, dixit domum fieri ex domo, id est, fieri secundum illud exemplar domus quod erat in mente domificatoris. Vel dicas quod res fit a sibi simili in specie, nam licet *aristoteles*, *primo ethicorum*, conetur improbare hydeas, vel fortassis melius dicam illos qui male intelligebant materiam [naturam?] hydearum, tamen dixit quod hic homo et per se homo non differunt specie intelligendo quod per se homo esset hydea hominis. Ita quod si concedatur hydea esset similis speciei cum omnibus illam hydeam participantibus, nec sequitur aliquid inconveniens ex hoc, immo habetur verissimum quod individua eiusdem speciei habent aliquid commune et essentiale quod precedit ipsorum existentiam. Et hoc patet per diffinitionem que nulli particulari convenit sed nature communi et talis natura communis falso diffiniretur nisi esset aliquid precedens ipsum esse existentie, unde philosophus, *VII° methaphysice, textu commenti 44*, dicebat, substantia rei sensibilis est substantia demonstrata propria rei sensibilis, sed quidditas est substantia communis, et sic quidditas non est substantia propria. Et *commentator, commento 45*, dixit quidditas est substantia que convenit pluribus, et ista materia satis agitur diffuse *ibidem, commentis 46, 47, 48*, licet Averois videatur loqui de universali.

Ad 4m cum dicitur quod de novo generatus de novo [*col. 2*] habet quidditatem, dicatur quod per quidditatem intendit formam universalem quam significat diffinitio, ut supra dixi, et ideo solum intelligitur de composito, quia illa forma sive quidditas est compositi. Nam humanitas est quidditas sive forma hominis, ut homo constat ex materia et forma, et non est quidditas materie hominis neque anime intellective, ita quod ipsa quidditas est forma quam significat diffinitio intelligendo de diffinitione reali. Diffinitiones enim cum ponuntur ex principiis propriis que sunt in re, ut dixit *Averois, prohemio de anima, commento V°*, nec loquimur hic de composito ex materia et forma ut tale, compositum est hoc aliquid sensibile sicut est plato et cicero vel hic equus ut patet, sed loquimur de composito cui corespondet quidditas in essentia, esto quod nullum particulare reperiatur, sicut dicimus quod nulla rosa existente adhuc rosa est pulcherrimus florum. Et ut istud clarius intelligatur nota secundum *commentatorem, VII° methaphysice, commentis 34 et 38*, quod duplex est prioritas, scilicet hominis et generationis, quod etiam colligitur a philosopho, *2° de anima*, cum dixit, 'Scientia inquam contemplationem generatione precedit,' et istam vocat ibidem commentator prioritatem materie ad formam secundum quam generatio incipit ab imperfecto et tendit ad perfectum. Alia est prioritas diffinitionis sive perfectionis quam vocat prioritatem forme ad materiam, quia incipit a perfecto et tendit ad imperfectum vel ad perfectum minus. Et quia talis prioritas est naturarum que sunt priores secundum naturam et simpliciter, ideo secundum hanc prioritatem fit diffinitio et demonstratio. Et quia prioritas prima est naturarum que sunt posteriores secundum naturam et priores quo ad nos, ideo secundum hanc prioritatem accidit quo ad nos prima cognitio, ut colligitur *prohemio physicorum*. Dico ergo quod prioritas forme ad materiam est prioritas in essentia, sed prioritas materie ad formam est prioritas in existentia sive in esse sensibili. Illi ergo prioritati forme ad materiam corespondet compositum secundum formam universalem, scilicet humanitati, et istud est compositum intentum. Sed prioritati materie ad formam corespondet compositum productum et est compositum secundum formam particularem. Et consyderare de composito secundum formam universalem per abstractionem a motu et generatione est consideratio methaphysica; [*fol. 84v*] consyderatio vero naturalis est secundum motum et quietem, et has duas differentias non transcendit philosophus naturalis, ut dixit *Averois, XII° methaphysice, commentis 5 et 8*, et *2° physicorum, commento 21.* Et sic habetur quomodo id quod de novo generatur, scilicet per unionem materie ad formam, et est compositum productum de novo, habet quidditatem secundum illud esse existentie. Non tamen oportet quod compositum intentum habeat novam quidditatem, quia non de novo intenditur, licet de novo in esse existentie producatur.

Ad 5m dico quod generatio est mutatio entis in potentia ad ens in actu non intelligitur nisi ut materia que est in potentia ad formam movetur et disponitur ad illam suscipiendam. Quando vero dicitur quod forma non est ens in actu, dico quandocumque ipsa est, est ens actu. Si quidem intelligeretur pro composito, istud esset falsum, quia materia non movetur ad compositum sed ad formam et ad perficiens et non ad perfectum. Et movetur ad illud quod appetit quoniam illo caret et appetit formam, ut patet per *Aristotelem et ipsum commentatorem, primo physicorum.* Quando autem dicit commentator quod generans non facit in materia formam, hoc est verum, sed introducit formam in materiam, et ideo fuit opus ponere agentia separata, neque facit illam ex materia, sicut nec forma artis fit ex ligno. Nam si illa propositio ex dicat partes, certum est quod materia non est pars forme. Si dicat terminum a quo, sicut dicimus ex nigro fieri album, hoc iterum est falsum, quoniam forma fit ex privatione tanquam ex termino a quo et non ex materia, ut patet per declarata *primo physicorum.* Si vero dicat commentator quo ex materia fit aliquid, dico quod est verum, quoniam ex materia fit compositum tamquam ex altera parte ipsum componente et intrinsecus constituente.

Ad 6m dico illud esse verum, iam enim concessum est compositum generari non principaliter sed consecutive, tamen forma est illa que principaliter generatur ex cuius introductione in materiam resultat compositum sensibile. Dico etiam consequenter quod quemadmodum per introductionem forme particularis resultat compositum sensibile, ita per formam universalem cum materia resultat compositum, scilicet homo cuius humanitas est forma que dicitur forma universalis. Sed ad maiorem istorum declarationem nota quod compositum [*col. 2*] potest consyderari dupliciter, uno modo ut est compositum ex materia et forma demonstrata que duo sunt principia individui, alio modo ut est compositum ex materia et forma speciei que est materia intelligibilis et non sensibilis. De primo consyderat naturalis et de secundo considerat methaphysicalis, et ideo *commentator, VII° methaphysice, commento 33 in fine et commento 38 in solutione diffinitionum mathematicarum,* dixit quod materia est duplex quedam sensibilis et quedam intelligibilis, et colligitur *3° de anima, commento VIIII,* et sic quidditas speciei habetur ex forma universali et materia intelligibili non sicut mathematica sed sicut naturalia abstracta.

Si quis dicat istud esse contra *commentatorem, VII° methaphysice, commento 36,* dicentem nequaquam posse intelligi quidditatem animalis sine carnibus et ossibus, et ibidem ab *aristotele textu commenti 38,* responditur dictum aristotelis debere intelligi pro materia sensibili, tunc aliter quidditates diffinitionum essent corruptibles et per consequens scientia non esset eterna, cuius oppositum habetur *VII° methaphysice, commento 52,* et *primo posteriorum,* et *VI° ethycorum.* Et patet consequentia quia materia est causa corruptionis, ut habetur *primo physicorum,* quamvis ipsa sit ingenerabilis et incorruptibilis, ut habetur ibidem. Ideo diffinitiones non sunt substantiarum sensibilium sed ipsarum proprie est generatio et corruptio propter materiam, ut habetur eodem commento. Ergo materia quam includunt quidditates diffinitionis non est nisi intelligibilis intellectu forme. Et non dico quod sit solum intelligibilis quia solum habeat esse intentionale; immo dico quod ipsa vero est materia et est ens extra intellectum sed nullo sensu immo solo intellectu percipi potest. Istud [dicit] *Avicenna VI naturalium, capitulo 3°,* dixit quod aliquis creatus perfectus subito cessantibus ab eo omnibus sensibus affirmabit esse sue essentie, non tamen affirmabit esse suarum partium quecumque sint partes intrinsece vel extrinsece. Ex quo dicto multi voluerunt eligere quod quidditas non includat materiam, quoniam secundum hoc dictum videtur quod homo affirmet suum esse preter materiam, quod dictum etiam ipse repetit *ibidem, tractatu Vto, capitulo VII°.* Sed si quis recte et totum advertat [*fol. 85r*] quod ibi Avicenna dixit, videtur id dixisse solum ut probaret actum intelligendi ut per operationem nos induceret in cognitionem anime, non enim ibi probat esse hominis sed sue anime intellective. Ideo intelligit Avicenna quod anima se esse affirmat per suum actum intelligendi quo se ipsam intelligit actu reflexivo; non tamen affirmat absque suis partibus hominem esse hominem, verum si velles intelligere de esse hominis, dicatur quod 'creatus perfectus' ut puta homo in specie sive separatus 'subito cessantibus ab eo omnibus sensibus,' id est omnibus particularibus et individuantibus remotis, 'affirmabit esse sue essentie' secundum consyderationem methaphysicam. 'Non tamen affirmabit esse suarum partium' quas habet in esse existentie sive sint partes intrinsece, ut materia et forma demonstratis, sive partes extrinsece ut sunt partes sensibiles et [etiam] accidentales.

Ad VIIm dicitur quod cum illud quod generatur sit forma, conceditur quod ipsum genitum non est hoc aliquid, id est individuum sive compositum sensibile, quia forma principaliter generatur, ut dictum est, tale non compositum resultat, et sic forma procedit a causa separata ut patet.

Ad VIIIm dicitur illud esse verum, scilicet quod principaliter agens immateriale non dependet a materia, et conceditur quod hydea generat sibi simile, nec sequitur ipsam hydeam esse hoc aliquid, quoniam ipsa non intendit compositum principaliter ut dictum est. Nec Averois habet pro inconvenienti quod forma generetur sed si ipsa generaretur et nullum compositum resultaret et sic effectus non est forma tantum, id est solus ita quod excludatur alius effectus.

Ad VIIIIm dicitur quod hydea transmutat materiam sed mediantibus instrumentis corporeis puta celo et particulari agente, aliter non produceretur esse existentie quod est esse productum non tamen principaliter intentum.

Ad Xm dicitur quod potentia pro nunc est duplex, scilicet subiectiva et obiectiva, et quod commentator intelligit de potentia obiectiva in illis duabus autoritatibus et sic agens [*col. 2*] non largitur multitudinem sed perfectionem et illud quod est in potentia deinde in actu non sunt duo diversa, quoniam albedo in actu non est diversa a se ipsa ut erat in potentia obiectiva. Sed loquendo de potentia subiectiva contingit oppositum, quia sic agens producendo formam de novo facit multitudinem. Item ens in potentia, scilicet materia, et ens in actu, scilicet forma vel compositum, sunt diversa, ut patet realiter distincta.

Ad XIm ut clarius respondeatur notandum quod inter generationem et creationem est differentia, nam creatio est productio inter ens simpliciter et nihil. Sed generatio est inter ens et privationem, que privatio, etsi nihil sit formaliter, tamen dicit aptitudinem et inclinationem naturalem in subiecto, et talem aptitudinem aut inclinationem non presupponit creatio nec talem privationem in aliquo subiecto, quia deus potest producere sine susceptivo, nec istud est contra philosophum aut commentatorem, cum non sit actio naturalis qua secundum omnes naturales ex nihilo nihil fit. Propterea dixit *beatus thomas*, *VIII° physicorum*, quod dicti philosophi non repugnant fidei. Nam si potentia dei excedit potentiam nature, profecto aliquid potest deus quod natura non potest. Et forte propter dictam causam dicunt quod forma naturalis a naturali agente producitur de potentia materie, non quod in materia sit aliquid forme sed quoniam agens naturale in generando non agit inter ens et nihil sed inter ens et privationem in subiecto dicentem talem aptitudinem vel privationem sive carentiam ut placuit beato thome. Et videtur sententia *commentatoris*, *VIII° physicorum*, *commentis vii et viii*, dicentis contrarium esse potentia suum contrarium, eo quod in uno contrariorum puta in aere est privatio ignis per quam redditur aptus ad susceptionem forme ignis ratione sue materie hanc privationem in se complectentis. Dicatur itaque quod productio illa est de nihilo propter hoc, tamen non sequitur quod sit creatio, licet generatio et creatio non distinguantur ex hoc quoniam utraque est de nihilo ut nihil dicit habitudinem termini, tamen differunt quoniam generatio respicit susceptionem quod non respicit creatio, ut patet per predicta.

Ad XIIm dicatur non semper esse necessarium quod res naturalis habeat principium activum intrinsecum sui motus, [*fol. 85v*] sed sufficit quod habeat principium passivum vel naturalem inclinationem ad illum motum. Motus enim vaporis sursum est naturalis et tamen non ratione forme vaporis, quoniam ipsa tunc movetur per se ad sui corruptionem, sed est naturalis ratione materie cui sicut inest naturaliter moveri ad omnem formam, ita est susceptiva cuiuslibet motus ad illam formam, et sic vapor habet principium passivum ad illum motum. Et si dicitur quod naturalia differunt ab artificialibus quoniam naturalia habent principium activum sui motus, artificialia ut sic non habent, dicatur quod ista non est differentia, sed quia in naturalibus est principium passivum habens determinatam inclinationem ad formam sed in artificialibus non. Nam lectulus sive tripos non est forma ad quam lignum habeat principium intrinsecum passivum per quod ad illam inclinetur sicut materia naturalis ad suam formam ab intrinseco inclinatur.

Ad XIIIm dicitur quod in materia est pars forme non formaliter quia sic forma esset divisibilis sed virtualiter quemadmodum dicimus calorem esse partem sanitatis. Vel dicas melius quod *aristoteles*, *VII methaphysice*, intelligit illud idem quod intellexit *2° physicorum*, scilicet quod privatio est quoddammodo forma et privatio est in materia, ergo in materia est quoddammodo forma. Et per hoc intellexit in materia esse aptitudinem ad talem formam, et quanto materia magis ac magis disponitur tanto redditur aptior ad formam suscipiendam et finaliter sic ad istam formam quod non ad aliam. In materia ergo propinqua et disposita est pars forme, id est, tanta dispositio ut naturaliter in talem materiam sic dispositam non possit alia forma introduci preter istam. Oportet enim concedere quod idem movens principale est quod disponit materiam et introducit formam sed aliter et aliter: disponit enim non immediate sed mediante corpore celesti et aliis multis minus universalibus instrumentis corporalibus disponat materiam, quoniam excepta prima intelligentia nulle alie possunt materiam corporalem alterare nisi mediante corpore. Corpus enim non fit ex non corpore nec nisi mediante corpore. Sed introducit formam nullo corpore mediante. Sunt ergo corpora facientia ad dispositionem et facta dispositione [*col. 2*] cessat ipsorum motus. Sed non faciunt ad introductionem quam appellamus generationem et subitam ad instantaneam productionem, nam a divisibili agi in indivisibile non videtur conveniens. Et ideo cum forma que introducitur sit indivisibilis et sua introductio fiat in instanti quod est indivisibile, videtur quod sua introductio fiat ab indivisibili et non ab alio.

Ex quibus salva semper doctiorum sententia ego concludo formam principaliter generari et ipsius inductionem fieri ab hydea modo supradicto. Ex quo sequitur conclusio principalis, scilicet quod ad generationem naturalem proprie dictum hydeas concurrere et eas non esse reiciendas, ut multi putant, de intentione philosophi et commentatoris.

Hoc tamen ultimo adduco. Si quis vellet recte interpretari illud verbum, 'forma educitur de potentia materie,' aliter quam communiter consueverit, dicat quod materia sumitur tribus modis: primo pro ea que est pura potentia que est pars inexistens rei naturalis; alio modo pro re quod est oppositum, id est pro eo ex quo fit aliquid et illud ex quo fit non inexistit, ut quando ex aere fit ignis; tertio modo pro naturali agente. Certum est quod ex prima fit compositum tamquam ex altera parte constituente. Ex secunda fiunt invicem elementa tanquam ex termino a quo, et de hac materia dixit *commentator*, *VIII° physicorum*, quod secum est coniuncta potentia rei in quam fit transmutatio, nam aer est potentia ignis. Ex tertia fit forma [argumenta] in generatione ita quod forma substantialis que generatur educitur de potentia materie, id est, de potentia activa materialis agentis, et per materiale agens intelligo more theologorum omne agens quod claudit in se imperfectionem qualia sunt omnia agentia citra primum. Et quia a nullo tali materiali forma humana educitur, quia solum per creationem infunditur, ut omnes concedunt, ideo dicimus omnes formas naturales preter ipsam educi de potentia materie, id est materialis agentis, humana vero advenit de foris per creationem immediate a deo qui est primum agens. Et si dicitur quod agentia separata sunt agentia [*fol. 86r*] immaterialia, dicitur hoc esse verum comparando illas substantias separatas ad agentia corporalia que talium substantiarum separatarum sunt instrumenta. Hec sunt que sentio, mi compater: tua modo intersit corrigere et emendare et emendata ad me mittere ut tua literatura fiam doctior.

Mihi carissimum atque gratissimum foret si opus quod ad defendendum platonem fecisse R. d. cardinalem credo multi dicunt ad me mitteretur, nam libenter illud legerem et lectum remitterem ei qui mihi mutuasset. Credo rem esse arduam, ideo pulchram et legi dignam. Tu vale, me ama, commatrem et cetero[s] tuos meo [nomine][13] salvas facias, et rescribito precor. Ex tuderto die Xa Ian. 1470.

Nicolaus fulginas
compater tuus

[13] The word and letter in brackets are not in the manuscript. I am indebted to Monsignore Mercati, Prefect of the Vatican Library, for suggesting this reading. The "cetero" is rather illegible, and some scholars to whom I have shown the photostat of the passage have suggested "atrio" instead.

APPENDIX 19

AD VIRUM PRAESTANTISSIMUM LAURENTIUM MEDICEM NICOLAI FULGINATIS OPUSCULUM DE IDEIS

Latin text from MS Laurent. Plut. 82, cod. 22, fols. 1r–47r.

ETSI CUIQUE vel docto [inquirere][1] licet, Laurenti clarissime, de ideis rectius an plato an aristoteles sit locutus, ne cui mirum sit, si et ego volo michi quamvis sciolo etiam liceat. Nam quanto res altior est tanto cupiditas ardentior animum excitat ad sciendum. Natura quidem nobis insitum est ut sapere cupiamus.

Cumque diebus hisce superioribus commentarios illos legerem quos disertissimos ac elegantissimos in ethicorum Aristotelis libros ad virum prestantissimum ac inter eos qui unquam vixerint celebratissimum, Cosmam medicem prudentissimum avum tuum, Donatus azarolus, [*fol. 1v*] vir et doctus et probus, rem edepol optimo philosopho dignam edidit et dicavit, inveniremque pulchre atque subtiliter prestantem istum hominem summa industria mirisque suasionibus indulsisse, quo vel tantos philosophos conciliaret quasi eadem suis opinionibus persentiscant, vel aristotelis dicta refelleret velut sub umbra videatur asserere mentem platonis aristotelem a vera sententia non paululum extorsisse, vel quod in eos invexerit qui ut verba sonant platonis animum intellexissent: — hec omnia cum sint a perypateticis interpretibus aliena, excitatus animus est apponere fundamenta platonis et quibus argumentis sectatores Aristotelis conentur illa dissolvere. fortassis hinc mens utriusque philosophi clarior apparebit.

Plato, vir divinissimus moribus et doctrina, voluit omnium artium cunctarum rerum generationis universeque scientie ydeas esse datrices, nec sue voluntati partim [*fol. 2r*] defuit Avicenna in hoc uno dissentiens qui solam et unicam intelligentiam posuit cui tale dicavit offitium, eam colcodream, id est formarum datricem arabico sermone, denominans et aliquando emanationem qua omnibus in rebus virtus producitur [quo][2] de potentia in actum exeant et existant. item causam precipientem illam sepissime nuncupavit et eam nominavit creatorem. Hinc ab aliquibus dubitatum est an voluerit deus sit vel ymago paterna vel aliqua una intelligentiarum que citra deum celorum motus exercent. At plato cuilibet rerum spetiei generique propriam opinatus quemadmo-

[1] Added in the margin.

[2] Added in the margin.

dum producendarum rerum speties sunt diverse, sic idearum multitudinem diversitatemque ostendere conabatur. Quare sicut homo leo bos serpens planteque variantur sic unumquodque suam habet producentem ideam et variam et diversam.

[*fol. 2v*] Aristoteles vero platone nequaquam inferior, licet Tullius ceteris omnibus ipsum preposuerit excepto platone, philosophus solertissimus cui fuit sublime acreque ingenium, putans absurdum esse ponere id cuius natura non eguit, que neque in superfluis abundat neque neccessaria omittit, quoniam deus et natura nichil faciunt frustra quos satis constat certo federe cuncta disposuisse, alienus ab ista sententia tales ideas ut rem in natura superfluam delere platonemque arguere nixus de hac ipsa re quoad potuit, que gravissima et altissima videbatur, multum diuque sollicitus quot in libris edidit, ut *methaphisice VII*, *ethicorum primo*, isthanc opinionem nititur improbare. quis horum iustius induerit arma nondum apparuit: hinc achademici platonis positionem custodientes, hinc perypatetici plurimum impugnantes sub dubio iudice causam relinquere.

Sed cum ego putem Speusippo vivente, [*fol. 3r*] qui platonis nepos extitit et successor, integro acrique philosopho nequaquam dubitante asserere platonem sine virili semine genitum extitisse multisque superstitibus clarissimis viris qui etiam si oportuisset pro platone oppetere non dubitassent, hanc de idea sententiam esse omnibus manifestam, minime reor de tanta opinione que velut divinum oraculum tenebatur aristotelem vel portiunculam detraxisse vel in aliqua particula fuisse mentitum. Amentis stultique fuisset edidisse publiceque legisse, in scriptis ad perpetuam memoriam reliquisse, quorum improbatio in promptu et per innumeros excellentesque philosophos evidentissima probaretur. Unde et mendax et reprobus tantus philosophus supervixisset ac perenni [3] notaretur infamia.

Benignius atque gravius ut opinor aiunt dantes operam qua tantorum philosophorum dicta in unum cohereant, licet calle diverso perrexisse videantur. Hi non [*fol. 3v*] perperam agunt, tamen in vanum laboravere, quoniam si aristoteles sensisset que plato reliquerat, frustra contra ipsum decertasset cuius viginti annos extiterat auditor. nec tot tantosque labores totque vigilias in vanum fuisset perpessus aut suum animum defixum apposuisset ut sua postmodum vana ac stulta improbatio nosceretur. longe quidem abest redarguendo dumtaxat velle alterius sententiam confirmare.

Qui vero credunt in illos invexisse philosophum qui ut sua verba iacent platonis sententias interpretabantur quasi non probe nec recte

[3] "Peremni" seems the spelling in the manuscript.

dixerint a mente philosophi sunt alieni, cum aperto marte platonem impugnaturus rationes adducat pene inrefragabiles et apertas.

Nec ista ad te scribo, prestantissime Laurenti, quo putem tibi otium superesse vel possis rebus huiuscemodi indulgere, quoniam [*fol. 4r*] onus rei publice que tuo nutu et sapientia gubernatur tenet tuum animum in grandioribus impeditum. Verum michi decentissimum visum est ut ad eos quorum gratia et suasu cum commentaria sunt edita tum textus e greco traducti quibus e latinorum mentibus multa ignorationis nebula est amota, si qua etiam disputanda sunt dirigantur ut eorum perpetue laudes supervivant.

Sed iam quibus divinissimus ille ad ponendas ydeas movebatur non erit inane subiungere. sunt quidem fundamenta perardua atque sublima. Exinde que in ipsum iaciuntur tela durissima aperte perquirere. Sic fortassis animus utriusque philosophi videbitur manifestus.

Hoc tamen unum abs te peto, vir [clarissime] gravissime, quod si non adsint que apud oratores quorum hec florentina civitas referta est nunc sunt in honore vocabula, minime stomacheris, cum huiusmodi rebus [*fol. 4v*] humanitatis nunquam indulseram, tum quia imbutus que a nostris commentatoribus habentur frequentius in eas plurimum dictiones sum dilapsus quas rhetorice sectatores utraque linqua et periti et docti vel nauci faciunt vel contempnunt, tum quia dantes operam philosophie videntur eloquentie litteras aborrere. at tempus est ut rem ipsam aggrediar.

SCIENTIAM ESSE perpetuam oportere ac de rebus eternis que nullam corruptionem patiuntur cum platonis mens divinissima perspicaci ratione cognovisset, quod etiam *aristoteles* ubique, maxime *in posterioribus* et *ethicorum VI°*, aperte confirmat, causas illius contemplatus nullo unquam tempore decessuras. Nam fortassis id supra vires hominum est indagare, quoniam coniectura mentis humane [*fol. 5r*] magna cum admiratione perquiritur, censuit de particularibus effectibus ad tempus paucum duraturis cum sint corruptibiles et caduci nullam posset perfectam scientiam exhiberi. Furor enim esset, horum mensuram si quis ausus fuerit attigisse, [quoniam imbecillitas humana hec nequaquam intellexisse potest, incomprehensibilia sunt ut *plinius secundus suo secundo libro* recensuit; propterea a generalissimis ad specialissima descendentes iubet plato quiescere, ut dixit porphyrius.] [4] Si quidem de aliquo eterna scientia potest haberi convenit illud perpetuo duraturum. Est quidem scientia verorum que corruptionem non patiuntur. particularia vero sunt suo tempore definita.

[4] The passage enclosed in brackets is added in the margin.

De rebus igitur eternis scientia est quales rerum ydeas plato credidit demonstrasse quarum eternitas in motu est sive mutatione continua, quia numquam motum relinquit quod vitam non deserit nec ab his dare vitam discedit in quibus agitatio vincitur esse perpetua. Nam si cessaret omnis generatio finiretur. earum est ut dixi virtus et producendi et conservandi omne quod factum est ut continuo res nove succedant et per generationem [*fol. 5v*] et corruptionem perduret a natura productum.

Preterea quod tale est per participationem neccessarium est ad id reduci quod per essenciam esse tale cognoscitur, cum vero particularia non essentialiter sed per participationem de sue spetiei essentia dicantur talia, opus est ut ad essentiam sue spetiei reductionem patiantur, quasi linee procedentes a circuli centro dependent illoque participantes esse quod habent ab eo suscipiunt. quo fit ut Cicero vel Sempronius achilles aut thersites nequaquam essentialiter sed participatione homines esse dicantur. quod etiam de individuis spetierum omnium affirmandum est. Hec igitur non sub certa scientia continentur cum illa sit ut diximus de universalibus et eternis. est quidem per se homo de quo scientia tradi potest quem homines cuncti participant. Nam quidditate et essentia omnes homines [*fol. 6r*] sunt unus homo que porphirii perstat sententia.

Rursus rerum particularium in naturam activa productio [aliqua est ex habentibus semina] [5] ut plantarum et animalium que perfecta sunt et non orbata nec spontaneam generationem habencia. Aliqua ex seminibus minime producuntur et hec triphariam vel quia sic nata ex putredine procreantur, ut vermes ex fimo et vespe ex asino putrescente, aut ab aliquo quod similem spetiem preostendit ut ignis ex igne, aut per alterationem ab extrinseco venientem sicut ignis ex durorum corporum concussione producitur et ex arundinum diverberatione a vento caniculari sole urente. quorum omnium in causam sibi spetie similem neccesse est quod productio reducatur.

Platonis enim, cuius mens pura perfecta et contemplatione non sensibus solum sed divino lumine replebatur, potissimum fundamentum est [*fol. 6v*] ymmo neccessarium: si quid generatur non ab alio quam a sibi actu simili procreari, quod et *aristoteles* videtur sensisse, *secundo de anima*, dicens fore naturalissimum simile sibi simile produxisse ut animal quidem animal, planta[m] vero plantam. In ideas rerum omnium tanquam in causas similes specialesque essentialiter generationem plato reduxit.

Placuit igitur illi summo philosopho fundamentum sue opinionis assumpsisse quod quecunque de potencia in actum, id est de non esse sensibus apparente ad esse quod per sensus apprehenditur, neccessario a

[5] These words in brackets are added in the margin of the manuscript.

causa sibi simili provenire. Clarum est enim que secundum essenciam inter se dissimilia sunt invicem quo ad nationem minime convenire. Numquam quidem ex lapide ut lapis est generabitur equus, nec elephas ex serpente, vel cignus ex corvo, nisi idealis impressio sit communis.

Cum presupposuisset tale fundamentum quod esse [*fol. 7r*] neccessarium ex omni philosophia tenebatur, sic suam ratiocinationem plato fundabat: omne quod educitur de potentia in actum sive de non esse ad esse a causa sibi simili produci neccesse est. Sed quedam producuntur in esse per motum [ut ignis ex motu lapidum erat quidem in lapide potentia ignis et ex motu est][6] actu fit ignis et multa sunt alia que cognitiones humanas exuperant. propterea propter imaginationem fortassis et non verissimam rationem ab hominibus intelliguntur.

Preterea quedam in actum essendi per putrefactionem eveniunt, ut mus et vermis, fit ut neccessario quod causa sibi simili procreentur. at motus cum igne non convenit, plus enim quam genere differunt, cum ignis substantia sit, motus vero accidens, neque vermis aut mus cum putrefacto conveniunt. relinquitur opus esse causam similem assignare quam ideam esse plato disseruit quam dixit formam quandam perpetuam exemplarque [*fol. 7v*] eternum rerum ut diximus omnium productricem. [Et *Aristoteles in posterioribus* monstram [*sic*] nuncupavit ideas.][7] dixit Albertus magnus in amphora milio plena que diutius undique clausa extiterat mures fuisse repertos, et *Avicenna, in libello de diluviis*, castorem dixit animal fuisse repertum in loco in quem numquam fuerat apportatus nec per se gradi potuisset, ac subiunxit post cathaclismos, id est universales aquarum undationes quas diluvia nominamus, homines natos ex putrefacta tellure principiis naturalibus minime repugnare, quam opinionem miris argu mentationibus exclusit Averrois.

Huius tamen generationis nulla causa verior assignari potest quam vel idea secundum platonem que eiusdem generis cum genito vel eiusdem speciei essentialem similitudinem habet, vel secundum avicennam dabitur colcodrea quam posuit formarum omnium creatorem, ut *VII et VIIII* [*fol. 8r*] *sue methaphisice* apertus asseruit.

Preterea cum nulla formarum substantialium sit complexio, nec sit aliqua primarum qualitatum, nec aliud iuxta mentem omnium philosophorum, petatur iste forme a quo producantur vel a se ipsis vel ab aliquo extrinseco.

Primum negandum est quoniam tunc forma fieret a non faciente; ante generationem quod fit non est et cum non sit agere non potest. Si vero fiat ab aliquo extrinseco, cum omne quod fit fiat a sibi simili, oportet

[6] The passage in brackets is added in the margin of the manuscript.

[7] The passage in brackets is added in the margin of the manuscript.

enim quod fit et quod facit in eandem naturam essentialiter convenire.

Dicenti tale faciens individuum esse speciei vel generis eiusdem reprobatio prompta est, quoniam constat ignem cum lapide vel motu aut genitum vermen cum putrido ex quo nascitur speciem neque genus habere communes nec ab individuo illorum esse progenitos. Stat itaque [*fol. 8v*] substantiam aliquam ab hiis separatam seorsumque existentem effectus taliusmodi procreasse.

Rursus que seminibus generantur nequaquam ab individuo similis generis aut speciei in naturam educuntur. alia quidem glandium species est, alia quercus et fagi.

Preterea palam est in ipso semine animam actu non esse sed potentia tantum, quapropter non apparet consonum dicere virtutem seminis animam in actum produxisse quod vere sensit philosophus, *II° de anima*, dicens, non est id potencia vivens quod abicit animam eaque vacat sed id quod ipsam habet.

Ubi dixit *Averrois*, *commento x*: cum dicit philosophus quod habet potenciam ut vivat, non intendimus per hoc sicut dicimus in eo quod habet habitum et formam quibus potest agere et pati quemadmodum diximus quod semen et fructus habent potentiam ut vivant et quod sanguis menstruus habet potentiam ut sentiat et moveatur quasi dicat seminis [*fol. 9r*] potentia ab actu est valde remota quapropter actu producere formam semen non potest.

Item illa anima vel producetur in actum ab anima generantis puta patris vel ab anima quam seminibus inclusam aiunt. primum non apparet quoniam generantis anima iam cessavit. nec secundo consentiendum est cum si adsit ibi anima solum potentialiter adest, et que sunt in potentia se ipsa in actum deducere non possunt, quoniam actus elicitur ab eo quod actu est, potentia expectat actionem agentis et idem respectu sui actus et potentia esse non potest.

Si quispiam dixerit murem ex putrido genitum a sorice quem mus genuit specie differre et ignem genitum ex collisione durorum cum igne qui ex igne nascitur eiusdem speciei non esse, vehementer errat. Congruens est omnium philosophorum opinio, ea quorum eadem sunt accidentia tam communia quam [*fol. 9v*] propria in idem genus eandemque speciem spetialissimam convenire. Nam mus uterque pernas rodit et caseum et latibulas queritans staturam similem habet et in sonitu oris et totius corporis figura alius ab alio non dissonat. Et ignis uterque calefacit ardet et urit, e combustibili flammas et fumum educit. ipsos ergo specie similes esse concluditur et in specifica essentia minime variari. talis essentia in quam coheunt quod ab individuo fiat a nemine peribetur.

Fit igitur ab idea utrumque formam suscipere et quod in illam participatione consentiant. Ex dictis luce clarius est quod si simile ex suo essentiali simili in naturam producitur, ideas generandarum rerum causas esse formarum per quas hec particularia sunt et degunt.

Insuper platonem voluisse peribent formas substantiales in materiebus inclusas vires actionis non habituras. Nam qualitatum [*fol. 10r*] primarum, scilicet caliditatis frigiditatis humiditatis et siccitatis, actio est et passio et earum que ex ipsis conflantur complexionum, quales melancolicam dicimus ex bili nigra congenitam, colericam ex bili rubea venientem. Item sanguineam rursus et flegmaticam que ex pituita nascitur. nec abest multas esse formas tam substantiales quam accidentales complexionibus que adduntur, ut gravitas terre, levitas igni, et grossities ligno et lapidi atque durities et liquidum esse et molle levum [*sic*] et asperum.

Constat queque natura componuntur actu existentia ut hic bos, hic leo, hec arbos formas suas substantiales includere et ab eis sibi similes particularibus que insunt minime procreari, si quidem active non sunt ut diximus nec a complexionibus vel formis aliis accidentalibus ortum suscipiunt, quoniam substantie ex non substantiis [*fol. 10v*] nasci non possunt, et tamen ut videmus quotidie producuntur, aliter individua non superessent. Sequitur ab ydeis tamquam a re divina atque perpetua eas infallenter nativitatem suscipere. Hec sunt que vir ille divinissimus voluisse testantur. Cui quamvis aristotelem commentaretur themisthius consensisse cognoscitur.

Alexander vero qui primus aristotelem exposuisse creditur et Averrois acutissimus commentator mentem aristotelis interpretantes a platonicis longe dissentiunt. Dixit quidem *Alexander in secunda parte sui tractatus de causis*, non esse necessarium illud simile actu existere a quo sibi simile essentialiter procreatur, quoniam in multis satis est similitudo secundum virtutem, et sic fundamentum platonis conatur diruere.

Spiritus enim qui gignitivus dicitur in se portat virtutem specificam et essentialem eius a quo semen deciditur. sic ex equi [*fol. 11r*] semine equus producitur ceteris ad generationem adiuvantibus que sunt locus in quem genitura diffunditur, ut in animalibus perfectis est femine membrum quod matricem appellant, et causa universalis puta celum quod influat neccesse est, non quidem idea verum Sol et homo generant hominem. Sic in multis terra mater est que disposita per concurrentem influentiam ex semine gignit arbustum quod ex radicibus sibi in specie similis [*sic*] etiam procreatur hac influentia concurrente.

Nec huic opinioni forsan obsistit plato cum dixit potentia parvum adesse patrem in semine nec de potentia passiva loquebatur ut opinor sed activa, quoniam cui accidit esse patrem activam continet potestatem. Sufficit ergo similitudo virtutis et innate potentie.

Rursus alexander duplicem actionem esse disseruit alteram scilicet que motus est, alteram que mutatio. priori solum qualitates [*fol. 11v*] primas formasque complexionales activas esse concessit que mensurata tempore alteratio nominatur. Hac dumtaxat accidentia producuntur que dicuntur communia, quoniam pluribus subiectis specie differentibus inesse possunt ut albedo unioni nivi et parieti. Sed alterationem quandam in instanti fieri vel in tempore quod a nobis est imperceptibile ut de illuminatione credimus minime dubitandum. Mutatione vero substantia numquam in tempore sed solum in instanti producitur ab ea forma substantiali que materia inclusa servatur. non negavit formas substantiales que particularibus innectuntur esse activas, immo concessit.

Palam igitur est quo pacto alexander fundamenta platonis dicebat non suscipere veritatem, scilicet quod simile generetur ab eo quod actu simile est, quoniam sufficit similitudo secundum virtutem et formas substantiales que sunt in materia vires ad agendum habere [*fol. 12r*] voluit, quod ut aiunt plato negaverat. Que cuncta sensit *averroys, methaphisice VII, et commento 30*, dixit quidem, cum consideraverimus quod forme substantiales sunt generantes formas materiales, apparebit quod semina cause sunt dantes formas generatorum ex seminibus per formas quas scilicet acceperunt semina a generantibus. In generatis autem preter semen et his que putredo procreat apparebit quod sunt corpora celestia.

Duo dicit averroys, primum quod forme substantiales in materia existentes sunt active, secundum quod similitudo sufficit que est secundum virtutem, qualis est in sole vel animalium vel plantarum quorum semen causa est ex inclusa in eo similitudine nativitatem suscipiunt quam in illo ab generante impressam esse tradidere, qualem etiam adesse contendunt dum ignis ex igne aut ex lapide gignitur aut unum elementorum ex alio elemento.

In hiis apparet [*fol. 12v*] actio que non est motus sed mutatio, quia forma substantialis producitur quacum non repugnat affectus quos passiones speciei proprias dicunt eodem instanti simul cum forma ipsa produci et generari, quamvis vel accidentia sint vel ad minus modum habeant accidentis.

Quo videamus vim argumentorum Aristotelis in platonem tria sunt disserenda. Primum an aliqua forma substantialis vel accidentalis alicuius operationis principium esse possit. Exinde utrum forma vel compositum generetur. Tertium si vi corporum celestium omni alio efficiente semoto fiant que ex putrefactione nascuntur.

His quidem manifestis palam fortassis erit quid in platonem possit aristotelis obiectio, cuius raciocinationes averroys et alexander in medium quasi irrefragabiles aperuere. *Primo posteriorum, Aristoteles* scriptum reliquit, Cuius [*fol. 13r*] vi agitur illud magis agere. At elementa cum agant primarum qualitatum virtutibus prorsus ille qualitates sunt activiores. Similiter vi suarum complexionum sunt activa.

In formis substantialibus idem est etiam evidens. nulli dubium est intellectum esse perceptivum eorum que intelligibilia sunt, et cum sic intelligere sit quoddam pati, scilicet perfectivum et non corruptivum, ut *III° de anima* clarum est, opus est dare formam agentem eiusdem generis, ut ibidem et *in libello de somno et vigilia* scripsit *Averroys*. Sed cum intellectus sit forma substantialis sive det esse sive operari, sequitur formas substantiales que sunt immerse corporibus esse activas. Preterea cum desinit alteratio agens complexionale suam deserit alterationem, igitur forme substantialis introducitur a forma [*fol. 13v*] substantiali. comperimus sedulo ignem de potentia materie puta de re que comburitur ignem educere. precedens alteratio non attingit formam substantialem. Igitur forma substantialis sibi similis est productiva. fit igitur quod forma substantialis est alicuius operationis principium.

Adhuc vel compositum est causa formalis vel forma compositi sive sit substantialis sive accidentalis. cum compositum, ut scribit *Galienus primo de iuvamentis membrorum circa principium*, sit instrumentum suarum formarum, talis causa esse non potest, quoniam cause instrumentali non attribuitur actio principalis, non enim malleus agit cultellum sed faber.

Accedit etiam quod si eadem actio duobus annectitur, necessarium est quod alteri principaliter alteri secundario tribuatur id est minus principaliter, sed omnis operatio que composito concessa est vel sibi tribuitur ratione materie vel ratione forme. sed cum materie nichil principaliter sit operari propterea [*fol. 14r*] formam esse dixerunt principaliter operantem.

Rursus si compositum esset operationis principium idem secundum quod idem ageret et pateretur et esset simul actu et potentia quod a cunctis philosophis esse posse negatur. Id sequi satis compertum est si summatur pars una que sit minima corporis quod vegetatur, loquor de minima secundum formam id est de parte illa sub qua forma illius speciei non tamen sub minori potest suas operationes perficere. Nam sub minori quanto illa forma nec stare posset neque salvari nemini dubium est quod, sicut totum est in continua alteratione propter suam formam complexionalem, ita et pars illa formalis, sicut scribit *galienus primo de regimine sanitatis* et notatur *in commento illius afforismi*, "*Epylenticorum iuvenilis*" etc., et *Avicenna de complexionibus etatum*. Si quidem in hac operatione forma non esset causa sed compositum, tunc simul tale compositum seipso movet et movetur, [*fol. 14v*] at omne quod movetur neccesse est ab altero moveri, ut probatur *VII phisicorum* sicut ibi dicitur de motu gravis. non igitur seipso motum agit et suscipit sic quidem esset simul in actu et in potentia quod apud philosophos dissonum est.

Preterea pars minima formalis corporis vivi ageret ac pateretur non per diversas partes quarum altera in alteram ageret, quoniam hec pars minima formalis in partes alias formales secari non potest, nam minimo amoto a minimo formali cessat esse formale, aliter non esset minimum. fit itaque quod si tale minimum alteratur, ut posito quod exiccetur, id evenit ab agente complexionali. Et sic patet quod a forma provenit operari.

Bene consideranti[s] hec ratio difficilis apparebit quoniam in formale minimum ab intrinseco provenit alterari sicut et suum totum ab intrinseco suscipit alteritatem. Verum talis alteratio a composito provenire non potest, istud enim compositum quantitativam divisionem non patitur [*fol. 15r*] cum habeat minimam quantitatem sub qua forma illa salvari potest et cum ipsum paciatur eius non est agere, nam simul inesset sibi actio et passio, quapropter apparet quod sua exiccatio fiat a forma videlicet a caliditate.

Eorum autem que nunc dicta sunt in contrarium videtur philosophus volens actiones a singularibus provenire quare non formarum sed compositorum actio peribeatur. dicit etiam *Averrois VII methaphisice, commento 30*, semina generationis activa per formas substantiales seminibus inexistentes, non dicit tamen formas esse generationis activas.

Multi sectatores huius opinionis, cum evadere nequeant quin forme sint active operationum, duo principia posuere, scilicet efficiens et formale. primum ipsum compositum statuerunt, secundum vero formam substantialem et accidentalem quorum positionem multi interpretes ad hoc ipsum retulerunt quod compositum actu agit sed forma virtute.

Tertii dixerunt ipsa composita mediantibus primis qualitatibus illis actionibus [*fol. 15v*] agere quarum terminus per motum haberi[8] potest ac que per mutationem acquiritur, formam substantialem sine actione forme substantialis introduci non posse. Volunt tamen formas accidentales a seipsis semoto quocunque alio actione carere. dicit quidem philosophus, *primo de generatione*, caliditatem a subiecto separatam nec agere nec pati, quoniam actiones sunt suppositorum et formas substantiales immediate non esse activas. firmant ex eo quod dicit *Averrois, VII° methaphisice, commento 30 in fine*, scilicet quod movet materiam immediate neccessario est corpus qualitatem aut formam activam in se habens. Unde *ibidem, commento 27*, intulerat ponere formas separatas propter generationem non oportere, cum non agant verum si agunt id efficiunt corpore interveniente.

[8] The word *non* has here been crossed out in the manuscript.

Ad id probandum si ratiocinationes adduxero non erit inane. Quelibet naturalis actio fit per contactum, *III° et VII° phisicorum*. cum nulla forma sive substantialis sit sive accidentalis preter corpus tangibilis cognoscatur, nullius erit forme [*fol. 16r*] preter corpus agere nec pati. non est etiam dare formam naturalem corpori non coniunctam. Nam illa forma vel esset in materia et sic extaret compositum, aut non et sic ipsam agere non contingit nec pati. Eorum enim que in materia coniunguntur actio est et passio, ut patet *primo phisicorum et de generatione*.

Adhuc unumquodque agit secundum quod est in actu, *II° phisicorum*, ubi dicit philosophus triplicem esse substantiam, scilicet quedam potentia est ut yle id est materia prima, quedam est actus ut forma, quedam ut compositum ex ambabus quod etiam dicitur *II° de anima in principio*.

Amplius si alicuius motus esset forma principium, tunc sola forma et nullum compositum fieret, quia forma et dimensio differunt genere remoto.

Et si dicatur corruptibile ab incorruptibili procreari, ut vermis a celo gignitur quamvis remoto genere differant, respondetur nos loqui de productione que immediata est, celum enim corruptibile gignit mediante [*fol. 16v*] corpore quod est corruptibile, ut *VII° methaphisice, commento 30*, Si forma compositum faceret, id esset composito mediante.

Contra id superius dictum, scilicet nullam qualitatem esse tangibilem que a corpore sit seiuncta, stat experimentum, videmus enim prospicientis acerba comedentem quod dentes obstupescunt quam dubitationem grandem perpulchram et difficilem tanquam ad propositum non facientem in tempus reservemus.

Nullas formas esse activas supra de divinissimi platonis intentione premisimus, quod de primis qualitatibus ipsum non intellexisse a multis ut dicunt compertum est, nam omnes aiunt frigiditatem a caliditate fugari. Si quidem ipse sunt elementorum instrumenta, non ab ipsis sed a primis corporibus principaliter provenit actio. Sic etiam formas substantiales complexionibus ut instrumentis mediantibus agere philosophus non negaret. hinc solvi potest quod primo dicebatur: propter quod unumquodque tale illud magis. Nam [*fol. 17r*] istud secundum *Albertum de causis finalibus* firmam certitudinem habet, si me dignum impensa putem que ad conficiendam domum congruunt et domum digniorem pensavero. Verum si in causis efficientibus id consentiant, dicatur veritate potiri, modo non sint cause instrumentales. at qualitates sunt instrumenta quibus elementa suas imprimunt vires. patet igitur platonem voluisse materiales formas immediate non agere nec pati, quod ut dixi summus aristoteles non negasset.

De intellectu dicitur quoniam substantia non est sed anime potentia sive virtus quapropter is non agit nisi quatenus sibi virtus ab anima imprimatur. Si vero velimus ipsum esse substantialiter animam intellectivam, dicendum est potentiis suis mediantibus esse activam et non aliter. dicunt omnes philosophi corpus esse subiectum anime et ipso velut instrumento uti.

Ad tertium dicamus id quod forme substantialis est subsceptivum ad generationem esse per alterationem predispositum nec alterari prius [*fol. 17v*] desinit quam sit forma introducta nec prius forma introducitur quam desierit alteratio predisponens. quis dubitat quod linea non prius dividetur quam erit divisa si in instanti fiat divisio sicut forme substantialis introductio, et introducitur virtute forme substantialis ut videtur placere philosopho qui contempnit ydeas. hinc albertus dicebat id quod est generare eo quo est. plato tamen vir sanctissimus diceret formas illas particulares que idealem virtutem participant in illo [changed from *nullo*] composito preexistentes quas seminales peripatheticus asserit solum dispositive ad sibi similem formam producendam concurrere. sic enim materia predisposita actionem suscipit ydearum que ultimam formam et specificam introducunt et sua cum participatione congenerant.

Cum divinis participare non negat philosophus cuius fuit intentio ut anima humana cum intelligentiis eternitatem participet, eam enim posuerunt peripathetici in infimo gradu intelligentiarum, argumento [*fol. 18r*] facile respondetur. quoddam enim instrumentum in se claudit agentem causam sicut corpus animalis est instrumentum in se continens animam in omnibus generibus causarum excepta materiali, ut habetur *ii de anima*, huic instrumento totique composito tribuunt operari. Sed instrumentum in se non claudens efficientem ut de malleo exemplum posuimus de se operari nequit. Multe sunt operationes anime corporique communes, sed cum corpus sit in actu per formas, putandum est illas operationes ab anima sive forma principaliter provenire. securi si removeatur acies non est amplius securis, et oculus amoto visu remanet equivoce oculus ac si lapideus esset vel depictus.

Hinc ad aliud habetur responsio, dicitur enim quod ratio principalis ad agendum est forma quamvis per compositum in actum producatur.

Ad quod de minimo respondendum est sermonem nostrum esse de parte formali seorsum accepta sed non de illa que suo toti continuatur, [*fol. 18v*] et non est pars actu sed potentia tantum et a forma totius et a toto motus est susceptura. Si quidem dabitur minimum naturale et formale per se in natura quod subsistat id actu existit de se compositum ex materia et forma et est totum et non pars ut apparet recte consideranti.

Summa dictorum est formas substantiales que in materia sunt per se immediate nec activas esse neque passivas, verum forte non repugnaret eas alterationem perfectivam et non corruptivam suscipere, sicut et visus a coloris specie perfective recipit immutationem.

Forma ergo materialis et substantialis non generat nec producit formam sibi similem materialem nisi modo quo diximus. Ac etiam satis consonat nec ideas immediate suorum effectuum esse productrices ex quo requirunt materiam preparatam ab agente particulari. actus quidem agentium in eo quod patitur et dispositum est recte suscipitur.

De formarum actionibus iam diximus et apparet [*fol. 19r*] partem probleumatis utranque probabilem, sed tamen videndum an forma vel compositum generetur. *Averrois, 3 celi, commento 52 circa finem*, et *primo phisicorum, commentis 62 et 64, ac etiam 68, 58, et 63*, dicit quod fit fieri in subiecto et ex subiecto. Idem sensit *alexander in libro suo de generatione, parte prima, distinctione VIa*, subiectum habet rationem materie, *2° de anima in principio*. Igitur quod fit non est compositum sed forma.

Sed *Averrois, eodem commento 64*, videtur sensisse contrarium ante secundam expositionem quam ibi declarat. Dixit enim quod non esse recedit a generato quod est forma. et *ibidem, in principio 31 commenti et commento 23 et 32*, et *12 methaphisice, commento 12 et 18 circa finem* expresse, et *VII methaphisice, commento 25*, et *primo phisicorum, commento 17*, formis attribuit generari.

Quod etiam ratione sic probatur. Componentia ex natura rei precedunt compositum et principia principiatum et cause suum effectum. Sed materia et forma sunt componentia, principia et [*fol. 19v*] cause, igitur compositum intelliguntur precedere. sed cum materia sit ingenerabilis et incorruptibilis, *primo phisicorum*, sequitur formam ipsam generari.

Preterea vel habetur forma per motum localem, ut multi putant, tenentes formas in materia latitare vel per motum alterationis et tunc forma substantialis esset accidens et in tempore moveretur, aut per generationem et tunc stabit propositum, vel habebitur per simplicem creationem et tunc materia prima non est necessaria in productione formarum.

Amplius post previam alterationem vel acquiritur forma vel compositum. non compositum, quoniam tunc post alterationem fieret aliquid materie quod esse non potest. Nam illud materie quod fieret fieret per generationem, quod non consonat, quoniam tunc eiusdem numero darentur due generationes distincte numero videlicet generatio materie et generatio forme vel compositi. dictum est etiam materiam esse ingenerabilem. vel per [*fol. 20r*] alium motum quod iterum est falsum. Dicit *Averrois, 12 methaphisice, commento 38*, quod materia est de essentia compositi. Quis dubitat formam non haberi nisi per generationem. hec sunt que *alexander* dicit in suo *de generatione*.

Fortassis quis dicet utrumque generari. huic tamen opponitur, quoniam due generationes invicem continuari non possunt, inter generationem forme et generationem compositi saltem secundum naturam tempus medium haberetur vel generationem compositi nulla precederet alteratio. habitibus existentibus in materia cessat alteratio, igitur habita forma substantiali motus quisquis absolvitur. At ubi compositum generaretur tunc id esset ens per accidens omne quidem materie formeque simul existentibus superadditum adesse accidentaliter testantur, et absurdum esset dicere tunc formam per quam compositum in esse constitutum est ad compositi productionem previam esse, quoniam forma existente in [*fol. 20v*] materia nondum cessasset motus et in illo signo quo forma inesset materie compositum non esset constitutum ac generatio quedam assignaretur per quam sicut tunc esset generatio compositi nullius forme fieret acquisitio. Quis dubitat generationem compositi si qua datur ratione nature generationi forme postponi cum forma sit causa compositum vero effectus.

Alexander, a quo dicta positio robur assumpsit, volenti formam compositi differre a forma simplici et post generationem forme materiam esse in potentia ad formam compositi et volenti has duas generationes duabus formis terminari, scilicet forma compositi et forma simplicis, sic satis opponitur. forme quarum conceptus specie differunt ipse etiam specie non sunt eedem sed conceptus forme simplicis et conceptus forme compositi sunt huiusmodi sicut conceptus anime intellective que est forma substantialis hominis et conceptus humanitatis [*fol. 21r*] que est forma compositi. conceptus primus est conceptus simplex non includens materiam. Secundus est conceptus complexus et includens materiam. Et subiunxit quod eodem modo queretur de forma compositi an precedat compositum an sequatur. Similiter omnis species dicit compositum et forma speciei est differentia posterior sicut forma hominis est rationalitas sive intellectus. Alia igitur erit forma speciei a sua differentia constitutiva, si alia erit forma compositi a forma simplici. hoc autem est falsum etiam auctoritate *Averrois*, *VII methaphisice*, *commento 42 circa finem*, volentis speciem esse talem per differentiam ultimam.

Amplius totum differt a toto per formam qua est totum, ergo homo differt ab equo non per intellectum sed per formam qua est tale compositum, et tunc forme substantiales erunt forme in potentia quia non erunt forme ultime, solum enim forme ultime sunt forme in actu ut vult etiam *Averrois ibidem*.

Tandem ab alexandro [*fol. 21v*] concluditur solam formam generari et quod in eam generatio terminatur via mutationis que est generatio. Sed compositum generationem terminat via intentionis nature.

Fundamentum ad istud assumpsit quoniam compositum habet materiam et formam que sunt ipsum essentialiter componentia. principium autem ex natura rei precedit quod ab ipso capit initium ob quam rem forma precedit compositum saltem ex natura rei. Verum cum forma per alterationem nec per motum localem haberi nequeat, cogimur neccessario concedere via generationis acquiri.

Preterea materia non compositi sed forme est susceptiva cum ad ipsam dependeat videtur quod forma fiat et non compositum. materia quidem ratione sue potentie et imperfectionis ad id inclinatur a quo perficienda est, hoc est ipse actus. is forma est. dicitur enim quod forma sit endelecchia, id est actus vel perfectio. Materia est quod perfectionis est appe- [*fol. 22r*] tibile habet adnexam privationem ut dicitur *primo phisicorum*. At perfectibile ad id naturaliter inclinatur quod eius est perfectivum et ad perfectionem non tamen ad quod perfectum est. nam tunc ad seipsam quodammodo dependeret, quoniam perfectum sive compositum in se materiam contineat, cum sit eius altera pars essentialis. At compositum perfectum esse dicitur, perfectio vero forma.

Rursis ait partem precedere totum cum forma sit pars prorsus totum precedit cuius est pars essentialis.

Alexandro satis opponitur dictum *Aristotelis, VII° methaphysice, textu commenti 30*, inquit enim si forma generatur et non compositum, tunc vel materia prima non necessario ad generationem concurreret, quod est contra philosophum, *primo phisicorum, commento 51*, dicentem tunc generationem esse simplicem, et *ibidem, commento 59*, dicit quod materia pars est generati quam sententiam ibidem firmavit *Averroes, commento 60*. Vel ex corpore fieret non corpus, quoniam ex habente [*fol. 22v*] dimensiones fieret eas non habens. Ac etiam sequeretur quod ibi dixit Averroes, scilicet quod si forma generaretur, tunc generatio esset non a materia. Accedit etiam quod si forma sola generationem susciperet, quod tunc eius productio non esset nisi a forma.

Verum istud concedunt platonici, negatur tamen a perypateticis, quoniam tunc immediate esset generatio a causa simili sicut corruptio fit a causa dissimili, saltem in generationibus que non sunt secundum accidens. generationes vero que per se sunt semper fiunt a generante simili, ut vult *Averroes, VII methaphysice, commento 27*. At secundum ipsum sufficit similitudo virtualis. illa vero non est opus quam ydealem platonici posuerunt cum sit quid superfluum in natura ut per ea que dicenda sunt apparebit inferius.

Ad rem tam arduam declarandam puto premittendum fore prioritatem tripliciter dici scilicet diffinitione, tempore et [*fol. 23r*] cognitione, nec abest quin addatur dignitate vel perfectione. Prius quidem diffinitione animal est quam homo vel leo. Et magis universalia minus universalibus sunt sic priora. dicitur hec precessio secundum naturam. diffinitio igitur generis antecedit hoc pacto speciei diffinitionem. similiter et differentie diffinitio quamvis differentia sub habitu quo differentia est minime diffiniatur. De hiis universalibus que sunt magis nota nobis non datur dicta prioritas.

Dubitanti an partes suum totum diffinitione precedant dicendum est, ut habetur *XII° methaphysice, commento 32 circa finem,* quod pars est duplex, scilicet quantitatis et qualitatis. partium quantarum diffinitiones preceduntur a diffinitione totius et a toto. At qualitative que sunt essenciales precedunt diffinitionem totius et ipsum totum quemadmodum totum universale totum particulare diffinitive precedit. Sic totius universalis diffinitio quod quidem totum universale pars est minus universalis ut genus speciei pre- [*fol. 23v*] cedit diffinitionem totius puta compositi. Partes autem secundum quantitatem sunt sicut duo semicirculi in circulo, sed qualitative se habent velut corpus et sensibile in animali.

Constat enim ut compositio secundum Averroim quod partes secundum quantitatem et earum diffinitiones sunt posteriores diffinitione totius cuius sunt partes, et sic etiam diffinitione totum ipsum subsequuntur. diffinitio quidem circuli diffinitione semicirculi prior est. At diffinitio partium secundum qualitatem precedit diffinitionem totius ut corporis et sensibilis diffinitio animalis diffinitionem precedit. Generatione vero partes quantitatis suum totum precedunt, ut intelligit commentator, et sunt eo posteriores diffinitione. Sed qualitative totum diffinitione precedunt quod generatione sequuntur.

Sed istud fortassis absurdum est, quia tunc prius esset socrates vel callias vel aliud individuum quam homo vel animal. Fortassis igitur prestat [*fol. 24r*] dixisse, has qualitativas partes suum totum et generatione et diffinitione precedere. consonat id philosopho dicenti prius embrionem vita plante vixisse, vegetatio pars est universalior, sensibilis vero minus universalis. demum vita intellectiva subsequitur que specifica pars est. saltem constat partes qualitativas suum totum diffinitione precedere.

De priori sicut absolvimus, ita de posteriori dicendum. Contingit prius diffinitione secundum cognitionem nostram esse posterius, ut patet his qui per effectus causas nituntur agnoscere, ut *VII° methaphisice, commento x,* et habetur *prohemio phisicorum,* et *2° de anima.* Materia formam et compositum tempore sive generatione precedit tamen illis est cognitione perfectioneque posterior.

Forma, ut dicamus in calcem, compositum perfectione ac diffinitione sive causalitate precedit. partes enim diffinitionis et ipsarum diffinitiones diffiniti diffinitionem ac etiam ipsum diffinitum conceduntur precedere, ut *VII°* [*fol. 24v*] *methaphisice, commento 31 in fine.* Si quidem forma eius quod est compositum actus est, ut habetur *VII° methaphysice, commentis Vto VII° VIII° et XXVII,* est quidem compositi tota quidditas. sequitur quod illo sit longe perfectior. Etiam dictum, est forma[m] cognitione perfectioneque quod materiam antecedit, id ex eo patet quia materia cognoscitur per analogiam ad formam et per ipsam perficitur. Cumque materia tam per se quam per accidens nequaquam generabilis sit neque corruptibilis, forma vero saltem per accidens desinat esse, videtur quod ad materiam sit posterior. Si motus precedit quod per motum acquiritur prioritate generationis et materia eadem prioritate precedit motum, sequitur quod materia generatione formam precedat. quoniam forma per motum acquiritur, generationem precedit alteratio. Dicitur etiam quod complexio precedit formam via generationis, at forma complexionem via perfectionis et diffinitionis.

Inquit tamen *Averroes*, [*fol. 25r*] *VII° methaphysice, commento 46*, quod qualitas nullo modo precedit substantiam et intellexit de qualitate que est accidens et non de illa que substantialiter qualificat.

Est etiam forma composito generatione posterior quia forma non generatur nisi mediante composito, ut dicit *Averroes, VII° methaphisice, commento 25*. plato id concederet quoniam ydea pressupponit compositum a composito predisponi. et etiam cognitione quoniam forma non cognoscitur nisi per operationem, ut dicit *Averroes in libello de substantia orbis*, sicut cognoscitur materia per transmutationem, ut *VII° methaphysice, commento viiii*. At cum materia sit ens in potentia, compositum vero sit ens actu, ipsam pressupponere via generationis non est absurdum quamvis compositum materia sit perfectius.

Licet de partibus quantitatem habentibus et de hiis que per essentiam suum totum constituunt dictum satis esse videatur, tamen ut de priori posteriorique sermo fiat apertior [*fol. 25v*] loquar iuxta mentem *Averrois, VII° methaphysice, commentis 34 et 36*, dicentis prioritatem esse duplicem, scilicet temporis et generationis, qua dicunt quod formam antevadit materia, quoniam generatio incipit ab imperfecto quod ad perfectum extenditur. Verum diffinitione perfectioneque forme materia postponatur qua ipsum perfectum ad imperfectum dilabitur. primam nominant prioritatem materie ad formam, secundam vero forme ad materiam. hec nomina commentantibus sunt in usu. prioritas forme ad materiam dicitur esse nature, id est eorum que sunt priora secundum naturam et dicuntur priora simpliciter, per que fit demonstratio potissima et essentialis, et ita diffinitio. verum prioritate materie ad formam ea priora dicimus que nobis sunt notiora, quibus nostram id est sensibus subiacentem dicimus esse noticiam. Earum partium que priores sunt secundum naturam diffinitiones precedunt totum cuius [*fol. 26r*] sunt partes, aliter non contingeret fieri demonstrationes quas potissimas vocant. eas quidem ex prioribus et notioribus tanquam ex causis haberi neccesse est et earum pars perfectior est medium, id est diffinitio de quo *primo posteriorum* traditur perfecta noticia. At partium que sunt secundum quantitatem diffinitiones non precedunt totum cuius sunt partes nec per ipsas fieri potest potissima demonstratio.

Premissis autem iis, scilicet quomodo forma precedit materiam et compositum et econverso, pro solutione iam mote dubitationis, scilicet an in formam vel in compositum generatio terminetur, est advertendum quod de tribus substantiis, scilicet materia forma et composito, consideratio duplex habenda est. Quarum altera dicitur naturalis que in se motum quietemque claudit. Alteram [*fol. 26v*] primus philosophus contemplatur tunc consideratio est de substantiis ut in primam et summam substantiam ordinantur. quod fuit de mente illustrissimi platonis, ut rentur dicentes tantum philosophum eas intellexisse ydeas omnium productrices formaliter, quas summus deus in seipso cognoscit et has cognoscendo cuncta producit.

Aiunt etiam improbe philosophum niti contra platonem, quoniam Aristoteles has ydeas vel minimo negasset, vel eas in deo esse si non meditaretur, non solum a theologia qualibet verum ab omni philosophia fuisset alienus. Et istud affirmantes, platonem argumento fuisse dignum autumnant, si vel in orbe signorum vel alibi locasset ydeas.

Ad istud postremo confugiunt nescientes modum alium quo philosophi rationes evitent, ignorantes ut opinor ubi plato ideas locaverit, quod declarans *Macrobius de somnio Scipionis* inquit, Anima cum trahitur ad corpus in hac sua productione silvestrem tumulum hoc est ylem influentem sibi incipit experiri. [*fol. 27r*] hec autem yle est que omne corpus mundi quod ubique cernimus ideis impressa formavit. Et *Servius primo Eneidos* inquit. Quam greci ylem vocant, poete nominant silvam, id est, elementorum congeriem unde cuncta procreantur. non igitur de hiis ideis que sunt in mente dei locutus est plato, nec istud scivit franciscus de Maironis qui sollicitus in Aristotelem nullibi ideas locatas esse disseruit.

Divisio date considerationis est *Averrois, 12 methaphysice, commento quinto et 38,* et *2 phisicorum, VIII methaphysice, commento 4° in principio,* ac etiam *VII methaphysice, commento viiii et 38,* et *2° phisicorum, commento 21.*

Considerare igitur quod forma prioritate diffinitionis vel perfectionis materiam antevadat ad methaphysicum pertinet, est quidem consideratio ab omni motu quieteve abstracta, quorum principium est natura, *2 phisicorum.* Et secundum hanc considerationem forme nulla tribuitur generatio neque corruptio, quoniam sic formam considerare, cum in hac [*fol. 27v*] meditatione quies et motum includantur, est philosophi naturalis. hac naturali contemplatione forma compositum non precedit. non movetur forma nisi per accidens ad motum compositi. Omne quidem quod per se movetur est corpus, ut habetur *VII phisicorum*,[9] corpus est igitur quod movetur, vel materia que in se continet dimensiones. Concludunt itaque prioritate generationis quam vocant prioritatem materie ad formam quod forma compositum antevadat. Volunt ut videor qui alexandri sententiam imitantur in formam quod ipsa generatio terminetur.

Tenentes compositum generari primo sic dicunt, quod de novo habet quidditatem, id de novo generatur, et cum forma nullam habeat de novo quidditatem sed ipsum compositum, apparet ipsum compositum generari.

Item si generatio est mutatio de non esse ad esse et habere esse advenit ratione quidditatis eius quod habet esse, forme autem nulla sit quidditas eo quod ipsa quidditas est prorsus, [*fol. 28r*] videtur compositum et non formam per generationem produci. nam si forme esset forma vel quidditas in infinitum esset abitio et tunc forma fieret ex aliquo in aliquo, ut arguit commentator, *VII methaphysice, commento 26.*

Amplius generatio est mutatio entis in potentia ad ens in actu, quoniam est actus entis, *2° phisicorum.* antecedens constat, quoniam illud quod mutatur in generatione est materia et materia est ens in potentia. dicit *Averroes, VII methaphysice* auctoritate Aristotelis, *commento 25*, quod generans in materia formam facit ex materia aliquid, ergo facit ex materia id est ex ente in potentia formatum, id est ens in actu. forma quidem non fit ex materia, quia tunc ex dimensionato fieret non dimensionatum.

Sed hic obicitur quia homo et sua quidditas sunt idem essentialiter sive compositum et sua quidditas, ut habetur *VII methaphysice, commentis 21 et 23*, sed compositum parte generatur, ergo et sua forma. apparet consequentia quia compositum et [*fol. 28v*] sua quidditas sunt idem, sed quidditas compositi est forma compositi *eodem VII, commentis 5, 7, 8 et 21.*

Quo istud clarius habeatur prorsus est advertendum formam esse duplicem. Nam altera est universalis sicut forma hominis quam humanitatem nominant, altera vero dicitur particularis sive singularis que signum est. sic hominis animam intellectivam esse designant. Prima forma dicitur quidditativa et hanc esse rentur compositi quidditatem que quidditas largo modo forma dicitur. Altera forma partialis simplex que compositi pars potior est et hanc proprie formam vocitant. Quam distinctionem *VII methaphysice, commento 34*, ponit Averroes volens hoc nomen forma de utraque dici, scilicet de universali que est speciei quidditas et de forma materie demonstrate, *VII° methaphysice, commento 52 in principio*, et capitur ex intentione Averrois primam formam universalem per diffinitionem significari [*fol. 29r*] eam que est singularis et de-

[9] In the margin is added: "istud tamen negasset Plato volens animam per se moveri."

monstrata non significat diffinitio. diceret Averroys ut opinor formam compositi quodam modo generari, alteram vero formam non esse quidditatem sed quidditatis partem. Utrum forma totius et forma partis realiter differant vel solum secundum rationem satis dubitatur, quoniam alteram partem ponit Albertus, alteram beatus thomas aperte defendit. Habite rationes utrunque generari satis suadent nec id abicit platonis ideas generationis non esse factrices.

Quis dubitat etiam secundum mentem philosophi, *2° de anima*, compositum esse velut subiectum ac materiam quandam eius que in ipsum introducitur forme nec per prius tale subiectum esse potest quam cum illa componatur nec prius componitur quam [in] illa introducatur. Ex his quidem duobus quomodo fiat unum sicut ex cera et figura nemo dubitat, sed unio est ab idea formam introducente simul et esse dante composito, quapropter [*fol. 29v*] consonum est utrumque generari et ab idea totum in esse constitui. alterum tamen generationem subiective terminat, alterum vero formaliter.

Hactenus que dicta sunt opinionem platonis nequaquam distermінant, nec ad ipsam abiciendam satis sunt que de artibus et scientia obicit philosophus, quibus, quoniam facilis est responsio, non me impediam dare contrarium. difficultatem facit an que fiunt ex putrido a celesti corpore producantur, quoniam si hoc cum agente particulari sufficeret, frustra poneretur ydea. Sed celum huius esse causam roboratur pressupponendo ipsum non contingenter agere sed necessario. Voluntarie quidem ageret et cum intellectu, si contingenter ageret, quoniam nunc sic et nunc non, eadem manente proportione. dicunt id esse non posse, quoniam celi per intellectum, id est intelligentiam ipsum agentem, est assimilari prime cause, quod in doctrina de celo et mundo satis colligitur.

Amplius si celum non [*fol. 30r*] necessario sed contingenter ageret, tunc esset dare aliquam complexionem que ad aliquam formam ultimo prepararet nec solum desineret movere sed a motu sine illa forma desisteret, quod absurdum esse autumnant posito lapidem in motu dispositionem ultimam ad habendam formam ignis acquisivisse et putridum suppremam habitudinem in putredine ad formam vermis. Si corpus celeste non agat necessario, tunc staret ultima dispositio ignis cum forma lapidis et vermis cum forma fimi, quod absonum putant.

Et cum ego ignorem quid tunc celum ab actione sua detineat, quererem an ipsum impediens sit in materia vel in ipso corpore vel in aere medio. non dabitur primum nec tertium, quoniam in eis pressupponitur nichil esse quod vetet, nec secundum, quoniam celestia corpora per se minime permutantur, ut habetur in libello *de substantia orbis*. Et *Avicenna, 3° canonis, fen 16, tractatu quinto, et capitulo primo*, dicit. [*fol. 30v*] Cum evadit materia et vestitur complexione, neccessaria est rectificatio quam tollerant figure et forme et non prohibetur eius propriatio a complemento naturali que pertinet ei ex factore potente. Et *4 canonis, fen prima, tractatu 4, capitulo primo,* dicit. Et causa omnium horum sunt forme ex formis celi facientes esse neccessarium illud cuius eventus ignoratur.

Ferunt Avicennam etiam dixisse *in suo libello de aspectibus* quod luna existente in tercio gradu tauri quilibet morbus tunc incipiens neccessario in omni aspectu tauri erit ille morbus magne mutationis ad salutem. de neccessitate celum agere videtur sensisse *galienus, 3 de creticis.* Et si videantur diverse operationes id est ratione multarum dispositionum sicut apparet de sole in diversis regionibus et diversis temporibus ut habetur *2° methaurorum* ad litteram.

Amplius pressupposito complexiones in instanti non posse corrumpi, quoniam quod acquiritur motu perimitur motu, sed qualitas complexionalis acquiritur motu, igitur non [*fol. 31r*] corrumpitur in instanti. Et sic stante eadem complexione neccessario dabitur forma cuius est illa complexio ut patet intelligenti. si complexio aliqua corrumpatur in instanti, tractandum est alibi. nunc vero dimittendum ne plura et longiora sint ipso opere que adiunguntur.

Ex dictis suasum est ex putrido generata fieri a corpore celesti, nunc vero contrarium inducentes dicamus corpus celeste non esse causam eorum que generantur ex putredine, quoniam tunc sequeretur animal ex putrido generatum ab extra non posse corrumpi. Contra philosophum *septimo methaphysice* dicit omnia particularia eo quod in materia participant apta nata corrumpi, quod sensit *hypocrates in libello de humana natura.* Similiter *galienus suo de elementis.*

At illud sequi sic probant, animalium corruptio vel ab intrinseco provenit vel ab extrinseco. primum contingit ratione complexionis que versus extremum sue latitudinis permutatur. Quam corruptionem [*fol. 31v*] *Galienus, primo de re sanitatis,* ex duobus provenire disseruit, scilicet ex calore intrinseco et aere extrinseco, quod firmavit *Avicenna, primo canonis, capitulo de complexionibus etatum.* Ab extrinseco fieri casu vel gladio vel a similibus causis quas procatharticas, id est primitivas, vocitant. Si quidem corrumpatur forma substantialis ipsius animalis a causa primitiva, sua complexio non permutatur. Sin vero ab intrinseco, sua permutatio incipit a complexione. Stantes in proposito dicamus: si corpus celeste generatorum ex putrefactione causa sit, generata sic corrumpi non posse. ponamus corpus taliter genitum quod sit scorpius qui a causa extrinseca corruptionem suscipiat, videlicet vel fuste vel ferro vel lapide, tunc queratur an eodem instanti corruptionis forme corrumpitur etiam sua complexio que preparabat ad formam scorpionis vel non. in eodem instanti non conceditur complexionis corruptio.

Nam cum alteratio sit motus in tempore, ut superius pressupponitum [*fol. 32r*] est, et complexio generetur et corrumpatur per alterationem, sequitur ipsam, in instanti quo corrumpitur forma, corrumpi non posse, quam ob rem amota substantiali forma supererit complexio que preparabat ad formam scorpionis, saltem pro aliquo instanti. Sed cum corpus celeste agat formas preparatis materiebus, neccessario fit post amotionem forme substantialis scorpionis eodem vel sequenti instanti per celeste corpus forma scorpionis in eandem materiam reducetur, quoniam eadem remansit complexio que preparabat ad formam.

Dubitationem non parvam hec ratio facit quam duobus modis conantur effugere, primo quod complexio animalis consideretur ut sequitur mixtionem, que complexio cum precedat anime vires, non abest quin forma corrupta supersit. Secundo ut ipsa complexio terminatur, id est ad determinatam formam determinatam habet proportionem, que ut sic formam subsequitur vel concomitatur, [*fol. 32v*] ut videtur mens *Avicenne, 2° canonis, capitulo executivo,* dicentis complexionem advenire post virtutem, que complexio ut sic forma simul abicitur, et sic scorpionis substantiali forma deperdita eodem instanti complexio ut ad eam formam limitata corrumpitur. ea propter [propterea?] corpus celeste eam regenerare non potest, licet ipsa eadem non tamen limitata sed ut sequitur mixtionem remaneat.

Hec fuga nullum habet vigorem. Cum enim corpus celeste formam substantialem in materiam ducit ob novam complexionem que in putrefactione acquiritur, nullum dubium quod illa complexio preparans ad determinatam formam nondum est determinata per formam, cum forma nondum adsit. quemadmodum igitur celeste corpus formam induit propter complexionem mixtionis acquisitam ex putrefactione, sic post corruptionem illius forme remanente illa complexione formam regenerabit.

Preterea per solam complexionem acquisitam ex putre- [*fol. 33r*] factione forma generatur a corpore superceleste, ita quod materiam lineat et ut instrumentum preparat secundum quod exigit dicta complexio ex putrefactione producta, donec illam materiam induat forma substantiali. multo magis induet formam illa complexione priori manente maxime stantibus lineationibus organizatione et compositionibus eisdem que preerant et ad illam formam requirebantur.

Quamvis ergo scorpius occidatur tamen superstantibus predictis etiam remanebit mixtionis complexio. Satis igitur haberi potest quod obicitur, scilicet quamvis remaneat complexio eadem tamen corrupta forma proportio illa corrumpitur que aderat inter formam et complexionem. est vile quoniam illa proportio sequitur formam et nullatenus preparabat ad formam nam complexio ut preparans acquiritur in mixtione tali. Complexio hec tamen non solum est prima complexio sicut calidi frigidi sicci et [*fol. 33v*] humidi simplicium vel compositorum corporum, sed est secunda et tertia sicut eas investigat *Averrois*, *Vto colliget*, *capitulo 39*.

Datur etiam altera fuga quod complexio que acquiritur motu potest corrumpi in instanti nam sicut stat aliquam qualitatem de tercia specie qualitatis subito et in non tempore introduci, sicut dicit *Averrois*, *Vto phisicorum*, *commento Vto*, ita stat etiam deperdi. Sed de hoc ut dixi magna est dubitatio.

Eorum que supradiximus contrarium ponit *Averroys*, *VII° methaphysice*, *commento 30*, volens in hiis que non habent causas generantes similes corpora celestia esse causas productivas.

Dicendum ad dubitationem secundum perypatheticos corpora celestia causas esse illorum que fiunt ex putrido. Quod probasse credunt, quoniam si hoc non esset, tunc ponerentur cause separate quas dari putant esse dissonum in natura. id probant quoniam si corpora celestia formas illas non influunt, nec ipsarum cause sunt individua specierum, tunc necessario dabuntur [*fol. 34r*] cause separate.

Tunc ad rationem que difficilis videbatur. Complexio preparans ad formam substantialem non corrumpitur in instanti, igitur illud animal cuius talis complexio preparat ad formam est incorruptibile. Stat consequentia quoniam virtus superior agit ex neccessitate. Dicitur quod qualitas que acquiritur motu potest deperdi in instanti et que suscipitur in instanti potest motu desinere. Et consequenter quod non repugnat alterationem esse instantaneam ut aliqualiter nunc dicetur.

Quando dicitur, si illud non esset, idee neccessario ponerentur, concedatur ac etiam omne illud ab ideis fieri et procreari. propter hoc nequaquam excluduntur idee que sint cause rerum que procreantur. Scimus enim quod corpus celeste ut corpus est neque activum esse neque passivum, quoniam quantitati nichil est contrarium, ut placet *Aristoteli in predicamento de quantitate*. Verum, si capiatur ut est tale corpus ut ab instrumento sue proveniunt operationes, est tamen [*fol. 34v*] instrumentum intelligentiarum que movent etiam ideis subserviens. Ex quo forma, que generatur vel in esse producitur, conditionum quas planete influunt est susceptiva, quamvis celum agat immediate non tamen principalius, quoniam tunc omne instrumentum esset maioris virtutis quam id cuius est instrumentum.

An alterationem contingat fieri in instanti multis rationibus suaderi potest. Substantia sensibilis potest in instanti corrumpi, ut *methaphysice VII°*, quod nemo negat. sed cum accidentis esse sit in esse sicut omnium sententia dictat, prorsus amoto subiecto ipsum neccessario corrumpetur.

Preterea luce clarius est affectus proprios cum sua forma desinere sed constat illam subito deperdi. igitur et accidens proprium quod secum connascitur. Insanus esset si quis opinaretur risibilitatem superesse rationali disiecto.

Rursus cum incipit calefactio, vel in primo mutato esse quicquam acquiritur aut nichil. Si quidem aliquid, vel illud erit caliditas vel [*fol. 35r*] dispositio. Si caliditas, igitur caliditas habebitur in instanti, quoniam mutata esse in motu sunt velut instantia in tempore. Si dicitur quod sit dispositio, tunc perscrutemur de 2° instanti quod si caliditas acquiritur stat propositum. si nichil, transeamus ad tertium instans et hoc modo si procedatur per totum motum in mutatis esse usque ad finem motus. quo fit quod vel complexio vel qualitas habebitur in instanti, vel nichil quod videtur absurdum, quoniam nemo dicet quod in ultimo mutato esse qualitas non sit impressa subiecto.

Sed adducatur ratio facta superius, videlicet, si alteratio nulla fieret in instanti, tunc animal putrefactione productum per causam primitivam non posset corrumpi. Si unumquodque producitur cuius cause productionis sunt in actu, tunc vero cum illud animal corrumpitur a causa extrinseca, cause sue generationis actu sunt, quia celum et complexio. ergo instanti eodem quo tale animal esse desinit regeneratur. maior istius rationis est nota [*fol. 35v*] sicut si posito igne cum stupa convenienter approximatis. minor est clara, viso quod cause vel causarum dispositiones ad omnem effectum neccessarie sunt tres sine quibus actio nulla conficitur et quibus adductis actio est neccessaria, sicut scribit *avicenna*, *primo canonis*, *doctrina 2a de causis*, *primo capitulo*, et *Averrois*, *4 colliget*, *capitulo de distinctione temporum morbi*. prima causa dicitur agentis fortitudo. Secunda dicitur aptitudo et preparatio pacientis. Tertia est possibilitas actionis per temporis durationem. Verum cum hec tres cause sint in actu eodem instanti quo vermis corrumpitur per causam procatharticam, quoniam adest propositum agens, scilicet celum et aptitudo passi, quoniam alteratio complexionis non fit instantanea et forma vermis corrumpitur, in instanti [10] quo vermis formam amisit vermis stat sub propria complexione, sed corpus celeste non quiescit stante preparata materia [*fol. 36r*] igitur etc. Ista pro nunc satis sint. res hec indiget longiori vestigatione quam deo dante alibi non effugiam.

Per ea que dicta sunt minime probatum est ideas non esse ponendas. non loquor de hiis quas volunt esse in mente divina, sed si citra ponantur sicut credo platonem contemplatissimum intellexisse. nunc de isto queratur maiori cum diligentia modo que brevissimo. Maius inconveniens per perypatheticos adductum est, quoniam si ponantur idee rerum quidditates, tunc res et rerum quidditates abinvicem separate longius inter se

[10] In the margin is added, "tunc eo instanti."

distarent. Accepit plato ydeam pro ratione diffinitiva ut refert Franciscus de Maironis quoniam diffinitio significat rei quidditatem.

Quamobrem nunc sciscitandum est, an quidditas quam significat diffinitio, que dicitur specifica quidditas, sit pars substantie sensibilis, id est quidditas rei demonstrate, id est ipsius compositi in esse producti. Quod ut [*fol. 36v*] clarum esse videatur, compositum dicamus dupliciter considerari, uno modo ut constat ex materia et forma demonstratis que duo sunt principia individui, altero modo ut constat ex illis prout sunt speciei principia. quo pacto non considerantur a naturali sed a primo philosopho, sicut placet beato thome de aquino sumenti fundamentum ut opinor ab *Averroi*, *VII° methaphysice*, *commento VIIII°*, dicente considerationem methaphysice non esse de causato ex materia et forma sed de causis, et intelligitur de causis non demonstratis, id est non limitatis ad rem aliquam unam particularem. Unde colligitur quod quidditates in eadem specie sunt due, scilicet quidditas primi compositi et quidditas secundi, et quod quidditas prima est quidditas demonstrata sicut sua principia demonstrantur. Verum secunda quidditas est quidditas universalis quam ex prima obiective cognoscimus. Adducatur nunc hec ratio, si compositio ex materia [*fol. 37r*] et forma demonstratis aliquid composito superaddat essentialiter et non per accidens, tunc compositum demonstratum, id est ipsum individuum, habet aliquam quidditatem. dicit quidem philosophus, *VII° methaphysice*, et commentator, *commento 59*, quod in compositis simpliciter id est essentialiter quidditas est quid additum componentibus. At istud additum accidens non est, nam tunc esset ut navalis quedam compago. fit ut sit substantialis, hec tamen quidditas non est quidditas quam diffinitio manifestat cum sit incorruptibilis. hec vero deperditur. illa substantie sensibilis non est pars. ista vero sic, ergo, etc.

De illa incorruptibili nunc querendum est quam plato posuit a singularibus separatam. Nec obstat quod *septimo methaphysice*, *commento 36*, dixit Averrois, scilicet animalis quidditatem sine carnibus et ossibus nequaquam intelligi. Ac *ibidem* dicit, *commentis 33 et 38*, ut Aristotelis littera sonat, quidditates quarum forme sunt in materia determinata materiam in seipsis continere, [*fol. 37v*] quapropter hec quidditates non intelligi possunt absque materia terminata, quibus dictis inferre nititur eadem esse principia utriusque quidditatis.

At responsio prompta est, si dicamus materiam esse duplicem, alteram scilicet sensibilem, alteram intelligibilem, ut ipse *Averroys*, *VII° methaphysice*, *commento 33 in fine et commento 38*, in solutione diffinitionum mathematicarum testatus est.

Dicendum igitur quidditatem speciei compositam esse ex forma universali et materia intelligibili, non sicut mathematica sed sicut naturalia abstracta. dicitur intelligibilis materia que per individuancia [or, *individuaticia*] non concluditur et ab eccaitatibus est semota, ut scotistarum utar vocabulo. aut cum illis non est comprehensio. forma vero universalis quolibet secluso individuo speciei se alligat.

Hec nunc satis neccessaria iam apparent. Cum dicit aristoteles quidditatem animalis sine propria materia nequaquam intelligi, si eam voluisset esse sensibilem, tunc quidditates quas significat [*fol. 38r*] diffinitio corruptibiles esse oportet, quapropter scientia non esset eterna, quod ipse negat, *VII° methaphysice, textu commenti 52*. At illud sequi satis declaratur, quoniam talis materia ob sibi adnexam privationem est causa maleficii, *primo phisicorum*, id est corruptionis. ideo diffinitiones de rebus sensibilibus que particulares sunt a philosophis non tribuuntur cum ipsarum sit generari et corrumpi propter materiam, ut ibi satis ostenditur. Materia ergo quam includunt diffinitive quidditates est solum intelligibilis et intellectu forme.

Multi dixerunt Aristotelem illud dixisse comparando naturalium quidditates ad mathematicas, ut hominis quidditatem ad eam quam circuli exprimunt geometra [*sic*] nam circuli quidditas materiam non includit. Et fortassis istud platonici non inficiarentur ponentes ideam esse quidditatem et formam specifiam a singularibus segregatam [nec dubitarunt mathematica esse rerum principia ut unum duo tres quod quomodo intellexerint alias dicendum] [11] Horum intellectus stare non potest. Nam si quidditas [*fol. 38v*] speciei ut hominis materiam quidditative non includat, tunc homo ab intelligentia specie non differret per hominis diffinitionem qua dicimus ipsum esse animal rationale. Consequentia deducitur quoniam si quidditas hominis nullam includit materiam, puta corpus hominis, tunc eius quidditas erit sola forma ipsius vel compositum. non compositum, cum ipsum includit materiam. Si autem hominis quidditas est sola forma, scilicet intellectus vel ratio, tunc quidditas hominis est quidditas intelligentie separate. Sed quidditas est idem cum diffinitione, igitur diffinicio hominis et diffinicio intellectus separati erunt hedem. Sed quorum diffiniciones sunt hedem illa sunt eadem.

Amplius si quidditas speciei materiam non includat, tunc compositum non habebit pro parte materiam. consequens est falsum, quoniam compositum non fit ex duobus actu existentibus, *VII° methaphysice, commento 47*, ergo materialis substantia [*fol. 39r*] quod materiam includat tamquam partem alteram non dubitetur. antecedens est notum, quoniam quidditas et id cuius est quidditas sunt idem essentialiter et non separabiliter, *VII° methaphysice, commento 21*. Si quidem intelligatur quidditas seclusa materia, simili pacto compositum cuius est quidditas intelligemus,

[11] The words in parentheses are inserted in the margin.

ut si humanitas non includit materiam et intelligitur ea semota, simili modo cognoscemus et hominem.

Preterea quidditas compositi vel est forma compositi vel materia vel compositum vel aliquid existens in composito additum principiis componentibus. Sed non est materia, quoniam quidditas eius est perfectio cuius est quidditas, materia perfectio non est, immo prestat imperfectionem sicut disputantes, *5 phisicorum*, affirmant. neque forma que materie coniungitur, quoniam est forma demonstrata et pars substantie sensibilis. Si quis dicat ipsam esse compositum aperte delirat.

Fit igitur ut sit aliquid additum quod accidens esse negetur, [*fol. 39v*] quoniam tunc compositum esset quid per accidens et tamen est substancia quare sequitur unum ipsum per se. Verum quodcumque unum ex duobus construitur illa duo ab ipso includuntur.

Hinc apparet ipsam quidditatem materiam formamve in se connectere.

prelibati viri suam opinionem in *avicenna* fundabant, quoniam *VI naturalium, capitulo 3° circa finem*, dicit, aliquis creatus perfectus subito cessantibus ab eo omnibus sensibus affirmabit esse sue essencie, non tamen affirmabit esse suarum partium quecumque sint partes intrinsece vel extrinsece. Et ex hoc visum est istis quidditatem materiam non clausisse, quoniam homo affirmat suum esse seclusa materia ut arguatur sic. Quod affirmatur differt ab eo quod non affirmatur, sed in homine affirmatur esse et non affirmatur sua materia, igitur esse hominis et materia differunt et unum non includit aliud in [*fol. 40r*] conceptu. prefatam sententiam *ibidem* repetit *Avicenna, tractatu quinto, capitulo VII°.*

Non intelligentes Avicennam ut opinor se male fundarunt. illa quidem non fuit mens Avicenne. Sed volens probare actum intelligendi ut per operationes nos duceret ad animam cognoscendam non probat ibi esse hominis sed esse sue anime intellective. Stante ergo casu dicendum quod tunc anima affirmabit se esse per actum quo intelligit seipsam qui est actus reflexionis, non tamen affirmabit absque suis membris se esse hominem.

Hec iam dicta palam fient si contemplemur an speciei quidditas sit pars substantie sensibilis, id est quidditatis compositi demonstrati. hec ab illa qua queritur an universale sit pars substancie sensibilis diversa questio est, quoniam per quidditatem intelligitur res que prime intentioni subiecta est. In animali prima intentio dicitur [*fol. 40v*] quod sit substantia animata sensitiva de se. res igitur que habetur per hunc actum intelligendi quidditas appellatur. per universale rem intelligimus que subicitur intentioni secunde. postea quidem intellectus habuit primam intentionem de quidditate generis aut speciei, statim secundo format in quidditate intentionem aliam que accipitur ab ipsa quidditate seu a proprietate reperta in illa quidditate, que est quedam convenientia, puta quod generis quidditas est communis quidditatibus differentibus secundum speciem, et quod quidditas speciei est communis quidditatibus singularibus differentibus secundum numerum. Demum secundum logicos statim in hac quidditate format quomodo illa de suis inferioribus predicantur, et hec tertia intentio dicitur tale predicabile quod genus vel species nominatur. Secundum has intentiones accipimus quidditates subiectas intentionibus. prime intentionis [*fol. 41r*] quidditatem manifestat diffinitio sive quod quid est per essenciam. Secunde intentionis quidditas est universale. Tertie vero intentionis predicabile.

Verum prime intentionis quidditas est essentialis. Alie quidditates velut accidentia quedam capiuntur. Et ideo in predicatione essentialis predicati includitur prima intentio essentialiter, verbi gratia cum dicitur Socrates est homo, in illo predicato homo includitur diffinicio quoniam predicatur in quantum est animal rationale. propterea sequitur est homo ergo est animal rationale. Sed in hoc predicato non includitur secunda nec tercia intentio quoniam minime sequitur ergo est universale vel predicabile. Et sic apparet quod quidditas speciei est pars substantie sensibilis.

Quecunque dicta sunt non adversantur platoni, quoniam quemadmodum lumen unum si ponatur in corona quoslibet in se manens seipsum diffundens adstantes illuminat et [*fol. 41v*] est unum in se ab omnibus participatum, sic idea est una in se, participata tamen ab omnibus quorum est idea, et sicuti illa sunt illuminata sic illa omnia sunt formata. et est lumen unum et idem in omnibus per participationem. Verum ut est in hoc non est in illo, que diversitas non est ratione luminis, sed contingit ob diversitatem recipientium puta ratione compositi demonstrati et per diversitatem que habetur merito individuantium.

Et ad argumentum quando ex illis duobus resultat una quidditas quam oportet esse compositam eo quod ex componentibus constat, dicitur quod ex illis nulla resultat quidditas, immo sic composita unam habent quidditatem illa componentia que connectit et salvat et est ut supradixi tanquam vis centri dans esse omnibus lineis que in circunferentiam contrahuntur, quantuncunque ad diversas partes circuli sint producte a centro tamen habent quidquid essentialiter [*fol. 42r*] habent, quod diversificatur non ratione centri sed ratione linee habentis aliud et aliud esse protractum ad partem istam circuli et non ad illam.

Si queratur an materia sit de quidditate compositi, dicitur quod sic quantum ad existentiam suam essentialem, non quantum ad essentiam formalem per quam istud est in sua specie determinatum. Nam determinatio est a forma, multiplicatio vero a materia, dico de multiplicatione secundum numerum. Ex quo dici potest quod quidditas illa est una non a pluribus abstracta sed in plura essentialiter diffusa.

Quod videtur ab *Avicenna, VI naturalium, tractatu 2°, capitulo 2°*, qui voluit esse essentie differre ab esse existentie, intelligens per esse essentie ipsam quidditatem simpliciter et per esse existentie ipsam quidditatem productam et limitatam que quoniam habetur ut hec et in re demonstrata in esse particulari et [*fol. 42v*] corruptibili propterea est corruptibilis non simpliciter sed secundum esse participatum.

At contra predicta non erit inane si colligantur argumenta philosophi, que *VII methaphysice* colliguntur, *commento 44*. Substantia rei sensibilis est substantia demonstrata propria rei sensibilis, sed quidditas est substantia communis, ergo quidditas non est substantia propria. Concedatur maior istius rationis, illud tamen est verum cum substantia sensibilis iam existit, id est habet esse existentie in rerum natura dearticulatum. Minor est vera si illa substantia simpliciter consideretur et non contracta nec participata quamvis sit contrahibilis et apta participari.

Sed si postea sumatur argumentatio qua dicitur quod substantia est una numeraliter, si ergo esset substantia multorum, tunc illa omnia essent eadem numero. Dicatur quod illa substantia est una numero essentie sed non numero existentie, de qua distinctione meminit [*fol. 43r*] *Albertus in suis universalibus* autoritate boetii, non ergo sequitur omnes substantias que ideam participant easdem esse numero materie quomodo individua inter se differunt.

Alia est ratio sua, *ibidem, commento 45*. Quidditas est substantia que dicitur de pluribus. Sed substantia sensibilis non dicitur de pluribus, igitur quidditas non est substantia rei sensibilis.

Respondetur quidditatem dici de pluribus uno modo, quoniam ab ipsa sumitur universale et exinde genera et species que sunt predicabilia, et isto modo dicitur de pluribus, id est ab ipsa sumitur predicabile cuius est dici sive predicari. alio modo, quoniam quidditatem significat diffinitio et ista nulli particulari convenit sed generi vel speciei que sub se plura continent. alio modo, quod illud dici est essentiale id est essentialiter et ratione participationis pluribus convenit. vel dicas ut habetur *ibidem, commento 46*, quod [*fol. 43v*] universale est dispositio dispositionum substantie sensibilis secundum quod est abstracta.

Et quando dicit *ibidem, commento 47*, quod si quidditas est substantia individui, tunc in individuo essent due forme substantiales.

Unomodo respondeatur negando illud sequi, quoniam est una et eadem substantia sed dearticulata et limitata nisi istud est inconveniens secundum diversam considerationem. Nam alio modo dicitur quidditas simpliciter sumpta puta hominis vel alius speciei que dicitur quidditas specifica et est per se ens in esse essentie immo est ipse homo. Et alio modo ut talis essentia in individuo clausa manet, quoniam tunc est ut tale compositum continet in se materiam et alia inidividuantia.

In commento 48, sic arguit, Vel ex substantia que est quidditas et substantia sensibili fit unum per se aut unum per accidens. aliter substantia que est quidditas non esset [*fol. 44r*] substantia rei sensibilis. sed non fit unum per accidens, quoniam tunc humanitas non esset substantialis ipsis individuis puta Socrati vel Ciceroni. Si vero fiat unum per se, tunc aut quidditas est substantia in actu vel in potentia. non in potentia, quia tunc esset materia. Si in actu, tunc ex duobus existentibus in actu fieret unum in actu, quia substantia sensibilis est unum in actu.

Dicitur quod fit unum per se et quod quidditas non est substantia in actu sed quod est actus et forma. Et negetur quod ex duobus existentibus in actu fieret unum in actu. Et dicatur quod ex isto actu et materia predisposita fit unum in actu, et hoc constitutum est substantia sensibilis, ita quod quidditas non advenit substantie sensibili puta quod substantia sensibilis sit aliquid in actu subsistens per aliquam ultimam formam individuum speciei perficientem. Verum talis est unione quidditatis contracte ad materiam predispositam [*fol. 44v*] Compositum istud tamen dissolvitur et desinit esse quidditate illa nequaquam corrupta, sed solum propter dissolvantia desinit operari, quoniam instrumentum ratione periodus provenientis ex compos[it]ione cum materia occasionata, qualis non est materia celi, semper versus corruptionem intenditur.

Nequaquam hoc dictum contrarium est philosopho, si Averrois de intellectu suam velit positionem defendere, scilicet quod sit unicus ingenerabilis et incorruptibilis ab omnibus individuis participatus semper tamen idem manens.

Franciscus de Maironis vir accutissimus et in Aristotelem infestissimus quasi velit se Aristoteli preferre dicta philosophi in platonem ad quatuor colligavit.

Primum est singularitas, scilicet Aristotelem dixisse de mente platonis ideam esse unum singulare individuum quod pluribus esset commune, nequaquam attendens species specialissimas [*fol. 45r*] in locis pluribus individua nominasse philosophum ad genus habentem analogiam. Si quidem dicit ideam esse individuum quod commune pluribus est, prorsus de specie et non de singulari significato philosophus loquebatur, nec fuit tam parve mentis Aristoteles ut non intelligeret quid importetur per singulare sic prolatum dumtaxat et per singulare quod pluribus esset commune. Sciebat enim philosophus, si non erat ignorationis plenus, quod singulare sibi ipsi et non pluribus convenit, et idem de seipso predicari potest, de pluribus autem non, quoniam, ut dicit philosophus *in primo posteriorum*, infra se nichil habet de quo predicetur, quod postea *porphirius in libro predicabilium* etiam confirmavit. Quod franciscus dicit a philosopho dictum non repperi verum divertenti animum non esset absonum illud inferre.

Secundum quod idea esset quid actu existens quod sit actus et forma non est contra platonem [*fol. 45v*] nec quod sit actu existens quando participata est et individuo suum esse prestabat. Sed dubium est an separata seorsum ab individuis existens habeat esse per se existens et particulare.

Verum plato intelligens per actum existentie suum esse per se quo nulli alteri est coniuncta per se ipsam existentem minime negavisset. non tamen concessisset eam ut naturale compositum ex materia formaque existere, quoniam tunc attribuisset illi corruptionem cuius predicabat eternitatem. Cum enim aristoteles sic intelligentiarum esse concesserit, prorsus in vanum franciscus de Maironis ob hoc nititur arguisse philosophum, qui quamvis ut opinor mentem philosophi cognovisset, tamen ut vir novi ingenii aliquando tamen perversi tanto philosopho contrarius esse voluerit.

Tertium quod idea esset localiter separata, et deum esse in oriente testantur philosophi et sic habere sedem constat, quoniam ad aquilonem [*fol. 46r*] malus angelus sibi sedem statuerat, quis dubitat alium esse dei locum, alium creature et intelligentiis orbes varios assignamus. Idea igitur in se non contracta non est in eodem loco cum individuis designatis, nullo ergo loco circumscribitur quamvis diffinitive sibi locum assignemus. Non fecit Aristoteles tam parvi platonem.

Quartum quod tempore mensuraretur idea quod si ex dictis platonis inferri potuisset fortassis non admirarer, verum legens que Aristotelis sunt nec ab ipso nec ab Averroi dictum invenio.

Petenti qua in re putavit philosophus platonem errasse dico quoniam si [ei?] verius apparebat et sufficientissimum esse ad continuam rerum successionem naturam in seminibus generationem posuisse concurrentem celorum influxu que generatio est univoca. Et disposita materia celeste corpus sua virtute concurrere ad generationem equivocam. [*fol. 46v*] propterea putavit ideas esse superfluas et superfluum aborret natura decet philosophos dicere causas effectibus equatas. quis dubitat quod a deo cuncta procedunt et in omnia influit et quod omnium est causa. sed longinquiora querimus quam optemus.

Ideo Macrobius, ut supra scriptum est, nequaquam fortassis errat nec etiam Servius ut comperio compagem elementorum quam ylem nominant ideis refertissimam posuerunt de intentione platonis in qua materia omnium formarum est origo. aliter non videtur quomodo forme de materie potentia educantur excepta forma humana quam volunt per creationem infundi. Quod in mente divina sint idee rerum omnium non dubitavit philosophus neque de hiis intellexit plato ut opinor, sed quod essent virtutes sive forme citra deum quarum vi hec inferiora in actu successivo salvantur.

Multi tamen, ut *Eusebius in libro de preparatione evangelica* [*fol. 47r*] dicit, ideas putaverunt esse virtutes celorum diffusas ad intelligentias a quibus orbes moventur. Nam he duo prospiciunt, scilicet ut suo factori similentur et ut hec inferiora salvantur [*sic*] motu continuo. [Visus est tamen *Averois, XII° methaphysice*, hanc sententiam tenens velle assentiri platoni, dixit enim proportiones et virtutes que fiunt in elementis a motibus solis et stellarum et aliorum sunt he quas plato reputavit esse formas et eas intendit.] [12]

Donato azarolo habeo gratias ingentes, laurenti clarissime, qui causa fuit ne hos paucos dies in vanum [13] pertransierim nec tempus in vanum triverim. Sed longe ingentiores tibi, si quidem has lucubrationes te intellexero benignius suscepisse, cui quantum sim obnoxius in maioribus demonstrabo.

Explicit.

[12] The words in brackets are a marginal addition.

[13] A *non* is inserted between the lines but apparently by some later hand.

APPENDIX 20

TABLE OF CORRESPONDENCES BETWEEN THE TWO TEXTS

VATIC. LAT. 3897, FOLS.	LAUR. PLUT. 82, COD. 22, FOLS.	NATURE OF THE CORRESPONDING PASSAGES
79r	6r–7r, 9v–10r	Plato's three basic arguments.
79r, col. 2	2r	Avicenna's "colcodrea."
79r, col. 2	7v	Avicenna, Metaphysics, VII–VIII, cited.
79v	7v	Spontaneous generation of a beaver.
79v	7v	Cites Avicenna, de diluviis, that men might be spontaneously generated after a universal deluge.
79v	9r–v	Mice generated from putrefaction are of the same species as other mice.
79v, col. 2	29v–30r	Argument against the stars acting contingently. Cites Avicenna, 3 Canon, fen 16, tract. 5, "Cum evadit materia . . ."
80r	30v	Cites Avicenna, 4 Canon, fen 1, tract. 4, cap. 1, "Et cause horum omnium . . ."
80r	30v–31r	Complexional forms not made or corrupted in an instant.
80r	31v	Both cite Avicenna, 1 Canon, cap. "de complexione," but not for the same detail.
80r	31r–32r	Were things generated from putrefaction by influence of the stars, they would be incorruptible *ab extrinseco;* example of the scorpion.
80r, col. 2	32r–35r	Answers the objection, "quod complexio preparans ad formam substantialem corrumpitur in instanti quantum ad proportionem quam habet ad illam formam."
80v, col. 2	12r	Averroes, VII Metaphysis, comment. 30, cited.
		Argument of Averroes that substantial forms are active, and virtual similitude sufficient.
81r	10v	Alexander, de causis, pars 2, cited.
81r–v	19r–22r	Whether form or composite is principally generated. Both the citations and the wording are identical in a number of cases and passages, and the order of treatment is roughly the same.
81v, col. 2	22r–v	Second argument, that form is not generated principally, with accompanying citations.
81v, col. 2	22v	Third argument, that then form would have to be generated from form.
81v, col. 2	27v–28r	Fourth argument, that a new generation has *quidditas.*
82r	28r	Fifth argument, "forma non est in actu."
82r	28r–v	Sixth argument, "compositum et sua quidditas sunt idem essentialiter."

TABLE OF CORRESPONDENCES BETWEEN THE TWO TEXTS (*Cont.*)

Vatic. Lat. 3897, Fols.	Laur. Plut. 82, cod. 22, Fols.	Nature of the Corresponding Passages
82r		Arguments 7 to 13 of the Vatican MS are omitted in the Laurentian, which proceeds immediately as follows:
82r, col. 2	28v	Form is duplex.
82v	28v	Averroes, VII Metaphysics, comment. 52, cited.
82v, col. 2, –83r	40r–v	Prime et secunde intentionis quidditates.
83r	41r	The foregoing illustrated by Sors or Socrates.
83r	42r	Avicenna, VI Naturalium, tract. 2, cap. 2, cited concerning *esse essentie* and *esse existentie.*
84r	42v	Aristotle, VII Metaphysics, comment. 44, cited: "Substantia rei sensibilis est substantia demonstrata . . ."
84r	43r–v	*Ibid.*, commentis 45, 46, 47, 48, cited. But the arguments in these citations are developed only in the Laurentian manuscript.
84r, col. 2	25v	Averroes, VII Metaphysics, commentis 34 et 36 (38?), cited: "Duplex est prioritas . . ."
84r, col. 2	27r–v	Metaphysical and natural consideration distinguished.
84v, col. 2	36v	The composite may be considered in two ways.
84v, col. 2	37v	Averroes, VII Metaphysics, comment. 33 et 38, cited: "Materia est duplex . . ."
84v, col. 2	37r	*Ibid.*, comment. 36, cited: "nequaquam posse intelligi quidditatem animalis sine carnibus et ossibus."
84v, col. 2	37v–38r	Quiddities of definitions are not corruptible.
84v, col. 2	39v	Avicenna, VI Naturalium, cap. 3, cited: "Aliquis creatus perfectus subito cessantibus . . ."
84v, col. 2	40r	Avicenna, tract. 5, cap. 7, cited.
85r	40r	How Avicenna's statement should be interpreted.

The remaining text of the Vatican manuscript is taken up with replying to arguments 7–13, which are passed over in the Laurentian manuscript.

APPENDIX 21

RUBRIC AND PREFACE OF GREGORIUS CHRISPUS *DE CULTU HUMANITATIS ET HONESTATIS*

From MS Laurent. Plut. 77, cod. 17, fols. 1r–7r.

Gregorii sapientis Tholosani bonarum artium ac totius philosophie studiosi ac precipue musici illustri ac regio domino Petro de Fuxo infanti navarre ac sedis apostolice protonotario De cultu humanitatis et honestatis libellus dicatur.

Cogitanti mihi sepenumero, illustrissime princeps, quenam essent illa studia que homines felices efficere possent, unicum tantum humanitatis et honestatis studium visum est sine quo neminem umquam felicem esse posse iudicavi. Nam omnes artes illas quas liberales vo- [*fol. 1v*] cant plane scire naturasque rerum omnium recte intelligere, et si quippiam emolumenti nobis in hac vita prestare potest, ad felicitatem tamen animi consequendam parum profecto confert. Posset namque quispiam omnis etiam istas artes et disciplinas edoctus et miser quidem atque infelix esse. Studia autem humanitatis et honestatis ea tantum sunt que et summum decus et ornamentum in hac vita prestare et eternam quoque felicitatem nobis in celo comparare possunt. Studium autem humanitatis et honestatis culturam accuratam et diligentem corporis et animi intel- [*fol. 2r*] ligo esse, sine qua omnes humanitatis motus indecori atque deformes sunt. Illa namque priora nature semina sive virtutum igniculi inculta numquam adolescunt. Opus est igitur ad hec recte perficienda morali philosophia. Nulla enim (ut inquit Cicero) vite pars est neque privatis neque in publicis neque forensibus neque domesticis rebus que morali philosophia vacare possit. In hac enim excolenda sita est vite honestas et in negligenda turpitudo. Cum igitur ea mihi consuetudo fuerit aliquid semper quod claros et prestantes viros [*fol. 2v*] oblectaret vel vulgari vel latino sermone scribere, interdumque amatorias cantilenas et metrico concentui et armonicis modis accomodatas aurium demulcendarum gracia ediderim, ingravescentibus iam annis quom rationis potentia facta esset validior, carmina illa ipsa etati iam non convenire existimavi. Quare et ad gravis historias philosophorumque et theologorum sententias et legendas et scribendas me contuli, quod quidem suavissimum animo meo esse pabulum cognovi.

Quocirca cum sepius optavissem aliquid dignum scribere quod tue sublimitati dedicarem [*fol. 3r*] quodque et te dignum et tibi gratum foret, in mentem venit ex philosophorum ipsorum amenissimis ortis ac fructiferis arboribus quasdam uberes frondes amputare et odoriferos suavissimos flores legere quibus sertum pulcherrimum conficerem quo tua egregia et illustria tempora et belle quidem et devote meo munusculo coronare possem. Non quod te inornatum cernerem sed ut et animo et corpore adolescentem favore quodam in ipso cursu velociorem [*volociorem* in the MS] facerem officioque meo erga te cuique nemo est me amantior nemo observantior aliquantulum satisfacere viderer. [*fol. 3v*] Accipe igitur libenter, vir amplissime, hoc ipsum meum munusculum libenter abs me tibi et devote quidem oblatum. Alii argenteas pelves aureosque creteres tibi offerant. Alii gemmatos anulos. Alii eburnea vasa margaritasque preciosiores. Ego hunc solum de cultu humanitatis et honestatis libellum tanquam observantie in te mee integreque fidei pignus sublimitati tue devotissime dedico qui nomen tuum immortalitati facile consecrabit. Neque enim magis proprie alteri cuique dedicandus erat, cum de humanitate et honestate tractet, quam tibi qui et humanissimus [*fol. 4r*] es et honestatem accurato studio colis, veneraris, amplecteris. In te enim esse scimus incredibilem quandam ingenii magnitudinem, cumulatam litterarum et bonarum artium eruditionem, elegantem et dicendi et scribendi copiam et facilitatem, divinam memoriam, precipuam religionem, integerrimam fidem, domesticam pietatem, parem quandam in omnis equitatem, et denique frugalitatem, liberalitatem, magnificentiam, que omnia unico nomine regium splendorem appellare quidem licet. Quam igitur ex tuis his divinis ornamentis efficit iam pulchritudinem eam quidem hunc libellum legendo poteris [*fol. 4v*] confirmare eternamque beatitudinem tibi hinc preparare. Cuius quidem facile comparande multa iam pre te fers argumenta. Nam ad virtutum splendorem eximium consequendum illustrem in primis atque regium sanguinem habes propicium tuorum maiorum exempla clarissima tibi non desunt quorum prestantissimas ymagines ita intueris ut animus tuus eorum exemplo perinde ac face quadam ad virtutes et honestates vehementius accendatur.

Tibi enim paternum maternumque genus et potentissimos reges et principes fortissimos et invinctissimos clarissimosque alios heroas edidit. Nam ut reliquos pretereeam [*fol. 5r*] quorum laudes attingere nequirem et quorum splendore et gloria domus de fuxo tua regias inter familias illustrissima iudicatur, quondam illum Petrum de fuxo avi tui fratrem et apostolicum senatorem ecclesieque maximum lumen et decus, virum quidem celo dignum et iam ut opinor inter sanctos relatum, tanquam tue professioni magis consentaneum tibi continue imitandum offers, ut nichil ad humanitatem, nichil ad honestatem, nichil ad virtutem, nichil denique ad perfectam felicitatem consequendam tibi deesse possit. Optime profecto tu illum imitari studes recteque [*fol. 5v*] intueris [*interis* in MS] ut non plus tuorum quam tua virtute glorieris. Quos enim sanguinis claritate equasti [*equasi* in MS], eos certe virtute non modo equare sed superare quidem conaris, et quos generis dignitate superas, iis te virtute inferiorem esse dedecorosum admodum iudicas. Recteque Socratis illam doctrinam sive monitionem observas qua discipulos suos ut se crebro in speculo intuerentur inducebat ut si qui fortasse corpore pulchri essent moribus turpibus non se dehonestarent. Si vero forma essent indecenti, se ita moribus ingenuis informarent ut vite sue et animi pulchritudine [*fol. 6r*] corporis deformitatem redimerent et absolverent.

Ut igitur natura tibi maxime fuit liberalis atque propitia que corpus tuum clara in primis ac regia stirpe, eximia forma, statura eleganti, coloris suavitate, et pulchritudine vultus, dignitate et venustate adornavit, ita tu nature munificentiam secutus indigne longe iudicasti avarum tibimet ipsi fore. Quamobrem te iis ornamentis virtutum que solum in nostra potestate sunt ita te ipsum decorasti ut omnis qui te cognoscunt dubitent quid magis vel corporis tui vel animi pulchritudinem admirentur [*fol. 6v*] et laudent. Cui si maximas gerendi res occasionem quandoque fortuna ut spero prestiterit, intelliget orbis quante in te virtutes sint, quanta modestia, quanta religio, quanta vite sanctimonia, ut non plus tibi dignitatis quam tu sibi tua domus sit allatura. Recte igitur tibi dicandus erat, amplissime domine, libellus meus de humanitatis et honestatis cultu pertractans. Si quid enim erroris aut inepte scriptum in eo tua sublimitas inveniet, corrigat et emendet, queso. Hec enim fuit una dedicandi causa. Si vero quicquam laude dignum contineat, [*fol. 7r*] soli deo optimo maximo a quo omnia bona defluunt et dependent tribuendum erit. Iam itaque tua amplitudo que sit hominis natura dignanter audiat.

APPENDIX 22

CONTENTS OF OLIVER OF SIENA *DE DEO ET RERUM NATURALIUM PRINCIPIIS ET SUMMA BEATITUDINE*

From MS Laurent. Plut. 82, cod. 21.

OPENING STATEMENT

. . . tractatulum hunc sexpartitum incipiam. Prima pars erit de diffinitione ipsius dei secundum famosiores positiones et theologorum veritatem. In secunda de factione spiritualis creature agam. In tertia de rerum naturalium principiis declarabo. In quarta vero de mundi creatione. In quinta quid sit summum bonum et in quo summa beatitudo consistat adducam (Et numquid eius ab eterno ydea fuerit in mente divina determinabitur).[1] Sextam partem et ultimam de rationali scientia naturalique philosophya atque de medicina pariter et de uniuscuiusque illarum fine breviter definiam.

THE CLOSING TABLE

de deo quid dicendum sit secundum omnes positiones et veritatem
de creatione rationalis creature et angelorum custodium [or, *custodia*]
de rerum omnium naturalium principiis
de eternitate mundi et eius creatione
de ydeis et formis exemplaribus
de summa beatitudine et fine summi boni
de morali sapientia et virtutibus moralibus
de rationali scientia atque eius utilitate
de naturali philosophia eiusque laudibus
de medicinali scientia et ipsius origine

Tandem de uno solo deo et trino per quem omnia facta sunt, a quo dependet celum et tota natura, qui vivit et regnat in secula seculorum. Amen.

[1] The passage in parentheses is added in the margin of the manuscript.

GENERAL INDEX

INDEX OF MANUSCRIPTS

INDEX OF INCIPITS

COLUMBIA UNIVERSITY PRESS
Columbia University
New York

FOREIGN AGENT
OXFORD UNIVERSITY PRESS
HUMPHREY MILFORD
Amen House, London, E. C.